CLINE, G.G.
Peter Skene Ogden & the
Hudson Bay company

HERTFORDSHIRE LIBRARY SERVICE

This book is due for return on or before the date shown. You
may extend its loan by bringing the book to the library or,
once only, by post or telephone, quoting the date of return,
the letter and number on the date card, if applicable, and the
information at the top of this label.

Please renew/return this item by the last date shown.

So that your telephone call is charged at local rate,
please call the numbers as set out below:

	From Area codes 01923 or 0208:	From the rest of Herts:
Renewals:	01923 471373	01438 737373
Enquiries:	01923 471333	01438 737333
Minicom:	01923 471599	01438 737599

L32b

THE AMERICAN EXPLORATION AND TRAVEL SERIES

PETER SKENE OGDEN
AND THE
HUDSON'S BAY COMPANY

PETER SKENE OGDEN
and the
Hudson's Bay Company

GLORIA GRIFFEN CLINE

UNIVERSITY OF OKLAHOMA PRESS : NORMAN

WATFORD CENTRAL

Library of Congress Cataloging in Publication Data

Cline, Gloria Griffen.
   Peter Skene Ogden and the Hudson's Bay Company.
   (The American exploration and travel series)
   Bibliography: p.
   1. Ogden, Peter Skene, 1790–1854.   2. Hudson's Bay Company.
I. Title.   II. Series.
F880.O34C53   971.2'092'4 [B]   72–9266
ISBN 0–8061–1073–2

For Jack

Preface

OF ALL THE FUR TRADERS who roamed the North American West in the first half of the nineteenth century, none, in my estimation, had more personality, more character, and more exciting and diversified experiences than Peter Skene Ogden. So often when one thinks about a fur trader, he pictures a tall, young man dressed in leather britches and a coonskin cap facing the hardships of the Far West, setting his traps in freezing waters, walking or riding miles on an empty stomach, or crouching in an arroyo attempting to escape Indian attack. He is the embodiment of the romance of Lewis and Clark, and he was called westward from farms in New England, Kentucky, or the new frontier developing in the Mississippi Valley to fulfill his and his nation's destiny.

Much of this is true of the American fur trade, but north of the United States there existed another trade in furs, that of the North West and Hudson's Bay companies. In many respects the employees of these organizations were the counterparts of the Americans for they were generally French Canadians from an agricultural background or Orkney Islanders seeking opportunity in the New World. Peter Skene Ogden, however, does not fit the stereotype of the fur trader. All his life from youth until his death in 1854 at the age of sixty-four was involved with the fur trade, but he was more than a trader interested only in economic gain. He was a brigade leader, an explorer, an executive of the Hudson's Bay Company, a political agent during the Oregon question crisis, and a representative of his company and country in Washington, D.C., after the United States received the Pacific Northwest south of the forty-ninth parallel.

Physically Ogden did not fit the stereotype. He was relatively short with a stocky frame, but he was as strong as any man in the West, red or white. His background also differed from that of most of his contemporaries. He was the son of well-born, well-educated parents who brought him up in a stimulating, intellectual environment, and his early years with his family in Montreal undoubtedly partly account for his introspective character and complex personality.

When I was quite young, the man whom Ross Cox called "the humourous, honest, eccentric, law-defying Peter Ogden, the terror of

Indians, and the delight of all gay fellows," captured my imagination. As I traveled with my parents through the Bitterroot Valley of Montana or along the British Columbian and southeastern Alaskan coasts, I wondered more about this trader. Then as a teenager riding horseback along the banks of the river discovered by Ogden, the Humboldt, not far from our ranch in Lovelock, Nevada, my interest grew more serious.

Peter Skene Ogden and the Hudson's Bay Company is the result of more than twenty years' research. During this time many people have been of great assistance. I am especially indebted to the Governor and Committee of the Hudson's Bay Company for their courtesy in allowing me access to their superb archival collection, and to their extremely competent staff, Mrs. Joan Craig and Miss Gwendolyn Kemp, for their aid, kindness, and consideration. I must, however, single out Miss Alice Johnson, who has been of unlimited help; her suggestions through the years as well as her reading of the final manuscript are greatly appreciated. I also wish to express my gratitude to retired Hudson's Bay Record Society editors, E. E. Rich, Master of St. Catharine's College, Cambridge, and K. G. Davies, professor of history, Bristol University, for their writings and illuminating conversation.

Also in England the late Miss Eldreth and her successor, Mrs. White, the representatives of the Public Archives of Canada in London, were most helpful. Too, I am grateful to the staffs of the Public Record Office and of the Record Room, County Hall, London, especially Miss Ida Darlington of the Record Room, for making pertinent material available to me. For information relating to the Royal Engineers, my appreciation goes to Brigadier M. L. Crosthwait, Royal Engineers retired, and now bursar of Darwin College, Cambridge, and to Lieutenant Colonel F. T. Stear, head librarian, Institution of Royal Engineers, Chatham, Kent.

For many years, I spent much time at the Bancroft Library, Berkeley, California, where many people were of great assistance, especially the retired director, George P. Hammond, as well as Robert Becker, John Barr Tompkins, and the late Helen Bretnor. At the Henry E. Huntington Library, San Marino, California, I remember Miss Fry and Miss Noya as being most helpful. Various state historical societies have contributed significantly to this work. I would especially like to thank Thomas Vaughan and his excellent staff of the Oregon Historical Society.

In Canada, Willard Ireland of the Archives of British Columbia, Victoria, and W. Kaye Lamb, retired director of the Public Archives of Canada, Ottawa, have been most generous in allowing me to use manuscript materials as well as pictures which are part of their splendid collections. My special thanks go to Archdeacon Guy Marston, Anglican

Diocese of Quebec, and his vestry clerk, A. E. Williams, who helped me solve the perplexing problem of Ogden's birth date by locating his baptismal entry in their old records.

During the course of these many years, three men in particular have given me inspiration and encouragement. For these important ingredients, my deepest thanks go to the outstanding Hudson's Bay Company and Commonwealth scholar, John S. Galbraith, professor of history, University of California at Los Angeles; Daniel J. Boorstin, Director of History and Technology, Smithsonian Institution; and Alan Cooke, Curator of Manuscripts, Scott Polar Research Institute, Cambridge University. Most of all I want to thank my understanding husband, John Charles Harrison, Jr.

Many other people deserve mention, as well as Mrs. Margot Chubb, Trinity College Library, Dublin, who supplied me with a desk in a scholarly environment where this manuscript was completed.

GLORIA GRIFFEN CLINE

"Silverdale," Bray, County Wicklow, Ireland
February 1, 1973

The publisher wishes to acknowledge with grateful thanks the assistance of Alan Cooke, of the Scott Polar Institute, Cambridge University, who read the proofs of this volume following the untimely death of Gloria Griffen Cline.

UNIVERSITY OF OKLAHOMA PRESS

Norman, Oklahoma
February 25, 1974

Contents

Illustrations

Maps

PETER SKENE OGDEN

AND THE

HUDSON'S BAY COMPANY

Prologue

With the beginning of the crusades in the eleventh century, men on the continent of Europe began to think in much broader geographic terms than those of a closed, rural society. This new way of thinking produced a new breed of men who began seeking sea routes to the rich spice lands of the East. Among them was Columbus to whom is attributed the discovery of the Western Hemisphere in 1492. In the 250 years following Columbus' voyage, the coasts of North and South America were explored, named, and settled by his followers, mainly adventurers from the Iberian Peninsula.

Although the coastal areas were soon charted, the extent of the new realm remained unknown until the late eighteenth to middle nineteenth century. The men who charted the coasts sought not spices but furs, for life-styles had changed considerably since Columbus' time. A sea route to the Spice Islands had been discovered through the pioneering of Vasco da Gama, but Captain James Cook's voyage three centuries later revealed the large quantities of fur-bearing animals in North Pacific America. Furs were much in demand for use in adorning clothes and in making felt for the hats that were coming into vogue in the late seventeenth and early eighteenth centuries, and now exploration of North America for the purpose of securing them could be carried on from both sides of the continent.

Shortly after Columbus' voyage of discovery, non-Iberian nations began to challenge Spanish and Portuguese power in the Western Hemisphere. The first were France and England. The French followed Cartier and Champlain up the St. Lawrence River, and the English followed Sir Humphrey Gilbert, Sir Walter Raleigh, and Captain John Smith to the Atlantic coastal plain. Many of the newcomers were not merely adventurers, but people who had decided upon a life in the New World because they were dissatisfied with their existence at home, either for religious, political, social, or economic reasons.

One Englishman who chose to leave the Old Country for the Colonies was John the Pilgrim, the great-great-great-grandfather of Peter Skene Ogden—a man little known in North American history but one who contributed substantially to it in his capacity as explorer, fur trader,

Indian pacifier, and chief factor for the Hudson's Bay Company. When John Ogden emigrated from England in early 1640, he and other emigrants settled on the southern shore of Long Island, where they founded the town of Southampton. From this vantage point, John Ogden noticed that North America was made up of isolated settlements, cosmopolitan in nature, which stretched from French Quebec and Montreal on the far north to the Spanish settlements in what is now Florida. In between, the Puritans and Pilgrims occupied New England and other Englishmen Maryland and Virginia, where they were separated from their countrymen by the Dutch and the Swedes, who had chosen the valleys of what was to become New York and Pennsylvania.

By 1664 the Dutch and the Swedes had lost their possessions. Isolated British communities now dotted the Atlantic coastal plain in an unbroken line between the northern French and southern Spaniards, and after spending twenty-five years in Southampton, Ogden decided to take part in the British expansion along the Atlantic seaboard, brought about by the return of Charles II to the throne and the expulsion of the non-English groups. In 1665 he moved his family to Sir George Carteret's emerging colony, named New Jersey after the latter's administration of the English Isle of Jersey.

By August, 1665, the energetic Ogden had begun the development of Elizabethtown, New Jersey, and the first proprietary governor established himself there with the "Ogden company."[1] Capable, intelligent, and well educated, John Ogden soon endeared himself to Governor Philip Carteret, who in October appointed "John Ogden Gentleman" justice of the peace of Elizabethtown. Carteret was so pleased with Ogden's administration that he promoted him to deputy governor the following month, and John was acting governor during Carteret's absence.

John Ogden's descendants carried on the family's tradition in New Jersey politics, and during the later seventeenth and first three-quarters of the eighteenth century, they were active in Elizabethtown and Newark. But as the Ogdens maintained their image as a "rich, powerful, influential, and cultured" family, life in North America was changing significantly. When the Seven Years' War (or, as the Americans preferred to call it, the French and Indian War) ended with a complete English victory over France in 1763, a new spirit became evident in the Colonies. The English took France's possessions in Canada, and the Americans, with the French menace to the north removed, became more belligerent. At the same time, England, aiming to increase her hold on her far-flung empire, introduced new economic measures, one of which was the Stamp Act of 1765.

The passage of this act aroused little interest in England, but the Virginia House of Burgesses strongly opposed it. Thomas Jefferson, at the time a law student at Williamsburg, Virginia, slipped away from his studies to listen to Patrick Henry's electrifying speeches to that body. Newspapers joined in opposing the tax, and the Stamp Act Congress was called in New York City to bring about repeal of the act. Peter Skene Ogden's grandfather, a Yale University graduate, was fifty-eight years old at this time, and although he considered himself a loyal subject of George III, he joined other colonial lawyers and refused to purchase stamps.[2]

With the success of the congress and repeal of the Stamp Act, many colonials felt that difficulty with the Crown had been averted, but great undercurrents of discontent remained on both sides of the Atlantic between 1765 and 1776. During these years the king fumed and ministries rose and fell, but in the interim Parliament, aiming to increase British control in America, vigorously engaged in passing new legislation or repealing that of its predecessors. In the Colonies virtually all British legislation was flouted, mobs rioted, liberals plotted and wrote political tracts. As Clinton Rossiter has so aptly put it, whether the American political situation was "calm or convulsed," it moved steadily ahead, and "the peaceful revolution that had been gathering momentum from the time of the first settlements moved irresistibly to conclusion, and the fighting revolution could now begin."[3]

As the pace of political events accelerated, Peter Skene Ogden's grandfather, who was a member of the King's Council for the Province of New Jersey and also served as judge of the Colonial Supreme Court after 1772, found himself in a dilemma. After the First Continental Congress in 1774, Lexington and Concord and the Second Continental Congress in 1775, and the Declaration of Independence in 1776 (signed by his daughter-in-law's brother, Gouverneur Morris),[4] the old judge could see that he would soon have to decide where to place his allegiance: with the Colonies or with England.

At first Judge David and all of his sons—Josiah, Isaac, Abraham, Samuel, Nicholas, and Peter—seemed to support the Patriotic cause. Isaac, Peter Skene Ogden's father, even delivered a stirring address to a mass meeting in Newark. But like many moderates, Judge Ogden wanted reform, not revolution, and he attempted to devise a plan for governing the Colonies after their submission to Great Britain, an event he deemed "certain and soon to happen, if proper measures were not neglected."[5] Surprisingly enough, his legal mind envisioned an enlightened government in which there would be a Parliament with authority to levy taxes, a power to be relinquished by England. David Ogden's background, however, caused him to insist that many of the aristocratic privileges in the Colonies remain.

As the war progressed, the old judge and sons Isaac, Nicholas, and Peter joined the Loyalists, and as a result their New Jersey property was condemned and sold. The Ogdens were naturally distraught at this confiscation and while Benedict Arnold was being pushed southward from Quebec and George Washington was crossing the Delaware and making winter quarters at Valley Forge, David Ogden was busy again with his pen trying to recover the family's property. Ogden's friends, among them William Franklin, the last Loyalist governor of New Jersey and the bane of his father Benjamin Franklin's existence, also tried to help David and his Loyalist sons, who meanwhile had taken refuge in British-occupied New York City.[6]

Meanwhile, Isaac Ogden was trying to keep his family together. With him were his three daughters, Mary Browne Ogden, Catharine Ogden, and Sarah Ogden, all children by his late wife, Mary Browne, daughter of the Reverend Isaac Browne of Newark. Now he and his new wife, the charming, rich, and socially prominent Sarah Hanson of Livingston Manor, New York, were establishing a family of their own. David, Henry, and Isaac had already come into the world, the latter two born in New York City while the family was in exile. However, with the rising cost of living, the family had difficulty financially for although Sarah Hanson had brought to her marriage "a large fortune which she inherited in her own right," since she and her family were Loyalists, they, too, like the David-Isaac branch of the Ogden family, had lost their wealth.

From New York City the Ogdens watched General Burgoyne move southward from Montreal and through the Hudson Valley, only to be defeated at Saratoga in October, 1777. By the latter part of 1778, however, the war had shifted primarily to the south. Things began to look more promising to the Ogdens when the British landed near Savannah and soon took South Carolina and Georgia. By the spring of 1781, General Cornwallis was able to move north into Virginia, but Washington and Lafayette besieged his position in the village of Yorktown, and with the prospects of no land or sea support, Cornwallis had no choice but to give up. With Cornwallis's surrender at Yorktown on October 19, 1781, the war virtually ended. The final peace treaty, however, was not signed until two years later, on September 3, 1783. With this conclusive act, the Ogdens felt that there was no place for them in the new nation, so on November 23, 1783, they and many other Loyalist refugees sailed for England.

For David Ogden's sons Abraham and Samuel, who had remained true to the Patriotic cause, life was much more pleasant. Abraham had married Sarah Francis Ludlow, the daughter of a wealthy New York citizen, just before Christmas, 1767, and by the time war broke out, they had four children. Their fourth child, Thomas Ludlow Ogden, was born on December 12, 1773, and had become a precocious and adventuresome boy by the time the Revolution was well under way. Seesaw battles between British and Continental forces were fought in New Jersey, and young Tom was fascinated by these and other events that were taking place around him. He was especially intrigued by the frequent visits of an angular-faced man with a commanding figure, none other than George Washington. General Washington took particular interest in Squire Ogden's son, and it has been said that he took Tom on his rounds among the troops, the boy mounted before him in the saddle.

When the war was over, Tom's father, already a distinguished lawyer, became even more prominent. Through his own ability and his family's friendship with Washington, he was appointed commissioner to study the relinquishment of much of the Iroquois Nation's title to land in northern New York state, a consequence of the Indians' strong support of England during the war. This gave Abraham knowledge of the country lying south of the St. Lawrence River and resulted in the purchase of a large tract of land by himself, his brother Samuel,[7] Gouverneur Morris, Nicholas Hoffman, Richard Harrison, and Stephen Van Rensselaer. In it was founded Ogdensburg, a place Peter Skene Ogden was to visit many times.

Samuel Ogden also fared well. His name became nationally known when he became involved in the intricate and complicated life of Newark-born Ogden family friend Aaron Burr, who unsuccessfully sought the presidency of the United States in 1800 against incumbent John Adams, Thomas Jefferson, and Charles Pinckney. After his defeat, Burr's political fortunes declined, and in 1804 he lost the race for governor of New York. Believing this situation had arisen because Alexander Hamilton had cast a slur upon his character, Burr killed Hamilton in a duel on the heights of Weehawken, New Jersey, on July 10, 1804. Burr's later actions in the West and his association there with Herman Blennerhasset and General James Wilkinson led him into serious trouble. By 1807, Burr was under arrest for treason for his part in an alleged plot

7

to establish a separate state west of the Allegheny-Appalachian mountain chain. Samuel Ogden assisted in Burr's defense when Burr was tried before Chief Justice John Marshall. As a means of rebuking President Thomas Jefferson, Marshall insisted that the constitutional statement of grounds for conviction of treason requiring either a confession in open court or before "two witnesses to the same overt act" be adhered to strictly. As a result, Ogden and his associates were successful in securing Burr's release.[8]

While Samuel and Abraham were finding fame and fortune, the Ogden refugees were facing postwar vicissitudes. For the first five years after their arrival in England, they missed North America greatly as they tried to adjust to living abroad. Then, in 1788, their fortunes changed when Isaac Ogden was appointed judge of the Admiralty Court in Quebec by George III.[9] So it was that because of eighteenth-century political changes in North America, Peter Skene Ogden was to be born in Canada instead of Newark, New Jersey, or London, England. Commercial activities along the bustling St. Lawrence River would push him toward the West and the frontier, where his adventurous spirit could be given full rein. It was an act of God which had repercussions in the development of the North American continent.

The Call of the Beaver

IMMEDIATELY AFTER HIS APPOINTMENT as judge of the Admiralty Court in Quebec in 1788, Isaac Ogden set sail for Canada. With him were his wife, Sarah, and three children by his first marriage: Mary, Catharine, and Sarah, whose ages at the time are unknown. The children of his second marriage also accompanied them: David, sixteen; Henry, six; Isaac, five; and Harriet, a babe in arms born that year.[1]

The Ogdens lived for six years in Quebec, a city of six thousand inhabitants established on the banks of the St. Lawrence River by Samuel de Champlain in 1608. Here two more members were added to the Ogden family: Peter Skene, born in 1790, and Charles Richard, born in 1791. (It has heretofore been accepted by all authorities, including the Hudson's Bay Company itself, that Peter Skene Ogden was born in 1794. However it now appears conclusive that he was born in 1790, since his baptismal entry in the "old records" of the Cathedral of the Holy Trinity in Quebec reads: "Peter Skeene, son of Isaac Ogden Esq. & Sarah his wife. Bapt. Feb. 12th. 1790."[2])

Peter Skene Ogden received his middle name from the Skene family of Skenesboro, New York, who had settled on the southern shore of Lake Champlain where Whitehall now stands. They were a distinguished military and literary family, and Andrew Skene, an eminent jurist, was Ogden's godfather.[3] Peter Skene Ogden took great liberties in the spelling of his middle name and it appeared variously as *Skene, Skeen, Skein,* and *Skeene,* but the archival collections at Beaver House in London and at the Oregon Historical Society in Portland indicate that he most often signed his letters and documents *Skeen.*

In 1794, Guy Carleton, first Baron Dorchester, who was governor of Quebec from 1786 until 1796, appointed Ogden's father puisne judge in the District of Montreal. So it was not Quebec, with its high hills, plains, and palisades breaking off abruptly to the water's edge, but the bustling city of Montreal that was Ogden's home during his early childhood. As he matured, his restless disposition and imagination were aroused by the activity along the mighty St. Lawrence, where sheds and warehouses fairly buzzed with men unloading and storing furs. When he walked past Dillon's Tavern, crowded with the usual group singing songs and trading gossip about their favorite topic, the fur trade, he longed to be a part of that scene. The Montreal of Ogden's youth was the center of the Canadian fur trade, and practically everyone had either a financial or social interest in it. Even more appealing to an adventuresome young man, however, the Montreal of the late eighteenth and early nineteenth centuries was alive with stories of exploration. Ogden listened attentively to reports of new rivers and mountains named after the enterprising men who had the courage and the ability to press westward under the auspices of the fur companies.[4]

Ogden wanted to be one of them, one of the first white men to see the great expanses of wilderness uncluttered by civilization. He was tired of his parents' efforts to make a lawyer out of him for the sake of family tradition. After all, two of his brothers were already in the profession. David, whom Ogden later resembled greatly, was in his thirties and well on his way to becoming a prominent Montreal attorney, and Charles Richard, though only three years Ogden's senior, showed both stability and a keen desire to become a well-known legal figure. Everyone else seemed to be doing what he wanted. Catharine had married a British army officer, as had Harriet, whose husband, Thomas Evans, became a general. Isaac had also joined the army, but he later resigned his commission and became a respected sheriff of Trois Rivières, later known by its Anglicized name, Three Rivers.

Only Ogden's father knew of his son's longing to see and be a part of the frontier. He understood him so well because he himself was intrigued by the North American West. The old judge's imagination was fired in England by talk about Captain Cook's last expedition, 1776–79, which was conducted during the American Revolution. His interest was naturally reinforced when he came to Montreal, the outfitting center for the North West Company. Enjoying splendid cuisine and vintage wines as a guest of members of the Beaver Club, he became more knowledgeable and more curious about the Far West. He was enraptured by stories of the River of the West and the Straits of Anían and of how Alexander Mackenzie, searching for the elusive Northwest Passage, bore northward in 1789 and pushed to the Arctic Ocean along the river that bears his name. Then in 1793, with considerable baggage, a leaky canoe, and ten men, Mackenzie pushed toward the Pacific, which he finally reached in present-day British Columbia on July 22.[5] Judge Isaac believed there must be a Northwest Passage somewhere out there, and after he met the eccentric Peter Pond, a splendid cartographer and explorer and developer of the Athabaska District, he believed there was a waterway between Great Slave Lake and the Pacific.

Although the old judge could sympathize with his son, he insisted that the boy receive a good education, which is clearly reflected in Ogden's character and tastes in later life. Little is known about Ogden during this period, but he studied and read law under the tutelage of the Reverend Doty, also Charles Richard's mentor. By the time Ogden was fifteen, however, it was clear that he disliked his academic life intensely, and his family, realizing that his restless, irrepressible nature could not be controlled much longer, relented.

The fur trade had changed tremendously since the sixteenth century, when Cartier sailed up the St. Lawrence and his men traded axes, knives, and a few trifles for walrus, bear, fox, and wolf pelts.[6] In their wake came fishermen–fur traders, who soon realized that prices for fish were small compared to those paid for furs. Furs were in great demand, not only among aristocrats, but also among the growing European commercial classes.[7] By the latter part of the sixteenth century, the fur trade had broadened. Not only were the entire pelts of various animals being used to ornament clothing, but the beaver was becoming particularly prized because its fur was an excellent material from which to make felt for the type of hats that were coming into style. Thus it was fashion which lured Peter Skene Ogden away from a legal career and made him a trader-explorer.

Many beaver skins were needed to make hats. Only part of a pelt could be used. When the beaver skin came from the trader, it was generally rough, greasy, and covered with coarse brown hair; underneath was the soft, fine, rich fur (wool) that is generally associated with this animal. The first step in hat making, then, was to shave both hair and wool from the skin. The wool and hair were separated by a blowing process, and the bare skin was sold to glue makers. Now the soft, loose wool could be transformed into felt. A suction device pulled it against a revolving perforated copper cone, after which the hood was removed from the cone and placed in a mold, where it was shaped and shellacked. To give it additional pile, more fine fur was added; then, to develop greater luster, brushes, irons, and sandpaper were used to add the finishing touches to the exquisite hat known as the beaver.[8] By the time Peter Skene Ogden had become a highly respected fur trader, more than 100,000 beaver pelts a year were consumed by the hat-making industry alone.

With such lucrative prospects for trade, many organizations were formed to exploit the virgin fur-bearing territories of North America. The first of any consequence was the English Hudson's Bay Company, which received its charter from Charles II on May 2, 1670. It is still in existence today, making it the oldest chartered organization in the world. Through the course of its long history, the North American establishment, which began on the shores of Hudson and James bays, changed, but the structure of the London policy-making body, composed of a governor, a deputy governor, and a committee of seven members, has remained the same. These directors were stockholders in the company, and their decisions and tenure in office were subject to the control of the entire body of stockholders, who met periodically as a general court.[9]

Another British organization interested in tapping the rich fur reserves of North America was founded in America much later. The North West Company was established in 1779 through an agreement by a number of Montreal merchants to pool traffic. After a series of subsequent agreements, by 1787 all the important fur dealers were brought into partnership. The North West Company had two classes of shareholders: the eastern partners, merchants of substance in Montreal and Quebec who supplied the capital for the venture, and the so-called wintering partners, who contributed the skill and leadership needed in the field. This company had become a giant by 1800. It employed almost two thousand men and maintained large warehouses at Montreal and Fort William, on the western shore of Lake Superior, thereby assuring its interior posts regularity of supply. The competition of the North West Company forced the Hudson's Bay Company to expand westward from its headquarters at York Factory, on Hudson Bay at the mouth of the Nelson River, for fear of losing trade with the western Indians. As a result, both companies began to push their operations west and to establish posts farther and farther from their home bases, so that by the end of the eighteenth century, each had traders on the Upper Missouri.[10]

Americans, too, were interested in the fur wealth of the West, particularly after its potential was pointed out by Lewis and Clark when they returned from their exploring expedition of 1804–1806. Following Lewis and Clark's trail up the Missouri were such prominent St. Louis traders as Manuel Lisa and Auguste and Pierre Chouteau, and by 1808 the Missouri Fur Company had been established by the Chouteaus, William Clark, and five others. In the same year in New York state, John Jacob Astor, the leading fur dealer in the United States, finally secured a charter for what he chose to call the American Fur Company. For years he had resented buying pelts on the Montreal market, for he figured that in addition to ordinary costs, he was giving profits to Canadian merchants, as well as paying tariff and transportation costs. Astor's company was capitalized at $300,000, of which he owned all but a few shares; the remainder were disbursed merely for qualifying directors of the company. He was now ready to move into the Old Northwest,[11] a region he had coveted before the signing of Jay's Treaty in 1794. He hoped to keep infiltrating Canadian trappers out of the area—a point which he hoped would be acted upon by Congress—so that the popular slogan "America for Americans" could be realized at last.[12]

Surprisingly, Peter Skene Ogden's introduction to the fur trade came through the American Fur Company, which after its formation continued Astor's operations in Montreal. Ogden received a minor position with the organization in that city through the good offices of an uncle, Nicholas Hoffman,[13] who had been a prominent New York merchant and a personal friend of Astor.[14] Living at home and working in a warehouse in Montreal, however, was not Ogden's idea of the fur trade. He wanted to follow in the footsteps of Alexander Mackenzie and David Thompson and the host of others who had blazed trails in the North American wilderness, so after a relatively short time, Ogden left the American Fur Company and joined the North West Company.

Ogden's desire to see the West was satisfied more quickly than he had anticipated. Soon after becoming a Nor'wester, he was sent into the interior of North America to serve as clerk at that company's post in the swampy lake country of Île à la Crosse in what is today Saskatchewan Province. It is difficult to follow the events in Ogden's life over the next few years, because most of the North West Company's records have not survived. Therefore, references to Ogden for the eleven-year period between 1810, when he joined the company, and 1821, when the North West and Hudson's Bay companies amalgamated, must be gleaned from the writings of Hudson's Bay Company employees. These men generally did not see Ogden as a youthful, exuberant, competent competitor who was fond of coarse practical jokes, but as an irritating, irresponsible individual who was capable of the most savage and cold-blooded crimes.

The sturdily built Ogden apparently arrived at his first wintering post in September, 1810.[15] Here he met the big, rawboned Scotsman Samuel Black, who was also a clerk at Île à la Crosse. Even though Black was ten years older than Ogden, the two men took an instantaneous liking to each other that was to last a lifetime, and the dreary life at the post in the Saskatchewan District to the east of Lesser Slave Lake was made pleasant for Ogden because of his friendship with Black.[16] Feeling keenly the rivalry between the Canadian North West Company and the British Hudson's Bay Company, both of which had pushed westward into the same territory, Black introduced Ogden to his favorite pastime: harassing the Hudson's Bay men. Shortly after Ogden's arrival, he and Black tried to amuse themselves at the expense of the Hudson's Bay traders; their effort was to make them well known and feared and was to have a brief but temporarily serious effect upon their careers.

On the evening of October 12, 1810, Ogden and Black sauntered over to the Hudson's Bay Company's post, which was near their own. As they approached the fort, they saw that its inhabitants were strengthening it by adding "6 Stockades" to those that had been put up during the summer. To irritate their rivals, the two young men decided to enter the post. As soon as the Hudson's Bay Company men finished putting up the stockade, Ogden and Black climbed over it, entered the garden, and proceeded to strut through it. They passed close to the "watchhouse," and a Mr. Campbell, who was there, saw them and sent a man to escort the two unwanted Nor'westers out. They left the fort quietly, but to show their defiance, "they remained at our [Hudson's Bay Company's] Front Gates near 10 minutes armed with Pistols & Daggers."

In Ogden's twenty-year-old mind, this type of activity must have seemed great sport, for ten days later he and Black were at it again. On the morning of October 25, they loitered outside the Hudson's Bay Company's gates but did not cause any immediate disturbance. In the evening they returned, well armed, "Black with a loaded Gun & 2 Pistols & Ogden with his Dagger," but this time they entered through the east gate and walked through the yard. Peter Fidler,[17] the thoroughly experienced Hudson's Bay Company leader, became enraged and "told them both to return the same way they came & that they should not pass thro' our yard in the Insulting Manner they intended." Black and Ogden were delighted that Fidler had risen to their bait, and they continued to walk around the company grounds. Fidler became so infuriated that he picked up a stick lying near by and hit Black with it two or three times. Ogden immediately came to his friend's aid: he pulled out his dagger, already well known, and "cut 2 Large holes in the Side & Back of [Fidler's] Coat & pricked [his] body." Then Black picked up the remainder of the stick that Fidler had broken over him and smashed Fidler's thumbnail. By this time quite a crowd had gathered, and Fidler noticed that "all our men [were] looking on the whole time without giving me any assistance." Satisfied with the spectacle they had created, Ogden and Black walked to the west gate, opened it, and, all eyes upon them, wished the men of the Hudson's Bay Company "a very miserable & unhappy winter."[18]

Ogden's first winter passed uneventfully. He and Black pursued their clerical work during the day and shared stories during the long, dark evenings. They had no more brushes with Hudson's Bay Company employees during the cold winter of 1810–11, but their competitors watched them closely. It was noticed that Ogden, who was considered a good shot, was sent out on a hunting expedition to Methy Portage on March 17, 1811. After being cooped up all winter, it was a pleasant diversion for Ogden to lead a party of seven Canadians with nine sledges, each drawn by three dogs. He was also elated by the party's success. When they returned to Île à la Crosse ten days later, the sledges were loaded with "Skins & Meat."[19]

As warm weather approached, Ogden's spirits became even more exuberant, and he returned to the newfound pleasure of harassing serious and often humorless Peter Fidler and the Hudson's Bay Company. As Fidler and sixteen men in three boats departed for one of the company's most important posts, Churchill Factory on Hudson Bay, Ogden and a party of Canadians in two canoes arrived on the scene. For the next six days the Ogden group taunted the British traders by keeping just ahead of them—in order "to get every thing from Indians that may be on the road, as they can go much faster than us," said Fidler. The Nor'westers were probably going to Fort William, for the Hudson's Bay and North West companies' routes were identical as far as Frog Portage. Here they separated, the Hudson's Bay men carrying on down Churchill River and the Nor'westers turning south to Cumberland Lake and then down the Saskatchewan River. This is undoubtedly what happened because when some Canadians arrived on June 10, Ogden "went away with them" and rid Fidler of his unwanted companions.[20]

Ogden's pranks were distasteful to the Hudson's Bay Company, but they were enjoyed and abetted by his employers. Virtually nothing is known about Ogden from June 10, 1811, until December, 1814, but he did quite well for himself during the period; he rose from clerk at Île à la Crosse to head of the Nor'wester post at Green Lake, a short distance south of his former station.

Now, four years after joining the company, Ogden's actions were becoming more deliberate and serious, and instead of mere pranks, they reflected the growing struggle between the two companies. In December, 1814, when James Spence, James Ross, and Andrew Setter of the Hudson's Bay Company were proceeding from Paint River (now known as Vermilion River) to Île à la Crosse to locate Joseph Howse, they encountered Ogden and six men returning from Île à la Crosse to Green Lake. Ogden became very belligerent, and in his distinctive voice, which could often be almost shrill, he asked James Ross "what business he had there." Ross replied that "he was come on his Masters business which he supposed did not concern him." Irritated by Ross's answer, Ogden turned to his men and gave them orders in a French Canadian *patois*.

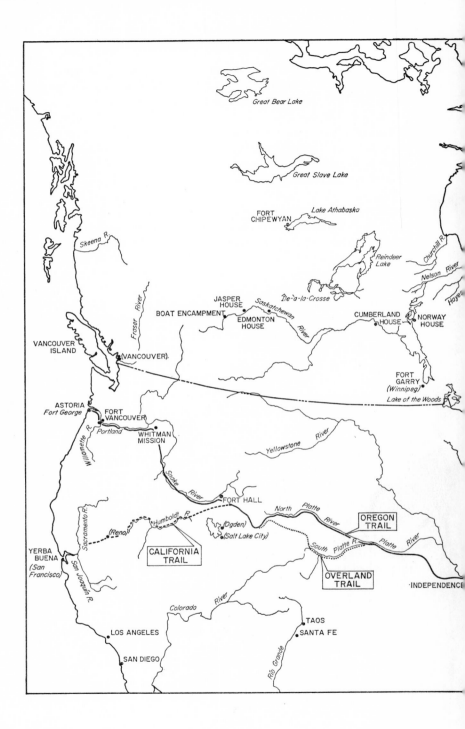

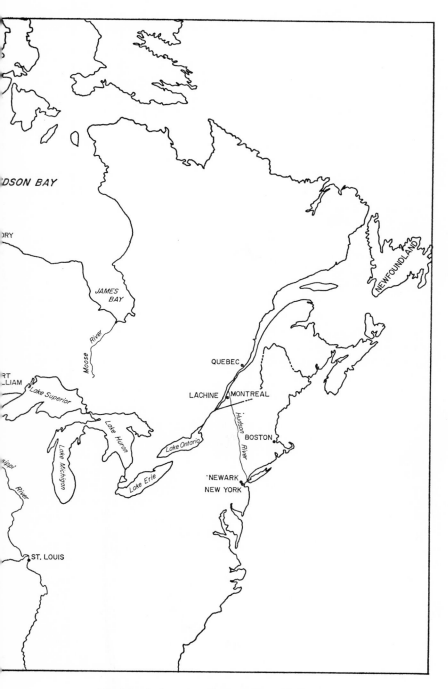

The North America of Peter Skene Ogden

Two of them grabbed hold of Ross, and Ogden, in what he considered a gentlemanly but forceful manner, struck Ross twice across the face. Then the same procedure was applied to Andrew Setter. Ogden told James Spence that "he had desired him not to come there again, that he had now come twice but if he came the third time he should never return home."[21]

About the same time, Ogden also harassed John Lee Lewes. When Lewes and his Hudson's Bay Company party were camped on Beaver River a short distance from Green Lake, Ogden and four Canadians "armed with Guns, Pistols, and Clubs" arrived and camped near by. The next morning, Lewes and his men continued on their way, but they had not gone far along the trail before Ogden and the Canadians overtook them. Then, according to Hudson's Bay Company reports, Ogden tried to push them off the road in order to provoke a fight. Ogden spoke to his men "in a language Mr. Lewis [sic] did not understand," a Canadian patois which Ogden spoke as fluently as he did English, and the Canadians began stripping "themselves on the Ice" and challenging "Mr. Lewis Men to fight." In all such encounters between the Hudson's Bay Company's men and the Nor'westers, the former could not fight for their leaders or the company because they were bound by rules issued in London. Thus the Nor'westers, who were under no restrictions, carried the day on many occasions.

In this particular incident, only one member of the Hudson's Bay Company party, Patrick Cunningham, took exception to the attitude of Ogden and the Canadians. He said that he resented the Nor'westers' insult and took on "the stoutest of the Canadians," but he "proved too weak and was obliged to relinquish the contest from having Dislocated his Thumb." During the fight, John Lee Lewes "said something to encourage his man who was fighting. Mr. Ogden took offense at this, some altercations ensued and Ogden struck Mr. Lewis who returned the blow and knocked Ogden down." Ogden's men were fiercely loyal to him and "seeing this jumped on Mr. Lewis, seized him by the hair and struck him such a blow on the Eye that he immediately lost sight of it." The rest of Lewes' men made no attempt to come to the aid of their leader. Finally the Canadians not involved in the fight interfered and "separated all combatants." Then "each party dressed themselves and Mr. Lewis continued his Journey." Before they departed, however, Ogden warned them that he planned to keep watch on Beaver River "and await Mr. Lewis on his return to Ile a la Crosse to give him and his men a beating, saying that no servant of the Hudson Bay Company had any right to be in Beaver River, and much more such unaccountable nonsense."[22]

Apparently this incident was later repeated, for on April 1, 1815, James Bird, who was keeping the Edmonton House journal, reported a similar occurrence which is enough unlike the first to make one think that it was a second fight. In the second instance, too, the same principals were involved: John Lee Lewes and his party and Ogden with "four stout Canadians." The Hudson's Bay Company group was composed of Lewes, Patrick Cunningham, Michael Rooney, John Flett, Andrew Setter, and James Spence. As the Hudson's Bay Company men moved from Île à la Crosse to Paint River, they were accompanied by two Canadians. When they neared Green Lake, one of the Canadians left for the North West Company post, presumably to tell "Mr. Ogden, who was living at Green Lake of their approach." Ogden and four Canadians headed for the British camp and bedded down near it for the night.

When dawn broke, Ogden walked over to the Hudson's Bay Company camp and said to Lewes: "I took the advantage which Superior numbers afforded me to beat you Men now I am come with two less than you have that you may take your revenge if you can."[23] Lewes replied that he had not come to fight, but to prevent his men from being mistreated by Ogden. Ogden drew himself up and said quietly yet indignantly: "It appears then that you are a Gentleman come to protect others." Said Lewes: "I am a clerk to the Hudsons Bay Company and I believe you hold a similar situation in the North West Service." With this, Ogden exploded: "What do you reckon yourself a Gentleman like me, you Play actor Son of a B——h." He advanced on Lewes, but Lewes was able to push him down. Then a Canadian half-blood jumped Lewes, who fell in the soft snow, and while he was down, the Canadian struck him on the eye.[24] Since Lewes' eye was injured in this encounter and the one described earlier, they may have been the same incident described differently. Nevertheless, these incidents illustrate Ogden's fierce, competitive spirit and unsportsmanlike conduct in his early Nor'wester days, as well as the devotion and deep-seated loyalty he received from his men.

Ogden remained at his Green Lake headquarters for the next few years, making occasional business and social visits to Île à la Crosse, where he enjoyed the companionship of Sam Black, who was still stationed there. He made one of these periodic visits in September, 1815, for he was in Île à la Crosse on September 13. The Hudson's Bay Company men watched his activities closely and noted that he and Black "stood in front of their post gazing at us as we arrived a little below their Buildings."[25]

Two days later Ogden and Black learned to their dismay that the Hudson's Bay Company had decided to build a post a short distance from the North West Company's fort on the main Indian trail. In charge of the project was Robert Logan, who took his goods by canoe to the point of land chosen for the establishment. Apprehensive and curious, Ogden and Black followed Logan and offered him "a house & even a small building" if he would disregard his company's decision and build alongside their post instead. The rivalry between the Hudson's Bay and North West companies was so intense by this time that employees of the two companies were willing to go to extreme lengths to keep their competitors from doing well in the Indian trade.

Logan rejected his unwanted visitors' offer and built his post, but he found himself being harassed by Black and Ogden when he went from Green Lake to Île à la Crosse. One way in which the two men were able to annoy members of the Hudson's Bay Company was to cut their nets, which, of course, interfered with their fishing. On March 20, 1816, Logan recorded in his journal that Ogden had arrived from Green Lake and that he took this opportunity to visit with the Nor'wester. Wrote Logan: "I had some conversation with him & *Black* the latter denies of having known any thing of the destruction of my Nets, there is no credit to be given to what they say."[26]

Logan was apprehensive about Ogden's appearance at Île à la Crosse, believing that he had come to confer with Black about the men Logan had sent to Paint River. The next day, March 21, Black and Ogden left Île à la Crosse with three of their men, probably to go to Green Lake. Logan was concerned because Ogden was still patrolling the Paint River region, attempting to keep Hudson's Bay Company personnel out of what he considered his territory. Logan's apprehension was unwarranted. No confrontation occurred in the Green Lake–Paint River vicinity in March, 1816.

Logan had good cause for worry, however, because Ogden's and Black's notoriety as rough competitors—in every sense of the word—was spreading. The Hudson's Bay Company men watched their movements even more closely. In April, 1816, Ogden was probably considered to have become especially violent, because James Bird's Edmonton House journal records a story he heard from some men who had been sent to Beaver River with a load of pemmican—the ground buffalo meat, preserved by fat and flavored with berries, that was the fur trader's staff of life on the trail. Bird's men did not witness Ogden's activities, but they learned of a serious incident at Green Lake from a Mr. McVicar and carried the tale back to Edmonton—the usual way stories moved hundreds of miles from post to post.

According to the McVicar account, the trouble started when two of

Ogden's Canadians stationed at Green Lake saw an Indian named Buffalo going toward the Hudson's Bay and North West companies' forts, which were located near each other. Since Logan had indicated that his new post "was opposite the N.W. Fort & exactly on the way of the Indians," Ogden had probably been losing trade because of his rival's strategic location. Ogden seems to have introduced a new method of securing trade. As Buffalo walked toward the two establishments, the Canadians decided to escort him to their own fort. Buffalo refused to go and told them "that he had been a Slave long enough, that he was old enough to think for himself and that in short he was now determined to go where he chose." The Canadians persisted until the Indian finally lost patience and fired at them. He missed.

The Canadians rushed to the North West Company post to report what had happened. Ogden immediately armed "six or seven Men," and all went to search for the Indian, whom they found "still continuing his way towards the Houses."[27] Ogden approached Buffalo and forced him to walk ahead of the little party as it began to return to Ogden's post. As they came opposite McVicar's home, which they had to pass in order to reach the fort, "the Indian who was still in possession of his Arms jumped to one side, ran off, and succeeded in gaining Mr. McVicars House where he expected to find protection." Ogden and his men went to the door and demanded that Buffalo be turned over to them. After some hesitation, McVicar consented, and "the Indian was turned out of the House *unarmed* to the mercy of Ogden and his worthy Companions." According to what appears to be a very biased Hudson's Bay Company report:

Ogden and his Men, who were principally Half Breeds, dragged the Indian out on the Ice of the Lake and there butchered him in a most cruel Manner. They first fired two Balls into his Body, then a Canadian half-breed stabbed him in the belly with a Bayonet and his Bowels fell out: The Indian then requested a gun that he might have a chance of revenging himself before he died, to which Ogden replied by ordering a Canadian to knock him down with an Axe. Still the Indian continued to his Feet till Ogden enraged tripped him, and when he was down stabbed him with his Dirk, after which a half breed literally cut him to pieces in revenge for the difficulty they had in killing him.[28]

This account seems unbelievable in many respects. It does appear credible, however, that Ogden and his men tried to keep Buffalo from trading with the Hudson's Bay Company, for throughout his career, Ogden displayed a fierce loyalty to his company and to his country, and he had a keen, competitive spirit. He also possessed sensitivity, particularly for human suffering, although it was disguised by a brusque, gruff façade. Nevertheless, whatever happened at Green Lake in the spring of 1816 had repercussions that greatly affected Ogden's career.

By 1818 a report of the Green Lake incident had reached Hudson's Bay Company's headquarters in Fenchurch Street, London, and was discussed at the executive level. By the time the story reached England, however, it was somewhat different, although the basic details were the same. According to the London version, an Indian visited the Hudson's Bay Company's post at Green Lake and was given a supply of British goods on credit. He was then invited to the North West Company's post to "drink some rum." He soon came running out, however. He had two gunshot wounds and took sanctuary within the walls of the Hudson's Bay post. Ogden and his men then went to the rival fort and asked that the Indian be given up, for "he was a murderer, having killed and eaten two Canadians." The Hudson's Bay Company employees had never "heard of this alleged murder," but for some unexplained reason, they forced the Indian to leave. Ogden and his men then seized him, dragged him to the lake, and killed him.

Governor Berens of the Hudson's Bay Company was incensed by Ogden's behavior. He wrote Lord Bathurst, the colonial secretary, in February, 1818:

> Other instances might be produced were it necessary, of similar acts committed by the North West Company's servants upon natives when trading with persons unconnected with that company, the perpetration of these outrages ... by no means confined to ignorant and half-breed Indians, but they are committed by persons who have generally received a good education, such at least as regularly to qualify them for commercial and mercantile concerns. Ogden a principal clerk of the North West Company, the son of one of the Judges at Montreal, cannot surely shelter himself under the plea of not knowing right from wrong, or grounding thereupon an excuse for murdering an Indian in cold blood, merely because the Indian was attempting to trade with British subjects not associated with himself or his employers.[29]

Undoubtedly, Berens' irritation resulted not only from Ogden's actions at Green Lake in the spring of 1816, but also from the fact that Ogden continued to fight savagely for his company throughout 1816 and 1817. John McLeod, the Hudson's Bay Company clerk in charge of the post at Île à la Crosse, and John McDougall, one of the servants stationed there, indicated "that a long course of violence had been pursued on the part of the North-West Company's towards that of the Hudson's Bay, by firing upon them at different times so as to alarm and insult them." One such incident occurred on January 2, 1817, when Sam Black, Ogden, Benjamin

Frobisher, another North West Company clerk, "and about thirty men, part of them armed . . . endeavored by words and gestures to provoke the Hudson's Bay Company's servants to come out and fight them."[30] This, however, was not nearly as serious as what happened two months later.

By 1817 competition was becoming particularly fierce and measures to reduce the advantages of the Hudson's Bay Company were becoming more stringent. On March 16, Black, theoretically operating under the orders of John Thompson, took possession of the Hudson's Bay Company's Île à la Crosse post. After securing the establishment and placing it in the hands of capable men, Black went to Green Lake. Ogden was especially pleased to hear of the turn of events at his former post and was exhilarated to learn that plans were under way to take over the British post at Green Lake as well. He and Black discussed how this might be accomplished, and then about noon on March 20, they walked over to the Hudson's Bay Company fort. They told a Mr. Ducharme, who was in charge of the post, to turn its keys over to them. He did, but to put himself on record, he said "Black . . . forced him to do so, which the latter acknowledged."

When Ogden and Black had made sure that Ducharme and his ten men could not escape, they unlocked all the doors to the fort's Indian shop and stores. There they found a "considerable quantity of goods and furs, principally beaver and martin skins, and ten canoes," which they took to their post. They displayed a modicum of compassion for their prisoners, leaving them some "provisions and tobacco." Two days later, Black put the Hudson's Bay men under heavy guard and escorted them to Île à la Crosse,[31] concluding another episode in the violent seesaw battle between the two rival companies.

While the Hudson's Bay Company men became more and more incensed over the capricious and violent activities of Ogden and Black and sent reports, memorials, and depositions to London, Ogden continued his activities in the Paint River area as far as its confluence with the North Saskatchewan River. It appears that he was now serving at Île à la Crosse because in July, 1817, he had a pleasant visit there from Dublin-born Nor'wester Ross Cox and his party, who were on their way to the Columbia River. They brought news and other refreshing topics of conversation.

Ogden especially enjoyed the arrival of visitors, for although he had a direct and somewhat irresponsible nature, he also longed for intellectual stimulation. He missed the long, spirited conversations in his father's drawing room, and at times he even missed his law studies. However, during the seven years since he had left Montreal for the wilds of

Saskatchewan, he had developed his own code of ethics and outlook on life.

During the long daylight evenings of late July, 1817, Cox listened in fascination to Ogden's steady stream of talk. He found Ogden to be a gracious and generous host, and he enjoyed the "excellent white fish, and tea without sugar," which was about the most lavish fare Ogden could offer at his interior post. Cox and Ogden had many lengthy discussions, during which Cox, who later became a writer and Dublin journalist, gained a good insight into Ogden's personality and character. He discovered that "the study of provincile jurisprudence, and seignorial subdivisions of Canadian property, had no charms for the mercurial temperment of Mr. Ogden; and, contrary to the wishes of his friends, he preferred the wild and untrammelled life of an Indian trader, to the 'law's delay,' and the wholesome restraints which are provided for the correction of over-exuberant spirits in civilised society."

Ogden told Cox many stories about his life in the Indian country. At twenty-seven, Ogden was a gifted and imaginative storyteller, and this talent made him a popular figure around campfires and in officers' messes throughout his life. Wrote Cox: "His accounts of his various rencontres with Orkney men and Indians would have filled a moderate-size octavo, and if reduced to writing would stagger the credulity of any person unacquainted with the Indian country; and although some of his statements were slightly tinctured with the prevalent failing of *La Guienne*, there was *vraisemblance* enough throughout to command our belief in their general accuracy."

Like virtually everyone else in the fur trade, Cox had heard of Ogden's drastic acts against the Hudson's Bay Company, and he attempted to rationalize them: "In a Country . . . in which there is no legal tribunal to appeal to, and into which the 'King's writ does not run,' many acts must be committed that would not stand a strict investigation in Banco Regis." He and Ogden discussed the subject at length, and Ogden told him that "my legal primer says the necessity has no law." Certainly this was the policy of expediency that Ogden had been carrying out very effectively against the Hudson's Bay Company. Ogden reinforced his basic philosophy by attempting to rationalize his actions on the basis of location. He told Cox that "in this place, where the custom of the country, or as lawyers say, the *Lex non scripta* is our only guide, we must, in our acts of summary legislation, sometimes perform the parts of judge, jury, sheriff, hangman, gallows, and all."

On July 29, 1817, Cox and his party departed Île à la Crosse for the Columbia. He must have felt sad because he wrote in his journal: "We bid adieu to the humourous, honest, eccentric, law-defying Peter Ogden, the terror of Indians, and the delight of all gay fellows."[32] Neither realized that Ogden would soon follow Cox west.

As Ogden was entertaining Cox, Hudson's Bay Company officers in North America and England were developing a policy which would attempt to arrest and bring to justice all persons who had taken hostile action against the company. By August, 1817, "McLellan, Mainville, Peter Pangman (Bostonois) and Seraphim LeMar" had been taken into custody at Red River and were being sent to Montreal, and the company was looking for "Alex. MacDonnell, Cuthbert Grant, John Campbell . . . [and] Peter Ogden who was guilt[y] of a most barbarous murder."[33] The North West Company decided that Ogden should be transferred to the Columbia River, where he would be out of the Hudson's Bay Company's reach. Thus ended the first chapter in Peter Skene Ogden's fur-trading career. The second was to be even more exciting.

Across the Great Divide

PETER SKENE OGDEN departed for the Columbia River in late summer, 1818. It was a sad occasion for him because he had come to think of the Green Lake–Île à la Crosse region as home; in fact, he had even started a family. Probably in 1815 or 1816, Ogden took a Cree woman as his wife. On January 18, 1817, their son Peter was born. What happened to Ogden's wife is not known, but young Peter was educated at the Protestant school at Red River and followed in his father's footsteps, becoming an important figure in the New Caledonian (British Columbian) fur trade.

Ogden's buoyant spirit was not dampened for long. Since he had never been farther west than the vicinity of Île à la Crosse, he considered his assignment to the Columbia an adventure. He had long been aware of the North West Company's keen interest in the Far West, and he knew that as early as 1804 it had made a resolute attempt to gain control of the Upper Missouri by sending François Antoine Larocque to win over the Sioux and Crow Indians. Larocque's party spent the winter in the Mandan villages, near which Lewis and Clark later made their camp. In 1805, Larocque passed beyond the Mandan villages to the Little Bighorn, the Bighorn, and finally the Yellowstone rivers, but the United States government refused to allow trade south of the forty-ninth parallel, so the North West Company had to continue its westward expansion farther to the north.[1]

The work of carrying the North West Company's trade to the Pacific Coast was entrusted to a group of able men, the most notable of whom was David Thompson. In 1807, Thompson crossed the Rockies and reached the headwaters of the Columbia. In 1809 he again crossed the mountains and built Kullyspell House, situated on the east shore of Lake Pend Oreille in what is now northern Idaho. From here he moved to Clarks Fork of the Columbia and in November built the first Salish House, which was located near the site of present-day Thompson Falls, Montana. Shortly thereafter, Thompson or one of his companions built Spokane House, Ogden's first seat of authority west of the Rockies. After carrying his exploration to an area above the mouth of the Snake River, Thompson claimed the entire region in the name of Great Britain.[2]

Ironically, ahead of Thompson at the mouth of the Columbia River was the first far western trading party of Ogden's old employer, John Jacob Astor's Pacific Fur Company, the Pacific Coast subsidiary of his American Fur Company. Although an American enterprise, it was under the command of Duncan McDougal and three other men, all former Nor'westers. The promising future of the Pacific Fur Company was abruptly changed by the War of 1812, however, and the North West Company's position was strengthened. When news of the outbreak of war was brought to them and a British warship was reported to be sailing toward their post, Astoria, Astor's associates in the Oregon country, undoubtedly influenced to some extent by their British citizenship and previous connections, decided that it would be useless to attempt to hold their ground. Therefore, in October, 1813, they sold Astoria and all of the Pacific Fur Company's interest in the region to the North West Company. When the British warship arrived, Astoria was renamed Fort George in honor of George III and began a colorful career as the major British entrepôt on the Pacific Coast.

Fort George was Ogden's destination in 1818 when he left Île à la Crosse and pushed out across what seemed to be an endless sea of grass drying in the summer's heat. After traversing hundreds of miles of this stark, unchanging landscape, he finally saw the Rockies rising majestically on the western horizon, a sight that never failed to inspire him. As he approached them, he could see their rugged crags and snowy peaks, and as he passed through them, he discovered that his narrow trail sometimes dropped off thousands of feet to a rushing river far below.

After many days of wrestling with the mountains, Ogden found himself being whisked down the Columbia in a planked boat. He had heard a great deal about this magnificent waterway of the West, and he recalled conversations about it in his father's drawing room in Montreal. It was much like the St. Lawrence, for it was a strong, wide river. He marveled at the thick stands of firs (later named after his friend David Douglas) that went down to the water's edge and the little islands, partly covered by gnarled trees, that dotted the river's lower course.

Finally he arrived at Fort George. This place that he was to call home for the next six months was a cluster of log buildings on an acre of land surrounded by a heavy stockade. It was similar to most other fur-trading forts in having a gallery around the stockade, with loopholes for musketry. On two diagonal corners were two-story log bastions, each fitted with an eighteen-pound cannon to give added protection to the lonely little outpost, perched on the south shore near the mouth of the Columbia. Conditions, however, inside the fort were far from forlorn, especially for the gentlemen, a class distinction which was rigidly maintained by all of the British fur-trading companies. Also within the fort's walls were a large dining hall, warehouses for trade goods and furs, a blacksmith shop, a carpenter shop, and a trading store. Ogden was pleasantly surprised that European delicacies were brought to Fort George by ship, for his educated palate had become tired of the simple and unexciting diet at Green Lake and Île à la Crosse.

Ogden found that the men at Fort George not only ate and slept well, but also enjoyed an extremely pleasant diversion. The story is that Donald Mackenzie brought to the post Chief Concomly's daughter, known as the Princess of Wales. She in turn brought with her ten female slaves. With an eye to material gain, she began to rent these women out, particularly to newly arrived men, and soon her business was flourishing. Ogden, who was still young and carefree and who enjoyed the company of a woman, undoubtedly partook of the offering.

Shortly after his arrival, Ogden received his first Pacific Coast assignment. Oskononton, one of the Iroquois who had been brought west by the North West Company,[3] revolted against Mackenzie. Not being able to get along alone among "foreign" Indians, however, he returned to the fort in a repentant state. He was forgiven and sent off to trap the Cowlitz River, a tributary of the Columbia, with some of his fellow tribesmen. Oskononton and his irresponsible comrades did more than trap the Cowlitz. They decided to sample the charms of the Cowlitz women, and while they were trying to capture one, Oskononton was killed. The party returned to Fort George and reported the matter to James Keith, who was in charge. Keith was a very capable man in many respects, but he did have a penchant for bungling. He now demonstrated it.

Keith decided to send Ogden to the Cowlitz with thirty Iroquois to investigate the situation. Ogden found the Indians virtually uncontrollable, and when they reached the Cowlitz camp, before he had an opportunity to give an order, the Iroquois began firing indiscriminately, killing twelve innocent men, women, and children. Chief How How had been very helpful in attempting to find Oskononton's murderer, but when he saw his people being slaughtered, he became enraged. Ogden reasoned with the Indians (a skill for which he later became widely known) and was able to convince How How to visit Fort George after promising that a "gentleman" at that post would marry his daughter.

When Chief How How arrived at the fort, accompanied by a company guard to protect him from his enemies, the Chinooks, Ogden congratulated himself that the situation was well in hand. In true storybook fashion, the chief's daughter is said to have happily married a white man, and How How, laden with presents, departed. But this time he was without an armed escort, and about three hundred yards from the North West Company post, a party of Chinooks, waiting in ambush, attacked him. In the confusion, the guard on duty at the fort thought it was How How and his men who were attacking and ordered the Nor'westers on the stockade gallery to open fire. Fortunately, the mistake was soon discovered and Chief How How reentered the post. Keith tried to explain this bizarre incident but to no avail. Relations between the North West Company and the Cowlitz Indians remained strained for a number of years.[4]

Sometime in the late fall of 1818, Ogden was ordered to take charge of David Thompson's old post, Spokane House,[5] at the junction of the Spokane and Little Spokane rivers about ten miles northwest of what is now Spokane, Washington. He was pleasantly surprised, for he found it to be just as Alexander Ross has described it: composed of "handsome buildings" and "there was a ball-room, even; and no females in the land so fair to look upon as the nymphs of Spokane . . . there were fine horses also."[6] What more could a man want?

Ogden undoubtedly agreed that Spokane women were especially attractive, and shortly after his arrival, Julia Rivet, a Nez Percé[7] and the stepdaughter of old François Rivet, who had first come west with Lewis and Clark, caught his eye. Ogden found the widow attractive and saw her as a capable woman who would be a helpmate as well as a good mother. His abrupt move from Green Lake and Île à la Crosse must have been a sobering experience, for he certainly showed great maturity in selecting an older woman as his "wife." Little did he realize that his choice of a Nez Percé would allow him in later years to effect the release of the Whitman Massacre hostages from the Nez Percés and would make his name immortal in the Northwest. He now took his job as the head of Spokane House very seriously, since he hoped that during the year 1818–19 he could equal "the returns of last [year]."

In the spring of 1819, Ogden headed east, probably to Fort William, the North West Company depot on the western shore of Lake Superior. Roderick McKenzie, Jr., of the Hudson's Bay Company encountered him not far from Lake Superior on his way from Point Meuron to Lac la Pluie (Rainy Lake). Ogden was traveling in a light canoe with one passenger and eight men at the paddles. Although he had become a more responsible young man during the course of the past winter in the West, he still harbored hatred for the Hudson's Bay Company. McKenzie later wrote that Ogden kept aloof from his party "& would not allow any of their Men to speak to my people."[8]

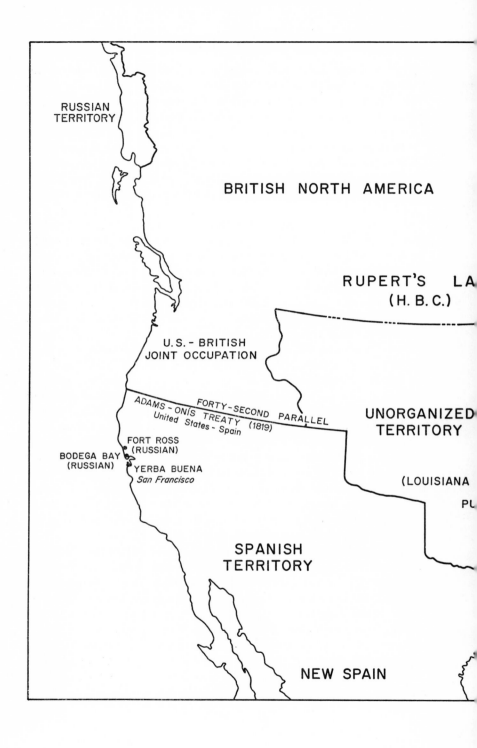

Ogden's Political Environment, 1820

By August, Ogden had completed his business in the East and was ready to return to the Columbia before winter set in. On August 26, 1819, Colin Robertson recorded that Ogden and John Haldane, the kindly but stern Scotsman who was so fond of Ogden, had passed Fort Cumberland and were headed for "the Columbia by way of Beaver River." The Nor'westers were sparing with Robertson and other Hudson's Bay Company employees, for he noted that "those worthies have thought it convenient to circulate, that their destination is Athabaska."[9] The astute Robertson was not fooled. When he was at Île à la Crosse two weeks later, he saw Sam Black making preparations for travel. "Haldane and that vagabond Ogden have gone across the Mountains," he wrote. "I presume Black will follow them."[10]

Black was not to follow Ogden quite so soon. While Ogden was on the Columbia, Black had been having problems of his own. The "involved maneuvres, outbreaks of violence, threats, bribery and interference with rival express packets" were continuing, and the Hudson's Bay Company men were equipping the Indians with trade goods and rum and even forcing the Indians to trade with them. Black continued his policy of intimidation, however, and on October 11, 1818, as Colin Robertson was reading a funeral service over one of his men, Black and Simon McGillivray broke into Fort Wedderburn on Lake Athabaska and took Robertson prisoner. He remained a captive for almost a year, but in 1819 he was able to escape and was back at Fort Wedderburn on Coal Island by September.

Meanwhile, Black attempted to cope with the failing fortunes of the North West Company in the Athabaska District, repeatedly writing to the company's agent at Fort William for more and better-quality trade goods. But the Colin Robertson affair was not over yet. In the middle of May, 1820, a Mr. Spence, a constable, arrived at Fort Wedderburn "with warrants against several of the N.W. Coy., for illegal seizure of my [Robertson's] person in October 1818. . . . Black unfortunately escaped the day I arrived, having drawn his pistol upon the Constable as he approached him."[11]

Black's escape route was virtually the same trail that Ogden had taken two years earlier. On June 12, 1820, he left the Fort Wedderburn–Fort Chipewyan region and headed for the west side of the Rockies. He immediately went to McLeod's Lake, then pressed on to Stuart's and Fraser lakes in New Caledonia, a region which he had not seen before but which he would come to know well, for some years later the region would be administered by Ogden and, ironically, Black would lose his life there.

Life was going smoothly for Ogden at Spokane House. When he returned from the East in the early fall of 1819, he learned that he had become the father of a son, Charles, born on September 5.[12] In addition, the North West Company was so pleased with his management of the post that it made him a partner in the company on July 12, 1820. Ogden was content with the way his family and business life were going, so much so that he was oblivious to what was happening elsewhere. Furthermore, since he was west of the mountains, he was isolated from news of events at Fort William and in Montreal and London. At the age of thirty, he was still thinking in terms of physical feuds with the Hudson's Bay Company and was not too concerned about the basic trade considerations involved.

By 1820 both the North West and Hudson's Bay companies, after having engaged in a protracted struggle for supremacy for more than a decade, felt severely the results of undercutting and overbidding. At the council of the Nor'westers held at Fort William in 1820, the wintering partners learned that their company was in dire financial straits, and there emerged a strong minority who were interested in coming to terms with the Hudson's Bay Company. In England, Edward ("Bear") Ellice and William and Simon McGillivray were joined by Dr. John McLoughlin and Angus Bethune, and the five men continued negotiations with the Hudson's Bay Company with this purpose in mind. As a result, the two companies merged under the name of the Hudson's Bay Company on March 26, 1821.

Probably no one was more surprised at the coalition than Ogden. His surprise soon turned to shock, however, when he learned that because of his violent methods of combating the Hudson's Bay Company, he, Sam Black, and Cuthbert Grant had been excluded from the merger. It was most irritating to him that those who had not taken the rivalry so seriously and had done their daily jobs methodically and were more interested in collecting their salaries than fighting, now made the transfer to the new company while he and his friends, who had given their all to the North West Company, found themselves unemployed.

Even though it refused to give him a job, the Company felt that Ogden was valuable. As the merger went into effect, the English organization began to worry about a replacement for him at the post on Thompson River (it appears that he had been sent to Kamloops sometime in 1820 or 1821). Since there was no one to take the position immediately, Ogden's old friend John Haldane, who had made the transition from the North West Company easily, wrote Ogden and asked him to continue to conduct business in his district for the Hudson's Bay Company. John

Dugald Cameron, who was in charge of Fort George, asked Ogden verbally to oblige the Company in this manner. Cameron was pleased that Ogden agreed "most Cordially notwithstanding the mortification that he must have suffered from his exclusion." Cameron added:

This must have been a great sacrifice on Mr. Ogden's part, His feelings severely wounded as they must have been; there are few Others who would have Continued in the charge: Besides the difference of living between Fort George (to which place Mr. Ogden might have retired to pass the Winter) and Thompson's River were such as would have enduced many others for much less cause than Mr. Ogden had, to relinquish a charge from which, according to the present agreement, he could derive but little personal satisfaction, and where he must suffer much from bad food.[13]

Although Ogden must have felt keenly the humiliation of being passed over, he did not panic, but thought seriously about the circumstances in which he found himself. He has often been considered an irresponsible person, but his ability to evaluate a situation, regardless of his emotional involvement in it, is certainly not characteristic of a temperamental individual, but, rather, the mark of a levelheaded, intelligent man. Ogden loved the fur trade, and he hated to think that perhaps he would be forced to give it up.

Ogden undoubtedly reasoned during the winter of 1821–22 that his doing a favor for the Hudson's Bay Company by looking after its interests on Thompson River would provide sufficient grounds for a review of his case. He also thought that if the Company would not have him, he, Sam Black, and Cuthbert Grant could develop their own organization and compete with the English giant. He knew, of course, that the Company was now much more powerful: since the merger, the British government had given it trading privileges which extended over three million square miles, or approximately one-fourth of the North American continent. It was probably for this reason that Ogden decided he would do everything possible to bring himself to the Company's attention, hoping that he would ultimately be asked to join.

In addition to his unofficial work for the Company at Thompson River, Ogden felt that a trip to London to plead his case at headquarters might help. His decision was undoubtedly influenced by the fact that his aging and ailing father had left Canada and was now living at Taunton in Somerset. Ogden had never been to England, almost seven thousand miles away, but once he had made up his mind, he was not to be deterred by mere distance.

By the spring of 1822, Ogden had finished his business at Thompson River and was ready to start east on the first leg of his journey. He first went to Fort Nez Percés, arriving there April 20. On April 23, he, John Haldane, John Lewes (whom he had treated so badly a few years earlier), and a party were ready to leave for York Factory on Hudson Bay.[14] By May 3 the group had reached "the first lake from the portage . . . to the Rocky Mountains" and all was going well.[15] They made good time crossing the mountains and the plains, and by June 15 they had reached Cumberland House on the Saskatchewan River. They stayed there overnight and set out early the next morning for Norway House, near the northeast end of Lake Winnipeg.[16] By June 25 they were at Fort Alexander, situated at the mouth of Winnipeg River, en route to Fort William and "on their way out to Canada."[17]

Although there is no mention of Sam Black's arriving at Norway House, he must have joined the party en route, for he was with Ogden at Fort Alexander. There has always been some doubt about whether Black accompanied Ogden to England, but no evidence has been found to support the theory that he did. Perhaps at this time—June, 1822—Ogden and Black were hoping to be reinstated in the Hudson's Bay Company without going to England; they had friends who were trying to help them achieve that goal. As early as April 3, John Dugald Cameron had written to Governor Simpson about Ogden's plight, mentioning how generous Ogden had been in handling the company's business at Thompson River.[18] However, Simpson was faced with the problem of an employee surplus, now that most of the former Nor'westers had been incorporated into the Hudson's Bay Company, and he had received a letter from London: "From the great number of young men now in the country, it will necessarily be a heavy burden upon the trade, and it is a matter of the greatest importance to consider of the *proper* mode of reducing the Establishment of Clerks and Servants to what may be necessary to carry on the trade in an efficient and economical manner."[19]

In answering Cameron's letter, Simpson noted that it was presented to him by Ogden's old friend John Haldane and that he had "laid [it] before the Council." When the Council of the Northern Department read Cameron's letter on Ogden's behalf, it indicated that it appreciated

Mr. Ogden's ready attention to the request of Mr. Haldane, but as they [the members of the council] are totally unacquainted with any agreement or understanding between the Honble. Committee and Messrs. Black & Ogden they must decline entering into the subject and cannot help remarking that the observations in your Letter relative to those Gentlemen are not sufficiently guarded and rather unseasonable; they however feel for their situation and could wish that they had been more fortunate.[20]

Simpson was not particularly interested in the Ogden-Black case. He was more concerned about economic considerations, partly because of his unbending temperament and partly because of his countinghouse experience with the London firm of Graham, Simpson and Wedderburn. Furthermore, he had been with the Hudson's Bay Company for only two years, and he was more eager to make a good showing for himself than to befriend two "vagabonds" or "ruffians," as Black and Ogden had been described. Thus when he wrote to Andrew Colvile of the London Committee, he was not at all sympathetic:

A party was attempted to be formed in order to petition the Committee to have Black and Ogden re-instated, but I do not believe they will proceed with it. Bird was applied to, but he would not join and Haldane sounded me but I gave him so little encouragement that the thing is likely to fall to the ground. Mr. Halket[21] I understand met those Gentn. also Cuthbert Grant at the bottom of the River Winnipeg on their way to Canada, he received them graciously and they in turn were very polite and respectful.[22]

Undoubtedly it was his returning to Canada in July, 1822, and finding that the Council of the Northern Department had not taken favorable action on Cameron and Haldane's pleas for his reinstatement that caused Ogden to make definite plans to go to London and discuss his case with the former North West Company representatives there and through them with the Governor and Committee of the Hudson's Bay Company. It is not known when or how Ogden journeyed to London. He left Montreal in the fall of 1822. Perhaps he sailed from this port before the freeze, or journeyed overland to Boston or New York and boarded a ship there. He was in England during the winter and early spring of 1822–23.

One wonders whether Ogden's ship sailed directly up the Thames to London. More than likely, it went to Liverpool, for most Company men sailed from New York to Liverpool at a cost of forty-five guineas and stayed at the Waterloo Hotel before going on to London or some other destination.[23] Regardless of how he reached London, Ogden decided to splurge and enjoy himself on his first visit to England. He had lived in the wilds of North America for the past twelve years under some rather primitive conditions, particularly at Thompson River. He had not spent much of his salary[24] since his needs were relatively few, so expensive indulgences on his first real holiday were perfectly understandable.

Ogden stayed at the London Coffee House on Ludgate Hill. The establishment, at 24 Ludgate Street,[25] was well known for many reasons. It was luxuriously equipped to serve the most discriminating guests, for it was "a large and superb mansion with a profusion of attendants, first rate cooks, the smartest chambermaids, hair dressers, porters and shoe blacks."[26] Ogden must have enjoyed seeing young, blond servant girls with smooth pink and white complexions, certainly a contrast to his attractive but older Indian wife, whose face was already becoming lined with wrinkles.

He found that the London Coffee House lived up to its reputation of being "the most elegant . . . in the three kingdoms," and he was enchanted by its history. James Boswell was a frequent visitor in the latter part of the eighteenth century, and, in 1811, Broadhurst, the well-known tenor, is said to have broken a wine glass on one of the tables while singing a high note. Ogden also found the clientele stimulating, since most of the people who stayed at the London Coffee House were successful men from different walks of life, but particularly "Physicians, dissenting Clergy, and masters of academies." During Ogden's visit a disagreeing jury from the nearby Old Bailey was probably confined there, a customary occurrence, since the London Coffee House stood within the Rules of the Fleet Prison.[27]

Ogden enjoyed himself thoroughly. He loved conversation on almost any topic and had been virtually starved intellectually for years, since few books or periodicals (much out of date) reached the western posts. In the Saskatchewan country he at least had Sam Black to visit and argue with, but they confined their discussions to subjects related to natural phenomena. Thus it was exciting to hear spirited talk about the death of George III, who was so well known in America and who had affected the Ogden fortunes so greatly, and about the accession of George IV, as well as discussions of the agricultural depression. Much more exhilarating for Ogden, however, who was a voracious reader, was to discover the wealth of new literature that had appeared in the years since Waterloo. As William and Mary Wordsworth, Samuel Coleridge, John Keats, Percy B. Shelley, Lord Byron, Jane Austen, Sir Walter Scott, and many others were discussed by his fellow conversationalists, he must have sat enthralled, even at the sophisticated age of thirty-two.

However much Ogden enjoyed his stay at the London Coffee House, he did not lose sight of the purpose of his journey. Shortly after his arrival, he called on three former North West Company agents in London: William and Simon McGillivray and Edward Ellice. They were sympathetic to his and Sam Black's plight and said they would try to help. Ogden did not know it but he was also receiving help from another and unexpected quarter. By the winter of 1822–23, Governor Simpson had changed his mind, perhaps because he had found a statement in Cameron's letter written many months earlier a little unnerving on closer examination: "I have reason to believe should Ogden and Black go out of the Country they will not [agree] to the arrangements for them last year [1821]. Hence we might soon expect an Opposition in the Columbia."[28]

On February 27, 1823, the Board for Consulting and Advising on the Management of the Trade met with Governor John Henry Pelly, William and Simon McGillivray, and Benjamin Harrison. "The Board then took into consideration the several letters referred to them by the Committee, and the application of messrs. Ogden and Black." The McGillivrays and Edward Ellice kept their promise to Ogden and told the board that they were willing to turn over to Ogden and Black "two of the three shares of the Profits under the 4th Article of the Deed Poll to facilitate their admission into the Service." With this kind of aid forthcoming from the North West Company's agents, the board "Recommended that Messrs. Ogden & Black be appointed Clerks of the 1st Class in the Northern Factory, with a Salary equivalent to the Amount of a Chief Trader's Share to be paid out of the said assigned Shares."[29]

Of course, Ogden did not know what was taking place at Hudson's Bay House, so he passed the time by taking long walks around London. He undoubtedly walked from Ludgate, which was presumably the eastern gate of the old Roman wall[30] that once surrounded the old city of London, to St. Paul's Cathedral. Here he marveled at the great structure begun in 1675 by Christopher Wren, an adviser to the Hudson's Bay Company. He must have wandered on to see Wren's monument to commemorate the Great Fire of 1666, perhaps even as far as the yellowish-white stone Tower of London, from which he could have seen the well-used passageway to the Thames and London Bridge, all so different from anything he had ever seen in Quebec or Montreal. There is no evidence to indicate that he was received by the Governor and Committee, but out of curiosity he must have walked up Ludgate Hill past St. Paul's Cathedral and on to Cannon Street, now a booming financial center, before making his way to Nos. 3 and 4 Fenchurch Street, where the Hudson's Bay Company's headquarters stood.[31]

Ogden was apprehensive during these days of February and early March, 1823, for he had written to the Governor and Committee on January 29 and had not yet received a reply. However, he was able to put some of his free time to good use. He made a trip to Taunton to visit his ailing, eighty-two-year-old father, his mother, and his half-sisters Mary and Catharine. The old man was delighted by the visit, but he realized that this would be the last time he would see his undoubtedly favorite son because Peter Skene was following the spirit of adventure that had fired his own imagination. On March 9 the old judge, who was to live for another year, wrote to Ogden:

The thought that we are separating forever in this world was so afflicting that I found myself unequal to take leave of you in Person, and indeed [to] bid you adieu in this mode fills my heart with grief which I cannot express. You have my blessing and my prayers that God of his great mercy & goodness may ever preserve you in all your perils & dangers to which you will be exposed. And that he will give you grace to be grateful for all the benefits & favours he may vouch safe to bestow on you, that you may repose your trust & confidence in him, and that through the whole course of your life you may be vigilant & careful to keep his commandments, to have faith in our blessed redeemer, and finally through his merits & atonement you may be eternally blessed & happy. You will as often as you have leisure think on these things, and that you may benefit & profit by those reflections, as being apointed [*sic*] to your present & future welfare.

Let me recommend to you to be careful of your health and not to expose yourself to danger unnecessarily. You will of course be exposed to many in the discharge of your duty, but let me entreat you not to court them or be a volunteer in any hazardous enterprise for which you will get little thanks & credit.

The old man knew his son well.

I long much to receive a letter from you. I suppose I shall receive one tomorrow.[32]

Ogden's letter not only thanked his father for a lovely visit, but also related some exciting news. On March 6, William Smith, secretary of the Hudson's Bay Company, had written to him to inform him that the Governor and Committee had appointed him "a Clerk of the first Class in the Northern Factory" and had even suggested to the Council of the Northern Department that his appointment be retroactive, indicating that he should "be admitted a Chief Trader from the 1st June 1821."[33] Ogden was especially pleased that his good friend Sam Black was to be similarly reinstated.

Although it appears, at least on the surface, that William and Simon McGillivray and Edward Ellice were Ogden's chief benefactors, Governor Simpson had undoubtedly swayed the Governor's and Committee's thinking to some degree. On March 10, 1823, four days after Ogden was informed of his appointment, London Committee member Andrew Colvile wrote to Governor Simpson and told him that the Governor and Committee had recommended "Blacke & Ogden to be admitted chief traders & that you should employ Cuthbert Grant as a Clerk. This has been done in great measure in consequence of your recommendation & from your representing that they had been rather the instruments than the contrivers of mischief." As a result of Simpson's comments, the

Governor and Committee were able to rationalize the three men's behavior: "Whatever might have been their delinquency they were not a bit worse than many who had been in the first arrangements."[34] Simpson was pleased to be recognized as the former Nor'westers' benefactor and acknowledged his actions when he wrote to Colvile, saying: "I feel highly flattered that so much attention has been paid to my recommendation, they will be very useful men and will prove they are worthy of the indulgence that has been shewn them."[35]

Until recently it was not known when or how Ogden returned to Canada, but if documentary information is diligently pieced together, it becomes clear that Ogden probably left London shortly after he received news of his appointment. The Governor and Committee apparently had confidence in him, for when he left the English capital, he carried packets to be delivered to York and Moose factories on Hudson and James bays, respectively, a common method of sending communications. Ogden traveled overland to Liverpool and boarded the ship *James Munro*, bound for the United States.

Other Hudson's Bay Company employees were aboard the ship, and one wonders how they treated Ogden. Chief Factor John Davis, who was also carrying Company packets, probably received him graciously. But James Bird,[36] who had written so critically from Edmonton House about Ogden's activities in the Green Lake–Île à la Crosse region and who had refused the previous year to join the York Factory group that wanted to reinstate Ogden, must have felt somewhat self-conscious.

The *James Munro* sailed into the East River and docked at New York City;[37] Ogden and James Bird now began their journey to Montreal. They probably chose the usual route, so beautifully described by Nicholas Garry in 1821. If so, they took the steamboat up the tree-lined Hudson River and admired the beautiful houses on the hills and at the water's edge. The 170-mile trip upriver took approximately twenty hours, so the men had a chance to enjoy the luxurious surroundings that the boat provided, to drink brandy, smoke fine cigars, and eat beautifully prepared and well-served meals. After spending the night on the vessel, they disembarked at Albany.

In Albany, they stayed at an excellent hotel, the Eagle Inn, run "by an Englishman." The proprietor undoubtedly wanted to hear the latest news from his homeland, and Ogden and Bird regaled him with stories about London. The next morning, they took a "light carriage" along the Hudson to Troy, then passed Waterford on the Mohawk River, and finally arrived at beautiful Saratoga Springs, where they dined. They did not stay at Saratoga, but pushed on to Sandy Hill, about fifty miles from Albany. On the following day, their fourth out of New York, they took a steamboat from Whitehall up Lake Champlain. This trip took almost as long as the Hudson journey because of the many stops at shore points. After arriving at St. Jean at the northern end of the lake, they covered the relatively short distance to Montreal by carriage.[38]

How long Ogden remained in Montreal is not known. He probably stayed there several days, visiting his brothers Charles and Henry and giving them the latest news about their ailing father. Perhaps he also saw his brother Isaac and Isaac's daughter Annie, who was two years old. Ogden later became extremely attached to Annie, so he must have met the child at this time, since he did not visit Montreal again until 1844, when he took Annie to England with him.

Ogden probably participated in the exuberant social life which was so much a part of Montreal. While he was there, probably in May, 1823, the social season was coming to a spectacular end before the summer holidays. Undoubtedly there was an endless succession of parties, balls, and theatrical offerings, all of which were on a lavish scale and well attended by the commercial elite, members of the British regimental garrison stationed there, and representatives of the government. The whirlwind of activity gave Ogden an opportunity to renew old acquaintances and make new ones.

Ogden's ambitious nature made him anxious to leave Montreal and assume his new role, so he and James Bird set out about the second week in May on their long trip to York Factory. From Montreal they proceeded up the beautiful and swift Ottawa River to Lake Nipissing, then pressed on to Sault Ste. Marie at the channel between Lakes Huron and Superior. Here they crossed to Fort William, the chief supply depot of the old North West Company, which Ogden viewed with nostalgia, and went on to Lac la Pluie, where they arrived "about 10 A.M." on June 8, 1823.[39] From Rainy Lake they moved along the fur-trade route to the mouth of Winnipeg River, up Lake Winnipeg to Norway House, then on to York Factory.

They arrived in time to attend the meeting of the Council of the Northern Department of Ruperts Land which convened there on July 5.[40] Here Ogden probably met Governor Simpson for the first time, since Simpson presided at the meeting.[41] During the course of the conference, Sam Black arrived. The York Factory Journal states that on "July 12 . . . arrived . . . Saml. Black Esqr., from England (via Canada)."[42] Here is one of those curious statements that indicate Black must have been in England, although it is strange that he came to the meeting alone and not in the company of Ogden and Bird.

Although he was not physically present, Ogden was much interested in the proceedings of the Council, for they affected him greatly. Through Resolution 123, Ogden and Black were reinstated in the Hudson's Bay Company according to the wishes of the Governor and Committee. Another resolution appointed Ogden to the Spokane House District, where he was "instructed to fit out a Trapping expedition next spring [1824] for the Snake country, for which 8 additional hired Servants to the present establishment, will be provided him, and that said expedition be placed under the direction of Alexr. Ross Clark."

The Council considered all eventualities and stated that Ogden should be "provided with a Canoe & 8 men for to convey him to the Columbia and that Rolls Tobacco and Guns be embarked by him along the route." While Ogden was assigned to Spokane House, Sam Black was appointed to accompany Donald Manson on an expedition "for the purpose of exploring a tract of Country laying on the west side of the Rocky Mountains from the head waters of Finlays Branch, to proceed as far North as the season will permit, then recross the mountains in order to fall on some of the streams leading into Mckenzies River."[43] The two old friends were to be temporarily parted again.

Before the Council meeting ended on July 22, Ogden embarked for the West. On the morning of July 18 he and John Work and a party of men set out for the Columbia in two light canoes, accompanied for a while by John Lee Lewes.[44] They followed the Hayes River–Norway House route to the top of Lake Winnipeg and arrived at Cumberland House on Cumberland Lake on August 5. Here they left Lewes and proceeded along the Churchill River to Île à la Crosse, which they reached eleven days later. Apparently they had eaten well, or at least sufficiently, since they consumed 1,035 pounds of venison pemmican after leaving York Factory.[45]

When Ogden and Work left Île à la Crosse, Ogden's major concern was the future, and as he moved west, he seemed to gain new vigor: he was eager to prove himself to his new employers. Simpson was fully aware of Ogden's attitude, for in a letter to Andrew Colvile dated September 8, 1823, he noted that "Ogden has gone to the Columbia and determined to do great things: he does not want for ability."[46]

While Simpson was writing to Colvile, Ogden and Work were encountering problems on the trail. Some of the pemmican they obtained at Cumberland House was moldy and inedible. When they reached Île à la Crosse, they learned that the post had very little dried meat to give them, and Ogden knew that it was a long haul to Moose Portage, where pemmican from Fort Edmonton was to await them. To make matters worse, they found the water in the North Saskatchewan River, which they were attempting to navigate, extremely low because it was the end of summer. They tried to pole their canoes over the mud and sand. This badly damaged the boats' frail bottoms, and finally the crews were forced to wade along and carry the canoes where the water was shallow or the river dry. They pushed on, however, with every hour of exertion seeming like ten. Their spirits began to rise when they neared Moose Portage, which meant pemmican in everyone's mind. But when they reached this spot, near the present-day Alberta-Saskatchewan border, there was no food.

Ogden and Work were grievously disappointed. They knew only too well that to try to continue on the trail without food was suicide. Therefore, they decided that Work should go to Fort Edmonton for the necessary supplies and Ogden should remain at Moose Portage with the party. As Work headed west, he became lost temporarily, so it took longer than estimated for him to reach this important prairie post, situated a few miles from the broad sweep of the North Saskatchewan River and a short distance from the eastern slopes of the Rockies. Upon his arrival he received another blow: even Fort Edmonton was experiencing a food shortage. However, he was given a small quantity of pemmican and was told that he and Ogden would find food in the second cache designated in their instructions.

During Work's absence, Ogden found himself in desperate straits. He felt miserable physically because he was ill, but even though he had fits of shivering at night, he was always up early, pressing his men to pick berries or try to catch fish. Finally he decided that he must move his party, and he was able to lead it to a spot where some Indians were encamped. In this vicinity Ogden encountered an Indian who was taking sixty pounds of pemmican to supply Chief Trader Connolly, who was then at Lesser Slave Lake. Ogden commandeered the meat and, with his party and himself in a very weakened condition, began to move westward. After passing Lac la Biche, Ogden met Bird's party returning from Fort Edmonton, so he was able to make good the pemmican he owed Connolly. Since he knew that he was on Connolly's route, he replaced the sixty pounds of pemmican that he had taken and paid Connolly a little interest in the form of fresh meat.[47] Now well equipped and with Work back in camp, the combined party set out for Edmonton House.

They probably arrived at Edmonton House about September 20. The Edmonton District Journal of Occurrences does not begin until September 24, 1823,[48] because of John Rowand's absence, so there is no mention

43

of Ogden's arrival there, which would indicate that the party passed through a few days before the journal was begun. When Ogden and Work arrived at Edmonton House, Ogden found his family waiting for him. It must have been a joyous reunion, for he and his wife had been separated for more than a year. The party left Edmonton House about September 22 or 23 on horseback and headed for Fort Assiniboine, which was then under construction. Situated on the shore of the rushing Athabaska River, the little post shrank below the towering, dark-brown mountains covered by glaciers. Here Ogden apparently took leave of his wife because Julia had returned to Edmonton House by October 4. She had a half-blood relative named Piccard, a freeman and hunter with the Hudson's Bay Company, and she visited him during October.[49]

At Fort Assiniboine, Ogden and Work left their horses and took boats up the Athabaska to Jasper's House,[50] located in what is now Jasper National Park. Here they made preparations to cross Athabaska Pass by packhorse, a precipitous journey through the Rockies. By October 10 they had negotiated the height of land at Athabaska Pass, and three days later they reached Boat Encampment. Here they met Chief Factor Kennedy and Alexander Ross. The combined parties now took boats and went downstream to the forks of the Spokane River, where Ogden and Work set out on horseback for Spokane House, where Ogden was to become intimately involved in the stresses, strains, and fortunes of the Hudson's Bay Company's Snake Country expeditions.

John Bull Meets Uncle Sam

In perfect autumn weather, on October 28, 1823, Peter Skene Ogden arrived at Spokane House where he was to carry out his duties as prescribed by Resolution 124 of the Northern Council. Life went smoothly at this northwest post, and Ogden's chief concern besides collecting furs from the area was to outfit Alexander Ross for a Snake Country expedition. Ogden had delivered dispatches to Ross in early October at Boat Encampment assigning him this mission. It had placed Ross in a quandary, for when he and the Kennedy party had met Work, Ogden, and their group, Ross had been with his family heading east of the mountains. But after much conversation, Ogden had persuaded Ross to lead the expedition.

Both men had misgivings about the assignment for they were familiar with this branch of the trade. Ross, who had been on the Columbia for some time, certainly was familiar with it, and Ogden had heard a great deal about it. It had been founded by his old employers, the North West Company, not by the Hudson's Bay Company. His friend Donald Mackenzie, who had been the first leader of this brigade for the Northwest Company, had in 1818 led the first party southward from Fort Nez Percés, near present-day Walla Walla, Washington, into the Snake Country and even farther south and east in order to trap the Bear and Green River valleys. This was at least five years before Jedediah Smith and the Americans penetrated the country. Ogden knew that Mackenzie had not had an easy time. His party had been relatively small, composed of 55 men, 195 horses, and 300 beaver traps. They had had a considerable stock of trading merchandise, but the party itself had been "without provisions or stores of any kind" and, therefore, had to depend upon the chase.[1]

Mackenzie had been a good leader, and under him the Snake Country Brigade prospered. In 1819 he had led the party again, this time on a thirteen months' expedition which had returned with excellent results, 154 horses laden with beaver. Mackenzie had taken only twelve days to rest his men and horses, and, while the Americans had been celebrating their Independence Day of 1820 in the East, he had started back to the Snake Country with a party of seventy men. The brigade returned to

Fort Nez Percés on July 10, 1821, with even more pelts than in the preceding year and without the loss of a single man.

Unfortunately we have very little information concerning these significant Mackenzie expeditions into previously unexplored country, although Mackenzie seems to have realized the importance of what he was doing in the Columbia and Snake River region. In a letter of July 30, 1822, he wrote that the height of his ambition was to end his "days in a snug cottage at some healthy situation with my book, my pen, my horse, my dog, my fishing rod and my gun and give the world a full narration of the fur trade."[2] This priceless narrative was never completed. While Mackenzie was writing his work, his wife, feeling that his literary efforts were impairing his health, burned his manuscript; and he, unlike Carlyle with his history of the French Revolution, did not have the courage or the energy to begin again. Thus Ogden was to write the first comprehensive accounts of the Snake–Great Basin country and life in this part of the North American West, a classic that has been little appreciated.

Ogden, comfortably situated at Spokane House, did not know that his journals would one day be read and copied and recopied. He was preoccupied with thoughts of Mackenzie's last expedition. Ogden knew what had happened in 1821 to change the fur trade. He had fallen victim to the amalgamation of the North West and Hudson's Bay companies. Nevertheless, the change in management, in both personnel and the locale of authority, wrought relatively few immediate changes in the field. The Snake Country expedition which had been founded by the old Nor'wester Mackenzie was to continue and even to grow in importance.

It was to be at least four years, however, before it would regain its former importance. With the joining of the two companies, Mackenzie left the Columbia to go east of the mountains, and it was another two years before another party set out for the Snakes. This first Snake Country expedition under the direction of the Hudson's Bay Company took to the field in the spring of 1823 under Finan McDonald and Michel Bourdon. They apparently followed much the same route as Mackenzie had, but they found the journey rough, and in one engagement with Indians, Bourdon and five others were killed. This was McDonald's first and only visit to the Snake Country, which apparently appealed to him little, for upon his return he wrote, "I got safe home from the Snake Cuntre . . . and when that Cuntre will see me again the Beaver will have Gould [gold] Skin."[3] In some respects McDonald's dislike of this region was justified. Service with this brigade was considered "the most hazardous and disagreeable office in the Indian country."

Ogden knew that McDonald had been unwilling to return to what is now Idaho and Utah and that as a result Governor Simpson had turned to Ross, then factor at Fort Nez Percés, to lead the brigade. Ross set out from Flathead Post near the present Thompson Falls, Montana, on February 10, 1824, with a party of 54 men and boys, 20 lodges, 62 guns, 206 traps, and 231 horses. Ross had misgivings about the success of the expedition. On the day of his departure he showed his apprehension regarding the personnel: "There are many of these people too old for a long Voyage. . . . The Iroquois tho' in general good trappers, are very unfit people for a Snake Voyage being always at variance with the whites . . . too fond of Indians and of trafficking away their property with the Natives."[4] Ross was not alone in complaining about the Company's use of Iroquois Indians in the trade. They were considered irresponsible and troublesome when not under very strict supervision.

Ross, who was later relegated to the position of school teacher at Red River, was not a wise choice as leader of the Snake River Brigade, especially in 1824 when this position was becoming even more difficult than in the past. Ross's predecessors had had to contend with severe climatic conditions, scarcity of food, and, in some cases, hostile Indians, but by 1824 the westward thrust of the American fur trade made Ross's task even more hazardous and also caused concern in high British economic and political circles.

American interest in the West was not new. The American fur trade, with its headquarters at St. Louis, had begun in the late eighteenth century with the activities of such prominent traders as Manuel Lisa and Auguste and Pierre Chouteau. After the Lewis and Clark Expedition, 1803–1806, revealed the economic potentialities of the Pacific Northwest, Manuel Lisa led a party up the Missouri to the mouth of the Bighorn, where he established a trading post. American activities in the area increased in the next few years when John Jacob Astor planted his Pacific branch of the American Fur Company on the Columbia. But with the War of 1812 and the Blackfoot depredations on the Upper Missouri, many trappers were killed and stocks of merchandise lost, causing the financially insecure American companies to curtail their operations.

In 1824, however, American expansion began again when Jedediah Smith, a member of the two-year-old Rocky Mountain Fur Company, followed up the Sweetwater River and made the effective discovery of South Pass, the natural gateway through the Rockies in what is now southern Wyoming. Thus the Americans were led into a lucrative trapping area generally free from hostile Indians. Smith did not know that the region immediately to the west of him had been visited by Donald Mackenzie as early as 1818 and had subsequently been revisited by the

British Snake Country expedition. If he had known that the British were in the area, Smith would probably have felt that he had equal right to trap this region because the Convention of 1818 between England and the United States gave both nations the right to trade and settle in the area between the Spanish-Mexican territory on the south and the Russian settlements on the north.

Governor Simpson had hoped to return to England in 1824 to get married, but he was ordered to visit the Columbia District and see about its improvement. The Governor and Committee of the Hudson's Bay Company were apprehensive about the Americans' westward movement, and as early as 1822 they had expressed concern about an American newspaper article stating that 150 Americans had left the Missouri on an expedition across the Rockies toward the Columbia. The Governor and Commitee also said that they had learned of the intention of the American government to establish a settlement on the Columbia and requested information concerning these developments.[5] Simpson, too, was worried about American activities, and he saw in the Snake Country expedition a chance to check the Americans. He said that this brigade, "if properly managed . . . would yield handome profits . . . which for political reasons we should [attempt to trap out] . . . as fast as possible."[6] Simpson's concern is also evident in a letter to the Chief Factors of the Columbia District: "The Snake Country Expedition has been fitted out under Mr. Ross, who should be cautioned against opening a road for the Americans."[7]

As Ross moved southward into the usual Snake Country trapping grounds with misgivings about the success of his expedition, Jedediah Smith was making his spring hunt on the Green River. After conducting a small rendezvous in June, 1824, back on the Sweetwater River, he sent Fitzpatrick, Stone, and Branch east to General Ashley with the accumulation of furs while he and his remaining six men moved westward for a fall hunt. In the late summer of 1824 in the vicinity of the present town of Blackfoot, Idaho, on the banks of the Snake River, Smith and his men encountered a party of Iroquois which had been detached by Ross from the main body of the expedition on June 12 (not June 16, as is sometimes stated). When Smith discovered them, the Iroquois were in dire circumstances as the result of a recent clash with the Snake Indians. The Snakes had stolen one of the Iroquois' horses. In retaliation the Hudson's Bay Company's Indians killed one of the natives. Learning of this, the Snakes set out to revenge their dead comrade, and when Smith came upon the Iroquois, they were "pillaged and destitute."

Smith was therefore able to strike a shrewd bargain with the Iroquois.

48

Peter Skene Ogden about age thirty-two. Daguerreotype
taken in London about 1822.

Courtesy Oregon Historical Society

Dr. John McLoughlin

Courtesy Notman Collection,
McCord Museum,
McGill University, Toronto

Father DeSmet

Courtesy Provincial Archives,
Victoria, British Columbia

John Work

*Courtesy Provincial Archives,
Victoria, British Columbia*

William Fraser Tolmie

*Courtesy Provincial Archives,
Victoria, British Columbia*

Fort Nez Percés, built on the banks of the Walla Walla River in 1818 by
Donald Mackenzie, was Peter Skene Ogden's chief outfitting
point for his Snake Country expeditions.

Courtesy Bancroft Library

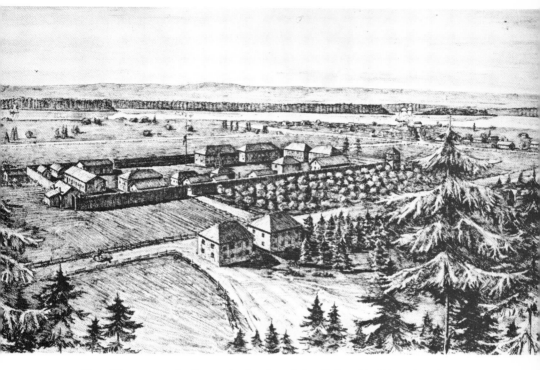

Fort Vancouver, built on the banks of the Columbia River in 1824, was the Hudson's Bay Company's Pacific headquarters.

Courtesy National Park Service

Fort Astoria, at the mouth of the Columbia River, was constructed by John Jacob Astor's American Fur Company. The fort was first visited by Ogden in 1818.

Hudson's Bay House, Nos. 3–4 Fenchurch Street, London. This was the Hudson's Bay Company's headquarters from 1795 to 1865. It was the Company's headquarters when Ogden visited London. From a painting now hanging in Beaver House, London.

Courtesy Hudson's Bay Company

Pencil sketch of Peter Skene Ogden at age fifty-five. Drawn by Henry J. Warre when Ogden was leading his party across Canada in 1845.

He agreed to escort them to Pierre's Hole, near the present tourist mecca of Jackson Hole and the Three Tetons, where the main body of Alexander Ross's expedition was to have been. As the group crossed the Snake Plains, they met a search party which had been sent out by Ross to find the irresponsible Iroquois. This group now led the Americans and the Indians across the Snake River Valley and past the Three Buttes to arrive at Ross's headquarters, close to the confluence of the Salmon and Pahsimai rivers near the present-day Idaho town of Patterson.

Ross must have been shocked to see his Iroquois "trapless and beaverless, naked and destitute of almost everything." He had done well after a poor spring hunt and had counted upon the hundreds of skins which he had expected the Iroquois to bring in to make a good showing for his expedition. The heaviest blow, however, must have come when Jedediah Smith and his six men rode into his camp with the Indians, for Ross wrote: "With these vagabonds arrived seven American trappers from the Big Horn River; but whom I rather take as spies than trappers."[8] Ross's doubts were confirmed when the lanky Smith, who was over six feet tall, announced that he and his men were fearful of Indian depredations and would like to accompany Ross to Flathead Post.

Ross felt that something was wrong when Smith asked to accompany his party. The twenty-five-year-old New Yorker appeared to be no novice to the fur trade and therefore must know his way around the country. Indeed, he was a veteran of the 1823 Arikara fight near Council Bluffs and had been on the Upper Missouri before making the effective discovery of South Pass. His appearance and habits also aroused suspicion. He was clean shaven when most men wore beards, and he was a devout Methodist who neither smoked nor drank. Little wonder Ross thought that this blue-eyed leader of men was a spy rather than a trapper.

Smith, who had been weaned on Lewis and Clark's exploits and thought constantly about exploration and cartography, must have felt that luck had smiled upon him when he met the unfortunate Iroquois. If he could accompany Ross to Flathead Post, he would have a chance to see a region which no Americans since the Astorians had penetrated and also an opportunity to obtain information concerning British operations. Ross, however, had no obvious reason for denying Smith's request, and the Americans did accompany him back to the Flatheads, where Smith picked up considerable information. He learned, for example, that the British had sixty men trapping the Snake Country and that in the previous four years they had taken out 80,000 beaver weighing 160,000 pounds.[9]

Ogden was surprised when he peered out of the front window of his accommodations shortly after his arrival from Spokane House to see Ross and the Snake Country Expedition ride into Flathead Post with the Americans.[10] Ross, too, was surprised the next day, November 27, when Ogden handed him a letter from Governor Simpson appointing him to take charge of the Flathead Post for the coming winter. Simpson also named Ogden to take Ross's place as leader of the Snake Country expedition,[11] and undoubtedly Ogden was elated. Simpson, who had argued for Ogden's employment by the Hudson's Bay Company, believed that the Snake Country expedition could be an important instrument of empire in the hands of a strong man such as Ogden. He felt that Ogden could lead this unruly body of men. Ogden had the reputation of being able to out-swear, out-brawl, and out-drink any man on the frontier, more than adequate recommendations for such a hazardous job. Along with these "talents," Ogden was also apparently attempting to become a good administrator. He made meticulous reports to headquarters on his assignment of 1823 and early 1824 and expressed opinions about the trade of the interior.[12]

Simpson's evaluation of a man could be very harsh, and he seems to have made up his mind about Ross even before Ross allowed the Smith party to join him, for he wrote regarding Ross's leadership of the Snake Country Expedition: "This important duty should not in my opinion be left to a self sufficient empty headed man like Ross. . . . A change of such consequence I therefore conceived should be in the hands of a commissioned Gentleman and knowing no one in this country better qualified to do it justice than Mr. Ogden, I propose that he should undertake it and it affords me great pleasure to say that he did so with the utmost readiness."[13] Thus it seems likely that Ross's replacement was part of an over-all plan to revamp the Columbia Department and make a stronger case for Britain in the area of joint occupation, the "Oregon Country."

Ogden, who had received his commission as Chief Trader in July, 1824, was enthusiastic about the prospect of leading the Snake Country Expedition. An ambitious young man, thirty-one years old, he had long hoped to have an opportunity to show his prowess to his superiors. His first assignment as factor at Spokane House had been pleasant enough but had not given him a chance to show his mettle. Now, after Alexander Ross's fiasco, Ogden hoped to be able to make the Snake Country Brigade an important part of the Columbia trade.

Ogden had only three weeks to put his expedition together. He arrived at Flathead Post on November 26 and departed on December 20. He was extremely busy during this period, especially in settling the freemen's accounts. It was the custom of the trade not only to send out paid employees but to have so-called "freemen" accompany the brigades. These men bought their traps, guns, and other pieces of equipment from the Company. Since they had no money, the Company sold them goods on credit, the debt to be redeemed when the trappers returned from their annual hunt. The hunters paid off the Company with the furs that they had trapped during the course of the expedition and then outfitted themselves for the new year's hunt. The clearing up of old accounts and the opening of new ones kept Ogden busy during the last week of November and the first week of December. Ogden was very shrewd in this aspect of the business. On December 6, Ross recorded in his journal: "To-day Mr. Ogden put several of the engaged men with families free, which will be a saving to the Company and make the Snake expedition for ensuing campaign formidable."[14] Obviously this would be a considerable saving. The drawback was that the only tie these men now had with the Company was strictly financial.

The freemen were always a problem on an expedition and frequently caused trouble in the field. Generally they loved horses and spent a great deal of time trading among themselves or with the Indians, to whom many of them were related. The trading mania could also be hazardous since the freemen would trade ammunition for horses, a fact well known to the Indians, who depended upon the freemen for ammunition. Most of the freemen were undisciplined in other ways as well. In many cases, they left their traps unattended while they raced their horses. Often when they returned to their trap lines, they found that some had been stolen by Indians or carried off by beaver. Since success of an expedition depended upon the number of traps in use in the water, a leader had to watch the freemen's activities carefully.

Probably the most provoking trait of the freemen, however, was their unwillingness to guard their horses at night. As a result animals were often stolen or simply wandered off. In this area of the West, where boats were of no value and horse transportation was essential, much time on expeditions was wasted in attempting to recover strayed animals. Ogden frequently complained about this characteristic, which was especially annoying to such a well-disciplined man as he.

The last week before the party left, preparations were well under control. By December 11 the task of equipping the Snake hunters had been completed, and that same evening William Kittson, the young man who was to keep a meticulous journal of the expedition, arrived at Flathead Post from the Kootenais. On December 14 final preparations for Ogden's departure were being made, and eighteen men were sent off to

Thompson's Plains to collect the necessary horses. All was in readiness by dawn of December 20.[15]

Ogden himself did not leave Flathead Post until the afternoon of December 20, when he rode eastward eight miles to the encampment. The camp was imposing; Ogden had a fairly large party with him: fifty-eight men who were equipped with 61 guns, 268 horses, and 352 traps as well as a number of women and children,[16] families of some of the freemen who were always part of such expeditions. The women, who were either half-blood or full-blood Indians, were a very useful and necessary part of an expedition. If canoes were being used, they sewed and gummed them; if snowshoes were needed, they made them. Their usual work, however, was skinning the catch and preparing the furs for shipment to the London market. They skillfully slit the beaver down the full length of its belly, removed the feet, and stripped the pelt from its carcass. Then, with an agility gained from years of experience, they scraped the pelt with a sharp knife or axe blade to clean it and stretched the animal on a hoop made by bending a willow into a circle and tying it tightly. The freshly killed beaver sewed to the hoop would dry rapidly and be resistant to insects.[17]

The group was augmented by a considerable number of Indians, Kutenais and Flatheads (Salish) who had come to Horse Plains to trade with the freemen of Ogden's party. On December 21 the combined parties started off for Camas Prairie, which was a favorite camping place for the northern Indians, especially at bulb-digging time. The plain had been named after the camas, a beautiful plant with a blue flower which produced edible bulbs considered a delicacy by the western Indians. Although the Snake Country Expedition and their Indian companions followed a well-known old Indian trail, they found the going rather rough after they left Flathead River. The passageway was slippery and rocky, making it difficult for their many horses to follow.

By December 22 the Kutenais, having finished trading with the white men, departed from Camas Prairie and headed north. Ogden and his men and the Flatheads, with the benefit of good weather, moved southeastward the following day, and on Christmas Eve, 1824, they camped on Wild Horse River, so named because of the great number of wild horses said to be in the vicinity. The party, not as squeamish as twentieth-century Americans, killed a few of the wild horses, and "all hands made a hearty meal."[18]

Christmas Day was spent in camp. Ogden thought about his "merry friends" and noted what a "dull time" he was having. Two days later the Flatheads left the expedition, and Ogden now began to move his party faster until they were averaging about fifteen miles a day. On December 29, when the group was encamped on the grassy plains to the north and west of the present city of Missoula, Montana, they were joined by Jedediah Smith and the six Americans who had returned to Flathead Post with Ross the preceding month. It had been agreed before departure that the Smith party could join Ogden's group and thus have the benefit of the protection of a larger party. Even though arrangements had been made in advance for the joining of the two parties, Ogden was not pleased at Smith's arrival.

It is quite clear from Ogden's writings that he did not like Smith. Part of his dislike was due to a personality conflict; the two were very different temperamentally and socially. Both were interested in exploration and the geography of the country, and both would have gained considerably if they had talked more freely to each other. Apparently there was some communication, for Smith acknowledges his debt to Ogden for information gained on several occasions, but Ogden never indicates that he learned anything from the laconic Smith.

Ogden's dislike of his new traveling companion was probably enhanced by Ogden's great competitive spirit. He saw Smith not as a man a few years younger than himself but as a competitor in the fur field and, worse yet, not just an economic competitor but a political one as well—a young Yankee representing a foreign company and a foreign country.

Over the years Ogden's dislike of Smith apparently turned to resentment. On several occasions Ogden complained about the severe hardships that he experienced as the leader of the Snake Country Expedition which reduced him to "skin and bones" and for which he received relatively small remuneration. On the other hand, he watched Jedediah Smith become a prominent member of the Rocky Mountain Fur Company and then in 1826 a partner after he and David Jackson and William Sublette bought out General Ashley. Smith's good fortune rankled in Ogden, who worked hard for less money and was surrounded by red tape.

On December 30, 1824, however, as the combined parties passed through the "Gates of Hell," the well-known narrow canyon east of Missoula, Ogden was simply irritated that he had seven strangers adding to his problems as the weather grew colder and the pace slowed. Even though temperatures were low on New Year's Day, the group's spirits seemed to be high. All the freemen paid Ogden "their respects in return they received . . . [his] best wishes for a good hunt and a long life."[19]

During the next two weeks Ogden and his men proceeded up the

53

heavily wooded Bitterroot Valley and along the rushing mountain streams of that area. They probably did not appreciate the grandeur of the scenery because of the cold weather and the ice on their trail. By January 13 they had reached Gibbons Pass, first used by William Clark in 1806 and later named after General John Gibbon, who pursued Chief Joseph and the Nez Percés through the pass before the Battle of the Big Hole in 1877.

Ogden and company now moved into the Big Hole country and continued in a southerly direction. By February 11 they crossed from the east side of the Continental Divide through Lemhi Pass, which is now a political boundary separating Montana and Idaho, and "encamped in a fine spot" where hundreds of buffalo were seen. It was an imposing sight. Ogden wrote that "as far as the eye can reach the plains appear to be covered with them."[20] On the following day the freemen had a marvelous time pursuing the lumbering buffalo. Ogden noted: "Many [buffalo] were killed this day not less than 30 but not more than 300 wt. of meat came in to camp, the temptation of running buffalo is too great for them to resist."[21]

On February 17 the camp became excited for a quite different reason. Two young members of the party who had been absent for several days returned and reported that they had been attacked by seven Blackfeet and in their escape had lost their traps and other equipment. Ogden immediately sent out a party of twenty men to retrieve the property and punish the Indians. The party found the missing equipment but no trace of the Indians. Before going to bed that night, Ogden wrote, "So far well no lives lost." To be more accurate, he should have added "one life gained" because here in the cold of winter near the Continental Divide, Mme. Montour, the wife of one of the freemen, gave birth to a "fine boy," and ten days later the number of the party was further increased by another birth.[22]

When Ogden reached the Lemhi River, he found that Alexander Ross's party of 1824 had trapped the area thoroughly. Ross had followed the Lemhi downstream to the Salmon; Ogden now proposed going southeast, a course which would take him upstream to the sources of the Lemhi. Ogden, however, was running into difficulties. Lately he was finding either no grass or grass of poor quality for forage, and the horses were becoming pitifully weak. On February 22 he recorded: "I feel anxious regarding our route. We are now but eight encampments from the main Snake River and all accounts agree that we can never reach it with our horses in their present State."[23]

The men apparently shared Ogden's apprehension, and the next morning all the freemen "collected" around Ogden's tent and presented their ideas about what should be done. Ogden decided to try to find a spot for encampment where the horses could recuperate and then make a second attempt to reach the Snake River by the originally proposed route. On February 28, he wrote: "I feel weary about the results of the expedition entrusted to my charge, but the many obstacles attending a winter voyage to the Snake Country are known to those only who undertake it."[24]

By March 19, Ogden had become so eager to cross the Snake River and begin his spring hunt that he decided to push on "even at the sacrifice of horses." All of this time Jedediah Smith and the six Americans had been in the Ogden camp, but now they left the British brigade and set out for the Snake. Undoubtedly fear that Smith and his men would beat his party to the Snake and make good catches spurred Ogden to make his decision. But even after the two groups separated, they were in sight of each other much of the time, especially after they had both reached the Snake. They were practically confined to this area since the route to the Bear River by way of the sources of the Blackfoot was still snowbound. A good example of this game of leap frog played by the British and the Americans is found in Ogden's April 17 journal entry: "The Americans followed us this day and have encamped three miles ahead, but this will avail them naught as independent of our party we have traps twelve miles ahead."

By April 20, Ogden reached the Portneuf River, which he trapped before following approximately the route later to be the segment of the Old Oregon Trail between the upper waters of the Portneuf and the great bend of the Bear River. They reached this attractive Great Basin stream in the vicinity of the present Alexander, Idaho, on April 26.[25] Continuing south and crossing into the present state of Utah near the modern town of Franklin, they left the main stream and trapped along Logan River and Blacksmith Fork before turning south again to pass through the present Hyrum and enter what was later to be known as Ogden Valley.

Smith had started up Bear River while Ogden and his party were going downstream. Smith soon reversed his course when he learned that some Americans had reached the Bear River the previous fall. Indians informed Smith that the group had wintered on the banks of this stream and were now trapping below. Hearing that some of his fellow countrymen were in the region and realizing that they could be members of his employer's company, he naturally wanted to make contact with them.

The identity of the trappers who wintered on the Bear River is one of the obscurities in the history of the fur trade which abounds in obscurities. To this date no substantial narrative by any member of the party has come to light, and only by piecing bits of information together has any identification been made. William L. Sublette has generally been considered the leader of this group, but it seems more likely that Captain John H. Weber was in command. The party was apparently part of the spearhead that had started up the Bighorn with Major Henry in the fall of 1823, but which was cut loose from its base when Henry abandoned his fort on the Bighorn. Only a few names of the members of the company who camped on the Bear River are known. It seems certain that John Weber; Daniel Potts, the letter writer who later illuminated Jedediah Smith's travels; and Jim Bridger, who became an institution on the Overland Trail, were among the party. As these men trapped, more or less independent groups of free trappers seem to have attached themselves to the party, one group of whom was headed by the belligerent John Gardner.

Ogden, however, was completely unaware that there were Americans other than Smith's men in the vicinity until May 4, when he met a band of Snake Indians who informed him that a party of twenty-five Americans had wintered nearby and had gone in the direction he had intended to take. These Indians had four guns which were old but in good working order, and they had ample ammunition, indicating that they had recently traded with the Americans in question. Ogden's only concern about the Americans was apprehension that the beaver population would have been decimated by such a large number of trappers in the area for so long a time. Ogden began to press his hunt even more. His interest in exploration took second place to his economic interest for the expedition. On May 5, Ogden and his men crossed a good plain which was covered with buffalo and thousands of small gulls, which Ogden thought "a strange sight" that indicated "some large body of water near at hand at present unknown to us all."[26]

This assumption was correct. Ogden was near the Great Salt Lake. Surprisingly, this gigantic body of water in the middle of a relatively arid region was still unknown to him and to the rest of the world, with the exception of a few individuals, although it had appeared on early maps and many legends had grown up about it. Indian myths told about a great lake to the north of Mexico which was said to be the land of tinkling golden bells and the home of Montezuma's Aztec ancestors.[27]

While camped on Cub River, Ogden found the region to be far from "the land of tinkling golden bells" and showed little inclination to search for the lake that must have attracted the gulls. Until relatively recently

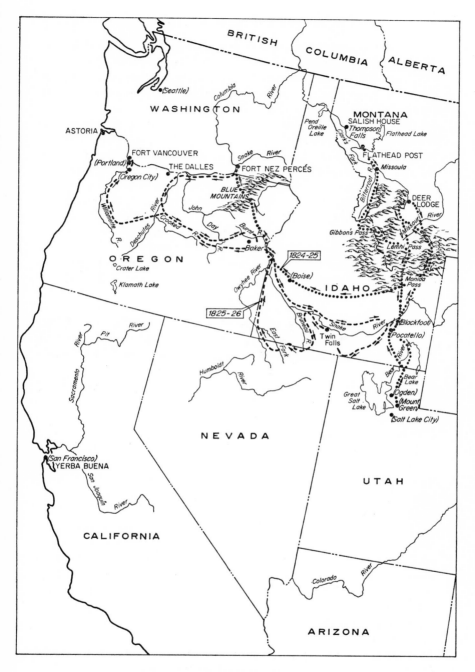

Snake Country Expeditions, 1824–25, 1825–26

many writers credited Ogden with discovering this lake which delights present-day non-swimmers because its saline qualities are so great that a body does not sink in its waters. This accolade, however, should rightly go to Jim Bridger, one of the trappers who had wintered on Bear River. One night while Bridger and his companions were sitting around a campfire in Cache Valley, they began to speculate about the course and outlet of Bear River, and several bets were made. In order to settle the argument, Bridger was chosen to follow the course of Bear River to its mouth. He descended the stream by bullboat to the point where it passes through a canyon from Cache Valley into Bear River Valley. Upon reaching the borders of the lake, he tasted its brackish waters and is thought to have said, "Oh! hell, I am on an arm of the sea!" It was probably from the region where Ogden was camped on May 5 that Bridger started his voyage of discovery.[28]

Now that Ogden knew that Americans were in the vicinity, he and his men trapped the upper waters of what was later named Ogden River in his honor and established campsites near the present Utah towns of Liberty, Eden, and Huntsville in Ogden Valley. From here, Ogden and his party continued southward, passing over the divide into Weber River Valley near the modern community of Mount Green, which marked the southernmost point of travel by Ogden's first Snake Country Expedition.

This area is not significant as the southern extremity of Ogden's route but as the site of a conflict between British and American trappers. On the morning of May 22, 1825, one of Ogden's men came into camp with two former Hudson's Bay Company freemen, Jack McLeod and Lazard Teycateycowige, who had deserted from Flathead Post in 1822. These men told Ogden that they were part of a group of thirty men who had been outfitted by Mexican and Missouri traders. They gave him some idea of the geography of the area and indicated that Ogden was now only fifteen days' march north of Taos, New Mexico, the outfitting center for the southern Rocky Mountain trade. Ogden does not seem to have thought much about this meeting. He was still preoccupied with economics. Twenty of his men were absent from camp, but he was not worried. He felt that this was a good sign, assuming that they were busy trapping beaver. The men, however, were otherwise engaged.

On May 23, Ogden decided to stay another day at the comfortable camp near the Weber River in order to give his absent men an opportunity to return. Early in the day, however, perhaps while Ogden was finishing lunch in his tent,[29] he heard a commotion caused by the arrival of François, an Iroquois chief who had deserted the Hudson's Bay Company two years earlier, with a party of fifteen men, including three Canadians, a Russian, and an old Spaniard. This cosmopolitan group was led by Étienne Provost, well known in the fur trade of the region. He and his partner, LeClerc, had launched trapping operations north-west from Taos into the Colorado Rockies. It is not known how far north and west the partners penetrated in 1823–24, but they did trap the eastern Great Basin in the fall of 1824 and perhaps got as far as the valley of the Great Salt Lake itself.[30] In this vicinity a band of Snake Indians attacked his party and only Provost and three or four of his men were able to escape. Now Provost apparently spoke brusquely to Ogden, blaming the British for the massacre of the preceding fall.

Shortly after this incident, the calm of the spring afternoon was again broken. Ogden was astonished to see a body of about thirty-nine men approaching him. At first, he could hardly believe his eyes. The men were making a great deal of noise as they marched behind several others who were carrying American flags unfurling in the May breeze. The bizarre little group approached within one hundred yards of Ogden's encampment. Then the self-appointed leader of the group, Johnson Gardner, came forward and stated in a loud voice that everyone in camp could hear that the British Snake Country men were in American territory. Therefore, all men were free whether they were engaged or indebted trappers of the Hudson's Bay Company. He also announced that the Americans would buy the British trappers' beaver for $3.50 a pound, eight times as much as the Hudson's Bay Company was paying, and if these trappers would like to join, they need not fear Ogden or the Hudson's Bay Company, since he, Johnson Gardner, and "his party were ready to stand by."[31]

Night began to fall and no more was said, but Ogden set a strict watch for the night. The next morning Johnson Gardner went to Ogden's tent and in an insulting manner told Ogden that if he "knew what was good for himself and party he would return home." Ogden's firm jaw hardened, but he kept his face otherwise unmoved and spoke in even tones. He had always found that when he became angry a certain calmness would come over him, and this was the case now.

At this moment Ogden evaluated his own position to judge how far he could go. After a few minutes of introspection, he realized that his plight was bad. If the Americans were offering the British trappers eight times what the Hudson's Bay Company paid them, why should the men not desert to the Americans? What loyalty did they feel to the Hudson's Bay Company? Very little, and perhaps rightly so. The Company had had no altruistic motives when it had established its fur prices, and when it had become the great fur-trade monopoly in North America in 1821, it had been able to set arbitrarily the payments to trappers. Now the situation was changing on this southwestern frontier. Perhaps the freemen would take advantage of it.

As Johnson Gardner continued his harrangue, Ogden decided that he had no advantage to press and must remain calm and aloof. Gardner said, "Do you know in whose country you are?" Ogden replied that he did not, "as it was not determined between Great Britain and America to whom it belonged." Of course, Ogden was referring to the Convention of 1818 which gave free right to both the British and the Americans to trade and settle in what was later termed the "Oregon Country." Gardner told him that the region had been ceded to the United States, and since Ogden had "no license to trap or trade," he must leave American territory. Ogden replied, "When we receive orders from the British Government we shall obey." Gardner ended the conversation by warning, "Remain at your peril," and departed.[32]

Ogden watched Gardner leave his tent and enter that of John Grey, with whom Ross had had trouble on the 1824 Snake River Expedition. Ross had called Grey "a turbulent blackguard, a damned rascal."[33] Ogden, concerned because he knew Grey's reputation, followed Gardner into the tent. Inside Ogden did most of the talking to Grey, who was half-white, half-Iroquois. Gardner, however, did point out to Ogden that the Iroquois and the freemen had been exploited by the Hudson's Bay Company, and Grey agreed. Grey added that Ogden was the only Company man who had treated him and his men fairly, but in spite of this fact the Iroquois were going to leave Ogden to take advantage of the more attractive trade terms, especially now that they had supporters. With this, Grey gave the signal for the Indians to raise camp, and "immediately all the Iroquois were in motion."

Gardner came forward again and began to assist some of Ogden's men who were also inclined to desert. Teycateycowige, the Iroquois who had deserted the Company, became agitated and called out that since the Americans and deserters were now greater in number than the Hudson's Bay Company's men, they should "fire and pillage them." He advanced with his gun cocked and pointed it at Ogden, but Ogden stood firm and unflinching until Teycateycowige backed down. The departing Americans and Iroquois called Ogden all kinds of names in their respective languages, but Ogden was determined not to allow himself to be provoked to action.

Even in the heat of passion, Ogden could see that his opponents were trying to goad him into firing, which would then give them an excuse to fire back. He realized that he was so outnumbered that once shooting started, the Americans and Iroquois would pounce upon him and take his horses and furs. His only hope was to hold his temper while the deserters packed up and joined the Americans in camp about half a mile from Ogden and his men. That night, May 24, Ogden was still concerned about the closeness of the camps. When someone brought word that the Iroquois and Americans intended to pillage his camp, Ogden made the rounds of the various tents, asking the free and engaged men to help him defend "the Company's property in case of attack." Greatly relieved that the men affirmed their support, he began making the "necessary preparations," setting a strict night guard.

The night passed without incident, and as the sun rose over the Utah horizon, Ogden gave orders to move camp. While the Hudson's Bay Company men were loading their horses, the Americans accompanied by three of the Iroquois deserters rode into the camp. What was on their minds is not completely clear, for they were quiet. Soon after their arrival, however, three of Ogden's men—Prudhomme, Clement, and Nicholas Montour, the father of the first baby born during the course of the expedition—announced their intention to join the Americans. With this, "they were immediately surrounded by the Americans who assisted them in loading" their furs and their belongings.

Ogden still remained aloof and mounted his horse in anticipation of moving camp. As he did so, the gloating Gardner rode over to him and said, "You will see us shortly not only in the Columbia but at the Flat Heads and Cootanies as we are determined you shall no longer remain in our territory." Ogden reiterated his statement that only when the Hudson's Bay Company received orders from the British government would they leave. Gardner could not resist one final jab at Ogden, and as he rode out of the Hudson's Bay Company's camp, he called out that American troops would oust the British from the Columbia by "this Fall."

As Ogden and the remnants of his once strong Snake Country Expedition moved out of camp, Ogden could not help thinking about the events of the past few days. The meeting with Gardner had been very costly. Twelve men had left him, and others would undoubtedly follow. And, indeed, they did. In all he lost twenty-three men, so that his party was reduced to about half its original size.[34] Financially his loss was great, too. The freemen had taken a large number of furs with them when they deserted,[35] which were later estimated as worth about £3,000.[36]

It has often been speculated why the Hudson's Bay Company did not seek compensation for the Gardner incident, but the explanation seems clear—Company officials believed that actually Ogden was in the wrong, that he was not in the "Oregon Country" but on American soil. The Company based this assumption on a letter written by Ogden on July 10, 1825, which indicated that he was at the "East Fork Missouri," which, of course, was east of the Rocky Mountains and therefore in American territory. The Company had never worried about American sovereignty in certain areas before. It was well known that Finan McDonald in 1823 and Ross in 1824 had traveled through American territory in going from Flathead Post to the Snake River. Indeed, the only practical route from Flathead Post to the Snake Country was through American territory, and as long as that post was used as the outfitting center for the Snake Brigade, its members could not avoid trespassing on Yankee soil.

The Governor and Committee in London, however, were concerned about the broad aspects of the trade in northwestern America and in international consequences and did not want to antagonize the Americans. Ironically, both parties seem to have been confused about where the Gardner incident took place. Gardner had pointed out to Ogden that he was on American soil, but Ogden himself believed that he was in the area open to nationals of both countries. Ogden was partly correct; he was west of the Rockies and thus not on American soil. Neither Ogden nor Gardner realized that they were in fact below the Forty-Second Parallel, the generally accepted northern boundary of the newly independent nation of Mexico.

Fur trappers operating out of Taos, such as Étienne Provost, carried word back to the New Mexican settlements of the British-American conflict in what is now Utah. The story was carried southward, and probably was embroidered many times before it reached Mexico City. As a result, the Mexicans became aware that British and American trappers were operating in their territory and protested. In 1825 they complained to the British government about this violation of sovereignty. The protest caused Dr. McLoughlin to order Ogden to "avoid any collision either with Americans or Spaniards as much as possible."[37]

Even before McLoughlin's directive, Ogden, realizing that his party was small and that perhaps even more trappers would probably soon desert, had decided to leave the area as fast as possible. As Ogden sat by his campfire on the evening of May 25, he was sorely disappointed at the turn of events. His high hopes of returning with an extremely large catch had been blasted by his encounter with the Americans. His hope of exploring was also blasted. Not very much was known about the Snake Country even though brigades had visited it during the past seven years and explorers from New Spain (Mexico) fifty years before had camped not far from where he was now sitting. Since his youthful days in Montreal and on the Columbia, Ogden had wondered if there really was a great river in this vicinity as Dr. McLoughlin believed. If there were, it would undoubtedly be full of beaver and would provide a water route to this part of the interior, for the Snake River with its rapids and steep canyons was not navigable.

Dr. McLoughlin had long been interested in finding such a river. He had studied maps of the Snake River–Great Basin country, which the Spaniards had explored and claimed in 1776, in the hope of improving returns from the area. Quite probably he and Governor Simpson had discussed this southern region when the Governor had been on the Columbia in 1824. Neither Simpson nor McLoughlin, nor Ogden, realized that the country was extremely complicated topographically. No wonder Gardner, Ogden, Dr. McLoughlin, the Governor and Committee of the Hudson's Bay Company, and later the British and Mexican governments were confused about where Ogden met the Americans, because within a comparatively small area which is not clearly defined by mountain barriers, streams rise which flow into the Gulf of Mexico by way of the Missouri, into the Pacific by way of the Columbia, into the Gulf of California by way of the Colorado, and into the Great Basin, which has no outlet to the sea, by way of the Bear and Weber rivers.

Indeed, even today this area is considered to be one of the most confusing regions hydrographically in North America, and there is little wonder that Dominguez and Escalante's cartographer in 1776 decided that the Green River, a tributary of the Colorado, probably did not run south but flowed west to the Pacific. Other hopeful thinkers such as Lewis and Clark, Zebulon Pike, and Alexander von Humboldt elaborated on this idea, and well-known cartographers followed suit. When Simpson and McLoughlin thought about the Snake Country, they had in mind Aaron Arrowsmith, the head of the prominent English family of mapmakers, and his map of the area. They had seen Arrowsmith's 1810 map of North America, which showed the Great Salt Lake, a remarkable feat in itself because the lake was actually discovered fifteen years later. Arrowsmith had even gone further and showed the San Buenaventura River, the mighty stream described by the 1776 Spaniards, and then added a dotted line to indicate tentatively that it emptied into the Pacific.

Simpson and McLoughlin disagreed with Arrowsmith and thought this watery avenue must be part of the Columbia, which would certainly be more convenient for the Hudson's Bay Company, whose headquarters were on the Columbia. Ogden's men and undoubtedly Ogden himself, however, did not believe that the San Buenaventura flowed into the Columbia. Nor did Jedediah Smith's employer, General Ashley. On May 8, 1825, before the Ogden-Gardner incident, Ashley wrote in his diary that he had met some Hudson's Bay Company men in the vicinity of the Great Salt Lake "who profess to be well acquainted with all the principal waters of the Columbia, with which they assure me these waters had no connection short of the ocean. It appears from this information that the river is not the Multnomah, a southern branch of the Columbia, which I first supposed it to be."[38]

In a letter, Ogden gave Dr. McLoughlin this same information. Now McLoughlin gave up his idea that the Buenaventura was a branch of the Columbia and came to agree with Arrowsmith. In October, 1825, he wrote the Governor and Committee in London that "it is certain when Mr. Ogden's men left him he was not on the waters of the Columbia and I think he was either on the head waters of a river that falls at St. Francisco or on those of a river said to fall into the ocean a little south of the Umpqua."[39]

As Ogden sat in his Great Basin camp on May 25 and speculated about the country, he realized that he could not immediately satisfy McLoughlin's curiosity about this country. He would have to revise McLoughlin's orders to make a swing around the interior and come out via the mouth of the Columbia. McLoughlin had instructed him to proceed "direct for the heart of the Snake Country towards the banks of the Spanish or Rio Colorado pass the winter and spring there and hunt their way out by the Umpqua and the Wilhamet Rivers to Fort George next summer sufficiently early to send the returns home by the ship."[40]

These instructions again clearly show the confusion in men's minds about the geography of this area. McLoughlin's orders indicate that he thought that the Umpqua and Willamette rivers had their sources far to the west, perhaps in Bear River Valley. Surprisingly enough, this geographical conception is depicted on William Kittson's map which was drawn during the course of this Snake Country Expedition. Kittson states that the "Bear River with all its branches enters the Pacific about 1 mile off Fort George, South side."[41] Because his party was so small, Ogden was aware that he could not afford to take such a lengthy route, even if it were to increase his and the Company's knowledge of the region. Ironically, it was to be Jedediah Smith who would be able to inform Dr. McLoughlin of the true course of the "San Buenaventura River" and even draw a map of the American West for him.[42]

While encamped near Weber River contemplating what he should do following his encounter with the Americans, Ogden came to another decision. He had already discarded Dr. McLoughlin's advice on the route that he should follow back to the Columbia. Now he decided upon a different time sequence. McLoughlin had wanted him back on the Columbia before the ship with the annual fur collection sailed for London, generally in August, though in 1825 it actually departed in October. Ogden, however, did not return to Fort Nez Percés, near the confluence of the Columbia and Walla Walla rivers many miles upstream from Fort George, until November 2. Undoubtedly he had decided to extend his hunt hoping that a greater number of beaver would exonerate him in the eyes of his superiors.

Ogden knew that he could not dawdle in this country infested by Americans. On May 26 he gave orders to raise camp, and the party proceeded northward following their outcoming trail. Although his party was moving rapidly, the "American fever" still had not worn off. Three days later three more men deserted in order to join the Americans. Their desire to depart was so great that they left their "women, children, horses, traps, and furs" behind them with Ogden.[43] So encumbered, Ogden continued up the Bear River, crossed to the Portneuf, and by June 5 was camped on the Snake. The party continued to move northeast, and five days later the group was stirred to see the three imposing peaks of the Tetons rising majestically on the eastern horizon above the plains. In the vicinity of this awe-inspiring scenery, Ogden met two Flatheads and one Kutenai chief with communiqués for him from Governor Simpson urging him to proceed to "Fort George by the Umpqua." Of course, Ogden could not comply, and that fact had a depressing effect upon him. He momentarily indulged in a little self-pity, declaring, "I alone appear doomed to be unfortunate."[44]

All along the return route Ogden met a number of Indians. As he was traveling in a northwestwardly direction and was camped near the Continental Divide in the vicinity of Camas Creek, he met a big party of them, about 150 Bloods and Piegans. The principal men in the party were members of the Blackfoot Nation and walked into Ogden's camp. Accompanying them were three freemen, Morrice Picard, James Bird, and Hugh Munro, the last of whom later had his Indian name, "Rising Wolf," given to a peak in what is now Glacier National Park and was made famous through the writings of James Willard Schultz.

The new arrivals sat around Ogden's campfire, and a pipe, beautifully carved in smooth stone with a few vividly colored porcupine quills wrapped around its long stem, was passed from one to another. Ogden traded a few beaver with the Indians and gave a piece of tobacco to each chief. After the formalities, they swapped stories as they sat around the fire until early morning. As the logs in the fire began to turn slowly to embers, Ogden told about his encounter with Gardner. Since Ogden was a masterful storyteller with a penchant for detail and a great deal of verve, the episode lost nothing in the telling. The trappers and Indians were greatly impressed and retold the story many times. When Morrice Picard arrived at Edmonton House on October 18, 1825, he was able to confirm to the Hudson's Bay Company men that the Ogden reports, which had filtered more than 1,500 miles to the northern station, were true.[45] The Edmonton House Journal recorded the story of Ogden's difficulties on October 19.

Ogden took advantage of his meeting with the Indians and the freemen to dispatch a letter to the "Gentlemen on the east side . . . York Factory," the Hudson's Bay Company's headquarters at the mouth of Nelson River on Hudson Bay. In this letter he described his difficulties during the course of his first Snake Country Expedition and the incident with the Americans.[46] Picard carried the letter to the Alberta post, from which it was sent eastward by the usual route via the Saskatchewan River and Norway House to York Factory.

Even after a late evening, early the next morning the Indians and freemen and Ogden's party were anxious to get underway. By July 2, Ogden and his men were climbing eastward through Monida Pass, so named because it straddles the present political boundary between the states of Montana and Idaho, and thus were moving back into American territory as they had the previous winter. In this vicinity Ogden wrote a few more letters, one of which was dated July 10 and was sent to Fort Vancouver to Dr. McLoughlin, who received it almost a month later, on August 8. Because Ogden wrote this letter while camped on American soil, Dr. McLoughlin, Governor Simpson, and the Governor and Committee thought that the Gardner incident had taken place in American territory.

Ogden was eager to get his furs back to a Hudson's Bay Company post in order to catch the shipment to London, and so he sent William Kittson with two engaged men to Flathead Post on July 16. The catch to date had not been too bad, and when Kittson pulled out of Ogden's camp, he led eighteen horses loaded with beaver pelts. With Kittson heading northward to Flathead, Ogden pressed his hunt in the vicinity of the present-day copper center of Anaconda, Montana, before turning north and west to recross the Continental Divide once again and resume his trapping in "legitimate" territory.

On July 30 the everyday routine was broken when a wife of an Ogden guide committed suicide in a fit of jealousy. Ogden dryly commented,

"He has three and can afford to loose one"; but he was concerned about her four motherless children and the loss of her help in camp.[47] Despite the encumbrance of babies and unattended children the party trapped around the immediate watershed of the Rockies for the next several months before turning westward into what is now the state of Oregon, where they set their traps in many of that area's fine streams.

By October 27, they had reached the Burnt River, which had long been known to the traders and the trappers. And by October 30, Ogden realized that he was getting close to Fort Nez Percés, which he estimated to be only three days' march from his camp. The following morning he took two men and, bidding farewell to the main body of the party, set off for the post built in 1818 by Mackenzie on the banks of the Walla Walla River. As Ogden approached Fort Nez Percés on November 2, 1825, he was impressed by the imposing site Mackenzie had chosen for this inland post. From the fort itself there was a commanding view of the heavily forested hills and rugged bluffs on either side of the Walla Walla River made even more picturesque by the towering rocks on the east side of the stream called "the twins" by the natives. Foremost in Ogden's mind, however, was his belief that he had failed in leading the Snake Country Expedition, and he could not help wondering what letters awaited him at the post.

In anticipation, he rode through the massive wooden gates at the front of the fort and crossed the square to the factor's office and the gentlemen's lodgings. Here he was relieved to learn that he was not to be reprimanded and that he was to lead another Snake Country Expedition. Governor Simpson gave Ogden and his men "a fortnight or twenty days" rest in order to relax and re-equip after almost a year in the field. Simpson had planned the new expedition a year earlier,[48] and Ogden now received orders to join Finan McDonald, a former Snake Country leader under the North West Company. Consequently, he left Fort Nez Percés on November 21, 1825, after only eighteen days at the fort.

At Nez Percés, Ogden discovered that the Company had taken his encounter with the Americans seriously. He realized that his superiors still had confidence in him and wanted him to continue leading the Snake River Brigade, but he was also aware that they were concerned about the brigade's trading practices in the Snake Country. As early as 1824, in Simpson's survey of the Columbia Department, it had been suggested that the Snake Country Expedition be outfitted at the Walla Walla fort rather than at Spokane House or Flathead Post primarily in order to reduce transportation costs. Also after Ogden's adventure with the Americans, the Governor and Committee were concerned that any party leaving Flathead Post for the Snake Country had to pass through American territory. Thus hereafter Ogden and his men would make their permanent outfitting point at this present-day Washington city. The only difficulty with the plan was the hostility of the Nez Percé Indians.

Ogden was surprised at the furor his meeting with Gardner had created. While enjoying a few comforts of civilization at Fort Nez Percés, he was especially pleased to learn that McLoughlin, George Simpson, and the Governor and Committee took his American encounter particularly to heart because the desertion of the freemen pointed out all too clearly a weakness in their system. McLoughlin immediately in 1825 began to develop a revised and more liberal policy in regard to free trappers, and he received support and encouragement from his superiors by 1827. The Governor and Committee pointed out that an "Esprit de Corps" should be developed among the members of the Snake Country Expedition and that the Hudson's Bay Company "can afford to pay as good a price as the Americans." If a similar meeting should take place, Ogden should "pay as much or something more" to avoid a repetition of the Gardner incident.[49]

Although these plans were not developed to their fullest for the next few years because of the time required for communications to cross and recross the Atlantic, Ogden was pleased at the curious change of fortune from his first Snake Country Expedition. As he turned in the saddle to bid farewell to Fort Nez Percés and to the Union Jack and the Company's flag which had just been raised over it on the chilly morning of November 21, 1825, he felt satisfied to be joining Finan McDonald and beginning another Snake Country Expedition.

Our Man in the Snake Country

EARLY ON THE MORNING of November 21, 1825, Ogden and Thomas Dears rode out from Fort Nez Percés along the wooded banks of the Columbia River. About ten o'clock they arrived at the encampment of Ogden's men, whom he had sent out the day before. The small group[1] had been waiting for their leader, and shortly after Ogden and his companion entered camp, all were ready to begin the 1825–26 Snake Country Expedition.

Ogden had been informed that in order to have a relatively strong party in the field this season, he and the remnants of his brigade were to join Finan McDonald, who had been ordered to the Klamath Lake region in what is now southern Oregon. Simpson and McLoughlin had other reasons in addition to strengthening the party when they devised this plan. The area had never been explored, and they were eager to gain more information about this mystical land of the Umpqua and/or "Multnomah" rivers. More important, they wanted their brigades to trap this virgin territory and make it less attractive to the Americans.

The executives of the Hudson's Bay Company knew that the American fur-trading companies were operating on a shoestring. The United States was only fifty years old and had already experienced several depressions. No vast amount of capital had been accumulated by its citizens, at least none comparable to the personal fortunes of many of the Hudson's Bay Company's stockholders. Therefore, if catches were small, Indian hostilities great, or other difficulties arose, American companies could sustain losses for only a few years, if that, before going bankrupt. Thus a "fur desert" policy was developed by the Hudson's Bay Company.

Heretofore the Company had trapped areas lightly so that the animals could reproduce, thus providing fur resources for a later time. The new policy was developed in the hope of discouraging the American trappers from pushing into the lucrative British trapping grounds of the Columbia and New Caledonia (British Columbia). Undoubtedly, the desertion of freemen from their interior posts during the early 1820's and the Ogden-Gardner incident caused the Governor and Committee to accelerate this program. A second consideration involved future boundaries between British and American territory. Increasingly since the Convention of

1818, it appeared that the southern portion of the region open to both British and American citizens would go to the United States when the Convention expired in 1828. No one knew just where the future boundary would be, but most informed persons believed that Britain could not hope for a more advantageous boundary than the Columbia. Why, then, should the Company leave hard cash in the form of beaver in a land that would likely go to the United States in 1828? These economical, political, and geographical considerations were foremost in Ogden's mind as he set out on his second Snake Country Expedition.

In mild but rather foggy December weather, Ogden led his men along the banks of the Columbia River through some of the most beautiful country in the world. The party moved rapidly, averaging about fifteen miles a day; little trapping was done on the southern tributaries of the Columbia which were crossed as the party moved westward and down river. Ogden, traveling light, believed that McDonald had most of the provisions; therefore, he stopped only to trade for salmon with the Indians whom he encountered almost daily. On December 2, 1825, Ogden decided to leave the Columbia and strike out for the south. He started south a few miles from The Dalles, the great series of falls where Indians once speared salmon as they jumped the rapids to go upstream to spawn, but where today the vast Columbia River hydroelectric system has installations.

After turning south along Fifteen Mile Creek and crossing Tygh Ridge and the Laughlin Hills, Ogden made camp late in the day on the banks of a small brook. His hunters had luck and returned to camp with two deer and a mountain sheep, and a good meal was anticipated after a long, rainy march. While dinner preparations were under way, Thomas McKay rode into Ogden's camp with four companions. Ogden was especially pleased to see the half-blood son of Dr. McLoughlin and to learn from him that McDonald was only a short distance away.

Because he wanted to rendezvous with McDonald, early the next morning Ogden gave orders to move camp, and his party began an eight-mile trek over hilly country until they came upon McDonald near the present Warm Springs Indian Agency in what is now Jefferson County, Oregon. McDonald, the hard-boiled old Snake man, was delighted to see Ogden, and the feeling was certainly returned. Each was under the impression that the other would be better equipped, and Ogden was appalled to find that there were very few animals and fish in the vicinity for food and that McDonald did not even have a guide.

As a result, Ogden decided to lead the combined parties to his trapping grounds of early that year along the Snake, but in order to do so, he

70

needed a guide who knew the country. Ogden had had an Indian guide with him from Fort Nez Percés, but because he was unfamiliar with this area, Ogden had sent him home. On December 11 Ogden finally found a guide—a Snake who had been living with the Cayuses. Weather conditions, however, prevented them from breaking camp until December 14, when they turned southeast and passed through hilly country covered with dwarf vegetation and strewn with stones which damaged the horses' hooves.

Trapping as they went, they suffered many hardships before reaching the confluence of the Snake and Burnt rivers on February 11. Trapping was not easy even under the best of circumstances. When a trapper noticed beaver activity in an area, he wanted to set his traps without frightening his prey. Therefore, the trapper waded in the water along the banks of a stream looking for a suitable place for his traps. In February and other winter and even spring months this chore was often unpleasant when the icy waters of the rushing stream lashed against his boots. When a likely spot was found, the trapper had to make a bed for his trap, which must sit firmly about four inches below the surface of the water. The trapper would probably have to build a mound in most streams, with the exception of the Snake River. When he did, he had to scoop out a place for his trap in the gravelly riverbed with his almost frozen fingers. His work still had only begun. He opened the strong jaws of the trap by placing a foot on each spring. The weight of his body pushing down forced the jaws to open, the spring to catch, and the trap to lie flat. Then he took the chain attached to the trap and secured it in deep water with what was known as a "float stick."

Next the trapper had to set the bait, usually a willow switch, which beaver like. In this barren area the profusion of willows that grow along the banks of the streams was most convenient. The trapper cut a switch long enough to extend from the banks directly over the pan of the trap. Then he scraped some of the bark from the switch and smeared it with castoreum, an oily substance from the beaver that the trapper always carried in his bait bottle. With his job completed, the trapper waded some distance from the set trap, made his way up the willow-covered banks of the stream, and waited for an unsuspecting beaver.

Although the odor of castoreum is barely discernible by human beings, it has great appeal to beaver, especially at mating time, and the animals can detect it from some distance. When a beaver swam up to the trap and lifted his nose toward the baited willow switch, one or both feet would press the pan of the trap. This released the spring, causing the heavy jaws of the trap to snap shut on the beaver's feet. The frightened animal would struggle to break free, but in so doing he would plunge into deeper water where the heavy trap would weight him down and he would drown.[2]

At this time Ogden was interested only in procuring more beaver and improving the condition of his party. He could do very little about the latter, however, for during most of the winter and spring the weather was cold and privations great. Because food was scarce and sometimes virtually nonexistent, Ogden and his men went without eating for lengthy periods, once for as long as four days. Ogden wrote that he and his men were "reduced to skin and bones and more beggarly wretched looking beings I defy the world to produce."[3]

After striking the Snake, the expedition moved southward and up this branch of the Columbia River but found that their privations were not justly compensated. Beaver were few. Their search for the luxuriantly furred animals pressed on until the following week they were on the Owyhee, called "Sandwich Island River"[4] by the trappers because of the death of Hawaiian natives in this vicinity.[5] By February 21 conditions were so bad that Ogden detached Jean Batiste Gervaise with seven men and Antoine Sylvaille with five men and sent them to trap other areas in the hope that their catches would be better. Their departure also reduced the food requirements of the main encampment.

By March 13, as they plodded along the banks of the Snake in what is now a very fertile farming region, Ogden thought that his luck had changed. As he made camp adjacent to broad stands of willow that lined the river, probably a little east of the present-day Shoshone Falls, Idaho, McDonald, Dears, and McKay with a party of twelve rode jubilantly in with thirteen elk. In the next few days more elk were killed, and the men put some weight back on their emaciated bodies.

Ogden's rejuvenation of spirit, however, was to be short-lived. While he was encamped on the north side of the Snake, east of the present Burley, thirty Indians paid a visit on March 20. The Indians reported "that a party of Americans and Iroquois are not more than three days march" away. Ogden shuddered at this news and thought bitterly of the meeting with Johnson Gardner the preceding year as he noted, "If this be the case . . . our hunts are damn'd." His apprehension grew as he tried to assess his plight realistically: "I dred meeting with the Americans, that some will attempt desertion I have not the least doubt after the suffering they have endured can it be otherwise."[6] Nevertheless, he hoped to avoid the Americans and continued with his plans for trapping Raft River.

Crossing the Snake was not easy. The river was broad and fairly swift with chunks of floating ice. Some means of ferrying men and supplies across had to be devised. On March 20, when the news arrived that

Americans were in the vicinity, Ogden's men were busily engaged in making a "canoe" out of willows. By March 22 the boat was dried and the trappers were able to cross to the south side and set over one hundred traps in the Raft River. Because of lack of wood, only one canoe could be built. Thus the tedious process of getting men, provisions, and horses to the south side was not completed until the next day.

On March 24, after successfully reaching the Raft, Ogden came upon a large Snake encampment near the mouth of the river. He decided to rest his party and visit with the Indians. He was surprised to see them displaying the Stars and Stripes, and his dread of the Americans increased when he noticed the Indians' delight with the knives and trinkets that the Americans had given them. The Americans with whom these Indians had wintered were members of General Ashley's Rocky Mountain Fur Company under the supervision of William Sublette. Ironically, Sublette had chosen the mouth of the Weber River, near the modern city of Ogden, Utah, as the site for the winter headquarters of his white trappers and their five to six hundred Indian companions.[7]

Because the Americans were thought to be on or near Bear River, Ogden decided that he must not waste time in trapping Raft River now, but must make haste in trapping out the Snake upstream. This was a bold plan because moving back to the Snake would increase the likelihood of encountering the Americans. Accordingly, the party moved up the river, passed the present-day American Falls, Idaho, and went on to the vicinity of the future Wyeth's and the Hudson's Bay Company's Fort Hall, a well-known stopping place on the Oregon and Overland trails.

On Sunday morning, April 9, while Ogden and his men were encamped on the Portneuf River, a party of twenty-eight men, some Americans, some Iroquois, and some French Canadians, as well as half-bloods, entered their camp. When he talked with Jim Bridger, Thomas "Broken Hand" Fitzpatrick, and other members of the Rocky Mountain Fur Company, Ogden was amazed to learn that they had not anticipated meeting him. Ogden had known that the Americans were in the area and had expected to see them at almost any time, although he had hoped to avoid them entirely. The Americans had thought that they had the entire field to themselves since the Johnson Gardner incident.

After a short discussion, the Americans, who had some of the Ogden deserters from the year before with their party, left his camp and set up their own a short distance away. The next morning and afternoon Ogden "had a busy day in settling with them and more to my satisfaction and the Company's than last year." He found the Americans to be quite amiable, and he gained from them in trade ninety-three large and small beaver as well as two seasoned otter skins. More surprising than the Americans' amiability was the fact that some of his deserters of the previous year wanted to settle their outstanding accounts with the Company. In this way Ogden obtained another 81½ beaver pelts as well as "notes,"[8] undoubtedly I.O.U.'s from Montour.

As Ogden also took all the skins in the possession of Gabriel Prudhomme and Pierre Tevanitagan in partial payment of their debts, he observed that the deserters seemed "tired of their New Masters" and would like to return to Hudson's Bay Company service;[9] otherwise the men would not have bothered to have settled their accounts with Ogden. Several factors undoubtedly account for this change of heart.

Although the Hudson's Bay Company deserters were freemen and were generally used to a carefree life, they still had many ties with the Company. They knew the Hudson's Bay Company establishments, were familiar with their policies and routine, and met their friends and often Indian in-laws in post stores. When they had met the Americans and heard the high prices that they were offering, they had felt that they had been exploited by the "Honourable Company" and had, therefore, been quick to change allegiance. However, they found life in an American trapping camp quite different from anything they had experienced. There was not the same formality as in a brigade camp, but the deserters were no longer part of an organization—they now sold their furs to Gardner and joined him and his companions as free trappers. American free trappers wandered where they wished and sold their furs to the highest bidder. If they were combing the southern Rockies, they would take their furs into the Mexican settlement of Taos or, more than likely, if they were near where Ogden's men had deserted him, they waited for the annual rendezvous.

The rendezvous was a unique institution brought to the West by the Rocky Mountain Fur Company. In order to save the cost of building posts and also of losing the time traveling to and from the trapping grounds, each year a valley was chosen as the site for the rendezvous or annual fair, and the company's trappers came to this appointed place. Free trappers and Indians were also invited. To this rendezvous came the caravans from the East—generally from Independence, Missouri—laden with equipment to supply the trappers for the next year's hunt as well as trinkets and trade articles for the Indians and a substantial quantity of liquid refreshment. While furs were being stowed for the return trip to Missouri, all dissipated themselves and their money until they were ready to take to the field again without a penny in their pockets.

Ogden's deserters had attended the 1825 rendezvous at "randavouze

Creek" (Henry's Fork) with their new-found friends. The number of trappers at this meeting totaled 120, including "twenty-nine who had recently withdrawn from the Hudson's Bay Company."[10] Undoubtedly the deserters enjoyed the festivities of the rendezvous, but one wonders if perhaps they were somewhat disappointed at not being more prominent at the gathering. The old-established hands probably did not have much time for pleasantries, if they had the inclination, especially since General Ashley himself had come out from Missouri to conduct this rendezvous. Too, important plans were being made by Ashley and Jedediah Smith regarding the future and leadership of the Rocky Mountain Fur Company. Finally, because the Americans felt that the Ogden-Gardner incident must have shaken the Hudson's Bay Company so much that its brigades would not venture so far south again, they did not worry about further cultivating the deserters' loyalty to the American "cause."

Because of home ties and, probably more important, because of the shortsighted American "policy," Ogden had no more desertions. When he gave orders to move camp on April 11, 1826, "not one of our party appeared the least inclined to leave us not even a hint was given."[11] This was partly because most of Ogden's men were engaged men this season rather than free trappers. Some writers attribute the peaceful meeting to the fact that Bridger and Fitzpatrick were simply not as forceful leaders as Gardner, and therefore the Americans were more subdued. It should be pointed out, however, that Bridger and Fitzpatrick were men of integrity, respected by their "colleagues," while Gardner was not a company man, but a free-lance trapper who led only a few individuals. In fact, not all the Americans at Mountain Green in 1825 had supported Gardner's actions; some had even found them a source of embarrassment. Thus, as Ogden moved out of his camp, he had the satisfaction of having won a moral victory for both himself and the Hudson's Bay Company.

After leaving the Americans, Ogden and his men moved down the Snake and began trapping Raft River as they had originally intended. On May 7 some of the men became suddenly ill with pains in the head and legs. The sickness was attributed to eating beaver meat. Ogden believed that the beaver had eaten the water hemlock growing on the banks of the river and it had tainted the flesh. The next day, May 8, more people were taken ill, and the sturdy Pierre, the Iroquois, was found unconscious near his traps.

In another day nearly half of the Ogden party were sick, and had to remain in camp because they were too weak to move on. On May 10 the brigade moved a few miles. They also moved on May 11, but now all but seven men were ill. Ogden was mystified. Examining the beaver very carefully, he found the flesh to be a little redder and oilier than usual. In order to test his theory about the illness, he decided to eat some of the beaver meat himself. Disappointed to find that the meat apparently had no ill effect upon him, he commented, "I cannot but regret I have escaped."

Ogden spoke too soon. On May 15 he recorded, "I was this day seriously ill from the effects of eating beaver. I never suffered more for three hours; the pain was great and it has left me so weak that I can scarcely crawl."[12] Undoubtedly the symptoms of languor and drowsiness, the prickling sensations and tremors, and the rigidity of some muscles frightened him. His men probably gave him the same remedy that he had prescribed for them: pepper mixed with gunpowder and water! From a modern medical standpoint, this unpalatable potion probably did not have much therapeutic value except as an emetic, but it did seem to put the men back on their feet rapidly. Even illness did not stop Ogden. On the day after his attack he gave orders to move camp, and the party traveled all day, not reaching the site of their new encampment until about midnight. Even though nearly everyone in camp was sick and men fell in the road in their weakened state, Ogden's orders to move were wise, for once they had left the Raft River they all quickly recovered.

By May 24 they reached the mouth of the Malade River, which trappers called "Sickly River" because they had often encountered the same problem that the Ogden brigade had found on Raft River. From either eating or touching the beaver or from drinking the river water illness often followed, but this time Ogden and his men were more fortunate than before. Here, too, they observed a strange Indian custom. They found a dead Indian who had not been buried but had been left on the ground to be devoured by wolves and scavenging birds. Concerning this practice Ogden wrote poignantly: "Nor is there any ceremony observed or their grief of long duration. How pleasant it must be to part with our friends without regretting them. Certainly the Snakes have the advantage over us in this respect. I certainly envy them."[13]

They then moved up the Snake and made a detour to the south, which brought them into the present state of Nevada, to trap the Bruneau and Owyhee rivers. Conditions were bad. The weather was cold even though it was June, and the few beaver that were originally in these streams had been pretty well trapped out. Also, the country was so strewn with stones that horses' hooves were badly cut. When they reached camp the animals would lie down even with a full pack. The country was virtually destitute of food, and Ogden remarked that probably some of the horses' suffering would be ended by putting them in the soup pot!

On June 27, on Burnt River, Ogden detached McDonald, McKay, and Dears, with orders to take the accumulated furs to Fort Nez Percés, leave their horses there, and proceed to Fort Vancouver by boat with the furs.[14] Ogden decided to remain with his main party. He wanted to examine the country that McDonald had visited the previous fall before he had joined him, and on July 15 he was due to meet Gervaise, whom he had detached in February.[15]

By July 13 the party had gone up the Burnt, moved to the middle and south forks of the John Day River, and crossed the Cascade Mountains. Now they were in beautiful country covered with stands of oak and pine, tall ferns, hazel nut, and berry bushes. On the horizon loomed the magnificent volcanic cones of Mount Hood and St. Helens covered with snow. On July 16 they reached the Willamette River and found encamped there a freeman who gave them the latest news. Ogden was pleased to learn that Sylvaille and his party, whom he had detached from the main body in February at the same time that he had sent Gervaise out, had reached the Columbia, but there was no information about Gervaise, with whom Ogden had planned to rendezvous the preceding day.[16]

The freeman lent Ogden two canoes so that he could reach Fort Vancouver by water. At daybreak on July 17, Ogden and a group of selected men cast off, and by 10:00 A.M. they reached the beautiful site on the Willamette where the water rushes over the rock-strewn riverbed to produce a series of falls. Here, surrounded by primeval forests and cascading water where later Oregon City would stand, Ogden exchanged his two small canoes for one large one. Ogden pushed off at noon, without any premonition that he would spend his last days in this idyllic spot and that in less than thirty years he would be buried not far from where the Indians now traded him some salmon.

As Ogden glided down the Willamette in the big canoe, he wondered what Fort Vancouver, the new headquarters of the Hudson's Bay Company on the Pacific Coast, would be like. He had heard a great deal about it and had received many letters from there, but he had never seen it since he had not been on the lower Columbia for the past two years. Fort Vancouver was begun in late November or early December, 1824, when he was at Flathead Post, and was dedicated when Governor Simpson broke a bottle of rum on its flagstaff on March 19, 1825, while Ogden was leading the first Snake Country Expedition southward.

Now, as the sun was about to set, Ogden's canoe reached the mouth of the Willamette and entered the wide but calm waters of the Columbia near the present site of Portland, Oregon. His men steered the canoe to the opposite shore and a little upstream, and there he saw the broad, fertile plain of Jolie Prairie and Fort Vancouver looming up in the dusk of the July evening. He was surprised to see that a large portion of the three-hundred-acre plain was already under cultivation and that potatoes, wheat, oats, barley, and garden vegetables were growing well.

As Ogden approached the fort, which was about a mile distant from the river, he passed cattle and large numbers of horses grazing. Later he saw the goats and pigs that Dr. McLoughlin was raising. He moved closer to the post and could see in the gathering darkness the fir log pickets, twelve to fifteen feet in height and about six inches in diameter, that formed the stockade around the enclosed three-quarters of an acre which was Fort Vancouver. He passed through the main entrance, the double gate on the south side of the palisade which overlooked the river, and moved across the large square court around which the buildings were ranged. Looking around him, he saw the sturdy blockhouses built in the northeast and southwest corners of the stockade, and he thought how much this post resembled Fort George, the old headquarters at the mouth of the Columbia. If the resemblance was complete, Ogden knew exactly where he could find the Chief Factor. He continued across the square, passing the Indian trading store and the men's quarters. At the northeast corner, facing the interior of the fort, stood Dr. McLoughlin's house.[17] The director of the Pacific Coast operations of the Hudson's Bay Company was delighted to see Ogden and treated him "with every mark of attention."

Even in 1826, Fort Vancouver was by no means completed. At first Dr. McLoughlin did not have enough workmen to press construction. Then he found out that Governor Simpson was not enthusiastic about building the Company's headquarters on the Columbia if the Joint Occupation Treaty was to be terminated and the Columbia should become the boundary between British and American territory. The Governor wanted the Company's chief depot to be on the Fraser River in what is now British Columbia. Here it would surely be surrounded by British territory. Thus the construction of permanent buildings at Fort Vancouver proceeded slowly.

As late as Christmas Eve, 1825, David Douglas, who was gathering botanical specimens for the Royal Horticultural Society, indicated that his bark hut was quite uncomfortable, and Dr. McLoughlin invited him to stay in his own half-finished residence.[18] By the time Ogden reached McLoughlin's house on July 17, 1826, it was nearly completed, but the lavishly set table and other amenities of civilization usually associated with Fort Vancouver were missing at this early date.

Because Ogden had only had a short period of rest the previous year, he now took two months' vacation. He spent most of this time at Fort Vancouver, which even in its rough state must have seemed like paradise to him after a year of virtual starvation and freezing temperatures. Ogden had many pleasant evenings with Dr. McLoughlin during which the two were able to discuss Company policy and other subjects of interest to them both. Ogden had not only missed the appurtenances of civilized life, but had been starved intellectually as well. He had a quick, alert mind which craved stimulation from both conversation and books. Some of the pleasant July days at Fort Vancouver were spent reading the books and journals that had been brought from the small library at Fort George. They included files of *Blackwood's Magazine*, a set of the *Library Museum*, and many newspapers, including the *Literary Gazette* containing "Voyage on the N.W. Coast of America" and a copy of *Harmon's Journal*.[19]

Probably of greater enjoyment to Ogden was his acquaintance with the Scottish botanist Douglas, who was still at Fort Vancouver during the summer of 1826. Douglas and Ogden spent much time together, and the former described Ogden as "a man of much information and seemingly a very friendly-disposed person."[20] During the course of their many conversations and probably even specimen-gathering "expeditions," Douglas nurtured Ogden's interest in nature, for Ogden's 1826–27 journal written immediately after his summer with Douglas and McLoughlin at Fort Vancouver shows much more concern with the flora and fauna of the country than before. He made many references in his diary to flowers seen and animals encountered; he even skinned a white heron while encamped at Goose Lake and hoped to carry the remains back to Fort Vancouver. Since Ogden was an active man, much of the day was spent outdoors, probably shooting the ducks which came in great numbers to the two ponds near the fort or fishing from the wharf which had been built on the river about the time of the erection of the post.

By September, Ogden was tired of this sedentary life and was eager to head out with another brigade. He hoped that the results of this third expedition would be as good as those of his last. As he and Dr. McLoughlin had sat by the firelight chatting, Ogden could see that his superior was pleased with the fur catch of his 1825–26 Snake Country Expedition. McLoughlin considered that Ogden had been especially successful that year. He had brought in 2,180 beaver pelts weighing 2,817 pounds and 79 pounds of otter.[21] Considering the cost of procuring these furs, including the wages of the officers and men, the reduction of debts and gratuities, and the like, the total cost amounted to approximately £1,515.9s.5d. McLoughlin pointed out that if the beaver could be sold for £1.0s.5d a pound, the Snake Expedition "would clear 100%." Ogden's brigade did return handsome profits; it cleared £2,500. McLoughlin's enthusiasm about Ogden and the Snake River Brigade seemed boundless: "Certainly in proportion to the capital required this is the best trade we have on this side of the Mountains, the Snake furs this year are the finest furs in the Columbia and will bear a comparison with most of those on the other side."[22]

By early September, 1826, plans were well under way for another Ogden expedition. On September 1, Thomas McKay started with a group of Snake men for The Dalles, where they were to meet another group of the party which had set out earlier to go to Fort Nez Percés for horses. On September 11, Ogden with twelve men left Fort Vancouver in two boats to begin the hundred-mile journey up the Columbia to the cascading water and portage point of The Dalles. The river current was so strong that it was not until early on the fourth day that Ogden reached the site where McKay was "anxiously awaiting" him while his men were encamped with many Indians from various tribes.

Ogden's objectives on this third expedition were slightly different from those of the preceding ones. Trapping beaver was a major consideration, of course, but the desire for geographical discoveries was also significant. In 1826, McLoughlin and Ogden, thinking that the Americans and their relations with the Hudson's Bay Company's freemen were not a great immediate threat, wanted to carry out long-needed explorations. Specifically, more information about the region to the south and more references to the "great river" below the Columbia had whetted Simpson's and McLoughlin's appetites. During the course of Ogden's 1825–26 expedition, Ogden had detached Gervaise and Sylvaille with a group of men. He had aimed only to reduce the number of men to feed, but these men had discovered rivers that were rich in beaver and thereby determined the course of Ogden's third Snake Country Expedition.

After leaving Ogden, Gervaise's party had trapped the Burnt and Crooked rivers and had apparently discovered a stream which abounded in beaver, but had been unable to trap it because their horses had been stolen.[23] Sylvaille and his five men were more successful. As they trapped the Owyhee and Malheur rivers, they moved westward and discovered a stream extremely rich in beaver that was to become known as Silvies River. A small river, it empties into Malheur Lake. Unfortunately,

Sylvaille and his men were unable to take advantage of their last find because their horses were already heavily loaded with some 800 skins. Now they were eager to return to this region, which they said was only seventeen "ordinary marching" days from Fort Vancouver.[24]

Ogden had thought about these discoveries during his stay at Fort Vancouver and wished to follow them up. As he was formulating his plans, Alexander McLeod returned from his unsuccessful Umpqua expedition, which had taken him only approximately 150 miles south of Fort George. Ogden now proposed that his Snake Country area and McLeod's Umpqua area should be examined carefully. Apparently he thought that one of the rivers of his area must flow into or through the territory assigned to McLeod but not yet explored by him, and Ogden suggested that the Company "fit out two trapping Expeditions" for the purpose.[25]

W. Kaye Lamb, in his introduction to *McLoughlin's Fort Vancouver Letters, First Series*, hints that the Ogden Snake Country Journals should not be analyzed completely alone. This point is well taken, for it seems, particularly after reading Ogden's suggestions in 1826 "Relative to the Improvements in conducting the Snake Country Expeditions,"[26] that the Umpqua Expedition along the Pacific Coast south of the Columbia and the Snake Country Expedition into the interior are two prongs of the same operation. Thus when Ogden left Fort Vancouver on September 11, he hoped to proceed "direct to the River discovered by Sylvaille (supposed to be a branch of the river said to fall in the ocean south of the Umpqua) thence towards Lac Sale make a circuit west and comes out about the Clamet tribe."[27] At almost the same time, September 15, 1826, Alexander McLeod with Michel La Framboise and a small party started southward, according to plan, to explore the coastal country.

Interestingly, Simpson, McLoughlin, Ogden, and McLeod were not the only persons who wanted to find the "great river" that was believed to flow from the interior to discharge into the Pacific. General Ashley had been eager to find the mythical Multnomah and/or San Buenaventura rivers, and in July, 1826, when he sold the Rocky Mountain Fur Company to Jedediah Smith, David Jackson, and William Sublette at the Cache Valley Rendezvous, he bequeathed this interest to Ogden's old adversary, Smith.

While Ogden was on the Columbia formulating his plans to explore the southern country, Smith and his partners were planning to extend their trapping operations to the south and west of the Great Salt Lake. Smith apparently also believed in the existence of the San Buenaventura River. He wrote about wanting to follow "one of the larger riv[ers]" which he thought emptied into San Francisco Bay.[28] Smith also seems to have believed that it would be extremely advantageous to discover this river. Not only would it serve as a transportation route, but also he might build a post at its mouth, which he hoped would be located "about the 43 degree of latitude."[29] This was not a new idea. John Jacob Astor had begun the practice fifteen years before at the mouth of the Columbia, and General Ashley himself had had such a project in mind.

Ashley and, later, Smith were especially enthusiastic about this idea. They would like to ship their furs from the Pacific Coast directly to the big Canton, China, market instead of overland to St. Louis, from which point many of the furs undoubtedly went to China. If they could establish such a post, they would have a distinct advantage over the Hudson's Bay Company. The Company shipped its furs from the Columbia River, around the Horn, and across the Atlantic to be sold at auction in London. Many of these furs, sold to individual dealers, were later consigned to the East India Company for transshipment to China, but because of the East India Company's monopoly in the Orient the Hudson's Bay furs could not be shipped direct.

Now that Ashley was no longer actively engaged in the Rocky Mountain Fur Company, Smith decided to try to discover the San Buenaventura River himself. While Ogden was still at Fort Vancouver, Smith and a party of fourteen men set out from Cache Valley on August 16, 1826. They moved southward to the Great Salt Lake, then to the Sevier and Virgin rivers and struck the mighty Colorado not far from the present-day gambling mecca of Las Vegas, Nevada. From this point they struck out across the Mojave Desert, following an old Indian trail that had been used for centuries by the Mojaves going to and from the Pacific Coast to gather iridescent shells.

When Smith and his party reached California in November, 1826, they found the Mexican provincial Governor Echeandia inhospitable, and they were ordered to return by the same route by which they had come. Smith, however, was so obsessed with the idea of discovering the great river that he disregarded the governor's orders and led his men northward through what is now the San Joaquin Valley. Smith believed that if he followed the western foothills of the Sierra Nevada, he would come upon the San Buenaventura, which he could follow back to the Great Salt Lake. He seems to have lost faith in the existence of this river after traveling three hundred miles to the north of San Gabriel Mission and finding that the Indians knew nothing of such a stream. Because the season was late, Smith left his main party and furs in California, and with Silas Gobel and Robert Evans he returned to the Rocky Mountain

Fur Company's rendezvous, which was being held in July, 1827, on Bear Lake.[30]

As Smith proceeded northward in California, he did not meet Alexander McLeod since the Umpqua Brigade had gone south along the Willamette and had then moved to the coast via the Umpqua River. They had explored much of the area to the west of the present-day town of Roseburg, Oregon, and had proceeded as far south as the Rogue River; thus they were always north of the Forty-Second Parallel, which was the northern boundary of California.

Meanwhile, Ogden proceeded southward from The Dalles, to the Deschutes and Crooked rivers, and on to his first objective, Silvies River. He did not realize that his old rival was also moving his trapping grounds farther to the west and that Smith was after the same objective. Ogden, like Smith, did not worry about the question of Mexican sovereignty. He crossed into California, but only into the northeastern corner in the vicinity of Klamath River and Lower Klamath Lake. Here he discovered nearby the beautiful volcanic cone of Mount Shasta, one of the most striking physical features in northern California. While Ogden was trapping in northern California, he came upon the headwaters of a river which Smith was to "discover" along its lower courses in 1828 and to which he was to give the name "Bonaventura."[31] Smith's "Bonaventura" or "Buenaventura," however, was the Sacramento of today. It is a large river which is navigable for many miles upstream, but it flows north to south, not in the east to west direction needed for trade in the interior.

Ogden's 1826–27 Snake Country Expedition is in many ways only the first part of a series of journeys into the country south of the Columbia. Actually during this Snake journey, most of Ogden's geographical objectives were not realized, and further exploration was postponed until his 1827–30 expeditions. After leaving Fort Vancouver in September, 1826, Ogden and his men went directly south to the Crooked and Silvies rivers. They then went south and west, back to the Klamath country and into what is now northern California. From there they moved north into the desolate Hart Mountain–Harney Lake area before turning east into the Snake River drainage.

On July 15, 1827, while encamped on the Snake near the present boundary of Oregon and Idaho, Ogden decided to leave McKay with the main body of Snake men with orders to lead them back to Fort Nez Percés, while he returned to Fort Vancouver to plan next year's expedition. Taking four men with him, Ogden started northward with the

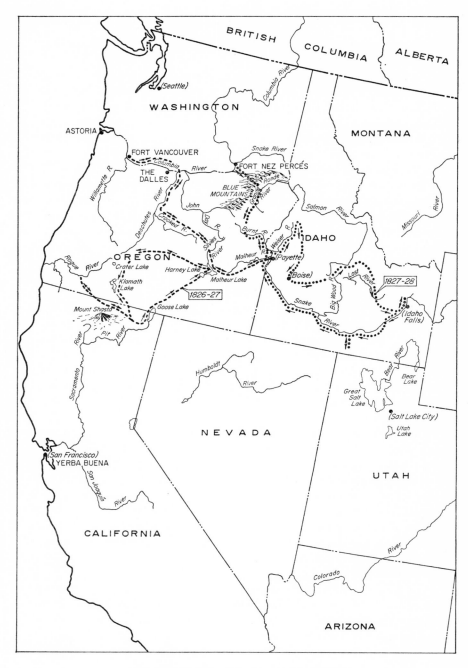

Snake Country Expeditions, 1826–27, 1827–28

1826–27 catch three days later. It was a long journey, and Ogden and his men did not reach the familiar gates of Fort Vancouver until August 5, in plenty of time, however, for their furs to be loaded on the *William and Anne* eight days later for London.[32]

Ogden did not remain long at the Columbia River post. By the end of the month, he and twenty-eight trappers left Fort Vancouver. By September 1 they were at Fort Nez Percés, and four days later they rode out of that post to begin a new Snake Country Expedition. The route for this year is easy to trace because the party followed an Indian trail from the Walla Walla River, across the Blue Mountains to the Grande Ronde Valley, and then traveled along the Burnt and Powder rivers. The brigade kept to the north of the route that was later utilized by the Oregon Short Line Railroad. They went up the Boise River to its source and then crossed Big Camas Prairie to Lost River. Because the winter of 1827–28 was long and severe, the detached party under the leadership of McKay which was trapping on the Salmon River could not rejoin Ogden until May. This expedition, which reached Fort Nez Percés on July 19, 1828, was successful, returning with a catch of beaver which amounted to three thousand skins.[33]

As Ogden and his men were returning to the Columbia in July and early August, 1827, they were ignorant of the negotiations between England and the United States taking place in London which were to have a decided effect upon the activities of the Snake Country Expeditions. In fact, they were off again on a new voyage, that of 1827–28, before word reached the Columbia of the settlement arrived at in London. It was known in the West, however, that after Simpson's visit to the Columbia in 1824–25, he had traveled on to London. Arriving there in the fall of 1825, he conferred with Governor Pelly of the Hudson's Bay Company, and the two decided to press Foreign Secretary George Canning to reopen negotiations with the United States regarding the Oregon country.

Canning was an advocate of the expansion of British influence and trade, and currently he was sympathetic to the Hudson's Bay Company and its aims, at least in part because of his growing antipathy toward the United States since the election of John Quincy Adams to the presidency in 1824. Adams, Canning's old diplomatic adversary, whose mentality was "so curiously like his own in assertive nationalism," irritated Canning and he wanted to press British claims in the Oregon country. Convinced in his own mind that the Hudson's Bay Company could develop an immense trade between its own establishments on the northwest coast and the Orient, when the East India Company's monopoly charter lapsed, Canning requested negotiations. William Huskisson, the cabinet minister who was president of the Board of Trade, and Henry U. Addington, the chief civil servant at the Foreign Office, represented Great Britain. Albert Gallatin, the former secretary of the treasury in the Jefferson cabinet and a man whose interest lay in the North American West, followed Rufus King as the American negotiator. Negotiations became deadlocked and were terminated in August, 1827, just as Ogden was returning to Fort Vancouver from his 1826-27 expedition. A negative agreement was worked out whereby the Convention of 1818 would be continued indefinitely but could be abrogated by either party on a year's notice.

Although the Americans ultimately gained more from the renewal of "joint occupation," and George Canning, the Hudson's Bay Company's last great spokesman for the Oregon country, died on the day of the signing of the agreement, the immediate results of the negotiations seemed to favor the Company and a new vigor is evident in the correspondence of the chief Company officials. Part of this renewed enthusiasm can be seen clearly in Ogden's 1828-29 and 1829-30 Snake Country Expeditions when Ogden led his men much farther into the field and into virgin territory many hundreds of miles from the nearest Hudson's Bay Company establishment.

By September 22, 1828, Ogden was ready to set out from Fort Nez Percés on the first of these expeditions. He was so experienced in preparing for these Snake Country voyages that the details were merely routine. Ogden, however, was particularly eager to begin this new expedition. He was looking forward to visiting the land to the south of the Klamath and Snake rivers, for virtually nothing was known about the region. The only white men who had crossed through the heart of the area were Jedediah Smith and two companions who had traveled from California to the Bear Lake Rendezvous in 1827. Little exploration had been done during this hurried trip, and little geographical knowledge had been gained in comparison with their daring exploits.

As Ogden and his party pulled out of Fort Nez Percés on a crisp September morning, they headed southward along their usual route, crossing to the Grande Ronde Valley and trapping along the Powder and Burnt rivers. When they reached the Malheur River, however, they changed their course. They moved into territory all but unknown to either American or English traders. They found the country confusing, and their confusion was increased by the fact that they had no guide.

Ogden had tried to obtain a guide, but an entry in his diary for October 7, 1828, indicates that the Snake Indian with whom he had negotiated did not appear. Annoyed at having to wait for the guide, Ogden led his men along the Malheur River, and on October 18 they struck out for the south. As they proceeded, they encountered Indian tracks and even some natives who gave them information. By October 26 they were in what is now Harney County, a rather bleak portion of the present-day south-eastern Oregon. That night they camped near Alvore Lake, which was a bitter disappointment to Ogden, for its waters were so salty that the men were not able to refresh themselves after their hard day's journey. The next day they continued southward hoping to find more pleasant country. On October 28 an Indian told them that they were heading in the direction of "a River well stocked with Beaver." This was good news, but Ogden did not hold a very high regard for the natives whom he met. He thought that they were the most ignorant and stupid people he had ever seen.[34]

Now the Ogden party pushed along through the sagebrush which covered the hills in all directions and made the landscape appear covered in velvet. But the sagebrush and the sandy soil were far from velvety for walking, and they proceeded slowly across the present-day Oregon boundary into the modern state of Nevada. By November 3, Ogden and his men reached the Quinn River, then crossed to the Little Humboldt. They followed the Little Humboldt down to its confluence with the Humboldt in the vicinity of present-day Winnemucca, Nevada. Looking about him, Ogden was not impressed with this small stream running between islands of gray sand and surrounded by thick stands of willow. He did not realize that the streambed filled with brackish water was perhaps the most important of all of his discoveries. The river with its vile-tasting water was cursed by future travelers, but in a large semidesert region it is the only river which flows in an east-west direction. Thus it later became the principal guide and source of water and forage for the Indians, fur trappers, emigrants, and forty-niners who passed through the maze of basin and ranges which form the area.

Ogden called it "Unknown River" because he did not know its source and course. This name, however, was applied only for a short time. For a while the river was called Mary's River after one of the trappers' wives, and later it was called Ogden's River by some persons in honor of its discoverer. Zenas Leonard of the Walker-Bonneville Expedition of 1833–34 felt that "Barren" better described the stream, but it was John Charles Frémont who gave it its lasting name in honor of Baron von Humboldt, the famous geographer who never saw the river that bears his name.

Although Ogden was curious about the course of "Unknown River," he decided that winter was coming on too rapidly for him to risk exploring its lower courses. Consequently, on November 12 he led his men eastward up the Humboldt through virgin territory. He planned to winter to the north and east of the Great Salt Lake, where he knew there were buffalo, though relatively few in number. On November 25, however, Joseph Paul, a member of the expedition, fell ill in the vicinity of modern-day Beowawe, Nevada, and the progress of the party was greatly hampered. Ogden was efficient in conducting the company's business, but the welfare of his men always came first. Therefore, he decided to make camp for a few days hoping that Paul would regain his health. By December 6, the weather was getting much worse, Paul had not improved, and Ogden felt obliged to give orders to move camp. The sick man was put on his horse and the party moved at a much reduced pace so that Paul could keep up. By December 10, Ogden sat by his fire near the present railroad town of Carlin, Nevada, and made a painful decision. Paul could no longer sit on a horse, and the party still had almost three hundred miles to travel to reach the Great Salt Lake country. In fairness to the other men, Ogden felt he must leave Paul behind. Leaving him in the barren stretches of the Great Basin in December was the same as signing his death warrant, but Ogden had no choice. He wrote in his journal, "There was no alternative. It is impossible for the whole party to remain here and feed on horse flesh for four months."[35]

Every man on the expedition knew when he left Fort Nez Percés that he might never see the old Hudson's Bay Company post again, but this did not make the decision easier. Ogden was pleased when two of Paul's friends came to him and offered to stay with the sick man. So, at last, the party left their Humboldt River encampment and said good-bye to the three lonely figures. Ogden knew that Paul would be cared for until he either got well or died.

The Snake Brigade moved rapidly up the Humboldt and then due east over the rugged Ruby Mountains via Secret Pass. By the end of the month they could see the Great Salt Lake, having traveled northward and crossed the present-day boundary between Utah and Idaho. On January 1, 1829, while encamped in the vicinity of present-day Malad City, Idaho, the two trappers who had remained on the Humboldt with Paul rode in with the sad news that the unfortunate man had died eight days after Ogden's departure.

By the latter part of March, Ogden was again able to see the Great Salt Lake, and he wrote that it "appears surrounded by Mountains, but beyond these mountains at the west and altho' the lake has no discharge I am of opinion there must be large rivers and probably an object worthy of exploration at a future day."[36] Although Ogden makes this positive statement regarding the discharge of the lake and refutes many contemporary geographers, his comment shows that he, like others, could not quite believe that a large stream did not exist in the barren country to the west of the Great Salt Lake.

Ogden and his party now continued in a southwestern direction, following their old trail in order to reach the sources of the Humboldt River. Ogden mentions on April 1 that they were also making use of Indian tracks that they encountered along their route because they now had to search for water, a problem which they had not had the preceding December when they were able to melt snow. Nevertheless, the group moved over their old trail rapidly, covering twenty-five to thirty miles a day, almost twice the daily distance they had averaged on their outward trek. They reached the Humboldt again on April 9.

This time, however, they struck the Humboldt not far from present-day Halleck, Nevada, and were now in new country. They began to move downstream, and on April 15 they reached Paul's grave and were relieved to see that it had not been molested by animals or Indians. Trapping was not very good, and they moved northward to the Owyhee, a tributary of the Snake. Finding few beaver here as well, they decided to satisfy their geographical curiosity and returned to the Humboldt with the objective of following it to its sink which the natives had told them about.

By the end of May they reached the source of the Humboldt River. Here they found that the stream, which had become increasingly narrow, passed through a swamp and then emptied into a flat basin which stretched for many miles to the west. High hills covered with sagebrush rose from the white, alkaline edges of the lake bed in virtually all directions. On May 30, while Ogden and his men were close to the shallow, flat sheet of water known as Humboldt Sink, they were surprised to see one of the men who had gone down to the lake running back to camp and shouting. With all of the commotion, Ogden rushed out of his tent. He learned from the almost breathless trapper that as he had been walking west to the lake, he had been startled by twenty Indians on horseback. The trapper had begun running toward camp, and the Indians had followed him shouting war cries.

As he listened to the man's story, Ogden looked up at the barren hills which surrounded his camp. There in the dwarf vegetation of the hillsides he could see hundreds of Indians watching the scene below. Soon a group of Indians came down to the plain and camped about five hundred yards from Ogden's temporary headquarters. Realizing that he could not let the Indians see that he was afraid, Ogden decided to take the initiative. He went to the Indian encampment, gave them a foot of tobacco which he hoped would appease them, and began talking to them. He was amazed to see that they had "rifles, ammunition, arms and other articles" which he thought "must be some of the plunder of Smith's party." He was thinking about the Umpqua River Massacre of July 14, 1828, when Jedediah Smith and two men had escaped the massacre of their Rocky Mountain Fur Company party, one of the worst disasters in the history of the fur trade. On the banks of the Umpqua, Smith had lost all of his furs and all his party except himself, John Turner, and Arthur Black. Undoubtedly Ogden wondered whether this would be his fate. If so, he knew that he would not have a friendly post relatively close for refuge as Smith had had.

Ogden's fears proved unwarranted. The Indians were fairly friendly and surprisingly well informed about the geography of the region. They told him about a river eight days' journey to the west, but because of the lateness of the season and worry about infringing on McLeod's Umpqua territory, Ogden and his men moved back up the Humboldt, and following roughly their trail of the preceding fall through northern Nevada and southern Oregon. From the Malheur River, they moved to the Silvies and John Day rivers. By July 4, Ogden was ready to start with two men on the well-known track to Fort Nez Percés.

During the course of this fifth Snake Country Expedition, Ogden covered a vast amount of territory, much of which had not been visited by white men. He experienced severe hardships and almost had a fight with Indians. Nevertheless, he had discovered a new river. He did not quite realize the significance of his discovery at this time, but Aaron Arrowsmith was impressed by the map that Ogden had drawn of this previously unchartered region. On his own 1834 North American map, the great cartographer depicted "Swamp Lakes & Is," the name which Ogden had attached to the lower reaches of the Humboldt River and its sink.

More important from the Company's standpoint and perhaps from Ogden's, this Snake Country Expedition was his most successful: he returned with a catch of four thousand beaver. Dr. McLoughlin was almost ecstatic. He declared that the beaver were greater in number than before and that they were "in the highest state of preservation which when it is considered some of these furs have been carried on horseback through the country since last fall, winter and summer, it is surprising and does Ogden great credit."[37] Thus, considering both the geographical and the economic aspects, the 1828-29 Snake Expedition must be considered the most successful in a long and colorful history.

After several months' rest on the Columbia, Ogden was ready to begin his sixth and last Snake Country Expedition. Like the previous voyages, this one took him over a great deal of new territory, but unlike his 1828–29 expedition, this brigade was ill-fated, and not a great deal is known about the route that was followed during the course of this year. Ogden's journal describing in detail the terrain, his thoughts and reactions to situations encountered, and other general observations was lost. Ironically the journal was lost on the return, only a short distance from Fort Nez Percés when a boat foundered in trying to navigate the precipitous, rocky passage of The Dalles. Only by piecing together information contained in letters written after Ogden's return to the Columbia River depot in July, 1830, and by relying on Ogden's sketch of life in the Snake Country written many years later can one gain some insight into what actually happened during the expedition. In September, 1829, Ogden began the Snake journey. Apparently he used the same route that he had taken in the fall of 1828 and the early summer of 1829, for he "lost no time in making the discharge of Unknown River," the Humboldt Sink.[38]

Ogden again found many Indians around the lower region of the Humboldt, but they caused him no trouble. These Indians were much less intimidating but also much less informed than the natives he had met here some months before. Because the weather was bitterly cold and the Humboldt was choked with snow and ice, Ogden decided to move his party southward into an area unknown to him. He asked the Indians for aid, but they refused to give him a guide and seemed to know almost nothing about the adjacent region. Ogden did not think long about what he should do. He was not well equipped to lead his men into virgin terrain about which he knew nothing, but only two days after he reached the Humboldt Sink, he gave the order to break camp. The party undoubtedly followed the creek bed that is filled in the spring months with the overflow from the Humboldt Sink to Carson Sink. They must have been surprised after crossing through this land of large hills and desert basins white with alkali to see the eastern slope of the Sierra Nevada Mountains covered with heavy stands of timber and the higher elevations with snow.

The party followed the eastern foothills of the Sierra southward to Walker Lake, the deep blue water surrounded by desert which was to be "discovered" a few years later by Joseph Reddeford Walker. From this lake named after the American trapper, the brigade moved southward again. It was probably after leaving the lake that difficulties "began to crowd" upon the party, and "their sufferings and trials" became "truly great." Ogden later wrote: "There were times when we tasted no food,

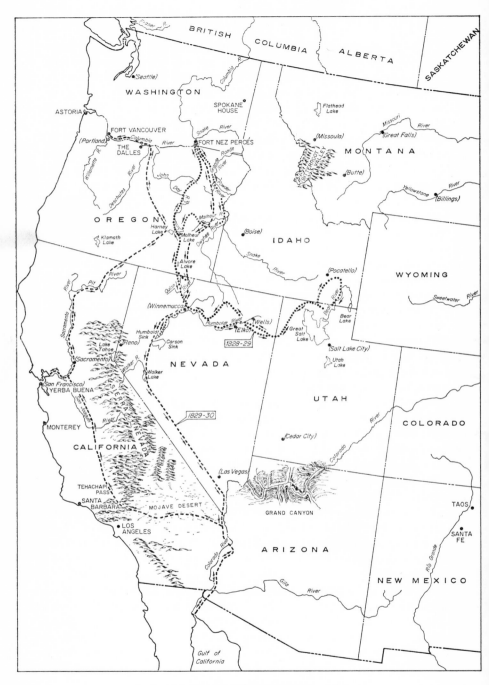

Snake Country Expeditions, 1828–29, 1829–30

and were unable to discover water for several days together; without wood, we keenly felt the cold; wanting grass, our horses were reduced to great weakness, so that many of them died, on whose emaciated carcases we were constrained to satisfy the intolerable cravings of our hunger, and as a last resource, to quench our thirst with their blood."[39]

Under such unpleasant conditions, the party continued to move southward. Their actual route is difficult to determine, but probably the Snake Country Expedition now passed through some of the most inhospitable country imaginable. They traveled through desert valleys flanked by high, arid mountains. They noted that the sagebrush of the north gave way to more desert species; creosote bush and Joshua trees now dotted the hills and bordered the white, alkaline-dried beds. They were probably traveling parallel to what is now the boundary between California and Nevada, and perhaps they passed through what has become the Las Vegas Bombing and Gunnery Range. Upon reaching a site to the north of present-day Las Vegas, they encountered a group of Indians. Ogden hired two of them in the hope that they would give him some information about this previously unexplored region. The natives did give him some general information, and Ogden rewarded them with a few baubles.

Ogden treated the Indians kindly, but he had some misgivings about this approach. He later came to the conclusion that if Indians were treated with great severity when they first encountered white men, they would be so awed that many lives would eventually be saved. At this moment Ogden did not feel frightened by these Indians, but, nevertheless, the next morning in his usual cautious manner, when the first rays of the sun appeared over the desert peaks, he had all his men roused, fires lighted, and all the horses collected. Shortly thereafter, a group of Indians approached and showered the Ogden brigade with arrows. With three of the party's horses injured, Ogden ordered one of his men to use his gun. The trapper aimed and fired, and an Indian fell. The shooting of their companion frightened the natives, and they fled. Showing restraint, Ogden did not let his men chase them and said, "I trust they were not only duly impressed with our superiority over them, but likewise with a sense of the lenient treatment they had received." Then he added in a philosophical tone, "From past experience, I could have little hope at the time that the effect of either would be very durable."

From this point the party traveled another three days "over a country as barren as ever Christian traversed," reached the rushing waters of the Colorado River, and proceeded along its stark, arid channel. Ogden concluded that the Indians whom he encountered on the Colorado were the ones who had massacred almost the entire Jedediah Smith party in the summer of 1827. Ogden knew that when the Smith group had reached the Mojave River, where they had spent fifteen days the previous year, they had found the hitherto friendly Indians restive. They were hired to transport Smith and his party across the Colorado River on rafts made of bundles of reeds, but they treacherously fell upon the white men in midstream, and only nine of the eighteen escaped. Ogden had learned all the details of Smith's encounter and escape from Smith himself when he had taken refuge at Fort Vancouver in the summer of 1828 following a second, even more harrowing massacre of a new party, this time on the Umpqua River. Ogden therefore decided to take special precautions now. Ogden furnished the members of his party, in addition to their usual firearms, spears to be used if necessary while reloading their guns after firing the first volley. Shortly after Ogden's preparations had been completed, one of the Hudson's Bay Company's guards was wounded by the natives, and at the same time an alarm went up that the Indians were trying to steal the horses. Ogden ordered his men to fire, and the Indians were so startled when so many of their companions "in a single moment were made to lick the dust, the rest ingloriously fled."[40]

With twenty-six Indians lying on the battlefield, Ogden gave orders to move camp. The party now followed the Colorado downstream along its twisting and turning canyons an undetermined distance, perhaps to its mouth in the Gulf of California. Ogden was certainly a long way from home. How different the Colorado—with silt-laden waters running through the red and yellow earth finally to reach an arm of the Pacific Ocean—was from his birthplace on the wooded St. Lawrence. Ogden preferred the water and timber country of eastern Canada and the Columbia. After trapping the thinly scattered beaver of this arid region, he decided to move his party northward.

As Ogden began to move away from the Gulf of California, his mind went back to 1825 and his meeting with Johnson Gardner. Remembering the admonition by the Governor and Committee regarding relations with Americans and Mexicans,[41] he steered his course northeast in order not to go "too near the Spanish settlements." The group probably proceeded through the broad Techachapi Pass and looked out upon the Great Valley of California stretching hundreds of miles to the north. Following the western foothills of the Sierra Nevada, which form the eastern boundary of the valley, Ogden was able to examine the various streams which flow from the mountains as Smith had done in 1827.

As the Snake Country Expedition proceeded northward, they were surprised to meet a group of Americans in this unpopulated area. The Yankees were led by Ewing Young, who had been outfitted by the Mexicans at Taos, New Mexico, or, as Ogden said, "St. Fee." Young, his 1829 passport signed by Henry Clay, seemed eager to take an active part in the trade of the upper Pacific Coast. He was moving up through California, trapping as he went, intending to go all the way to the Willamette. His spirits were so dampened when he met Ogden and later in the vicinity of the Upper Sacramento River when he saw tracks made by McLeod's Umpqua Brigade that he decided instead to spend the year in California.[42]

The Young party accompanied Ogden for about ten days or more, perhaps going as far north as the Pit River with him. When the combined parties reached the region of the San Joaquin–Sacramento rivers, they separated. Ogden was fascinated by this river system and decided to follow the important watercourses along their confusing lower extremities. It is regrettable that the 1829–30 journal is not available to give Ogden's reaction to the magnificent expanse of San Francisco Bay, but apparently he immediately grasped the economic potential of this protected harbor. In later years he was an advocate of Hudson's Bay Company trade with what was to become San Francisco.

After exploring the Bay area, Ogden moved up the estuary and the Straits of Carquinez to the Sacramento River, Smith's "Bonaventura." He followed it and its tributary, the Pit, up to the point where he struck his 1826–27 trail to Fort Nez Percés. Even though he still had to cross some difficult terrain which he greatly disliked, Ogden felt that he was almost home. The party reached the Columbia and the familiar Dalles safely, but just as the men were thinking about the fine time they would have when the expedition was over, disaster struck. One of the boats was caught in a whirlpool as it negotiated the series of rapids and falls. It began careening down the cascade. At first, instead of springing to their paddles, the men in the boat sat as if hypnotized. Then they panicked and dropped their paddles. The boat skittered along madly and then went down stern first, taking ten men, five hundred skins, and Ogden's journal and papers with it.[43] Only one man emerged from the frothing water alive; the other nine had traveled thousands of miles and experienced great hardships only to drown a short distance from Fort Nez Percés.

The depressed party continued the journey, reaching the idyllic Jolie Prairie and the gates of Fort Vancouver on July 6, 1830. Ogden had traveled through more territory than on any other Snake Country

Expedition, but he had found relatively few beaver. His returns had been small even before he lost the five hundred skins at The Dalles, and the final returns were "less than they have been any previous year."

Thus, after Ogden told his story to Dr. McLoughlin, he must have been relieved to receive orders from Governor Simpson transferring him from the dreadful interior trade to that along the northwest coast. Six years in the Snake Country with its great privations and hostile Indians had been more than enough for him. Ogden recognized the Snake Expeditions as a necessary evil, but he felt sorry for John Work, the dour Irishman from County Donegal who was succeeding him; the poor fellow "deserves a more substantial reward," he wrote.[44] Nevertheless, he thanked God that he had been rescued from the bitter winters and scorching summers of the semiarid region of the interior, and his thoughts turned to the Pacific Coast where his life would be spent among Indians and Russians in the forests to the north.

The Threat of the North

WHILE OGDEN was pushing his Snake Country expeditions farther and farther southward as a result of the negotiations in London, a great deal was happening on the Columbia. The extension of the joint occupation treaty between the United States and Great Britain gave the Company a new vitality, particularly regarding its policies on the Northwest Coast.

Governor Simpson, after his visit to London, was eager to return to the Pacific Coast and develop firmer British policies. When he had visited the Columbia in 1824, he had been chiefly concerned with pulling back Hudson's Bay Company posts from south of the Columbia River because he had felt that the Columbia would soon be Britain's southern boundary in the Oregon Country. Consequently, Fort Vancouver had been built on the north side of the river to replace Fort George on the south side of the river's mouth, and Ogden's old friend Sam Black had been ordered to move Fort Nez Percés across the river to the "British" side.

By 1828–29 when Simpson again visited the Columbia, his main concerns were New Caledonia (British Columbia), the Fraser River, and the development of trade along the northern Pacific Coast. These were not completely new concerns. He had been worried for some years about the presence of American trading ships along the coast and the Russian occupation of the northern coastal strip. The captains of the American vessels in this region proved to be tough opponents, but since the United States had no claim to the present British Columbia–southeastern Alaskan area, Simpson concentrated on the Russian "menace."

Russian expansion had pushed westward to the Pacific and had followed explorers Bering and Chirikov across the Bering Straits. By 1799 the newly formed Russian American Company had been granted a monopoly of the trade on the coast north of 55 degrees latitude and its members empowered to extend their operations southward into unoccupied territory. These operations were successful under the direction of the able manager, Alexander Baranov. Although Simpson considered the Russians a threat, he had respect and admiration for this now deceased little Russian of lowly birth but great talent whose boundless energy had given the Russian American Company a firm footing in the north.

In 1799, Baranov, at the age of fifty-three, had led a force of 1,100 men in the Aleutian skin boats called bidarkas, along the rocky, magnificently forested coast of southeastern Alaska from Kodiak Island to the island that now bears his name. From the fort of New Archangel (Sitka), re-built in 1804, the Russians pushed southward from Baranov Island to build a post at the open roadstead of Bodega Bay, California, in 1810. Two years later they established Fort Ross on the rocky promontory near Bodega Bay and just north of San Francisco Bay.

Even before Simpson's return to the Columbia in 1828, McLoughlin was aware of and preoccupied with Russian and American activities on the coast, but he was not able to do anything about the situation until 1827. That year he obtained the services of the capable thirty-four-year-old Æmilius Simpson of the Royal Navy, who was a "distant relative of George Simpson for he was the step-son of Mary Simpson, sister of the Governor's father." Æmilius had served well for ten years during the Napoleonic Wars, and, when he arrived on the Columbia in November, 1826, he was appointed superintendent of shipping on the West Coast. The young naval lieutenant charted the Columbia River from Cape Disappointment to Fort Vancouver and then took command of the *Cadboro* after her arrival from England in early June, 1827.

Simpson was then sent in the *Cadboro* to the Fraser River with the materials to build a fort there. While he was at sea, Chief Trader James McMillan was pushing overland from Fort Vancouver to the Fraser via the Cowlitz and Puget Sound with three clerks and twenty-one men to build and man the new post. Simpson and his men on the *Cadboro* waited on the Fraser River to give the land party protection from the Indians while the stockade, bastions, and a small store which were to form Fort Langley were erected.

Æmilius Simpson left the newly established Fort Langley in September, 1827,[1] and returned to the Columbia. Then because Dr. McLoughlin was too short of goods to outfit the *Cadboro*, he was sent to collect information about the possibilities of trade with California. McLoughlin wanted to find out what contacts the Americans and Russians had made with the Mexicans. Too, he was interested to know whether the Hudson's Bay Company could sell salmon in California and, if so, at what price. McLoughlin also instructed Simpson to try to collect a cargo of salt and butter which he hoped could be used to induce the Spaniards to trade on terms favorable enough to cancel Spanish debts to the old North West Company.

From Monterey, Simpson went back to Fort Langley, then along the northern coast, and then back to the Fraser River post. In 1838 he made his report on the coastal trade. He recommended that the Company make some arrangement with the Russians. He also believed that American trade could only be curtailed by building a strong and permanent Hudson's Bay Company post in the rich fur-bearing region of the Nass River. The chief problem here, however, was that the large number of Indians in the area were hostile to all white men but the Americans, who had already presented them with a substantial half-blood population.

While Ogden was returning to Fort Nez Percés from his fourth Snake Country Expedition and Æmilius Simpson was at sea, Governor Simpson was about to begin a trip that was to have a profound effect upon Ogden's life. Simpson adjourned the meeting of the Council of the Northern Department at York Factory on Hudson Bay on July 10, 1828. Shortly after midnight on the following day, he was ready to leave for the Columbia. His party was sent off with three cheers and a seven-gun salute, and to the tunes of his own *voyageurs'* songs they disappeared into the summer twilight.

Simpson's trips were never enjoyable for the people who accompanied him. They always broke camp at 2:00 A.M., had breakfast at 8:00 o'clock, and their midday meal at 1:00 P.M. Lunch was always rushed, an eight- to ten-minute stop when the men swallowed a few mouthfuls of pemmican and Governor Simpson had a slice of something cool and a glass of wine. The afternoons were more pleasant when Colin Fraser, Governor Simpson's private piper, played a few tunes. Simpson was not always pleased with these performances and sometimes complained that "the piper cannot find sufficient wind to fill his bag."[2]

Simpson's trips showed his great organizing abilities and also his endurance. It was not unusual for his party to cover ninety to one-hundred miles a day. In a little over three weeks they reached Île-à-la-Crosse, Ogden's old haunts, and by September 11 were at McLeod's Fort, the easternmost post in New Caledonia. Simpson wanted to find out if good communications could be established between this area and Fort Langley near the mouth of the Fraser, so in typical Simpson fashion he decided to explore the possibilities himself.

The Simpson party's explorations proved that the Thompson and Fraser rivers with their rapids, cascades, and narrow defiles were both unsuitable means of communication with the sea. Simpson in his 1828 visit to the Northwest determined that the Columbia was the only navigable water route for the Hudson's Bay Company to both the interior and the Pacific Ocean.

He was also interested in following up Æmilius Simpson's report. He came to agree that the only way to secure the coastal trade from the Americans and to keep New Caledonian land furs from the Russians was to build a permanent post at Nass, but he had to consider communication with the interior. His exploration had ruled out the Fraser River, and the Columbia might eventually fall to the Americans. Perhaps establishing a post at the mouth of the Nass River might accomplish two objectives—trade could be protected and a water route to the interior might yet be discovered.

Ogden was in the Snake Country at this time and thought that he would probably be there for many more years. He did not realize that the plans taking form in the minds of Governor Simpson and Dr. McLoughlin on the Columbia would affect him greatly. He would have been greatly surprised to learn that in the next few years he would lead the expedition to Nass to secure the northwest trade for the Hudson's Bay Company. In October, 1829, writing to McLoughlin about the establishment at Nass, the Governor and Committee stated, "The compliment of people should not be less than fifty in all, and from Mr. Chief Trader Ogden's enterprising character and active habits, we consider him well qualified for the charge."[3]

Simpson had hoped that his plans for capturing the northwest trade could go ahead with great speed, but circumstances caused delay. Simpson had planned that the *William and Ann*, a cedar brig of about 161 tons, and a chartered ship would be sent from England. The former could be sent to New Archangel to visit the Russians and then investigate the Nass River in order to find a suitable site for the proposed post. In the spring of 1829, however, Æmilius Simpson arrived at Fort Vancouver and informed the inhabitants that the *William and Ann* had struck South Spit as she was about to enter the mouth of the Columbia and had broken up in heavy seas with the loss of her captain, mate, and crew together with fourteen English men and boys and twenty-six Hawaiians.[4]

On May 8 the *Ganymede*, the chartered vessel, entered the Columbia and narrowly missed the same fate, when Captain Hayne mistook Chinook Bay for the Columbia. The Indians tried to encourage him in the error in the hope that his ship would be wrecked and they could plunder it. Upon her safe arrival, however, it was found that much of her cargo had been stowed near the salt and had been greatly damaged. To make matters worse, Dr. McLoughlin had only limited supplies at Fort Vancouver. Thus he had to sit by while the American Captain Dominis in his brig *Owyhee*, joined by another American vessel the *Convoy*,[5] monopolized the coastal trade.

Simpson realized that this turn of events upset his plans for the British coastal trade in 1829 and the founding of Nass, which he had proposed for 1830. He now pleaded for another vessel. The Governor and Committee responded by buying the *Isabella* for £2,900 and sending her out around the Horn, but on May 2, 1830, catastrophe struck again. The *Isabella* had almost reached her destination when Captain Ryan mistook Chinook Point for Cape Disappointment. Therefore, he tried to go through the breakers south of the channel. The ship's rudder broke off, and the wind and tide drove her on the shoals. Afraid that the ship would break up during the night, the captain ordered the abandonment of the ship. Dr. McLoughlin was irritated when Captain Ryan arrived at Fort Vancouver on May 4 with this depressing news. McLoughlin with all of the available men from the Columbia depot rushed to the scene, but they were unable to move the vessel from where she had run aground. At least the crew was safe this time, and McLoughlin and his party were able to salvage the greater part of the cargo.[6]

Even with these adverse conditions, McLoughlin was still determined to investigate Nass. He began preparations to send the remaining ships in the area to the northern coast. As a result, when Ogden, depressed about the loss of his nine men at The Dalles and the poor returns of his Snake River Brigade, entered Fort Vancouver on July 6, 1830, he was surprised to find the post a beehive of activity. Six years in the Snake Country had taken their toll on Ogden. He had lost a great deal of weight. His once round face was thin, and his usually sharp, mischievous eyes were dull with worry and responsibility. However, he listened intently to the gossip at Fort Vancouver, for much had happened while he had been away. He was surprised to learn that Æmilius Simpson had gone to the Russian settlement of New Archangel in September, 1829, where he had been graciously received by Governor Chistakov. Chistakov had welcomed the proposals that Governor Simpson had put forth in a letter delivered by his namesake and suggested that arrangements should be made between London and St. Petersburg.

The day after Ogden's return, McLoughlin wrote Æmilius Simpson ordering him to take the *Vancouver*, the sixty-ton schooner built at Fort Vancouver, the *Eagle*, and the *Cadboro* and proceed to Fort Langley with that post's trade goods. He was then to go on to Nass to "examine the harbours and rivers that fall in it as high up as you conveniently can and endeavour to find a good situation to build a trading establishment on its banks or on the shores of the harbour."[7] Because Simpson was allotted only a short period of time on the coast, he sent the *Vancouver* to Fort Langley, and he in the *Cadboro* with the *Eagle* arrived at Nass on August 28.

Simpson took the *Cadboro* up the river seven or eight miles to a point where the channel narrowed. Here he thought would be a good place for the post, for the ship would lie within pistol shot of the shore, an important consideration if there were hostile Indians nearby. He noted also that the site had a southern exposure so that vegetables could perhaps be grown and make the fort more self-sufficient. Any fears of the Indians proved groundless. Although Simpson and his men were able to stay only three days at Nass, they developed a lively trade with the natives who began to surround them, and they were able to accumulate two hundred beaver weighing 296 pounds, forty martens, and thirty land otters.[8]

By October, Simpson and his ships had returned to the Columbia, where they found malaria raging at Fort Vancouver. Mosquitoes breeding in and around the swamps of the lower Columbia had carried the disease, known here as "intermittent fever," to the Indians and the whites alike. By the fall of 1830 about three-quarters of the entire Indian population around Fort Vancouver had died, and fifty-two Hudson's Bay Company men were severely ill. It must have been a dismal sight for Simpson and his men as they moved upriver. The surviving Indians had abandoned their dead and dying to the birds and beasts of prey and had fled in terror to the seacoast. As one Indian explained the situation to James Douglas, "Every village presented a scene harrowing to the feelings; the canoes were there drawn up upon the beach, the nets extended on the willow-boughs to dry, the very dogs appeared, as ever, watchful, but there was not heard the cheerful sound of the human voice."[9]

After his severe privations in the Snake Country, Ogden was in a weakened condition and quite susceptible to malaria. By October, McLoughlin, writing about the widespread illness, noted, "Even Ogden was down."[10] As Ogden lay in bed with his thin body racked with chills and fever, he had only limited medical attention. The hospital which is so often thought of as part of Fort Vancouver was built three years later. Then, as a result of this and other epidemics, Doctors McLoughlin and Meredith Gardner began what is considered the first effort to build a permanent hospital in the Pacific Northwest.[11] Gardner and Dr. William Fraser Tolmie were not at Fort Vancouver at this time—they did not arrive until 1833. The physically fit at Fort Vaucouver had to care for the sick. Dr. Richard Hamlyn—a friend of Benjamin Harrison, the treasurer of the famous Guy's Hospital of London—left the fort during the epidemic to return to England.[12] Probably Dr. McLoughlin was the only man left with medical knowledge. McLoughlin had studied medicine for four and one half years with Dr. James Fisher of Quebec and then received a license "to practice in Surgery and Pharmacy or as an Apothecary."[13] That had been twenty-seven years earlier, however, and, with the burden of directing activities for the whole Columbia Department, McLoughlin could not have relished the departure of the dilettantish Dr. Hamlyn, which left him with added responsibility.

McLoughlin and the able James Douglas undoubtedly took care of Ogden while he was ill. One wonders if McLoughlin experimented with dogwood, whose astringent bark can be used as a substitute for cinchona, which, of course, was not available in the Columbia River Valley, since by 1832 dogwood bark was known to have similar properties and was used when other epidemics struck the area. Perhaps even in 1830, Ogden was given this medicine. Whatever the treatment, he survived and was put on the "convalescent list" by the middle of October, 1830.[14] During his long recovery, Julia, his wife, and their little daughter, Sarah Julia, now almost five years old, tried to cheer him.[15]

Because of the epidemic, McLoughlin sent the two-hundred-ton Isle of Wight brig, the *Dryad*, on a winter voyage to California and dispatched the *Vancouver* to the Hawaiian Islands. The establishment of Nass had been delayed, but by the spring of 1831, Ogden was well enough to command the Nass party which was to establish Fort Simpson. The *Dryad* and the *Vancouver* had returned from their winter voyages. On April 10, 1831, McLoughlin wrote to Æmilius Simpson to proceed with these ships to the Nass River, where he was to disembark Ogden and his party. McLoughlin ordered Simpson to remain with Ogden until he "can dispense with your assistance." Then if time permitted Simpson was "to examine Stikine and ascertain if as reported a large River falls into the ocean at that place."[16]

McLoughlin had grandiose plans for the coastal trade. He hoped that once Fort Simpson was established, the two schooners, the *Vancouver* and the *Cadboro*, could visit the various harbors where there was a large Indian population and make trade in these shallow coastal waters unprofitable for their American opponents. Too, he hoped that the large ship at his disposal, the *Dryad*, could be used to transport goods and supplies to forts Langley and Simpson and perhaps even carry timber and salted salmon from these northern posts to California, Peru, Chile, Mexico, and the Hawaiian Islands. Thus Ogden and Simpson's mission was only one part of a well-laid plan to advance the Hudson's Bay Company's trade along the Pacific Coast at the expense of the Americans and the Russians.

When Ogden left Fort Vancouver in the spring of 1831, he left domestic problems and sorrows. Much sickness had been experienced by the family during this winter, and on January 5 his and Julia's baby boy had died at Fort Colvile from an abcess in its stomach.[17] Now, as the *Cadboro* pushed out into the main channel of the river, Ogden knew that Julia was pregnant again and that when he returned to Fort Vancouver, he would welcome another child.[18]

Ogden did not have much time to think about his home life. A great deal of work had to be done. After more than a month's voyage, the ships finally reached the estuary of the Nass River and all hands were eager to land even if the country looked forbidding. The river was a chalky color caused by the glacial milk being carried down from the rugged and precipitous mountains that surrounded its channel. The summits of the mountains were covered with snow; the lower elevations with dense stands of pine. The site chosen for Fort Simpson was a flat space of about two or three acres on a rocky point which projected into the eastern channel of the river about forty feet above the high-water mark. Because it had a bold breastwork of rocks facing the sea, it was considered a good site. No one realized that it would bear the full fury of the northeast gales that were so frequent here in winter.[19]

Now, however, the weather was pleasant, and during the long summer evenings in this northern outpost under construction, Ogden and Simpson enjoyed each other's company. They mainly talked about the trade on the northwest coast and just where and how they were going to fit into it. Simpson knew much more about international problems and the objectives of the British, Americans, and Russians than Ogden, who had been in the Snake Country for years and away from any center of influence. Too, as Superintendent of the Marine on the Northwest Coast for the Hudson's Bay Company, Simpson had to keep himself informed about foreign affairs. During the balmy evenings of the summer of 1831, Simpson brought Ogden up to date.

Ogden learned that old Baranov had been an expansionist who had planted the Russian colonies at New Archangel (Sitka), Bodega Bay and Fort Ross in California, the Farallones Islands near the entrance to San Francisco Bay, and on Oahu in the Hawaiian Islands. Americans along the Pacific Coast traded liquor, guns, and ammunition to the natives in the neighborhood of the Russian settlements and caused the Russians a great deal of annoyance. Not only did they jeopardize the property and lives of the Russian American Company's servants, but their competition forced the Company to pay higher prices for furs. Consequently, the company forbade intercourse between its colonies and the Americans. This had a humiliating effect. The Russian American colonies were not self-sufficient and were soon in dire circumstances; this resulted in the Russian-American Treaty of 1824, which placed the southern Russian boundary at 54° 40′ north latitude and reopened New Archangel to American trade.[20]

Meanwhile men of the North West Company and later the Hudson's Bay Company were moving into the interior of what is now British Columbia. No point of conflict had developed because the British and the "British French Canadians" had no posts west of the Continental Divide, north of 54° 30′ north latitude, or west of 125° west longitude. In its early attempt to frustrate American trading the charter renewed by the Russian government on September 13, 1821, had extended Russian sovereignty in the form of the Russian American Company to the "shores of northwestern America which have from time immemorial belonged to Russia, commencing from the northern point of the Island of Vancouver, under 51° north latitude to Behring Straits and beyond them."[21]

Although this ukase was primarily directed against the Americans, the Russian maritime and territorial claims were not acceptable to the British Foreign Office, and it was only after years of activity on the part of the Hudson's Bay Company and governmental officials, particularly George Canning, that a treaty was finally signed on February 28, 1825. The treaty placed the boundary between Russian and British North American colonies at 54° 40′ north latitude and followed the Portland Canal to its head at 56° north latitude and then by a line no more than ten leagues from the coast to the 141st meridian. Both British and American subjects were given the right to trade at New Archangel and in the Russian coastal waters south of Mount Saint Elias for a period of ten years. The British were not particularly happy about the ten-year provision, but they were pleased that they now had the treaty right to travel to and from the interior of New Caledonia controlled by the Hudson's Bay Company through the Russian coastal strip and also the right of free navigation on the rivers that flowed to the coast.

As a result, Governor Simpson was eager to increase Anglo-Russian trade in the northwest. Æmilius Simpson told Ogden that he had been sent to Sitka or New Archangel in 1829 to discuss the British-Russian treaty. He had pointed out to Governor Peter Chistakov that the treaty forbade both nations to sell spirits, firearms, and ammunition to the Indians, but the Americans, who were not bound by the treaty, had been supplying the natives. The British and the Russians should co-operate to stop this. Governor Simpson's letter which Æmilius had delivered and the younger Simpson's conversation with Chistakov also suggested that the Hudson's Bay Company send out fifty to one hundred tons of manufactured goods from England, four to five thousand bushels of grain, and salt beef and/or pork. The purpose of this generosity was the elimination of American competition. Since the American traders' home port, Boston, was a long way off, they were heavily dependent upon the Russian trade. They needed Russian harbors in order to operate in the Pacific. They had gained access to these in the past by supplying the articles the British were now offering.

If the Americans were eliminated and the Russians stood alone, could the Hudson's Bay Company gain control of the Russian trade? Æmilius Simpson had been impressed by Sitka. It stood on a high, broad, flat knoll overlooking a fine harbor. At the top of the hill there was a rough bastion with twenty guns. From here stairs led down to the main settlement, which was enclosed on the landward side by a strong stockade. Twelve ships had been in the harbor, and Simpson had seen a shipyard in full production ready to launch a 280-ton ship.[22] As Simpson talked, Ogden tried to picture the Russian settlement. He could not foresee, of course, that in several months his companion would be dead and he would be taking his place.

In September, Simpson and the *Dryad* had returned to Nass after two months on the coast, and Simpson had been pleased to see the progress made in building Fort Simpson. A well-worn path went from the landing to the fort gate, near which some Nass Indians had pitched their lodges. The inside of the post was a pleasant sight. There was a large square edged with buildings and a "dwelling house" with roofs of cedar shingles. Even pathways had been made with cedar logs;[23] these would make walking much easier in winter and especially during the mucky thaw of late spring. Simpson tried to show enthusiasm about what his friend had accomplished during his absence, but it was difficult because he was sick. He was having increasingly sharp pains in his back. At first he had not thought they were serious, but he was soon found to be suffering from a liver inflammation. A few days later he was dead.

It was unpleasant for Ogden to write Dr. McLoughlin to inform him of the untimely death of the vigorous Superintendent of the Marine.[24] From time to time he walked down the pathway to the shore where his men were preparing Simpson's grave on the rocky, forlorn coast which Simpson himself had chosen as a suitable site for the Hudson's Bay Company establishment.[25] Immediately after he received Ogden's letters, McLoughlin began one of his long, precise letters in reply. Ogden was surprised when he received it. He knew that McLoughlin liked him, but he was taken aback to read: "In the present situation of our affairs we will attack [attach] the coasting trade to Fort Simpson, you will assume the management of both." Later Ogden realized that Dr. McLoughlin had few others whom he could trust to stamp out American and Russian competition on the northwest coast. McLoughlin repeated the Company's plans for the coastal trade that he had discussed with Æmilius Simpson in April. He told Ogden to use the two schooners, the *Cadboro* and the *Vancouver*, constantly in the coastal trade. Their use would cause the Americans to lose a great deal of business and perhaps "make them drop it."[26]

The Governor and Committee in London were shocked by the news of Simpson's death and worried about their policy on the northwest coast, though they approved McLoughlin's judgment in naming Ogden to replace Simpson. They knew that Ogden could handle men well, but there was a difference between maintaining discipline in a land party and commanding drunken seamen who the Governor and Committee thought "conducted themselves in a very turbulent manner." Too, what did Ogden know about ships? They wrote: "We are not aware that there is at present on the coast any officer fully qualified to superintend the Naval department of the Service; we shall therefore endeavor to engage a Lieut. or Master in the R[oyal] Navy, who from his habits will be fully able to enforce order among the people under him."[27]

Ogden would have been pleased to know the opinions of the Hudson's Bay Company's officials in Fenchurch Street in London. He was finding his new double assignment tedious. He was low on provisions and trade goods and had no prospects of getting more until spring.[28] In addition, McLoughlin was pushing him to expand the coastal trade and begin new explorations. McLoughlin wanted him to explore the Stikine River, which had figured in Æmilius Simpson's report on the coast, and he ordered Ogden "to ascertain if there is a situation eligible to erect an establishment on its banks about 30 miles from the ocean and also at Port Essington."[29]

McLoughlin really did not need to tell Ogden how to push the coastal trade. Four American vessels were trading along the coast dispensing large quantities of alcohol, guns, and gunpowder. Ogden decided to retaliate in kind despite Company policy and the Russian-British agreement prohibiting trade in these commodities. Soon he was writing to Fort Vancouver for more "trade goods," for his supply of rum was getting low. His methods proved effective. By 1832, even though the Americans still dominated the coastal trade, Ogden's schooners which were following the American ships into the shallow inlets and bays of the northwest coast had cut into their business considerably.

Ogden did not believe in selling liquor, guns, and ammunition to the Indians. He had been in the fur trade long enough to know their effect upon the Indians and ultimately upon any unfortunate white who met a well-armed drunken Indian. But by December, 1831, McLoughlin himself was convinced of the necessity of Ogden's actions and condoned them. He even ordered that if the Russians complained about the dispensing of liquor and weapons, Ogden should tell them that we "are obliged to do so in consequence of it being done by the Americans, and to prove to all that the Hudson's Bay Company is adverse to supplying these Indians with arms, ammunition, and liquor, you will propose to the Americans collectively to discontinue issuing and selling of these articles to which if they will accede you will also conform."[30] Simpson agreed and told the Governor and Committee that the Company must either follow Ogden's policy of combating the Americans or abandon the coast.[31]

At this time, McLoughlin's chief concern was in supplying Ogden with these trade goods, but problems kept arising. The *Vancouver* had to turn back on her way out, and the *Cadboro* was not yet ready to sail. McLoughlin wanted Captain Sinclair to get through with "the articles most required by Mr. Ogden . . . provisions, rum and ammunition."[32] Sinclair did get through, and by spring Ogden was pleased with his coastal trade. During this period at Fort Simpson, he reread the correspondence between the Governor and Committee of the Hudson's Bay Company and the directors of the Russian American Company which had been forwarded to him by McLoughlin. With these documents the old doctor added a personal letter encouraging Ogden "to cultivate a friendly understanding with them" and to visit Sitka if the opportunity presented itself.[33] After Ogden read this, he decided to visit the Russians at their New Archangel headquarters.

Very little is known about Ogden's activities in 1832 and 1833. Most of the pertinent letters and ships' logs apparently have been lost since they are not in the Hudson's Bay Company's archives, and Fort Simpson did not begin keeping an adequate journal until 1834. Thus Ogden's activities can only be discovered by piecing together the few references that are available. Ogden did visit Sitka. He sailed out of the mouth of the Nass River in the latter part of April in the *Cadboro* under the command of Captain Sinclair and arrived at Sitka by May 8, 1832.[34]

One wonders about the reception he received. If it was like the one that greeted him upon his visit to Sitka in September–October, 1834, he fired one of his guns to announce his arrival as his ship entered the harbor. Then a skin bidarka containing a paddler and a harbor pilot, one of whom was on duty both day and night, came out to the vessel and escorted her in. After safely anchoring, Ogden had his men fire a nine-gun salute to the governor, and this was returned by the Russian land garrison.[35] Ogden lost no time in seeking out the governor for he wanted to begin discussions with him. Walking toward the governor's house, which was still known as "Baranov's Castle," Ogden noticed the well-laid-out streets, the individual houses, and the wooden sidewalks. Pigs, descendants of those given to old Governor Baranov by King Kamehameha of the Hawaiian Islands, grazed quietly in a field nearby. The air was filled with the sounds of hammers on anvils and of the whipsaws creating boards out of logs.

The bustling and humming of Sitka was the work of the new governor who had replaced Peter Chistakov the year after Æmilius Simpson's visit. Baron Ferdinand von Wrangel, the distinguished Baltic German explorer and scientist, had taken office in 1830. It was he, a small, testy man with red hair and a red beard, who greeted Ogden. Wrangel had been eager to meet Ogden. From his vantage point at Sitka he had been watching Ogden's actions along the coast and his building of Fort Simpson. Ogden had figured prominently in Wrangel's communications to his board of directors, and it was probably with "a mixture of admiration, anxiety, and envy" that the Russian greeted the determined Ogden.[36]

Wrangel received Ogden graciously. It is not known whether he brought out the Union Jack to greet Ogden in the old Baranov custom of displaying foreign flags in honor of foreign visitors. Ogden probably enjoyed a hearty meal and a number of good drinks. The Russians were known to "drink an astonishing quantity," which one writer stated taxes "the health of a person,"[37] but Ogden would not have complained about this. Having dispensed with the pleasantries, the two efficient men got down to business. Wrangel offered to buy from the Hudson's Bay Company all of the wheat that it could provide because the Russian colony at Fort Ross had been a disappointment as a source of agricultural production. This post, on the rocky California coast which is so often shrouded in fog, was a poor producer, and even today the land is primarily used for sheep grazing. Wrangel also offered to buy "goods on credit at prime cost at Sitka." When Dr. McLoughlin read this proposition, he blurted out: "I think Mr. Ogden must have made a mistake in copying the Baron's proposal."

Wrangel pointed out to Ogden that the Russian American and Hudson's Bay companies had a great deal in common and that they should operate jointly to oppose the Americans. When Ogden reported this second proposal, McLoughlin saw a shrewd plan on Wrangel's part: "There is no doubt in my opinion but the Russians . . . would be as well pleased to see us leave the coast as the Americans."[38] The Governor and Committee did not appear as shocked as Dr. McLoughlin. They calmly stated that the Russian American and Hudson's Bay companies must keep their "dealings separate." They had no objection to selling the Russians goods at cost, but the Russians would have to pay the freight charges.[39] As a result, the Ogden-Wrangel talks came to nought, and the Russians were told to negotiate with London. Ogden meanwhile was pressed by Dr. McLoughlin to find a site for a post at Stikine and at Port Essington.

Ogden spent the whole summer on the coast "on board the 'Cadboro' with Sinclair."[40] They tried to follow McLoughlin's orders and sailed to Stikine, but Captain Sinclair became ill, and they were unable "to examine the entrance of Stikine River." Too, probably because of the captain's condition, they did not examine, as McLoughlin later complained, "Port Essington or its vicinity as I suggested."[41] The *Cadboro* returned to Port Simpson. By October she sailed again to visit Port Essington, about which McLoughlin was so concerned. Ogden sent his assistant, Donald Manson, in the *Cadboro* with a party of eleven Canadians to examine the Skeena River, at whose mouth lay Port Essington, in the hope that they would find a suitable site for a post. At noon on October 19, 1832,[42] Ogden said good-bye to the *Cadboro* and hoped that the party would be successful and that Dr. McLoughlin would be satisfied at last. By October 31, Manson was exploring the entrance to the Skeena River with "some Indian chiefs' sons," and by November 6 the entire party was safely back at Fort Simpson.[43]

The year 1832 had gone well for Ogden but he was tired. He applied for leave, and, as each ship arrived at Fort Simpson, he hoped that it would carry the letter that would let him go east of the mountains in 1833. He had been operating from the Columbia for the Hudson's Bay Company for almost ten years. He wanted a change of scenery and release from responsibility. Shortly before Christmas, 1832, the brig *Lama* sailed into the harbor.[44] Captain McNeill, the American skipper who virtually had come with the ship and who later discovered the harbor of Victoria, presented Ogden with the long-awaited letter, in which McLoughlin stated, "You will see by the minutes of the Council that you are permitted to go to York next spring." McLoughlin went on, "If you avail yourself of this permission," put Donald Manson in charge of Fort Simpson and attach the *Cadboro* and the *Lama* to whichever post is considered the most advantageous.[45]

One can imagine that Ogden celebrated that night with Captain Mc-Neill, Donald Manson, and a few others, and later with his wife, Julia. There has been some question whether Julia was at Fort Simpson, but it seems likely that she was, because in July, 1833, she gave birth to a son, Charles,[46] named after Ogden's brother. Since there is no indication that Ogden left the northwest coast in the fall of 1832, Julia must have been there with him.

Ogden's leave did not materialize, however. On January 4, Ogden had sent Donald Manson in the *Dryad* to Fort Vancouver, giving Manson and Captain Kipling, the ship's captain, instructions to stop at Milbanke Sound on their way south to examine it as a possible site for a future Hudson's Bay Company establishment. They encountered bad weather and reached Milbanke only on February 12 and then went on to the Columbia River. They found a suitable site, and in March, McLoughlin sent them off again to set up a post at their proposed location. On May 5, Finlayson, with Donald Manson, James Birnie, William Caulfield Anderson, thirty-one Canadian laborers, and ten Hawaiians, sailed for Milbanke. From there Finlayson was to go on in the *Dryad* to Fort Simpson. McLoughlin said that Finlayson's "arrival at Fort Simpson, will determine if Mr. Ogden will be here in time to overtake the Express, before it leaves Colville."[47] McLoughlin appears to have been less than enthusiastic about Ogden's leave. He informed him that Finlayson would arrive at Fort Simpson quite late. This would make it difficult for Ogden to catch the brigade going East. If he decided to winter on the Pacific Coast, it "would facilitate our proceedings very much."[48] Needless to say, Ogden remained at Fort Simpson.

Ogden spent most of 1833 aboard ship and left the trade at Fort Simpson to Donald Manson, who had returned from his explorations. During the course of his voyages, Ogden examined the Stikine River, going upriver about forty or fifty miles. He was not pleased with what he saw and said, "It will not altogether meet our wishes."[49] By the fall Ogden decided to return to Fort Vancouver and discuss his findings with Dr. McLoughlin, who noted that "Mr. Ogden has unexpectedly made his appearance."[50] At this time, Ogden was still hoping for a leave the following spring, but fate again decreed otherwise. Probably while he was still at Fort Vancouver, a letter arrived from the Governor and Committee in which they commented on the many leave requests: "The removal of so many commissioned gentlemen from the same district in one season would be exceedingly inconvenient, and might prove injurious to the business; we therefore desire that if this gets to hand in time in the event of Chief Factor McLoughlin's coming out next spring, Messrs.

Ogden and McDonald may remain until the following . . . year."[51] Thus Ogden had to remain on the Pacific Coast and lead an expedition for the establishment of a post at Stikine in 1834.

By May 10, 1834, Ogden was ready to begin this new adventure. On that day he and Dr. Tolmie, the newly arrived Scottish physician, with five men and one boy arrived at the mouth of the Columbia River in a gig from Fort Vancouver and boarded the *Dryad*. By May 28 they were at Fort McLoughlin discharging cargo. The weather turned bad after they left the post, and they made slow progress up the coast. The boredom of the voyage was broken for them a few days later when the *Dryad* met the ship *Lagrange* under the command of Captain Snow of Boston, who had just come south from Sitka and Fort Simpson.[52] On June 4 the young Yankee captain invited Ogden and Dr. Tolmie to the *Lagrange* for dinner. They spent a happy evening together. Ogden especially enjoyed the pleasant conversation and "good ale, wine, etc.," while Dr. Tolmie satisfied his sweet tooth with "lots of pastry" and "cheese and tart."[53]

By June 9, Ogden reached Fort Simpson. As the *Dryad* approached, the crew fired a shot to make its presence known.[54] Ogden and his party stayed almost a week at the fort that he had founded, making last-minute preparations to start north to establish another one. Two days after leaving Fort Simpson, on June 17, they reached Clarence Strait. Ogden observed that the country was less rugged here. The mountains became flat, low points as they approached the sea, and here and there were bays surrounded by sand. Certainly it was a more hospitable environment than that around Fort Simpson.

The next day Ogden's opinion changed. Perhaps Clarence Strait was more pleasant topographically, but certainly not socially. As the *Dryad* approached Point Highfield late on the afternoon of June 18, Ogden stood on deck in the rain and watched the scene around him. He glanced toward the shore and was surprised to see "a shapeless mass of logs or planks" with a few huts around it built on a grassy point about sixteen miles away. While wondering what these strange buildings could be in an area that had not been "laid down in Vancouver's chart," he saw a boat leave the shore and come toward the *Dryad*.

The men of the Hudson's Bay Company's vessel had hardly dropped anchor when the boat, which proved to be a long whale boat, pulled alongside. Mounted on a swivel in its bow was a gun manned by "four stout men." A youthful man who appeared to be in command of the little party came aboard. He presented himself to Ogden and handed him a large paper which stated that British and American ships were prohibited from trading in the vicinity.[55] This was Baron von Wrangel's decree of May, 1834, which stated:

Governor of the Russian-American Colonies, Post Captain of his Imperial Majesty's Navy, Baron Wrangell does hereby announce to Commanders of Foreign Ships, that the Honorable Russian American Company's Brig "Tschitshagoft" [*Chichagoff*] Captain Sarembo and Schooner "Cheelkat" Captain Coornetsoff have orders to take their stations in the Straits within the territory of Russia, that is to say . . . northward of 54° 40' latitude, where no foreign ship or vessel has now a right to trade with the Indians by virtue of a sanctioned convention concluded between His Majesty the Emperor of Russia, and the president of the United States, as well as with His Majesty the King of Great Britain, which convention the Governor of the Colonies hopes will not be violated by any English or American Vessel.[56]

Ogden decided to put himself and the Hudson's Bay Company on record in regard to this decree. He wrote a note stating that "he was determined to proceed according to the treaty,"[57] that is, the treaty signed by England and Russia on February 28, 1825. He handed his answer to the Russian, and with that the young man went over the side and headed the whale boat back to the Russian establishment.[58]

Not long after the long boat had disappeared, an Aleutian skin boat pulled alongside the *Dryad*. There were three men in the small boat. In the bow and in the stern were paddlers. Between them sat a thin, elderly officer dressed in a blue surtout with a white vest. The man climbed up the net on the side of the vessel, accompanied by a "short thick set good-natured vainlooking man" who was the Russian's Indian interpreter. The Russian officer knew only a few words of English and had difficulty making his ideas clear to Ogden, who knew no Russian. Ogden tried to talk to him in French, which he spoke fluently, but found that the dark Russian could not speak French. With his limited English vocabulary, however, the elderly man did explain to Ogden that if he attempted to go up the Stikine River, he had orders to "boxum," which apparently meant to oppose Ogden "by violence." He meant to carry out his orders, but in the meantime he enjoyed his visit with the English, and "Boxum," as Ogden and Dr. Tolmie called him, remained aboard ship and consumed more than a pint of brandy drinking toasts of good health to the Hudson's Bay Company's traders.

Hardly had "Boxum" left when the whale boat appeared again, armed as before. This time the young Russian was not present. His place had been taken by a tall, thin, stern-looking man dressed in a threadbare surtout. With him was a man who spoke a little Spanish and whom Dr. Tolmie could partly understand. After much conjecturing, they learned that because no one at the Russian fort could speak English, French, or Latin, a bidarka had been sent to Sitka to inform headquarters of Ogden's arrival and to ask for further instructions.

Early the next morning, the last visitor the evening before returned and invited Ogden to the Russian post of Fort Dionysius. Ogden decided against going himself but sent Dr. Tolmie and Captain Duncan with four well-armed men to the Russian fort. When the Hudson's Bay Company men came around the point near the Russian post, they were surprised to see a light brig, the *Chichagoff*, lying at anchor "about a stone's throw from the fort." As they approached, they were directed by gestures to proceed to the brig, where they met Lieutenant Sarembo standing at the head of the gangway in a navy blue uniform. They were ushered along the deck, where they saw twelve cannons and four swivel guns, and at each gangway "a brawny fellow stood, armed with cutlass and pistols." Lieutenant Sarembo, who spoke a few words of English, indicated that the Ogden expedition would not be allowed to trade in Stikine Sound or proceed up the river. He informed them that Ogden's answer to Baron von Wrangel's proclamation had been sent to Sitka and that it would take eight to ten days to receive a reply. In the meantime, he would stand by his original orders.

On the following day, June 20, Ogden wrote to Baron von Wrangel:

> Your proclamation dated 15th May, 1834, from Sitka, prohibiting British Vessels from trading in these Straits is now before me, and I have to remark that my instructions from the Governor of the Honorable Hudson's Bay Company, residing in Columbia River are to trade and form an establishment ten marine leagues inland, in accordance with clause *2nd* Art. 4 of Convention entered between Great Britain and Russia . . . . And in regard to Art. 7 which does not expire before February 1835, I am, as a British subject, and in accordance with my instructions, determined to avail myself of; and should any impediments be placed in my way contrary to said condition, you, sir, must hereafter be responsible for the consequences.[59]

These were harsh words, but Ogden was determined to state clearly his and the Hudson's Bay Company's case. He thought that Wrangel must be trying to bluff them. Why else would he interpret the Russian-British Convention of 1825 in such a way? Wrangel did know that he was straining the terms of the agreement, but he was disturbed that the Russian government had made such generous allowances to the British. He realized that if the Hudson's Bay Company built posts within ten leagues of the coast, they could intercept furs coming from the interior which would otherwise be traded to the Russians and hence Russian trade would be affected greatly.

As Ogden and the *Dryad* remained in Stikine Sound, Ogden thought that his problems in establishing what was to have been Fort Drew, to be named after a member of the Committee, would never cease. The warlike Stikine Indians were becoming hostile. On June 19, Seix, the tall Stikine chief, with his flowing, jet-black hair, bushy whiskers, and mustachio came on board wearing a fox-skin robe. He and Ogden had a short visit. Two days later he returned again. The British, he admonished, could establish a post at the mouth of the Stikine River, but under no circumstances would he allow them to build upstream.[60] The Russians had played upon the Indians' fear that if the British were allowed to build an inland post, they would intercept land furs coming from the interior Indians and exclude the coastal Indians from their "middleman" trade.

On the evening of June 28, two boats arrived at Fort Dionysius, and early the next morning a letter from Captain Adolf Etholine was delivered to Ogden. Etholine informed Ogden that Baron von Wrangel would be away from Sitka until the end of August. He repeated Lieutenant Sarembo's warning that Ogden would be forcibly prevented from going upriver and that he had no right to trade or navigate in the vicinity of a Russian establishment. In the afternoon Ogden visited Lieutenant Sarembo, who corroborated the Wrangel-Etholine statement and asked Ogden to leave Stikine Sound as soon as possible. Shortly after his return to the *Dryad*, Ogden decided that because of both Russian and Indian obstruction, "it would be highly imprudent to persist in the undertaking." He then issued orders to sail back to Nass in order to move Fort Simpson to a better locale.

On July 14, 1834, Ogden and the *Dryad* sailed into an inlet in British territory south of the Portland Canal. The country looked promising, and during the following week Ogden sent his men out to survey for a new Fort Simpson. As work went ahead on the post, Ogden found he needed spars. These could not be obtained in the immediate vicinity, and on July 30 he sent a small party of men across the channel to search for suitable timber. As the Hudson's Bay Company's men began cutting timber near the Russian settlement of Tongass, however, they were driven off by employees of the Russian American Company.[61] Here was another indication of Russian hostility. Now Ogden decided to go to Sitka and lodge a formal protest with the governor himself. Since Baron von Wrangel would not be in Sitka until the end of August, Ogden returned to Nass Strait and to old Fort Simpson. The post was dismantled, and on August 29, Ogden ordered the saddest part of the operation, exhuming the coffins of Æmilius Simpson and Donald Manson's little daughter.[62]

Early September was spent repairing the *Dryad* and completing the new Fort Simpson. The fort was about two hundred feet square with a bastion at each corner mounting a total of four guns. The massive gates were about six or seven inches thick, studded with large nails, and had small doors in them so as to admit only one person at a time as a precaution against the hostile Indians in the region.[63] By September 17, Ogden was satisfied that the ship was in good shape and that the fort construction was proceeding well. He was now ready to pay the long-planned visit to Baron von Wrangel.

Ten days later, on September 27, at 10:00 A.M., the *Dryad* arrived outside of Sitka harbor.[64] The crew fired two guns to call for the pilot, who arrived three hours later. By 4:00 P.M. they were in the harbor, and by 8:00 P.M. they had discharged their pilot and were anchored. At eight the next morning, Ogden had his men fire a nine-gun salute in honor of Wrangel, which was shortly returned by the Russian shore garrison. At noon on the same day, September 28, Ogden disembarked and went directly to "Baranov's Castle," the governor's residence, where he stayed until seven o'clock that evening.

Although Wrangel was gracious to Ogden, whom he admired from their conversations two years before, he remained determined to obstruct the Hudson's Bay Company's plan for a post on the Stikine. As the two men conversed in French, Wrangel, flushed with success after his recent visit to St. Petersburg, told Ogden that the provisions in Article 11 of the Russian-British treaty of 1825 justified his position, especially since the true nature of the Hudson's Bay Company's project on the Stikine was to undermine and attack Russian trade.[65] On October 2, Wrangel returned Ogden's visit when he came aboard the *Dryad*. Nothing important was accomplished by this conversation, and the Hudson's Bay Company party made ready to depart.

Because of calms, they were delayed in Sitka until October 7. They reached Fort Simpson one week later, after conducting business along the coast, taking on furs, spars, and passengers at Fort Simpson. They then proceeded southward to Fort McLoughlin and continued sailing down the coast against fogs and heavy gales until they reached the mouth of the Columbia. Here they encountered John Townsend and the famous scientist, Thomas Nuttall, whom Ogden told about their prolonged journey from Nass and how "they had been on an allowance of a pint of water per day, and had suffered considerably for fresh provision."[66] Their visit was brief, and soon the Ogden party crossed the bar at the entrance to the river. Then, Ogden, Captain Duncan, and ten men set off in the "Jolley bots [*sic*]" for Fort Vancouver,[67] which Ogden was eager to reach in order to report his difficulties to Dr. McLoughlin.

Three days later, on December 14, Ogden reached Fort Vancouver.[68] It was a jubilant day for Dr. McLoughlin. He had become worried about Ogden and only the day before in a letter to Peter Warren Dease had written: "It is with feelings of deep anxiety and distress that I inform you that I have no accounts from Mr. Ogden since he left this in May for the North West Coast and as he was to have been here in the latter end of September or beginning of October—I have every reason to fear some misfortune has happened in that quarter."[69]

After Ogden's return, he and Dr. McLoughlin spent long hours discussing the Stikine situation, and McLoughlin began formulating a most impressive case against the Russian American Company. With McLoughlin's prompting, Ogden made a formal report to his immediate chief in which he emphasized the great cost of the operation to the Hudson's Bay Company:

> In conformity with your instructions dated Fort Vancouver 10th, May, 1834, addressed to me, to proceed to Stikine River, which discharges in Clarence's Straits, to erect an establishment on British Territories, ten marine leagues from the ocean, as by right granted to British subjects in Article 3 of convention between Great Britain and Russia. Having for this express purpose in Fall 1833 with considerable expense ascended the Stikine River, and formally taken possession of a spot suitable for erecting an establishment, I accordingly after considerable derangement of our affairs on the coast, attended with an enormous expense in goods and provisions and serious loss of time, collected a party of sixty four servants and eight officers, and reached Stikine River on the 18th June; and I now beg leave to refer you to the enclosed documents for its not having been in my power to comply with your instructions.[70]

With this information in hand, McLoughlin now prepared a statement of expenses of the "*Dryad* Affair" for the Governor and Committee. McLoughlin estimated that the Company's loss was:

1—The wages for 38 men for a year's period came to _____£818
2—The expense of bringing the said men from Europe and
    Canada to the Columbia for the express purpose of building
    Stikine. At the cost of £25 a piece would come to _____ 950
3—Salary of three officers engaged in the same project for a year 265
4—Expense of bringing the officers to the Columbia _____ 150

5—Provisions for the "above 41 persons from the date of their arrival at Fort Vancouver on October 22, 1833 to June 1, 1834 . . . 221 days at 1/6 per man . . ." _____ 679/11/6

2,862/11/6

6—Wages for Captain Kipling and the crew of the "Dryad" (4 officers and 26 men) from October 1, 1833 ("the date on which the vessel would have been sent to England if it had not been considered necessary to keep her for the purpose of establishing Stikine") to June 1, 1834—8 months at £93/5/8 per month _____ 746/3/4

7—Provisions for the crew . . . 243 days at 2/6 per man _____ 729

8—"Eight months services of the Brig Dryad" _____ 1,200

2,675/3/4

After totaling the cost of the land and sea operations, the expense was £5,537/14/10. Then Dr. McLoughlin estimated that the expense of sending Ogden to Stikine in the *Lama* in 1833 came to £250. Of course, the outfit forwarded to Fort Vancouver for Stikine had to be considered as well as the Company's loss of interest on their money at 5 per cent which brought the grant total to £22,150/10/11.[71]

The correspondence and documents that substantiated the Hudson's Bay Company's stand on the "*Dryad* Affair" reached London in October, 1835, and Governor Pelly immediately filed a formal protest with the Foreign Office. Lord Palmerston, the foreign secretary, was delighted with the Company's strong case and ordered Lord Durham, the British ambassador to Russia, to press St. Petersburg for indemnification.

Now the situation at Stikine in 1834 was virtually out of Ogden's and McLoughlin's and the Company's control, and was being handled through diplomatic channels.

While the diplomatic representations were being made, the Governor and the Committee in London were considering new strategies of their own to defeat the Russians in America. They concluded that no further attempt should be made, at least at present, to establish a post at Stikine, for this might endanger the diplomatic proceedings. Instead, they decided to pursue the trade through the back door—by expanding activities in New Caledonia (British Columbia) and in this way obtain the pelts from the interior before they reached the coast.

When Ogden reached Fort Vancouver, he received a letter from Governor Simpson who praised him and expressed the Company's "unqualified approbation of the very effectual manner in which you have performed the important and hazardous duty of establishing the Honorable

Company's trade upon the North West Coast." As a result of his fine work, Simpson continued, Ogden would probably be promoted to a Chief Factorship, and he was given orders to take charge of the New Caledonia District. Now, because of his excellent work on the Pacific coast, it became Ogden's job to pressure the Russians on their rear flank.[72]

New Caledonia, 1835-1844

OGDEN HAD MISGIVINGS about his new assignment. He knew the New Caledonia District well. He also knew its reputation as a more wretched station than the convict colony of Botany Bay in Australia. Its isolation would certainly be a contrast to the bustling Fort Vancouver, which had changed greatly in the last few years.[1] A schoolhouse, the first in the Oregon country, had been built in 1832. There Dr. McLoughlin's son and some of the boys at Fort Vancouver were taught by John Ball, the American who had come West with Nathaniel Wyeth in that year. The village around the fort where the tradesmen, boatmen, and laborers had always lived had expanded and now had thirty or forty log huts with "broad lanes or streets between them" which formed a "neat and beautiful village."[2] Many American visitors now came to the fort both by sea and overland across the continent.

Some Americans came with the idea of staying. In October, 1832, Nathaniel Wyeth, a successful Cambridge, Massachusetts, businessman, visited Fort Vancouver. Two years later he returned, this time at the head of the Columbia River Fishing and Trading Company. He was accompanied by the Reverend Jason Lee of the Mission Society of the Methodist Episcopal Church, his nephew Daniel Lee, also an ordained minister, and two other Americans, Philip L. Edwards and Courtney M. Walker. In the same year Hall J. Kelley, the so-called "Prophet of Oregon" arrived with Ewing Young, whom Ogden had met in California in 1830, and a disreputable group recruited in Monterey and San José. Dr. McLoughlin welcomed all of his visitors graciously and was a most generous host.[3] He helped the Lees establish themselves in the Willamette Valley and at The Dalles. Ogden thought seriously about what was taking place at Fort Vancouver. He liked Americans individually, but he could not help wondering about the political implications of the arrival of so many of them.

In the first week of July, 1835, however, his thoughts had to turn from Fort Vancouver when he reluctantly left the Pacific headquarters and started for the north. Goods for the various New Caledonian posts were loaded into planked boats about twenty-five feet long and started slowly upstream to Fort Colvile, built in 1825 near Kettle Falls on the Columbia, a site which Governor Simpson had chosen for its strategic location and good farm land. Now, ten years after Colvile's founding, Ogden discovered the post to be a thriving agricultural community with fields of potatoes and wheat and even a gristmill in full production. Simpson's efficiency was apparent again. When the Ogden party reached the gates of Colvile, they were greeted by the one-eyed brother of Arctic explorer John Rae, William Glen Rae, who three years later was to marry Dr. McLoughlin's daughter Eloisa.[4] He was an odd man who had fits of depression and later committed suicide in San Francisco.[5] Now, however, he enjoyed Ogden's company and was a gracious and charming host, so that Ogden had a pleasant time during his brief stay at the upper Columbia River post.

From this point the brigade continued upriver until they reached Fort Okanagan, built near the junction of the Columbia and Okanagan rivers. Ogden was impressed as the Express, the brigade responsible for communication and supply lines for the Company, passed the rich farmlands surrounding the fort and the hundreds of fine horses grazing in the pastures nearby. Okanagan was an important horse-producing area, for it stood at the head of navigation. Here Ogden was to leave his boats and proceed on horseback into the heart of New Caledonia. He was delighted to reach Okanagan after an arduous twenty-day voyage for another reason. At the gates of Fort Okanagan his oldest and dearest friend, Sam Black, the boisterous companion of Île-à-la-Crosse days, was waiting for him. Ogden had been looking forward to seeing Black again since he had first learned that Dr. McLoughlin had asked Black to come to Okanagan from his post at Kamloops.[6] Black was one of the few people that Ogden always found compatible and yet exhilarating. They not only had their years in the North West Company to discuss, but books, magazines, and exploration. Although Black did not have a classical education, he was astute and observant and a man of literary attainments. It is easy to understand why he and Ogden were such close friends.

That evening as the men sat down to dinner, Ogden was surprised to notice that his friend placed a loaded pistol underneath the tablecloth. He asked about this. Black told him that because the natives of this region were extremely hostile, he carried "dirks, knives and loaded pistols concealed about his person" and always placed one on his dining table and in his bed at night. Ogden remembered that Black had never liked Indians even in the Green River–Île-à-la-Crosse days and that the Indians had been frightened of him, but he had never seen his friend so suspicious and on his guard.[7] Black felt that he had good reason to be wary of Indians. Indian troubles were an old story at Kamloops. As early as 1815, Charette, a Nor'wester in temporary charge of the fort, had been killed by a young native. In 1822, when Chief Trader John McLeod arrived at Kamloops, he found himself in a dangerous position; the tribes of the district were fighting following the death of a notable chief. Intertribal clashes were still frequent. They caused the white men great concern for their safety, and seriously interfered with trade.[8]

Shortly after his arrival at Okanagan, Ogden had to start north again, this time with a two to three hundred horse pack train. Each horse, sleek and fat and in almost perfect form and color, carried two packs weighing approximately eighty-four pounds and containing goods brought from England to entice the natives of the interior.[9] This imposing party moved over the Okanagan Trail. The trail was not too difficult. It had been worn through the years, and the Ogden party was able to average about fifteen miles a day.[10]

Upon arrival at Kamloops the large horse contingent with all of its accouterments was run into the stockade, which was large enough to hold the whole pack train. The fort, compact and well palisaded, stood a short distance from the stockade, but Ogden knew that traders were not enthusiastic about serving at this so-called "capital of Thompson River." Trade had fallen off greatly since its peak year of 1822, yet it had to be maintained because of its strategic location, since it was considered a division point on the brigade route from the Columbia to New Caledonia.

At Kamloops, Ogden left Sam Black, and the long and impressive train set out again toward Fort Alexandria on the Fraser River. The Fraser below the fort was not navigable, especially in the summer, with loaded boats, so this post had become the most feasible point where the Express could leave its horses and proceed upstream by water. Ogden's canoes now began the three-hundred-mile boat trip which took about twenty days to Fort St. James on Stuart's Lake. This old post, established thirty years before by Simon Fraser and John Stuart, was to be Ogden's headquarters for almost a decade. From here the goods brought up by boat were distributed to the various outposts in the vicinity by "large and small canoes, horses, dog sleds and men's back."[11] Ogden was relieved to arrive at his destination, for the trip had taken almost two months.

Fort St. James was built like most fur-trading posts. It was enclosed by a high, strongly built stockade and had bastions at the diagonal corners. Inside the fort Ogden found a two-story house made of squared timbers which was to be his home. Also built around the square were one-story buildings which were the clerks' and servants' quarters, a salmon shed, and a meat house. The Ogden children loved their new home, but Ogden himself knew that service as Chief Factor in New Caledonia would not be idyllic. That was why he was receiving an additional stipend. Even Governor Simpson, who often could be callous about assignments, showed compassion about duty here and wrote, "The situation of our new Caledonia Friends in regard to the good things of this Life, is anything but enviable."[12]

Ogden, in his usual efficient manner, began to take stock of the situation. His first thought, now in September with winter coming on, was an investigation of the food supply. He learned that here as at other posts in New Caledonia the diet was primarily fish. In the spring when navigation opened, carp could be caught, and by summer a small species of salmon about the size of a herring was running. By autumn larger salmon, weighing about five pounds, could be caught. In the winter a few white fish could be obtained. These were a great treat when served with berry cakes made by the natives. The greatest treat, reserved for holidays, was dog meat.

The food situation thus did not seem to present great difficulty, but Ogden soon learned that the real problem was not variety but quantity. His people were often reduced to a half-allowance or even a quarter-allowance, and on a few occasions they had no allowance at all. Many accounts mention the scarcity and unpalatability of the food. Men complained that they lived on "dried salmon and cold water," and Thomas Dears in 1831 moaned that "many a night I go to bed hungry and craving something better than this horrid dried salmon."[13]

One of Ogden's first acts in the New Caledonia district was an attempt to secure an adequate winter food supply. He estimated that a stock of about 30,000 salmon would be needed to meet all the demands for men and sled dogs, and he began sending two men with four horses and carts to transport salmon from the Babine River to the portage point. At the portage three men from Fort St. James met them and carried the collected salmon back to the Stuart Lake post. If salmon were running in Stuart's Lake, they were also caught and put away for future use. If properly cared for, salmon could be preserved two or three years, though the fish lost most of its flavor, but as Ogden said, "When one years staff of life is secured for the next your mind is relieved from a heavy load of anxiety."[14]

While worrying about his food supply, Ogden was also concerned about the Indians of the district. The chief tribes were the Babines and the Carriers, and, to a lesser extent, the Chilcotins. The Babines were curious people whose name came from the French "*babine*," meaning the chop or pendulous lip of an animal. A Canadian, Jean Baptiste, who Ogden thought had "a nice eye for analogy of form," gave them the name because they wore plugs of bone or hardwood between their teeth and their lower lip.[15] Since their territory was primarily around Babine Lake and River and the Bulkley River and Lake, Ogden at this time was more interested in his immediate neighbors, the Carriers.

The Carriers, like the Babines, were a group of Western Dénés. They had developed a means for obtaining a food supply adequate enough to allow them to live in large villages within easy reach of one another. Village society was dominated by hereditary noblemen who lived in large houses made of a framework of poles covered with bark with a door at each end of the dwelling and a hole in the roof to allow smoke to escape.

Ogden found that the individual villages had a communal *esprit de corps*, but the tribe as a whole had none. Villages often fought each other. It was difficult for a trader to keep informed about the situation. The Carriers were great traders. They had a long-established system of bartering even when Alexander Mackenzie visited them in 1793. They traveled in their aspen-wood or cedar-bark canoes all the way to the coast, where they exchanged furs for copper, woolen garments, and sea shells (wampum) which when strung together served as the currency for the area.

The custom that most distinguished the Carriers from their neighbors was their practice of forcing a widow to pluck the bones of her late husband from his funeral pyre and carry them in a leather wallet or satchel upon her back. It was this practice that prompted their French Canadian name *Porteurs*. Paul Kane has vividly described this ceremony:

The dead body of the husband is laid naked upon a large heap of resinous wood, his wife is then placed upon the body and covered over with a skin; the pile is then lighted, and the poor woman is compelled to remain until she is nearly suffocated, when she is allowed to descend as best she can through the smoke and flames. No sooner, however, does she reach the ground, than she is expected to prevent the body from becoming distorted by the action of the fire on the muscles and sinews; and whenever such an event takes place she must, with her bare hands, restore the burning corpse to its proper position; her person being the whole time exposed to the scorching effects of the intense heat. Should she fail in the due performance of this indispensable rite, from weakness or the intensity of her pain, she is held up by some one until the body is consumed. A continual singing and beating of drums is kept up throughout the ceremony, which drowns her cries. Afterwards she must collect the unconsumed pieces of bone and ashes and put them into a bag made for the purpose, which she has to carry on her back for three years; remaining for the time a slave to her husband's relations, and being neither allowed to wash nor comb herself for the whole time, so that she soon becomes a most disgusting object. At the expiration of three years, a feast is given by her tormentors, who invite all the friends and relations of her and themselves. At the commencement they deposit with great ceremony the remains of the burnt dead in a box, which they affix to the top of a high pole, and dance around it. The widow is then stripped naked and smeared from head to foot with fish oil, over which one of the by-standers throws a quantity of swan's down, covering her entire person. She is then obliged to dance with the others. After all this is over she is free to marry again.[16]

Fortunately, Ogden believed, this custom had been dropped by the time he arrived at Fort St. James. He found the Indians burying their dead rather than cremating them, a change which saved many a bereaved widow from being scorched at her husband's funeral pyre.

When he arrived at Fort St. James, Ogden also found the Carriers living up to their reputation for troublemaking. He stated that "they attacked me as a matter of course on my arrival," but he was able to get along with them and soon gained their respect. Ogden was one of the few traders in the American West who had some liking for Indians and seemed to understand them, but he did not like the Carriers. He thought that they were "a brutish, ignorant, supersticious beggarly set of beings." Yet he felt rather sorry for them. He noticed immediately that they were under the debt system. In this type of trade they received ammunition and tobacco on credit, generally in the summer. In the autumn they received guns and ammunition to aid in their hunt for food so that they would have more time to trap fur-bearing animals. Credit was extended with the idea that the Indians' debts would tie them to a specific post and that they would hunt harder in an effort to extinguish these debts. This system had been introduced to New Caledonia very early. No one had tried to abolish it for fear that the Carriers would take their furs to the coast and trade them to the coastal Indians, sell them to the Americans on vessels in the area, or even sell them to another Hudson's Bay Company post. The last would be a lesser evil, but would still deprive the "home" fort of its commerce.

Shortly after Ogden's arrival, he began to think about the Carriers' problems. He then told them that they had his permission to leave Fort St. James if they wished after they paid their debts. Studying the Carriers and the debt system, Ogden decided that the Indians could not really understand this Anglo-Saxon institution. He noticed that even if the Indians had debts, "not one in ten will absent himself from his village and in winter in lieu of employing themselves trapping will lounge and idle their time in gambling, feasting and sleeping." Ogden also concluded that although some considered the debt system a great evil of the fur trade, the Company actually profited little better than the Indians. He noted that "guns, axes, tranches, moose skins and traps" were lent to the Indians, but "the Carriers scarcely ever returned an article loan'd them but always have some plausible excuse ready when called on." This debt system was so firmly established, however, that it took Ogden almost four years—until 1839—to abolish it completely.

Under his new system direct selling took the place of the debt-credit policy. Ogden now sold traps to the natives for four beaver apiece. Theoretically, under the previous practice, the natives had paid six skins per trap, but generally they had not paid the Company. Ogden found the discounted direct-payment system effective: "Returns have not diminished and our indent on the last article has been decreased one half." Too, as Ogden improved the method of transporting salmon across Babine Portage, he was able to reduce costs from sixty salmon for one beaver to ninety salmon for each pelt, and he observed: "The Carriers know too well their own interest . . . and finding we can obtain our supplies independent of them, they now willingly sell them to us." In addition, Ogden made the price of traps and salmon at Fraser Lake, Stuart's Lake, and the Babine posts uniform, and the Indians of the vicinity were no longer discontented about the disparity of prices at the different posts. These reforms benefited the district. The Company's profits increased and Indian unrest decreased.[17]

As Ogden studied trade practices of the New Caledonia District, he was surprised to note that great quantities of leather, a scarce commodity in British Columbia, had been brought from the plains of what are now Alberta and Saskatchewan over the Rockies to New Caledonia at an early date. He remembered that the famous Colin Robertson, who, when he opened trade with the New Caledonian natives in 1819–20, had introduced dressed leather. Leather had grown in importance as a trade item over the years. The natives of this western region had become very attached to the parchment, buffalo robes, pack cords, snowshoe lines, and other leather goods, which came to them via Fort Edmonton on the North Saskatchewan and Fort Assiniboine on the Athabaska and then over Tête Jaune (Yellow Head Pass) or the so-called Leather Pass. In 1831 the trade route was somewhat changed and the leather began going to New Caledonia by the Peace River Route via Fort Dunvegan and Finlays Fort. In that year, 650 dressed moose skins, 100 pounds of babiche snares and beaver nets, 2,000 fathoms of pack cord, and large quantities of sinews and grease went through Finlays Fort. Ogden complained that he had to send seven men and a leader to Dunvegan to procure the leather supply allotted to him, but generally he kept a year's supply of leather on hand which he left "en depot at McLeods Lake," from where it was transported to Fort St. James in June.[18]

Ogden found in his assessments that this leather trade was very expensive. Analyzing the situation, he came to realize that much of the dressed leather that came into New Caledonia actually went to company servants, who "were in the habit of trading and wasting more than half," in some cases for a maiden's favor. Therefore, he now allocated his men sufficient leather for "one pair of shoes for fifteen days" which in one year would mean the "saving of more than one hundred skins" and "a gain on the trade."[19] Ogden may appear hard on his men in this action, but he made it up to them by taking pride in their actions and having the courage to write:

> The servants of this District have almost from the first year the country was established been represented as most worthless dishonest disolute set of beings; having been now some years with them with few exceptions they are by no means so bad as represented and when we seriously take into consideration the hard duty imposed upon them food of an indifferent quality and no variety, temptation great it is not surprising that they should occasionally deviate from the right path and under these circumstances some allowance ought to be made for them.[20]

Ogden's concern for his men can also be seen in his attempt to add variety to their "dried salmon and cold water" diet. He began to develop agriculture and to encourage his men to do so as well. In 1835, as a result of Ogden's efforts, Sam Black at Kamloops began farming with a small potato patch in the Schiedam valley.[21] There were no two more unlikely farmers than Ogden and Black, but now in middle age, the formerly boisterous men of old Nor'wester days were happy to see their potatoes and wheat grow. Ogden was pleased when he was able to build a flour mill at Okanagan—the first to be built in what is now British Columbia —in order to take some of the pressure off Fort Colvile, New Caledonia's supply center. Even at Fraser Lake, fifty miles from Fort St. James, "there were good gardens in the vicinity of the fort in which potatoes, tomatoes, turnips and other vegetables with barley and even wheat came to perfection."[22]

Now Ogden was able to give his men a more varied diet. Each married man connected with the brigade received one hundred pounds of flour and each bachelor fifty pounds from the Okanagan mill.[23] Inland servants received twenty-five pounds of flour apiece. Interpreters were privileged characters and received the same as bachelor members of the brigade. Sugar was also an important staple, and the men generally received ten to fifteen pounds. An exception was old Jean Baptiste Boucher, a French-Cree half-blood who had come to Stuart's Lake with Simon Fraser in 1806. He was given "½ Keg Sugar gratuity and ½ keg on account" because Ogden felt that Boucher's contributions as "Gendarme ... in New Caledonia" had earned him extra rations.[24]

Even though conditions were improving, Ogden found "the same miserable solitude" during the winter at Fort St. James. When Stuart's Lake froze over and the trees became laden with snow, Ogden usually filled his days cajoling the Indians into tending their traps, but during the long, dark evenings he could only read and reread the few available books and English periodicals in front of the fire.

Ogden was occasionally able to spend some more pleasant evenings in thoughtful games of chess or backgammon or with a few lively hands of whist, or just sitting and talking. If anyone at the post had musical talent, he probably attended "Musical Soirees" as in the days of Peter Warren Dease's directorship of the Stuart's Lake fort. Other recreations included "dog racing, canoe sailing [in nicer weather] and l'amour; sometimes politics; now and then an animated discussion on theology, but without bitterness." Sometimes the monotony was broken by a feast given by Kwah, one of the few great Carrier chiefs. Such feasts featured roast bear, beaver, marmot, berries mixed in rancid salmon oil and fish roe that had been buried for at least a year. These winter feasts, however, were becoming infrequent. The ever efficient Ogden, thinking more about Hudson's Bay Company business than personal pleasure, worked at persuading the Carriers "to make their feasts in the month of June which does not interfere with their hunts."[25]

When spring came, Ogden was ready to lead the Brigade out from Fort St. James on their long trek to Fort Vancouver. About April 22, 1836,[26] the boats laden with the year's accumulation of furs pushed off with Fort Alexandria on the Fraser River as their immediate destination. The trip was rough, but they still made good time. They were at the post named after Alexander Mackenzie in early May and were able to join the Thompson River party by May 12. Because Ogden had left Fort St. James so early in the year, he was able to send some of his men from Fort Okanagan, after their arrival there, to assist "in bringing down the Boats from Colevile." Ogden considered this a good plan. It supplemented the original crews, and "with strong crews [we] are less liable to accidents in that most dangerous part of the river and with our weak bowmen for the safety of life and property too many precautions cannot be taken."[27]

When Ogden arrived at the Columbia River depot in June, he noticed that many changes had taken place during his eleven months' absence in New Caledonia. One of his chief interests was the S. S. *Beaver*. It was the first steamship used in the North Pacific and had arrived at Fort Vancouver from England on March 25, 1836. Simpson had urged building such a vessel for the American Pacific coastal trade as early as August, 1832, and Ogden, who had then been Superintendent of the Marine for the Northwest Coast, had agreed with him. Ogden was pleased when he looked over the 109-ton ship with her massive elm keel and two thirty-five horse-power engines supplied by the celebrated firm, Messrs. Bolton, Watt and Company.[28]

Ogden's enthusiasm about the arrival of the *Beaver* became even greater when he was invited to make a short excursion aboard her just before she sailed for the northwest coast on June 18.[29] He, with "a party of ladies and gentlemen," boarded the *Beaver*, under the command of Captain Home, and steamed down the Columbia to the mouth of the Willamette near the present city of Portland, Oregon, "then into the middle branch of the Multnomah [Willamette] and through it, into the Columbia, and back to the fort." The passengers were greatly excited, and the Reverend Samuel Parker commented: "The gaiety which prevailed was often suspended, while we conversed of coming days, when with the civilized, all the rapid improvements in the arts of life should be introduced over this new world." Ogden shrewdly observed that it was not only the advent of the *Beaver* but the presence of people like the Reverend Parker who were going to change the Oregon country.

Upon his return to Fort Vancouver, Ogden wanted to talk to Dr. McLoughlin about the "Stikine Incident" and to learn if the old man had received any news from London regarding Ogden's difficulties with the Russians two years before. McLoughlin told him that he had received a letter from the Governor and Committee stating: "The Russian Government disavow the construction which their authorities had out upon the stipulations of the Treaty of 1825; and that they promise to convey to those Authorities without delay His Imperial Majesty's disapprobation of their proceedings together with such further instructions as shall be necessary to prevent the recurrence of a similar cause of complaint."[30] Ogden was disappointed that more decisive action had not been taken, but he was pleased that his activities had not been censured. Now he returned to work and began preparations for the brigade's two-month return trip from cheery Fort Vancouver to gloomy Fort St. James.

The winter of 1836–37 was very much like the previous one at the New Caledonian post. The fish supplies were brought in, and Ogden continued to try to keep the Carriers in the field as much as possible and to improve the balance between expenditures and profit. When the heavy winter snows began to melt and the air became balmy, great activity began at Fort St. James. Spring had come, and the furs collected during the winter had to be baled and made ready for shipment to Fort Vancouver on the first leg of their journey to England. In April, 1837, Ogden again pushed off with his fur-laden boats and headed south for forts Alexandria, Okanagan, and Colvile on his way to the Columbia, which he reached on June 7.

This year Ogden found the trek to Fort Vancouver more difficult. Sam Black met his party and told him that the Thompson River Brigade had been coming out to meet the Ogden party but had had trouble with Indians. Between Thompson River and Okanagan, an Indian had stolen a horse from them, and the Hudson's Bay Company men had pursued him. They overtook a group of Indians and one of them came forward and tried to arrange a settlement. Somehow in the heated situation, the mediator had been killed. No one knew who had killed him or which side had fired the first shot. Just as Black was telling his story, Indians suddenly appeared and opened fire on Ogden and his men. One Hudson's Bay Company man was killed, and Sam Black, who already hated Indians, had his horse shot out from under him. The Indians soon stopped firing, and Ogden led his men out of the region as fast as possible.[31] Ogden was glad to reach the safety of Fort Vancouver.

This year he found that even greater changes had taken place. The marks of "civilization" were even more pronounced, but he was most surprised at the missionary zeal that prevailed in this previously wild country. He knew that Samuel Parker, a young missionary from Ithaca, New York, was at Fort Vancouver. He had met him the previous year and had talked with him while aboard the *Beaver*. Now Parker had been joined by others. In fact, when Ogden had almost reached Fort St. James in the fall of 1836, other American missionaries had arrived at Fort Vancouver. These people, who were eager to bring "enlightenment" to the Pacific Coast Indians, were members of the Whitman-Spalding party. Marcus Whitman, Doctor of Medicine from Wheeler, New York, was a friend of Samuel Parker who had become interested in Parker's Columbia River Indian project. When Whitman crossed the Plains, he brought with him his new wife, Narcissa, and the Reverend Henry H. Spalding and his wife, Eliza, the first women to cross the North American Continent above Mexico. All was not harmonious within this missionary contingent, however, for Henry Spalding was an old schoolmate and thwarted suitor of Narcissa Whitman.

Upon arriving at Fort Vancouver, the Whitmans and the Spaldings decided to separate. When Ogden arrived on the Columbia in early June, 1837, he learned that the Whitmans had settled among the Cayuses at Waiilatpu, the Indian name for "the place of rye grass," about twenty-five miles east of Ogden's old Snake outfitting point of Fort Nez Percés. The Spaldings were living among the Nez Percés about one hundred miles to the south on a small prairie where Lapwai Creek flows into the Clearwater. Ogden was surprised to learn that Dr. McLoughlin had been very hospitable to the newly arrived Americans. He had given them bedding and clothing and permission to draw on Fort Colvile for grain and flour for a two-year period. He had even let Narcissa live as a guest of the Company at Fort Nez Percés while her husband was building his mission nearby.[32]

Ogden knew that another minister had reached Fort Vancouver the previous fall and wondered about him. When he learned that the Governor and Committee had sent out the Reverend Herbert Beaver to the Pacific Coast to act as the Hudson's Bay Company's chaplain and missionary, his dry sense of humor caused him to remark that the minister had a "very appropriate name for the fur trade." Although a Beaver as chaplain at a fur trading establishment might seem appropriate, the man's temperament and personality certainly were not.

Beaver was a small man with light brown hair, gray eyes, and "a feminine voice, with large pretensions to oratory, a poor delivery, and no energy."[33] He was thirty-six years old when he arrived at Fort Vancouver with his wife, Jane, on September 6, 1836. Within weeks of his arrival, he was criticizing the people of the fort generally and, more specifically, the lack of attention to him and his wife and the lack of physical comfort, as well as the lack of religious and educational facilities.[34] Almost immediately he and Dr. McLoughlin, who had been baptized a Roman Catholic and had instituted French services for the Roman Catholic Canadians at the fort, disliked each other for both personal and religious reasons.

Ogden did not feel the same antipathy as others for the self-conscious, pompous minister. They had many conversations after Ogden's arrival at Fort Vancouver in early June, 1837. Much of Ogden's tolerance was the result of not taking the Reverend Beaver seriously. Also, he had a problem with which he hoped that the minister would help him. Ogden was playing Cupid. By 1837 he had successfully recuperated from the rigorous years in the Snake Country and with middle age setting in, his figure made him well suited for this role. An old friendship cast him in the part. James Birnie, Ogden's Scottish friend of old Nor'wester days, had a daughter, Elizabeth, by his Indian wife. A young man, Alexander

Caulfield Anderson, had fallen in love with her when they first met at Fort Simpson in 1834. Anderson vowed to marry her "as soon as she is marriageable."[35] By the summer of 1837, the girl was almost sixteen years old. Anderson, who was now serving under Ogden as clerk in charge of the Fraser Lake post, asked Ogden to bring the girl back to New Caledonia when the brigade returned.

Ogden, who generally did not have any deep religious convictions, did believe in observing the sacraments. While he was at Fort Vancouver in June, 1837, he asked the Reverend Beaver to baptize the girl before she left for New Caledonia to join her betrothed. Beaver, in his usual pompous manner, was shocked and spoke of Elizabeth "being consigned over to the state of concubinage."[36] He refused to baptize her because she was not "acquainted with the principles of religion."[37] Ogden would not stand for any such nonsense, however, and told the younger man that if he took this position, Ogden, with his power as a magistrate, would perform the service himself. When the brigade left Fort Vancouver in July, Elizabeth Birnie accompanied Ogden. She married Anderson the following year, and they lived a long and fruitful life together in what later became the state of Washington and the province of British Columbia.

Retracing his steps northward over the now familiar route to Fort St. James, Ogden thought about changes that had taken place on the Columbia in the last five years, particularly the influx of Americans. First there was the optimistic trader and former ice dealer from Massachusetts, Nathaniel Wyeth, who had arrived at Fort Vancouver in October, 1832. He had spent the winter as the guest of Dr. McLoughlin and in the spring of 1833 had accompanied the Snake Country Expedition southeastward, but he left some of his men behind him. John Ball became a school teacher at Fort Vancouver before turning to farming in the Willamette Valley with his former traveling companion, John Sinclair. Solomon R. Smith and Calvin E. Tibbetts also decided to remain in Oregon rather than return to the East with Wyeth.[38]

On his way out, Wyeth had met Captain Benjamin L. E. Bonneville, the French-born American army officer who had been befriended by the Revolutionary pamphleteer, Thomas Paine. Bonneville, with New York capital and a large number of trappers, was "on leave" from the army and was making his way to Fort Nez Percés to obtain supplies. As Ogden recalled the gossip, old Pierre Pambrun had been in charge of the Walla Walla post at the time. He had received the Americans cordially and even traded a roll of tobacco and some dry goods in exchange for furs. He refused, however, to re-outfit his competitors, and Bonneville later unjustly maligned Pambrun and the Hudson's Bay Company.[39]

In 1833, Wyeth returned. This time he came as the leader of the Columbia River Fishing and Trading Company, with seventy hunters and two Philadelphia scientists, Thomas Nuttall and John K. Townsend, and the missionaries Jason and Daniel Lee. On their way west, they had built a trading post on the Snake River near present-day Pocatello, Idaho, which they chose to call Fort Hall. Here they planned to outfit trappers and take away part of the Hudson's Bay Company's interior trade. They then continued on to the Columbia and built another post, Fort William, on an island at the mouth of the Willamette. Even though Wyeth obtained an agreement from McLoughlin to share part of the Snake Country, an agreement of which Governor Simpson and the British Governor and Committee took a dim view, Wyeth still met with so many difficulties that by this year, 1837, he sold out his interests to the Hudson's Bay Company.

Ogden believed that it was not the American ships' captains or the missionaries or even the settlers, but people like Hall J. Kelley and Captain Bonneville who gave the Company a bad name to Americans. He thought about his recent conversations at Fort Vancouver with Dr. McLoughlin and how the kindly old doctor had somewhat jeopardized his own position by befriending the many Americans. While visiting Dr. McLoughlin, Ogden had learned of an even more significant arrival, that of Lieutenant William A. Slacum, a former purser in the United States Navy. Slacum had been sent to the Pacific Coast by John Forsyth, secretary of state in President Andrew Jackson's cabinet, to "obtain some specific and authentic information in regard to the inhabitants of the country in the neighborhood of Oregon, or Columbia river; and generally, endeavour to obtain all such information, political, physical, statistical and geographical as may prove useful or interesting to this government."[40]

James Birnie, the father of Ogden's traveling companion Elizabeth, had greeted Slacum cordially on December 22, 1836, when he arrived in the brig *Loriot* at Fort George at the mouth of the Columbia River. James Douglas, McLoughlin told Ogden, had been at Fort George at the time of Slacum's arrival. He had brought Slacum in his private canoe to Fort Vancouver, arriving on January 2, 1837. Every courtesy had been extended to the young American. McLoughlin had even furnished him with a canoe, a crew, and provisions so that he could go to Champoeg to visit the Reverend Jason Lee and to French Prairie to visit the other American settlers.

Ogden knew that Slacum had stayed in the Fort Vancouver area for only six weeks, but by the time he left on February 10, he had traveled widely and had gained a great deal of information.[41] Ogden wondered how the Company's hospitality to Slacum would be repaid. He, Dr. Mc-Loughlin, and other employees along the coast believed that Slacum was an American spy. His visit would surely have political repercussions. These came sooner than anyone had anticipated. In December, 1837, Slacum's long report, the first detailed American account of the Oregon country, was presented to Congress. It received a great deal of attention and marked the beginning of a new era on the Columbia. Slacum described the Hudson's Bay Company as a great "foreign" monopoly which had such extensive powers that individual American traders could not hope to compete with it. Slacum strongly urged that the United States insist upon the Forty-ninth Parallel as its northern boundary and thereby gain control of the fine agricultural land of the Columbia and Puget Sound. Senator Lewis F. Linn of Missouri was greatly impressed by Slacum's views and began advocating American military occupation and settlement of the region in a harangue that would not end until 1846.

While agitation continued on the floors of Congress in Washington, D.C., Ogden went on performing his usual duties at Fort St. James. American activities in the Pacific Northwest annoyed the Hudson's Bay Company most, but Ogden's old feud with the Russians most rankled him. Reports were circulating in London, Montreal, and in the West that Ogden had failed to establish a post at Stikine because he had acted with "too much caution." In February, 1838, Ogden displayed his bitterness about being unjustly maligned when he wrote Dr. McLoughlin:

Had I last year called upon you for your opinion respecting my conduct in the discharge of my duty as connected with the Stikine Expedition, you might probably then have considered the application as premature. . . . The circumstances in which that affair was enacted have now, however, been thoroughly investigated and in justice to myself in common with the gentlemen attached to the Expedition under my command, I can no longer defer doing so. Reports, I am informed are current throughout the country insinuating that I acted with "too much caution" or in other words with cowardice, whence it would appear that an impression is entertained by many that the failure of the expedition in question is attributable to unworthy conduct on my part.

Under the unfavorable aspect which opinion has apparently assigned with regard to the share I bore in the transactions alluded to, I deem it proper, nay indispensible [sic] . . . to call upon you for an official answer to the following queries which, in justice to all concerned, I doubt not will unhesitatingly be accorded answer viz; Whether the part I adopted under the peculiar circumstances wherein I found myself placed, of withdrawing without having carried into effect the instructions I had received, be attributable to cowardice or not? Again: what in the opinion of Governor Pelly and yourself is the line of action I ought to have pursued in order to avoid the foul stigma which has been so charitably affixed to my name? And finally: whether, even admitting the question of my physical desparity to have been less obviously unfavorable to me, I could, without infringing on the provisions of the Convention, or consistently with the duty which I owe to myself as well as the Gentlemen who accompanied me, have acted in a manner more conducive to the ultimate interest of the concern of which I am a member?[42]

On April 22, 1838, Ogden left Stuart's Lake for the Columbia. He followed his usual path to Fort Okanagan, and here he was reunited with his old friend, Sam Black. Together, they proceeded first by horseback and then by boat to Fort Vancouver, which they reached on June 5.[43] During the next three weeks, Ogden and Black wined and dined and generally enjoyed the fine table and good companionship that Fort Vancouver always provided. One familiar face was missing this year. Dr. McLoughlin had been called to help the Governor and Committee and the British government settle Ogden's "Stikine Incident" with the Russians.

The Russians, Ogden knew, were now contending that when he was at Stikine in the *Dryad*, it was his fear of the Indians, not Russian threats of force, that had kept him from building a post on that river. The Governor and Committee had asked McLoughlin to come to London "as early as possible" and to bring with him "such books, accounts, affidavits and other documentary evidence, as may enable you to substantiate the account."[44] Dr. McLoughlin arrived there in late May. He found the Governor and Committee eager for constructive advice. They were especially interested in settling the dispute and supplying the Russians with goods and wheat at a price low enough to eliminate American competition on the coast. Armed with information from McLoughlin and his own ideas, Governor John Henry Pelly of the Hudson's Bay Company's North American operations decided to visit Russia with Overseas Governor George Simpson.

Pelly and Simpson left London on July 17, 1838, for St. Petersburg, where they remained for more than a month. The two governors had many difficulties. Neither could speak Russian, and upon their arrival at the Tsarist capital they even had trouble finding the Russian American Company's headquarters. When they did, they were amazed to find it housed in a building in one of the most elegant quarters of St. Petersburg. The smart address at 72 Moika Quai, was in a quarter where Tsar Alexander I had taken his daily walks and was quite different from the commercial Fenchurch Street of London from which the Hudson's Bay

Company directed its operations. Upon entering the building, once a private mansion, they were even more amazed to see opulent surroundings of costly furniture, rare rugs, and objects of art.

After many delays, Governor Pelly and Simpson met Wrangel, with whom Ogden had dealt five years before at Sitka. Although they found him dressed in his full regimental uniform, their opinion of him was similar to Ogden's. He appeared to them to be "very thin, weak and delicate, but evidently a sharp clever little creature." He was indeed clever. The diplomatic aspects of the "Stikine Incident," he said, were entirely in the hands of Count Nesselrode, the Russian foreign minister. He could only discuss matters of trade. Then, when Pelly and Simpson brought up the subject of the Hudson's Bay Company supplying the Russian American Company with goods and wheat, Wrangel said that "he had made an arrangement at Chili by which they would be supplied with grain at lower prices." Not to be outdone, the wily old Pelly threw out bait by suggesting that the Russians buy Hudson's Bay Company furs from Fort Simpson, "which they could import as produce of their own Colony on the N.W. Coast and thereby be admissable to entry for Home Consumption or Sale to the Chinese free of duty. This threw a new light on the subject, the little Baron opened his eyes as if wakened from a dream caught at the thing instantly."[45]

Thus, while the winter winds of 1838–39 howled around Ogden's post in New Caledonia, the Anglo-Russian negotiations continued. The Hudson's Bay Company was finding itself in a better position almost every day. The Governor and Committee knew that the Company had an irrefutable claim for damages as a result of the incident. Also, the Russians were not in a firm position to bargain with the English. The Russians were becoming afraid of isolating themselves diplomatically from the other European powers. Evidence of this can be seen later, in April, 1839, when the Middle East crisis centering on Mohammed Ali intensified. The Russians might have been able to invade Turkey and establish a protectorate, but they chose not to antagonize Great Britain, France, Austria, and Prussia.

These international considerations as well as the validity of the Hudson's Bay Company's claim caused Baron von Wrangel to agree to negotiate with Governor Simpson in Hamburg, the appointed place for discussion. On February 6, 1839, an agreement was signed. It gave the Hudson's Bay Company the privilege to trade and navigate on the Alaskan coast from Cape Spencer in the north to 54° 40′ north latitude to the south for a ten-year period beginning June 1, 1840. At long last the British were to have access to Stikine and even the Russian post at Point

Highfield which had caused Ogden so much trouble. The Hudson's Bay Company was also given the right to sell to the Russians 2,000 *fanegas* (a *fanega* is a 126-pound weight) of wheat in 1840 and 4,000 in subsequent years as well as other agricultural produce.[46] In exchange for these concessions, the Company was to renounce financial claims related to the "Stikine Incident" and was to pay an annual rent of two thousand seasoned land-otter skins. Ogden's difficulty of 1834 had now given the Hudson's Bay Company a monopoly of trade on the northwest coast.

Meanwhile, Ogden and Sam Black carried on as usual. In April, 1839, Ogden left Fort St. James to meet Black and the Thompson River Brigade. The united parties reached Fort Vancouver June 3. After three weeks of enjoying themselves and preparing for the return trip, they left on June 22 for the interior.[47] In 1840 the trip to and from New Caledonia was without incident, but the visit to Fort Vancouver was special. In June, after her father's arrival, Ogden's favorite daughter, Sarah Julia, now fourteen-years old, married a Scot, Archibald McKinlay.[48] Ogden was very fond of his new twenty-four-year-old son-in-law. He was a frequent visitor at their home and spent the last days of his life with them.

Ogden and Black expected these rough but enjoyable journeys to continue for several more years, at least until one of them took a leave or was transferred, but 1840 was the last of these trips. Sam Black, who had always feared Indians and had become even more suspicious of them through the years, was shot in the back by an Indian. Ironically, Black had been planning to leave the West for some time. Dr. McLoughlin had written from Red River on June 12, 1839, that "should C. F. Black, who complains of indisposition, wish to with draw from the Columbia either in 1840 or 1841, it will be necessary to relieve him." Black, however, put off leaving his post of Kamloops because of his "wife," the former Angelique Cameron, their younger children, and his friend Ogden.

Trouble at Kamloops first began in the summer of 1840 when Tranquille, a chief of the Shuswaps, the most important Salishan tribe in British Columbia, applied to Sam Black for a gun which he said the owner, a North River Indian, "had made over to him." Black told the chief that he could not comply with his request until he had further proof. The chief went away, and nothing more was heard from him until January, 1841, when he reapplied for the gun. Black gave Tranquille the same answer, and an argument began. Angrily Tranquille left Kamloops and went to his camp "at the Pavilion of Fraser's River." Five days later the Shuswap chief was dead. Before he died, Tranquille said: "If I have a sorrow it is that I may not take by the hand before I die my best friend, Mr. Black, and ask his forgiveness for the hasty words spoken when we last met."

Thus Tranquille died kindly disposed toward members of the Hudson's Bay Company. He even wanted a white man's funeral, and Black complied by sending two men, Edouard and Fallerdeau, to help bury him. The Indians, however, were becoming restive. A rumor among the natives that Tranquille had died as a result of the white men's bad medicine was insidiously propagated by the medicine men. In this case the death would have to be avenged. Shortly after Tranquille's burial, the Indians of the village calmed down and seemed resigned to their chief's death. Many of them were long-time friends of the Company. But not Tranquille's nineteen-year-old nephew, who had lived in the old man's tent. Goaded by Tranquille's widow and by his own love for his uncle, he decided to avenge the chief's death. On February 8, 1841, he stripped off most of his clothes, wrapped himself in a blanket, blackened his face, and rushed off to Kamloops with his rifle.

The arrival of the black-faced youth in scanty clothing on a bitterly cold February day must have seemed strange, but surprisingly, the usually cautious Black did not pay much attention. He was most gracious to the young man. He invited him to sit by the fire in the Indian Hall and had food, a pipe, and tobacco sent in to him. While the youth was brooding before the fire, Black went on about his work and spent most of the afternoon in his apartment, writing and studying while Leprade, a fellow employee, picked over sprouting potatoes from the cellar, which was reached through a trap door in the floor of the Indian Hall. From time to time Black left his desk, walked through the hall, and exchanged a few words with Leprade. Towards evening, when Black passed through the hall, he stooped down in order to open the door of the cellar. Black had his hand on the door knob and his back to the fireplace when the sullen youth suddenly shot him. The bullet entered the small of Black's back and exited below his chest. Black staggered into the next room and fell dead before his wife and children.

Leprade immediately took measures to make Kamloops safe from attack in case the shooting of Black was part of a plot. Then he sent word of the calamity to Archibald McDonald at Colvile, who in turn informed Dr. McLoughlin at Fort Vancouver. Word soon spread throughout the Oregon country. On the Columbia, McLoughlin took immediate action. Donald McLean and McPherson with seven men were sent off to Okanagan on their way to Kamloops. Ogden, who was greatly shocked and grieved by the news, started back southward to Kamloops, trying along the way to "pacify the natives, and smooth over any present difficulties."[49]

Ogden was greatly distressed by the death of Sam Black. He wrote:

B[lack] was one of my oldest and worthiest friends. Our intimacy had commenced some twenty-five years ago, and had been ripened by time into the warmest friendship. We had shared in each other's perils; and the narrow escapes we had so frequently experienced, tended to draw still more closely the bond of amity by which we were united. It was our custom to contrive an annual meeting, in order that we might pass a few weeks in each other's company. This reunion naturally possessed charms for both of us; for it was a source of mixed joy, to fight like old soldiers "our battles o'er again," over a choice bottle of port or Madeira; to lay our plans for the future, and, like veritable gossips, to propose fifty projects, not one of which there was any intention on either part to realize.[50]

Ogden felt the loss even more when he returned to Fort Vancouver in the summer of 1841 without his old friend. It was disturbing to think that his drinking partner and convivial companion of so many years was wrapped in horsehide and in a rough-hewn coffin on Thompson River.[51] Thinking philosophically some years later, Ogden said:

Thus perished my old companion, with whom, for so many years, I had been united in the strictest bond of friendship. Thus without the interval of even a moment, after the death blow was dealt, was his spirit ushered into the presence of that dread Being before whose tribunal . . . a just, but yet a merciful one . . . we must one day all appear. What my feelings on this sad occasion must have been, I shall not attempt to describe; the lapse of time has only alleviated the poignancy of my grief, and I am now resigned to the hope, that when a dark futurity shall no longer be to me as "future," I may meet my friend in another and a better world, where ruthless revenge, and very dark passion of our nature, shall be unknown.[52]

It was also disquieting that because his old friend had not left a proper will, his relatives soon began clamoring for his money. Black left a fairly sizable estate for a British fur trader. He had a sum of £7,877.11s. 10d. on the Company's books, which included the retirement provision for a chief factor, a full share of the profits of an expedition in 1840, and a half-share for the next succeeding six outfits, those for the years 1841–47. Complications arose because Black's parents were dead and other members of the family considered that he had never married even though he had seven known children and had probably fathered at least one more. His Scottish relatives, shocked when they learned of Angelique and her illegitimate children, instituted a "friendly suit" against James Keith, one of the executors of Black's will.[53] Ogden was repelled by the bickering and vowed that this would never happen to him. In making his own will, he drew upon the experience and upon some rusty recollections of his own legal studies. His bequests are specifically stated and detailed. He even anticipated the death of his principal beneficiaries and made provisions for the distribution of money in that event. In conclusion, Ogden wrote:

Now I have to request should any relation of mine or any other individual attempt to dispute this my Last Will and Testament I declare that I disinherit them as fully as the Law authorises me and should there appear an ambiguity or misapprehension as to my meaning or intention I desire the same may be cleared up by the decision of my said Executors.[54]

By June of 1841, Ogden had made his usual routine trip to Fort Vancouver, but it was a dreary trek without the companionship of his good friend. He tried not to let his grief show and acted very much like his old self. Lieutenant Charles Wilkes of the American naval expedition which was examining the Pacific northwest coast in 1841 commented that when he returned to Fort Vancouver from reconnoitering, Ogden and his brigade had arrived. Thus

The fort had, in consequence, a very different appearance from the one it bore when I left it. I was exceedingly amused with the voyageurs of the brigade, who were to be seen lounging about in groups, decked in gay feathers, ribands, etc., full of conceit, and with the flaunting air of those who consider themselves the beau-ideal of grace and beauty; full of frolic and fun, and seeming to have nothing to do but to attend to the decoration of their persons and seek for pleasure; looking down with contempt upon those who are employed about the fort, whose sombre cast of countenance and business employments form a strong contrast to these jovial fellows.

Ogden and Wilkes got along well together, and Ogden took Wilkes in his boat to Cowlitz Farm. Wilkes was impressed with the departure ceremony:

We were all summoned to the great dining-hall by Dr. McLoughlin, to take the parting cup customary in this country. When all were assembled, wine was poured out, and we drank to each other's welfare, prosperity, etc. This was truly a cup of good fellowship and kind feeling. This hanging to old Scotch customs in the way it was done here is pleasant, and carries with it pleasing recollections, especially when there is that warmth of feeling with it, that there was on this occasion. After this was over, we formed quite a cavalcade to the river-side, which was now swollen to the top of its banks, and rushing by with irristible force.

On reaching the river, we found one of Mr. Ogden's boats manned by fourteen voyageurs, all gaily dressed in their ribands and plumes; the former tied in large bunches of divers colours, with numerous ends floating in the breeze. The boat was somewhat of the model of our whaleboats, only much larger, and of the kind built expressly to accommodate the trade; they are clinker-built, and all the timbers are flat. These boats are so light that they are easily carried across the portages. They use gum of the pine to cover them instead of pitch.

Wilkes found the journey pleasant and informative:

I must express the great indebtedness I am under [to Mr. Ogden] for his attentions and kindness to Mr. Drayton, as well as for the civility he offered him for obtaining information during their progress up the Columbia. I am also under obligation to him for much interesting information respecting this country, which he gave me without hesitation or reserve. . . . Mr. Ogden is a general favorite; and there is so much hilarity, and such a fund of amusement about him, that one is extremely fortunate to fall into his company.[55]

After leaving Wilkes and Drayton, Ogden began the long trip back to Stuart's Lake. While he was traveling to Fort St. James, Governor Simpson, now Sir George, was making his way across the American continent on the first part of a journey around the world. He arrived at Fort Vancouver in the latter part of August, 1841, but he stayed only a week on the Columbia. He then inspected the Company's farms in what is now the state of Washington, and from there, Fort Nisqually, he embarked on the *Beaver* to visit the Russian settlement at Sitka. At the time it was rumored in New Caledonia that when Simpson returned to the Columbia, he was going to take Ogden with him to St. Petersburg and then to London,[56] but the rumor had no foundation.

Ogden spent the winter of 1841–42 at Fort St. James very much as he had the previous ones. In the spring, he was again ready to start for Fort Vancouver. This year for part of the journey he had the company of the Jesuit, Father Pierre Jean DeSmet. Father DeSmet had not been able to obtain sufficient provisions or clothing for the mission of St. Mary's that he had established in the Bitterroot Mountains in what was later Montana. On April 13, 1842, therefore, he began the thousand-mile journey to Fort Vancouver. By the first week of May he had reached Fort Colvile where he remained until the end of the month doing missionary work in the vicinity. To his good fortune, several weeks after his arrival, Ogden came in with the New Caledonian Brigade.

Realizing that Father DeSmet could not go on to Fort Vancouver by land because the melting snows had flooded much of the lowlands, Ogden offered to let the priest accompany his party down the Columbia.

Ogden took an instant liking to the charming Jesuit. He invited him to ride in his boat when they were ready to push off from Fort Colvile on May 30. On the voyage downriver and around the campfires in the evenings, Ogden and Father DeSmet found in each other stimulating intellectual companionship, something for which each was starved. The Belgian priest found Ogden to be a most gracious host. He said that he would "never forget the kindness and friendly manner with which this gentleman treated me throughout the journey, nor the many agreeable hours I spent in his company." Ogden regaled his companion with stories which Father DeSmet found to be "instructive" and "his anedotes and bon mots enterprising and timely."

The physical trials of the trip to Fort Vancouver were harsh. As the brigade approached the Okanagan Dalles, disaster struck. Father De-Smet, alarmed by this swift-running channel which he called a "pro-longed narrow torrent" between two steep rocks, asked to be put ashore while the boats negotiated the treacherous water. Making his way along the rock-strewn banks, he saw one of the boats suddenly strike something which caused it to stop so abruptly that the rowers could hardly keep their seats. He stood transfixed and watched the boat being carried into

the angry vortex; the waters are crested with foam; a deep sound is heard which I distinguish as the voice of the pilot encouraging his men to hold to their oars—to row bravely. The danger increases every minute, and in a moment more all hope of safety has vanished. The barge, the sport of the vortex, spins like a top upon the whirling waters—the oars are useless—the bow rises—the stern descends, and the next instant all have disappeared. A death-like chill shot through my frame—a dimness came over my sight, as the cry "we are lost!" rang in my ears, and told but too plainly that my companions were buried beneath the waves.[57]

Ogden, too, was stunned to see the five men go down, but, unlike Father DeSmet, he had witnessed this kind of tragedy before. He waited quietly and patiently to see what the whirlpool would disgorge and what bodies and equipment could be retrieved from the swirling mass. After order was restored, the saddened party continued on downstream and finally reached Fort Vancouver on June 8, 1842.[58] Ogden was de-lighted to gain the peace and security of the Columbia River post, and Father DeSmet was overjoyed to reach his destination, where he found "two respectable Canadian priests," the outstanding Oblate fathers, Blanchet and Demers.

After a short rest, Ogden left Fort Vancouver for Fort St. James. He thought that this return would be his last. He had applied for a leave, and the Council had granted it. Therefore, during the winter of 1842-43 as he compiled his "Notes on Western Caledonia," he expected to take it, for he wrote, "I am now on the eve of taking my departure." For some unknown reason, however, he changed his mind and decided to stay another year in what is now British Columbia.

Why he declined the leave he had wanted so long is not known, but the reason must have been personal. The Hudson's Bay Company's administration was willing for him to go, and Simpson wrote, "It is to be regretted that C. F. Ogden did not avail himself of his rotation of Furlough this season while the means of relieving him were placed at your disposal. That gentleman has expressed a desire to obtain leave of absence or an exchange of furlough next year, which has been granted him, as pr. the 67th Resolve of Council."[59] McLoughlin, on the other hand, was pleased to see Ogden arrive at Fort Vancouver on June 4, 1843, and was "happy to find [that he] had not availed himself of his rotation."[60]

Ogden and his party stayed at the Columbia River post until June 28, when they began the inevitable return to New Caledonia. Misfortune again dogged their steps. When they reached The Dalles, one of the boats was caught in a whirlpool, and one of the men, Arcouet, was drowned and most of the property in the boat was lost. On the following day, another man setting his pole in a rapid, let the pole slip. It knocked him overboard, and he drowned.[61]

This was to be Ogden's last winter in New Caledonia, and he was happy to turn over the chore of bringing down the interior furs to Fort Vancouver to Chief Factor Archibald McDonald and Chief Trader Donald Manson.[62] Ironically, he began to feel some nostalgia when he came to leave Fort St. James after so many years, particularly when his men showed that they felt bad about his departure. Sentimentally, he read the letter that he had received from Alexander Caulfield Anderson which said: "Permit me . . . in the name of the several gentlemen attached to this district, and in my own name, to express the satisfaction which we have individually experienced while serving under your command; and to bear testimony to that urbanity and friendly feeling which have throughout characterized your deportment towards us during the period of your administration . . . a period, it may be added, distinguished no less by the substantial increase of our private comforts than by the several public improvements which you have so successfully planned and carried through."[63] Nevertheless, Ogden wanted to leave this country, at least for a time, after so many years of physical deprivation and the lack of intellectual stimulation since the death of Sam Black. Therefore, he decided to return to England after a twenty-one-year absence and see some of his old Nor'wester friends and reminisce about the friends and the days of his youth.

VII

Disappointment at the Cape

IN THE SPRING OF 1844, Ogden joined the Express, the brigade which was the life line of communication between Fort Vancouver on the Pacific and York Factory on Hudson Bay over three thousand miles away. He went up the Columbia by boat, changed from boat to horse at Boat Encampment, passed on to Jasper's House in its idyllic Rocky Mountain setting, and then traveled on to Edmonton and across the plains to Red River. By the middle of June, he had arrived at Red River and attended the meeting of the Council of the Northern Department which had opened there on June 12.[1] He found the sessions interesting. He had an opportunity to see his old friends, and he was pleased to hear Resolution 74 read. The resolution mentioned that his son Peter, who was now a clerk with the Company, would "accompany the Saskatchewan Brigade [from Fort Edmonton] to the Columbia."[2] He remained at Red River for only a short time. Then, for some unknown reason, he embarked for Norway House, which he reached by boat on June 25, accompanied by Donald Ross.[3]

Ogden apparently stayed there for the next six weeks. Because none of the journals of the area mention Ogden's activities, it is not known exactly when he left Norway House. All the other post diaries along the route to Lachine for this period are also missing, but from a letter written by Simpson, we do know that Ogden arrived at Montreal from Norway House in the third week of August, 1844. Ogden was pleased to reach Montreal; he had been concerned about his family and friends. As early as 1835 he had said:

I was strolling on the banks of Stuart's Lake, anxiously looking out for the arrival of our annual Canada express, which was now momentarily expected; my thoughts occupied, as may easily be imagined, with many and sometimes sad reflections on the nature of the intelligence that would reach us. Of how many dear relations and friends might not death have deprived me during the lapse of the long year since I last heard of their welfare; and what important changes in the political world might not have taken place, affecting the interests of that country, and of those dear friends, at all times present to the mind of a poor, secluded exile.[4]

Ogden was right. Great changes had taken place in Montreal since

145

he had last visited it in 1822. His brother David, a prominent lawyer, whom Ogden greatly resembled, had died, as had his half-sister Sarah. The rest of the family, half-sisters Mary Browne Ogden and Catherine Ogden, as well as Henry, Isaac, and Harriet, lived much as they had before, but Charles Richard, three years Ogden's senior, was experiencing stormy years. Charles had followed the family tradition by becoming a lawyer and had had a meteoric career. In 1815 he had been appointed a king's counsel, and in 1818 the Duke of Richmond appointed him crown attorney general for the Three Rivers District. More important, in 1833, when Ogden was on the northwest coast, King William IV had appointed Charles attorney general for Lower Canada. The appointment had been confirmed after Queen Victoria's accession to the throne. Charles Richard, however, became involved in the Anglo-French conflict in Canadian politics and ended his career as attorney general of the Isle of Man and as the district registrar of Liverpool.[5]

During the winter of 1843–44, Ogden was more preoccupied with his long-sought leave than with his brother's activities. He looked forward to his trip to England, but he did not want to travel alone. Years before, he had become fond of Isaac Ogden's daughter, Annie. He now decided that she would make an ideal traveling companion for him and that she would enjoy a trip to England. This was arranged, and while Annie was preparing for the trip, Ogden spent his time looking around Montreal and visiting places and friends he had known as a boy.

The route Ogden and his niece took to London is unknown. Several possibilities were open to them. They could have gone to New York City via Lake Champlain and Albany and embarked there, the reverse of Ogden's return route from England in 1823, or they could have sailed from Montreal on the St. Lawrence River. It seems most likely, however, that they traveled overland to Boston and took ship from there. Nicol Finlayson, who had been at the Red River Council meeting with Ogden, sailed from Boston for England aboard the *Hibernia* early in September, 1844.[6] Although Finlayson does not mention that the Ogdens were passengers on this vessel, they might well have been aboard.

However they went, Annie seemed to enjoy the trip, and Ogden was proud that she "proved herself a good sailor." Once in London, they found suitable lodgings and set out to see the sights. There also Ogden decided to combine business with pleasure and took his niece to call upon Sir George and Lady Simpson, who were in residence in their London home. Some years before, Governor Simpson, the dynamic director of the Hudson's Bay Company's operation in North America, and his wife had forsaken Lachine, Canada, for long periods. It was here, at their London home, that Annie Ogden first met Edward Hopkins, Simpson's hard-working secretary, whom she was to marry a few years later.

At this time, however, Annie did not have much opportunity to visit with Hopkins. Ogden wanted to leave London for Scotland, and early in November, 1844, they embarked upon a ship for the north. The trip to Scotland appears to have been made in nearly record time. Ogden stated, "In 37 hours we landed here it is said and the newspapers corroborate the same a remarkable quick passage. . . . I will venture to add without fear of contradiction a most stormy one." Annie was sick during most of the voyage, and Ogden was concerned about her.

As soon as the voyage was over and Annie had recovered from her seasickness, Ogden was eager to show her around Edinburgh, which he considered a "superb town." But the Ogdens found that the "horrid" weather with its "superabundance of rain" was not conducive to "enjoying the grand sights." So they concentrated on the social side of their visit to Scotland. All of Ogden's old Nor'wester friends were delighted to see him again and to meet his niece, to whom they were "most kind and attentive." Ogden observed, "My niece is so truly well pleased with all that she feels rather reluctant to leave it."[7]

Ogden, however, was eager to visit Haddington in East Lothian, a short distance to the east of Edinburgh. He wanted to see John Haldane, who had been his chief benefactor at the time of the coalition and shortly thereafter. The Ogdens did visit the old gentleman, but little is known about their conversations. It must have been gratifying to Haldane to have Ogden, whom he had championed more than twenty years before, call upon him and show that he had not forgotten his kindness. Seeing Ogden, Haldane was also pleased to find that his judgment had been correct. Ogden was now a shrewd and intelligent fur trader with depth of character that few men could match.

After visiting Haldane, Ogden and his niece returned to Edinburgh and tried to do some sight-seeing, but as the weather remained poor, they decided to return to London in the second week of November. Ogden had apparently developed a greater liking for Governor Simpson, for he wrote Simpson: "I am anxious to see [you] . . . on my arrival in London [and] shall loose no time in paying you my respects."[8]

Ogden and his niece traveled overland to London. Miss Ogden did not want to board another ship after her unfortunate experience on the trip north. Land travel was more arduous, but Ogden apparently did not have much to say about the matter. The fragile Annie could twist her robust uncle around her little finger, the only woman who could do so. In his correspondence he often makes a statement and then qualifies it by saying, "Should not Miss O. direct otherwise."[9]

Upon arriving in London, the Ogdens had a most enjoyable time. They visited frequently with Sir George and Lady Simpson and a keen affection developed. Sir George had always liked Ogden, but not so much for his personality and character as for his usefulness to the Company. In 1832, twelve years before this London visit, Simpson had in fact written about Ogden with some misgivings. He had described Ogden as

a very cool calculating fellow who is capable of doing anything to gain his own ends. His ambition knows no bounds and his conduct and actions are not influenced or governed by any good or honorable principle. In fact, I consider him one of the most unprincipled men in the Indian country, who would soon get into habits of dissapation if he were not restrained by the fear of their operating against his interests, and if he does indulge in that way madness to which he has a predisposition will follow as a matter of course.[10]

By 1844, Simpson had come to have a quite different opinion of Ogden. He saw that Ogden had character and fine principles which were partly hidden by his utter frankness and sometimes coarse jokes. Ten years later, at the time of Ogden's death, he wrote: "Out of his own family, few persons I believe knew him so well or esteemed his friendship more highly than myself—our regard for each other had been the growth of years, on my side increasing as I became more and more intimately acquainted with his character and worth; his loss to me is greater than I am well able to express more particularly as I had been looking forward to his early return from Oregon in the hope that for years to come we might enjoy much of each other's Society."[11]

Even though this letter was written just after Ogden's death, it can be considered an honest expression of Simpson's feelings since Simpson certainly was not given to false sentimentality. One probable reason that Simpson was so slow in recognizing Ogden's worth as a man was Ogden's habit of always saying what he thought regardless of the rank of the person to whom he was speaking. The pompous Sir George found this trait most irritating. Ogden was one of the few people who had the audacity to criticize "The Little Emperor," and in 1850 Sir George wrote to Ogden:

I perceive that, even when writing on business, you must have a fling at someone, and in this instance you strike about you in great style, right and left. The rule which is applicable to cookery holds good in letter writing, viz: that a little spice may be agreeable, but that dishes when over-peppered are apt to be rejected. I do not, however, reject your late letters, notwithstanding the many spicy passages they contain, which I shall pass by without further remark, beyond making this gentle protest against a too highly seasoned style of letter cookery.[12]

Thus, even though Sir George criticized Ogden occasionally, he came to consider his frankness refreshing. He also respected Ogden's knowledge of the Hudson's Bay Company's Pacific Coast operations, and while Ogden was visiting him in 1844, he took the opportunity to question him about developments in the Oregon country. The Governor and Committee invited Ogden to their headquarters in Fenchurch Street and also asked him many questions. This visit must have taken place in the latter part of November, because on November 30, Archibald Barclay, the secretary of the Company, stated: "From Mr. Ogden the Governor and Committee have obtained much useful and interesting information respecting the State of the Company's affairs in the Columbia Department."[13]

The Governor and Committee in their discussions undoubtedly asked Ogden about Dr. McLoughlin and his opinion of McLoughlin's management of the Oregon country. Ogden was very fond of McLoughlin and loyal to him, but he must have felt obligated to tell the Governor and Committee that Dr. McLoughlin was becoming more dogmatic in his actions and more defensive. Everyone in the higher ranks knew that McLoughlin and Simpson had been clashing. McLoughlin believed in setting up many posts along the coast to control the trade while Simpson believed that control could be achieved much more cheaply by deploying more ships in the region. Simpson wanted to close the Hudson's Bay Company establishment at Yerba Buena (San Francisco), which was under the direction of McLoughlin's son-in-law, William Glen Rae, but McLoughlin had taken no action to do so. Simpson believed that the steamship *Beaver* would increase trade along the coast, but McLoughlin contended that steamships required too many repairs and that their crews were unreliable and often drunk. Dr. McLoughlin's friendliness toward the Americans was also a source of controversy, but the really important issue was bad feeling about the events surrounding the death of McLoughlin's son, John, Jr.

McLoughlin had a problem family, and John was the chief problem. As Archibald McDonald wrote to Edward Ermatinger on March 15, 1843, "Edward we are all unfortunate parents. Instance the awful shock of mind our old friend the Dr. lately experienced from the irregular and inveterate habits of his unhappy son John, after spending £2,000 on his education in foreign lands, too."[14] Dr. McLoughlin first sent his son to

Dr. Simon Fraser who lived near Montreal to receive his education. Governor Simpson was kindly disposed toward the young man, and through his influence John obtained a job in a Montreal counting house after he left Fraser. The young man lasted only about a year in the position. Then, in 1829, his father sent him to Paris to study medicine under his uncle, the distinguished physician David McLoughlin. John showed signs of ability, and in 1834 he received the degree of *bachelier ès lettres*. For some unknown reason, he then returned to North America, and after an unsuccessful plundering campaign at Red River, he joined the Hudson's Bay Company in 1837.

Once in the service, he was sent to the Russian post on the Stikine River which was now open to British traders. Young McLoughlin seems to have gotten along well there at first, but after the departure of Roderick Finlayson, his assistant of solid character and temperament, he seems to have begun drinking heavily. In April, 1842, when Governor Simpson was making his tour of the West, he sailed into Stikine harbor and found the flags at half-mast out of respect for young John, who had been murdered the day before. Simpson found the fort in chaos and the Indians of the vicinity menacing. He took depositions from witnesses. Then, because the murder had taken place on Russian soil that had only been leased to the Hudson's Bay Company, he turned over the accused murderer, Urbain Heroux, to the Russian authorities. Afterward, callously, or at least so Dr. McLoughlin thought, he announced that both the murderer and the victim had been drunk and that young McLoughlin's violence when drunk was so well known that the incident obviously was justifiable homicide. Dr. McLoughlin was infuriated by Simpson's attitude, and after this event McLoughlin's growing antipathy toward Simpson turned into hate.

In addition to the McLoughlin troubles, Ogden also discussed the American problem in Oregon with the Governor and Committee. Undoubtedly he was able to give them some fresh information, for he had been observing intently what was taking place on the Columbia every year when he returned to Fort Vancouver from New Caledonia. Ogden and the Governor and Committee had noticed great changes taking place during the last six or seven years. From the time Slacum made his report to Congress in 1837, and Senator Lewis F. Linn introduced his bill in 1838 for the military occupation of the Columbia and the creation of a territorial government for Oregon, the interest of the American public in the Pacific Northwest seemed to be increasing. Then the Reverend Jason Lee went back to the East with a petition composed by Philip Edwards and signed by thirty-six Americans living south of the Columbia. Senator Linn placed the petition before the United States Senate in 1839. While Lee was in the East, he made a speaking tour. In Peoria, Illinois, his speech fired the imagination of Thomas J. Farnham, who resolved to raise the American flag over Oregon. Farnham made a trip to the West, and although he accomplished little, he did bring back a memorial signed by seventy settlers who prayed for the United States government's protection. Farnham also published his *Travels* which were widely read and did much to increase popular interest in the Oregon country.

Meanwhile, the "Manifest Destiny" lobby of Senator Linn and others tried to force President Martin Van Buren to support American claims in Oregon. Linn told the President that the United States had a right to Oregon, and territorial status accompanied by American laws should be accorded the region. Linn asked Van Buren to give notice to the British government of the termination of the Joint Occupation Treaty and by presidential proclamation to create a regiment to send to the Oregon country.

News of Linn's resolutions reached London by packet boat from Nova Scotia in February, 1840, and Governor Pelly immediately took up the issue with the Foreign Secretary, Lord Palmerston, who "had already displayed his penchant for the virile foreign policy that made him the epitome of John Bull in the admiring eyes of the masses and an irresponsible blunderer in the view of those who believed that foreign affairs should be conducted with tact and discretion."[15] Palmerston, however, took no action, and the Americans became more militant. On February 17 and 18 the inhabitants of the Willamette Valley met at the Reverend Jason Lee's mission and elected a judge with probate powers, a clerk, a sheriff, and three constables. They actually accomplished little because Father François Norbert Blanchet refused to co-operate with them and Lieutenant Charles Wilkes, who was then on the Columbia, advised the Americans not to try to form a government while they were in the minority. When Simpson toured the Columbia River Valley during the summer of 1841, he was appalled at the number of American missions and their great economic prosperity. He also observed that in addition to the missionaries, there were 150 other Americans in the Willamette colony.[16]

The number of settlers increased after the grave agricultural depression in the Mississippi Valley following the Panic of 1837 in the United States. Beginning in 1841, American emigrants began the long overland trek to Oregon and California. The first really sizable migration came in 1842, when the Reverend Elijah White, who had been appointed Indian agent for Oregon by the United States government, led 120 men westward across the mountains. This was only the beginning. In subsequent years thousands of people converged upon Independence, Missouri, ready to start on their long journey to Oregon.

Alarmed by what was taking place in Oregon, Simpson suggested that the Company establish a post at the southern end of Vancouver Island, away from the Americans in the Willamette. The Governor and Committee accepted Simpson's advice and established Fort Victoria in 1843 in this region. Several factors dictated their decision. The bar at the entrance to the Columbia River was making navigation to Fort Vancouver increasingly difficult. The proximity of Americans to the Company's Pacific Coast headquarters was a consideration, but the decision seems actually to have been primarily motivated by an economic concern—Fort Victoria certainly would be more conveniently located for the coastal trade.

The bellicose Americans in Oregon were also not the main concern of the two governments. Daniel Webster, secretary of state under Tyler, and Lord Ashburton, representing the British government, were involved in trying to settle on a boundary between Maine and New Brunswick, a matter of great importance to Americans and Canadians. Their failure to negotiate about a northwestern boundary was at this time of interest only to the Hudson's Bay Company, a few American missionaries and settlers, and the handful of "Manifest Destiny" politicians.

These last two were, however, active and vociferous. In Oregon in the late winter and spring of 1843 what were called "Wolf Meetings" took place.[17] At the "Second Wolf Meeting" on May 2, 1843, a legislative committee of nine members was elected to formulate a code of laws and to report their findings at a meeting to be held at Champoeg on July 5, 1843. The code drawn up by the committee was based upon the old Northwest Ordinance of 1787 and the laws of the state of Iowa and was to be the "First Organic Law" for "Oregon Territory."

About the same time, July 3–6, 1843, a convention of about one hundred delegates from six Mississippi Valley states met in Cincinnati to discuss the most effective means of winning the Oregon country for the United States. The result of this meeting was the adoption of a series of resolutions which affirmed the right of the United States to the territory from 42° north latitude, the northern border of the Mexican province of California, to 54° 40′ north latitude, the southern boundary of the Russian possessions. This suddenly popular attitude was also expressed in President Tyler's annual message to Congress on December 5, 1843. Tyler repeated the United States' claim to this region. In the summer of 1844 the Democratic candidate for president, James K. Polk, also came out for what he called the "re-occupation" of Oregon as well as the "re-annexation" of Texas.

The Hudson's Bay Company and the British government had no intention of letting British interests in Oregon be flouted. While Ogden was in Montreal preparing for his trip to England with Annie, Dr. McLoughlin was improving the defenses of Fort Vancouver. He added a bastion to the Columbia River depot to make the fort impregnable to attack. He explained that this was a necessary precaution against the Indians, who had become more restive since the large American migrations. Too, the post was put on a strict military footing with a twenty-four-hour guard. Then on July 15, 1844, the British sloop of war *Modeste* under Commander Thomas Baillie entered the Columbia and anchored opposite Fort Vancouver. Although Baillie stayed there for only three weeks and did not display any great interest in Oregon, he and James Douglas did visit the Willamette settlement. This caused the Americans to believe that Great Britain was still committed to protect the Hudson's Bay Company in Oregon.

Ogden was able to have his pleasant visit with Governor Simpson during the fall and winter of 1844–45 because Governor Pelly and the Committee had called Simpson back to England to discuss the Oregon question. Since Polk's election in the fall of 1844, the Americans in the Willamette Valley were becoming more belligerent and anti-British. In England, Simpson drew the attention of Sir Robert Peel's government to the situation on the Pacific Northwest Coast. In a memorandum dated March 29, 1845, Simpson proposed to the Earl of Aberdeen, foreign secretary in the Peel cabinet, a plan for British defense of the region. Simpson was afraid that the Oregon dispute would lead to war, and, if war came, it would spread along the whole frontier. Therefore, he recommended that the British government send a force of regular troops to the Company's strategic colony at Red River. These men would be reinforced by a rifle company recruited from the half-bloods who lived in and around the colony. He also suggested that the British government send two steamers and two sailing ships with large contingents of marines to Oregon, and that Cape Disappointment, at the entrance to the Columbia, be occupied. When this was accomplished, an artillery battery should lay its guns to command the river.[18] Simpson's urgings for troops finally proved successful, but ironically the Red River garrison sailed from Cork, Ireland, on June 26, 1846, ten days after the Oregon boundary settlement had been concluded.

During the spring of 1845 the newly elected President Polk and Secretary of State James Buchanan seemed to be intent upon living up to their campaign slogan of "Fifty-Four Forty or Fight." Lord Aberdeen and Prime Minister Peel both felt that war with the United States was imminent. On April 2, 1845, Simpson called at Peel's residence, and at this meeting and at a later one with Aberdeen, a British plan for the Oregon country was evolved. One or two army engineers would accompany Governor Simpson on his annual tour of the Hudson's Bay Company's establishments in 1845. In order not to arouse American suspicions, it would be made to appear that the young officers were in North America on a hunting holiday.[19] Peel and Aberdeen also authorized Simpson to spend up to £1,000 to insure British control of the mouth of the Columbia River.[20] Undoubtedly before Ogden left London, Simpson discussed with him the role that he was to play in the drama to hold the Columbia River.

The exact date that Ogden and Annie left London is not known, but it was probably some time in late March, 1845. Simpson, who was also important in the Company's Oregon plans, probably left London a few days after the Ogdens. Peter and Annie arrived in Boston around the middle of April,[21] and Simpson did not arrive until April 22.[22] Ogden started north to take Annie safely home. Simpson, in his usual rapid and efficient manner, went south to confer with Pakenham, the British minister to the United States.

After discussing the Oregon question with Pakenham in Washington, Simpson returned to Montreal. He was pleased to learn that the governor-general of Canada, Lord Metcalfe, and the commander of the British forces in Canada, Sir Richard Jackson, had followed the problems on the Pacific Coast and were "quite alive to the necessity of being prepared in Canada for any outbreak in the United States."[23] With Metcalfe and Jackson in such prominent positions, Simpson was most fortunate, for they were capable men. Metcalfe, often called "Old Squaretoes," was born in Calcutta in 1785, the son of Theophilus Metcalfe, a major in the Bengal Army and a director of the East India Company. He was educated in England and stood high in his class at Eton. In 1834, when Lord George Bentinck resigned as governor-general of India, Metcalf held an interim appointment to that position, which he filled until the arrival of his old schoolfellow, Lord Auckland, in 1836. In 1839, Metcalfe became governor of Jamaica and in 1843 governor-general of Canada.

Jackson had had a long army career. He entered the service in 1794 and distinguished himself in the Peninsular War. He was appointed commander-in-chief of the British forces in North America in 1839 at a critical time in Canadian history. He proved to be not only a good soldier but a good administrator as well. Twice he took control of the government of Lower Canada during absences of Lord Sydenham, who was governor-general of Canada from 1839 to 1841.[24]

Unfortunately Jackson died of apoplexy on June 9, 1845. Charles Murray Cathcart, a son of Lord Cathcart, succeeded him. Cathcart was an excellent soldier and had distinguished himself at Waterloo, receiving the Russian order of St. Vladimir and the Dutch order of St. Wilhelm, as well as being made a Companion of the Bath. He was a member of the Royal Society and showed great interest in science.[25] Simpson was fortunate to have officers of the stature of Metcalfe and Jackson to aid in the mission.

Originally the two men who were to travel incognito to Oregon were to be selected in London, but then it was decided to leave the matter up to Lord Metcalfe, who in turn deferred to his military commander, Jackson. Just before his death Jackson chose his aide-de-camp, Lieutenant Henry J. Warre, a young man of fine family with a brilliant future. Warre had been brought up in a military tradition. His father, Lieutenant General Sir William Warre, was Colonel of the 94th Regiment of Foot. He was also socially prominent both through his immediate family and his aunt, who was the Countess Mulgrave and wife of the lord lieutenant of Ireland.

Young Warre had advanced his career in the usual nineteenth-century fashion prior to the abolition of purchase of commissions in 1870. He had bought his way into higher rank and increasingly prestigious regiments. Nevertheless, he was a fine soldier and later distinguished himself at the siege of Sebastopol in March, 1855, when he led the 57th Regiment in the assaults on the Russians' Redan fortifications. In 1858 he again commanded the 57th in the attack on the line posts on the Taptee River in co-operation with the Central India Force. In 1861 he played an active role in the New Zealand Maori War, and before his death he rose to the rank of major general and had been made a Companion of the Bath.[26]

The second member, Lieutenant Mervin Vavasour of the Royal Engineers, also came from a military background, but one not nearly so distinguished as that of Henry Warre.[27] Vavasour had been commissioned in the Engineers on March 19, 1839, as a second lieutenant and promoted to lieutenant on February 23, 1842. He was later active in surveying Ireland and then Great Britain before spending several unpleasant years in the West Indies. In 1853 ill health forced him to go on sick leave, and he died at Henley-on-Thames in 1866.[28]

In 1845, he was considered a capable young man and had been recommended for the Canadian reconnaissance by the commander of the Royal Engineers, Colonel N. W. Halloway. Nevertheless, Vavasour seems to have been an unhappy choice. He had many weaknesses and he apparently did not get along well with Warre. Two years later, in 1847, Warre in writing to Simpson indicated that the expedition across North America and the subsequent report made by himself and his fellow officer would have been "better" if there had been "unanimity" between them.

While Warre and Vavasour were preparing themselves for their trip westward, Ogden was returning to Montreal. Upon his arrival, he learned that another member of his family had entered the Hudson's Bay Company. His nephew Henry Ogden had become an apprentice clerk, and now, in May, 1845, he was about to leave for service at one of the King's Posts in what is now eastern Canada.[29] Ogden must have been pleased that his enthusiasm about the fur trade had inspired his nephew as well as his own son, but he was preoccupied with thoughts about Oregon.

It is often thought that Ogden met Warre and Vavasour at Red River when he arrived there from the Columbia and that he then led the two lieutenants back to the Columbia. Actually Ogden spent the winter of 1844–45 in England and Scotland. He returned to Canada via Boston in mid-April, 1845, and thus came to Red River from the Atlantic Coast. Because Warre and Vavasour were to make a meticulous reconnaissance of the West which would be of central importance to the British government and the Hudson's Bay Company, the Company's officials, under whose auspices the officers were to travel, wanted to make the trip as pleasant as possible. Therefore, Governor Simpson decided that he and Ogden would accompany the officers as far west as Red River. Then, as he told Warre and Vavasour, Peter Skene Ogden, "an influential officer of the Hudson's Bay Company," would lead them to the Columbia.[30]

Warre and Vavasour's commanding officers had insisted that they prepare themselves well for this important mission in the West. Warre was "recommended to read with attention and reflect upon the 'Reports' contained in a manuscript book now lent to him exhibiting the spirit of military surveying by very able officers." He was also instructed to read extracts from the journal of Colonel Henry Dodge, who in 1835 had traveled from Fort Leavenworth in present-day Kansas to the Rocky Mountains and returned via the Arkansas River. At this time, the British government and the Hudson's Bay Company were concerned about the movements of John Charles Frémont of the United States Topographical Engineers. Thus Warre was told that "it would be desirable for him to read" Frémont's *Report of the Exploring Expedition to the Rocky Moun-*

tains in the Year 1842 and to Oregon and North California in the Years 1843-44 which was published in that very year, 1845.

Frémont's survey of the route to South Pass in 1842 and his expedition of 1843-44—which led from Kaw Landing, now Kansas City, across the plains via the South Platte, Bent's Fort, South Pass, and Fort Hall to the Columbia—had caused much speculation in British circles. Frémont's arrival at Fort Vancouver had caused some well-justified apprehension. Frémont had not only surveyed the Oregon Trail during the course of this expedition, but his report had engendered in the United States enthusiasm for expansion and was referred to in debates in the Senate by his father-in-law, Thomas Hart Benton, the well-known "Manifest Destiny" senator from Missouri. Now Frémont was again on the trail west. Warre's superiors felt important that he should be familiar with the man and his activities.[31]

Colonel Halloway of the Royal Engineers gave Lieutenant Vavasour specific instructions so that he could best utilize his specialized training. Vavasour was told to examine and report on all existing British posts describing "their availability for defensive purposes or the means of making them available." As an engineering expert, he was also told to examine carefully sites Simpson might suggest as naturally suited for defending the whole country, and "to keep in mind the necessity of haste in the construction of such defenses."[32]

Warre and Vavasour were paid by the British government, as were all of the Hudson's Bay Company's servants taking part in this mission, and the two British officers were under Governor Simpson's control. To allay any American suspicion about army officers crossing Canada to the Oregon country, Warre and Vavasour were ordered to travel as "private individuals—seeking amusement." At the same time, they were instructed to "examine well the important parts of the country, referred to, so as to guide the prosecution of Military operations, should such operations become necessary." In addition to these orders, the two men also received instructions from the British War Secretary and from Jackson which were communicated to them "confidentially."[33] In an effort to keep Warre and Vavasour's mission secret, Simpson gave the young officers a letter to present to the supervisor of each of the Hudson's Bay Company's establishments indicating that they were in the West for "field sports and for scientific pursuits."[34]

By May 5, 1845, Simpson and Ogden, along with Edward Hopkins, Simpson's secretary, and Warre and Vavasour were ready to depart from Lachine. Shortly after dawn, the party got into two large white, birch-

bark canoes and proceeded up the Ottawa River. The canoes were pro-
pelled up the clear, swiftly flowing Ottawa by fifteen paddlers of Indian
and Canadian origin. Soon the quiet and tranquility of the wooded river-
bank was broken only by the *voyageurs'* French-Canadian songs which
rang out in rhythm with the dipping paddles. They went up the Ottawa
until they reached the Mattawa River, where they crossed by land to Lake
Huron. They went along its northern shore to Lake Superior. They then
pushed on to Lake of the Woods, Rainy Lake, and on down Winnipeg
River until they arrived at Fort Garry on June 7, a little over a month
after their departure. Fort Garry in the Red River Settlement was the
chief Hudson's Bay Company post in the Great Plains and had about five
thousand inhabitants.[35]

Simpson planned to separate from Ogden, Warre, and Vavasour at
Red River, and shortly before their arrival at Fort Garry, he gave specific
instructions for carrying out the mission to Oregon. While they were
encamped at Rainy Lake, Simpson meticulously spelled out his orders.
He prepared a letter for Ogden, directing that he lead his party out of
Red River not later than June 12, "so as to reach the Pacific as early as
possible." Simpson was anxious for Ogden and his military companions
to reach Oregon quickly, "with a view of anticipating Lieutenant Frémont of the United States Army, who I understand was to have left St.
Louis on the 25th April for the same destination; and by a steady prosecution of the journey, I am in hopes you may reach the Pacific by the
12th August."

Simpson told Ogden that his first objective was to occupy Cape Disappointment at the mouth of the Columbia River "on behalf of the
Hudson's Bay Company . . . ostensibly with a view to the formation of
a trading post and pilot's look-out." The big question was whether the
cape was already occupied. Simpson was especially eager for the British
government and Hudson's Bay Company to seize the mouth of the
Columbia even though Pakenham had advised Simpson in Washington,
in April, 1845, that it would be very unwise for the Hudson's Bay Company to take possession of the cape by force in peacetime. Consequently,
in Ogden's instructions, Simpson indicated that if Cape Disappointment
was not already settled by Americans:

You will be pleased to employ Mr. Lane [Richard Lane] and the servants
who accompany you, in the building of a house on the Cape, taking possession,
by a rough fence, of the headland and the Isthmus connecting it with the back
country, running a slight fence along the shore of the ocean, so as to enclose
as much of the interior as may be desirable for the exclusion of strangers;

likewise enclosing, for the same object, any high ground in the rear, within cannon range, which may command the Cape.

Ogden also was to take possession of Tongue Point, if Warre and Vavasour thought it expedient. Ogden was cautioned, however, that "neither Cape Disappointment, Tongue Point, nor any other place is to be taken possession of by the Hudson's Bay Company if already possessed and occupied on behalf of the United States Government or its citizens."[36]

Ogden had been directed to leave Red River not later than June 21, but because more time was needed for preparations, the group did not depart until July 16. Perhaps at this time, while preparations lagged, Ogden first developed the dislike for the two officers which was to grow greatly as they moved west and particularly after they arrived on the Columbia. Ogden, though now fifty-one years old, was still virile and rugged after years on the frontier, and he was irritated when his young companions complained that "our daily journeys commenced with the early morn . . . and ended where a sufficient supply of wood and water could be obtained to prepare our frugal meal—a tent our only covering."[37]

Their complaints had some validity. To someone not hardened to frontier life, the journey from Red River to the Columbia was arduous. Approximately sixteen hundred miles were covered by horseback and boat in a little over two months. On the first leg of their journey from Red River, they traveled on horseback from Fort Garry out across the plains. Here, Warre and Vavasour must have been impressed by the seemingly unending stretches of undulating country covered by tall stands of grass. Perhaps it was here that they saw a prairie fire, a frightening experience, which was later recorded by Warre in one of his magnificent tinted lithographs entitled the *Burning Prairie*. Too, as they proceeded westward, they must have been impressed by the large, burly buffalo which had so captured the European imagination. Again Warre was able to capture his thoughts graphically when he drew the excellent picture entitled *Buffalo Hunt*.

The party used the usual route up the Saskatchewan and reached Edmonton House, not far from the bluffs overlooking the northern fork of the river. Here they got sixty fresh mounts and started on what proved to be the most difficult part of their journey. They again went southward, this time across Wolfe and Red Deer rivers, and then turned westward across the plains towards the blue haze atop the Rockies which loomed up on the far horizon. They then crossed the mountain barrier at the headwaters of the swiftly flowing Bow River, today the delight of all western Canadian tourists. The magnificent scenery was difficult for them to appreciate when they looked from some rocky precipice thousands of feet below, or when, from time to time, a fearful pack animal lost its footing and fell, "rolling in some instances many hundred feet into the foaming torrent beneath."[38] Between Fort Edmonton and Fort Colvile on the Columbia, the party lost thirty-three horses, and many of the remaining twenty-seven that had left Edmonton were so exhausted and footsore that they could barely walk.

The Ogden party, which consisted of Ogden, a clerk, six servants, and guides, interpreters, and hunters, pushed on,[39] and by early August they were on the Pacific slope of the Rockies. By August 9, 1845, they were in the Flatbow country, and, as they came out of the heavily timbered mountains into a forest clearing, Ogden, who was riding at the head of the column, was startled to see Father DeSmet, with whom he had had the pleasure of traveling three years before. The Jesuit looked up immediately in surprise when he heard someone shouting his name through the wooded stillness.

Father DeSmet was on the other side of a small river when he heard his name called, and from the distance he could not make out who was calling him. He "returned the gracious salutation" and asked "to know whom [he] had the honor of addressing." The voice answered, "Wait until I reach the opposite shore, and then you will recognize me." DeSmet watched the men in "tattered garments" cross the clearing and come toward him. He noticed something familiar about the erect figure leading the party, but he still could not identify the man in "tattered garb and sloughed hat." Suddenly he realized that it was "one of the principal members of the Honorable Hudson Bay Company, the worthy and respectable Mr. Ogden." Father DeSmet was most interested to hear that Ogden had only recently returned from the British Isles and listened eagerly to the news of Europe that Ogden was able to give him.

In regard to Lieutenants Warre and Vavasour, Ogden had been instructed to keep the mission "strictly confidential and that the object of Messrs. Warre and Vavasour's journey be not disclosed, but that it be given out that, they are known to us only as private travellers for the pleasure of field sports and scientific pursuits."[40] Ogden generally observed all instructions from his superiors scrupulously, and it is difficult to believe that he was indiscreet enough to tell Father DeSmet, now a naturalized United States citizen, the real purpose of the trip. In any event, whether hints were dropped carelessly in conversation or whether the story of the pleasure trip was too implausible, the astute priest discovered the true object of the expedition. On August 17, 1845, he wrote

Bishop Hughes about his meeting with Ogden, Warre, and Vavasour:

It was neither curiosity nor pleasure that induced these two officers to cross so many desolate regions, and hasten their course toward the mouth of the Columbia. They were invested with orders from their Government to take possession of Cape Disappointment, to hoist the English standard, and erect a fortress for the purpose of securing the entrance of the river in case of war. [Then he philosophized]: In the Oregon question, John Bull, without much talk, attains his end, and secures the most important part of the country; whereas Uncle Sam loses himself in words, inveighs and storms.[41]

After leaving Father DeSmet, the party continued to Fort Colvile on the Columbia River, which they reached on August 16. Then they went to Okanagan, 180 miles below Colvile, then to Nez Percés, and finally to Fort Vancouver on August 26.[42] Ogden was irritated that the trip had taken so long, and his dissatisfaction with Warre and Vavasour had grown as he kept prodding the two officers forward. Simpson had planned the trip from Red River to the Columbia to take between forty and fifty days, and Ogden knew that in 1841 Simpson himself had crossed this stretch of country in only forty-seven days.[43] Even with Ogden's pleading and cajoling, it had taken his Warre and Vavasour party seventy-two days to reach Fort Vancouver. The next year, Ogden wrote to Simpson:

I had certainly two most disagreeable companions and I almost doubt you could have selected another that would have been so quietly submitted as I did, but from a sense of duty I was determined not to lose sight of the object of our voyage and was silent to their constant grumbling and complaining not only about their food which was as good and abundant as any man could wish for or desire, but also in regard to promises made by you and on one occasion I was obliged to check the Engineer [Vavasour]. I shall not however trouble you with further particulars, suffice it to say, I would rather forego the pleasure of seeing my friends than submit to travel over the same road with the same companions.[44]

Undoubtedly Warre and Vavasour were delighted to reach the plains of Jolie Prairie and the comfortable confines of the Hudson's Bay Company's Pacific Coast headquarters. They were surprised by the social amenities observed on this distant frontier and by the beautifully laid table and the sparkling conversation which accompanied dinner in the officers' mess. England did not seem so far away when the massive and dignified Dr. McLoughlin presided at the table and sometimes led them in a toast with excellent vintage wines. The two young officers were particularly fond of Dr. McLoughlin and James Douglas, who they felt treated them in "the kindest manner."[45] They were probably delighted to visit with these gentlemen after months of Ogden's company, for Ogden's dislike of them was heartily returned, and they were pleased to forgo his company.

Ogden felt that the party should immediately go on down the Columbia to its mouth in order to fulfill the purpose of the expedition. Warre and Vavasour, however, elected to stay at Fort Vancouver and play fully the part of "private individuals" traveling for "field sports and for scientific purposes." Naturally they had to dress appropriately, and it seems likely that their zeal in attiring themselves was enhanced by the fact that the British government was paying the bills. Thus, in their efforts to make themselves appear as "plain citizens," they bought "superfine beaver hats, at $8.88 apiece; frock coats, at $26.40 apiece; cloth vests, figured vests, tweed trousers and buckskin trousers, tooth brushes, nail brushes, hair brushes, fine handkerchiefs, shirts, shoes; also tobacco, pipes, wines, whiskies, extract of roses."[46]

Ogden was disgusted by this display, which must have added to his general dislike of European travelers in North America. Some years later when he compared the arduous activities of a fur trader to the wanderings of sophisticated gentlemen, who in many cases had large entourages, he said:

> True, indeed, we could not boast of India-rubber pillows or boots, nor of preserved meats and soups, which many others deemed indispensable adjuncts introduced by modern travellers. However, let me confess at once the vast difference between those who travel in pursuit of amusement or science, and men like us who only encounter these hardships for vile lucre. Though we must need content ourselves with the blanket and the gun, we do, at least, possess this advantage over them, that we usually *succeed* in our arduous undertakings.

Then he added bitterly, "On the other hand, we descend unnoticed to the grave, while honours and titles are lavished upon our rivals in enterprise."[47]

Several days after his arrival at Fort Vancouver,[48] Ogden left what he considered the suffocating atmosphere of the Columbia River post and headed for Cape Disappointment in an effort to carry out his instructions. He was apprehensive about American activities in general and those of Captain Frémont in particular. The British were well aware that the "Oregon Question" was only one part of a scheme for the annexation by the United States of much of North America, a project which had been in the back of many Americans' minds for the past twenty years. Texas had revolted from Mexico in 1836 and was waiting for statehood after failing to achieve a self-sufficient economy. As late as 1844, Lord Aberdeen had been ready to guarantee a loan to the independent "Lone Star" Republic if it would agree to abolish slavery. He had wanted a stable and independent antislavery state in the American Southwest which he hoped would block American expansion to the Pacific Coast. But only a month after Ogden, Warre, and Vavasour prepared to leave Red River, Texas ratified her annexation to the United States. Six months later Texas entered the Union. At this very time, President Polk, through Secretary of War William Marcy, ordered the United States Army under Zachary Taylor to deploy south of the Nueces River in the disputed territory between the "Texas–United States" combination and Mexico. Also, at this time California, with its magnificent harbor of San Francisco, was attached to Mexico by a thread so thin that the Americans hoped to cut it soon. George Bancroft, the American secretary of the navy, expecting war to break out on the Texas frontier, sent confidential instructions to Commodore John D. Sloat, the elderly commander of the Pacific Squadron, ordering him to seize San Francisco and blockade the other California ports if war broke out between the United States and Mexico.

Ogden did not know, of course, about these secret instructions, but he did know that the United States wanted Texas, California, and Oregon. He also knew that while he and his party were on the trail, farther to the south thousands of American homeseekers, impoverished by the agricultural depression of 1837, were marching westward. He wondered what role Frémont was playing in all this. Approaching Cape Disappointment in September, 1845, Ogden did not know exactly where Frémont was, only that he was somewhere in the West. If Ogden were to take possession of the mouth of the Columbia River, time was of the essence.

Actually Frémont was not to be a source of difficulty. He was in the West, but California was his chief concern. In the spring of 1845, Frémont recruited a party of fifty picked men. Such legendary frontiersmen as Kit Carson, Joseph Reddeford Walker, Alex Godey, Lucien Maxwell, and Basil Lajeunesse had worked with him in the past. Some of the new recruits such as Edward Kern and Richard Owens were soon to become famous by having their names given to some of California's best-known rivers, lakes, and valleys. The party left Bent's Fort in June, 1845, at the same time that Ogden, Warre, and Vavasour were in the vicinity of Red River. From this southwestern outpost, the expedition traveled up the Arkansas River into the heart of the Colorado Rockies, pushed on to the Great Salt Lake and through some of the desolate stretches of modern Nevada which Ogden had visited almost twenty years before. During this time Frémont, the "Pathfinder," changed the name of Ogden's River to

Humboldt River in honor of the great European geographer who had never been north of Mexico.

Ogden did not know that Frémont was crossing his old exploring grounds hundreds of miles to the south. He was sure that Frémont had the same objective as he did: taking possession of Cape Disappointment. The American House of Representatives had introduced a bill on February 5, 1845, for the organization of Oregon as a territory of the United States. Warre and Vavasour had pointed out in their second report: "We understand from several respectable emigrants that Lieut. Frémont, U.S. Topographical Engineers, had accompanied the present emigration with the intention of taking possession of the headland on behalf of the United States Government. The importance they attach to this point has induced us to urge the Hudson's Bay Company, through Mr. Ogden, to take immediate possession of so important a position in order to prevent the American Government obtaining it."[49]

When Ogden finally reached Cape Disappointment at the mouth of the Columbia River, he found that American citizens had moved into much of the region and had erected shacks to strengthen their claim to the land. Much of the land of Cape Disappointment was held by James Sanler, who lived there in a crude dwelling. Ogden approached Sanler with an offer to buy the tract from him and was surprised to find the man willing to sell him the property for two hundred dollars. Ogden agreed immediately, and the first, and probably the most important, part of his mission had been accomplished. In his usual capable and business-like manner, he set off up the Columbia and then up the Willamette to where Oregon City now stands to file his claim to Cape Disappointment at the Registry Office.

Any jubilation he felt soon turned to consternation when he learned that the property really belonged to Messrs. Wheeler and McDaniell, two Americans, and that Sanler was only their employee who had been settled on their claim to protect it. Wheeler and McDaniell, Ogden soon found, were also willing to sell, but their price was much higher, nine hundred dollars. Ogden thought this price was outrageous and refused to pay.

Meanwhile, the pace of events on the Columbia was accelerating. The Foreign Office had written to the Admiralty suggesting that a British naval vessel, perhaps even Admiral Sir George Seymour's flagship the *Collingwood*, should visit the northwest coast. Seymour, however, thought otherwise, and he dispatched Captain John Gordon, the youngest brother of Lord Aberdeen, commander of the fifty-gun frigate *America*. Gordon's ship arrived in Oregon waters after a voyage from Honolulu in late August, and on September 2, 1845, Gordon wrote to Dr. McLoughlin: "I have been directed, by the commander-in-chief in the Pacific [Seymour] to come here, and to assure all British subjects of firm protection in their rights."[50]

Actually, Gordon himself was not particularly interested in Oregon. He did not visit either Fort Vancouver or the Willamette Settlement. Instead, he sent two young officers, Lieutenant William Peel, the son of the prime minister, and Captain Henry William Parke of the Royal Marines to make a survey of the country. Parke "was a well-knit, capable man of unlimited service." He had served with the Royal Marines from 1822 until 1847, when he transferred into the Royal Marine Artillery. Peel was younger, fine looking, and well bronzed after his stay in the Hawaiian Islands and the epitome of what a naval officer should be. Before his untimely death in 1858 at the age of thirty-four, he had received the Victoria Cross and had been made a Companion of the Bath for his outstanding service in the Crimean War and the Indian Mutiny.[51] He was also brilliant. When he was commissioned in 1844, Sir Thomas Hastings praised him publicly and Sir Charles Napier gave him a flattering notice in the House of Commons. Gordon had selected capable men to make the reconnaissance.

At the start of their survey of the Oregon country, Peel and Parke visited the Hudson's Bay Puget Sound Agricultural Company's establishments at Fort Nisqually and Cowlitz Farm. They then went to Fort Vancouver, eighty-five miles away, where they were entertained by Dr. McLoughlin. Undoubtedly McLoughlin was pleased by the two officers' firm attitude toward defending Oregon. Their attitudes probably reflected those of Admiral Gordon. Even though Gordon believed that the country was not worth "five straws" and was "surprised that the Government should take any trouble about it," he had told Simpson that "our government are determined not to allow their rights to be encroached on." Parke, when dining with Dr. McLoughlin and the officers of the Hudson's Bay Company at Fort Vancouver, reiterated this point of view and said "no stone" shall "be left unturned. Well, Doctor, if they persist in bringing this on, we shall hit them harder than we would other people."[52] Dr. McLoughlin replied that he was most happy to learn that Gordon and company had been sent to Oregon "to assure Her Majesty's subjects a firm protection of their rights."

When Peel and Parke expressed a desire to see the Willamette settlements, Dr. McLoughlin sent Mr. Lowe, one of the Hudson's Bay Company's officers, to guide them. From Fort Vancouver, Peel and Parke pushed on to the Willamette where they could see the center of recent

American infiltration. They were well received by the Americans and spent two nights in the home of the famous old cowman, trailbreaker, and Oregon legislator, Jesse Applegate, who had come to Oregon as part of the 1843 immigration. Peel and Parke spent many hours with Applegate. They were intrigued by his personality and eager to learn his views. They questioned Applegate closely about his overland journey, and Peel particularly "was greatly interested." In trying to understand the vast overland American migrations, Peel, Applegate noted, "could hardly believe that the men would undertake and carry out such a journey without assistance and supposed the Government would have sent an escort with us; and thought that the Govmt. should at least have sent an officer to command each party." Applegate then told Peel that "he was somewhat mistaken in the character of the people—they were probably brave enough, but would never submit to discipline as soldiers." He then said, "If the President himself had started across the plains to command a company, the first time he should choose a bad camp or in any other way offend them, they would turn him out and elect some one among themselves who would suit them better."[53]

While visiting the Willamette settlement, Peel and Parke met Warre and Vavasour, who were being shown the region by James Douglas during Ogden's absence at Cape Disappointment. The five got along well, and Warre, Vavasour, and Douglas decided to join the naval officers' party. On September 24 they arrived aboard the *America*, which was anchored at Port Discovery. The socially conscious and ambitious Warre wanted to become better acquainted with Peel, the prime minister's son, and to meet Captain Gordon, Lord Aberdeen's youngest brother.

Douglas conferred with Gordon for three days and then departed. Warre and Vavasour decided to stay aboard the *America* for a voyage through the Strait of Juan de Fuca and to Vancouver Island. Probably now, or perhaps even earlier, Warre and Vavasour told Gordon and Peel that they were British officers who had been secretly sent west to take possession of Cape Disappointment.[54] The officers discussed the "Oregon Question" and, like many of their countrymen, did not have much enthusiasm for the region. Gordon observed that California with her splendid natural ports of San Francisco and San Diego, not Oregon, was the gem of the Pacific Coast.

Upon completion of the voyage to Vancouver Island, the *America* discharged her passengers, Warre and Vavasour, and prepared to sail. The *America* sailed from the Oregon Coast for the Hawaiian Islands on September 26.[55] In Honolulu, Gordon ordered Peel to carry reports and letters to the British government. On October 22, 1845, Peel sailed from

Honolulu to Mazatlán, crossed Mexico, embarked another ship at Vera Cruz on the Gulf of Mexico, and finally arrived in London on February 13, 1846. Upon arrival, he lost no time in presenting to the British government an oral report as well as a written one and letters from Captain John Gordon and Dr. McLoughlin.

While Peel was on the first leg of his voyage, Warre and Vavasour were making their way back to Fort Vancouver, and Ogden was returning from Oregon City. On October 1, 1845, Ogden arrived at the Columbia River post. He decided that even though Warre and Vavasour had not shown much interest in Cape Disappointment, he should at least explain the situation there to them, and on the day after his return, he wrote to Henry Warre: "I regret to state that my purchase of the Cape is now null and void. The man I purchased it from had no right to dispose of it. Two men Americans viz Wheeler and McDaniell had a prior claim. They however proposed to part with it for 900 dollars, which I refused having no Authority vested in me to negotiate. At all events, in my opinion by not appearing over anxious to obtain it, we can before spring, secure it at a lower rate; on this subject more when we meet."[56]

In this letter Ogden set forth the contradictory arguments that he was to use on several occasions to explain his failure at Cape Disappointment. Governor Simpson and the Hudson's Bay Company, he insisted, had not given him authority to take any action if Cape Disappointment were occupied by Americans. He did, however, take it upon himself to buy the property from James Sanler for two hundred dollars, and when he found out that Sanler had no right to sell the property, he offered the real owners, Wheeler and McDaniell four hundred dollars for it. But when they asked nine hundred dollars, Ogden's business instinct and his knowledge of Governor Simpson's frugality made him decline the offer.

Warre and Vavasour were not at Fort Vancouver on October 2 to receive Ogden's letter, and they found out about the situation only upon their return from Puget Sound on October 17. By this time Ogden was away from the Columbia River depot and did not return until November 9. Shortly after his arrival, he and Warre had many long conversations about what action should be taken regarding Cape Disappointment. Apparently during the last month, Ogden had had an opportunity to reflect upon the situation and had concluded that he should not jeopardize his position by assuming sole responsibility. After all, Warre and Vavasour were as accountable for protecting Cape Disappointment as he. In this vein, Ogden wrote to Henry Warre on November 17: "I have now to inform you, without you afford me, sufficient Security and Authorize me to purchase the Claim on Cape Disappointment in my name, which

I am most ready and willing to do; I cannot, from the tenor of my instructions take any further steps in securing the Cape, for the British Government; should you decide on making the purchase, no time should be lost, for by longer delay, the present owners of the Claim may be induced to enhance its value."[57]

When he received Ogden's letter, Warre realized that Ogden was trying to shift the responsibility to him, and he made a note that "it will be necessary to keep copies of this correspondence." He was probably pleased that, in writing a short report to Governor-General Metcalfe several weeks before, he had already managed to place the responsibility on Ogden. He had told Metcalfe that in regard to Cape Disappointment, "Mr. Ogden, to whom Sir G. Simpson gave Instructions, on this subject being absent, has also delayed our operations in that quarter."[58]

Nevertheless, Warre felt that Ogden's letter deserved a reply, and he went into conference with Vavasour. They decided that the best way to check Ogden's efforts was to restate Simpson's instructions even out of context. Thus they copied Simpson's statement: "Mr. Ogden has private instructions from me to take possession of that headland *on behalf of the Hudson's Bay Company*, ostensibly with a view of forming a 'Trading Post or Pilots Look Out' thereon—and if, after you have made an accurate survey, it be found, that any part of the back country overlooks the Cape Mr. Ogden has been further instructed to take possession of such commanding positions also."[59]

Correspondence between Warre and Ogden now became bitter although both gentlemen always maintained rigid politeness. On November 18, Ogden, somewhat irritated, sat down at his desk to answer Warre's letter of the day before. He continued to insist: "Still I cannot consider myself authorized to purchase the Claim on Cape Disappointment, although most anxious to meet your wishes." Then he decided to quote Simpson himself and included his remark to Ogden: "You will distinctly, understand, however, that neither Cape Disappointment, Tongue Point, nor any other place, is to be taken possession of by the Honble. Hudson's Bay Company, if already possessed or occupied on behalf of the United States Government or its citizens." He then turned the responsibility back to Warre, writing that this "binds me down and deprives me of all power or authority, under existing circumstances to act; and should you not consider it, of sufficient importance to authorize me to purchase the claims, I cannot, situated as I am, take the responsibility myself."[60]

November 19 was a busy and frustrating day. In the morning Warre replied to Ogden's letter of the preceding day and pointed out the inconsistencies of his actions: "Having duly received your (confidential) letter of yesterday's date, declining to take upon yourself the responsibility of purchasing Cape Disappointment on behalf of the Honble. Hudson's Bay Company in consequence of the Confidential Instructions received by you from Sir G. Simpson, May I beg you will favor me, with a statement of the late transactions, regarding the purchase of that headland from J. W. Sanler which I have reported to the Higher Authorities as in progress."[61]

Ogden must have felt uncomfortable when he received this note. He had realized from the first that his zeal in trying to take Cape Disappointment had caused him to act inexpediently if his original argument was to hold. He answered Warre immediately, hoping to get the whole difficult problem behind him. He retold the story of his negotiations with Sanler, but he still refused to answer clearly the crucial question of the extent of his responsibility and authorization for these activities. Then rather weakly and much unlike himself, Ogden wrote: "As my duty may require me shortly to absent myself from this place, it would be desirable you decide on the measures you intend to take in regard to the purchase of Cape Disappointment."[62]

Warre undoubtedly was pleased that his arguments had carried the day. Immediately upon the receipt of Ogden's letter, he wrote a curt reply: "As Sir G. Simpson's letter to M. Vavasour and myself is rendered nugatory by your interpretation of his instructions to you, and my private instructions not anticipating such an occurrence; I cannot consider myself justified in authorizing you, *individually* to purchase Cape Disappointment."[63] So the question of British occupation of the northern entrance to the Columbia River was dropped for the time being.

Ten days after Warre's reply to Ogden, Warre and Vavasour received naval reinforcements. The eighteen-gun British man-of-war *Modeste* commanded by Captain Thomas Baillie reached Fort Vancouver.[64] Ogden had disliked Warre and Vavasour from the beginning, and his dislike had increased after his correspondence with Warre. But after the arrival of Captain Baillie, they became insufferable to him. He wrote to Simpson: "My two officers have not left any deep impression of regret here prior to the arrival of the 'Modeste.' " Warre was tolerable until then, "but with the arrival of the British ship he . . . considered it highly important to assume an air of importance and self, his uncle Sir Richard and the latter's cook at five hundred a year was the constant topic of conversation. However, like all men who assume a character they cannot support or entitled to, the Naval gentry soon discovered him as well as Vavasour and held them both in very low estimation. Master V. supported his character to the last hour, a disagreeable puppy, and at times most disquieting, particularly when under the influence of brandy and opium, truly a noble specimen of Her Majest's Forces."[65]

However the arrival of the *Modeste* affected Warre and Vavasour's manner, the ship's crew certainly brightened the life at Fort Vancouver. Captain Baillie was very much a gentleman, as were his fellow officers, many of whom came from old navy families. Two of the young officers who were with Captain Baillie on the Pacific Coast in 1845 were Midshipman A. DeHorsey, who later became Admiral DeHorsey, and First Lieutenant T. M. Rodney, who was the grandson of Admiral C. R. Rodney. Because the American settlers in the Willamette Valley resented the arrival of the British war vessel, the officers and the men, following the advice of the Hudson's Bay Company, gave a series of entertainments to which all were invited. Soon performances of such plays as *Three Weeks after Marriage, The Deuce Is in Him,* and *The Mayor of Garrat* were being performed by young Oregon women and personnel from the *Modeste,* using scenery painted by the ship's crew. These performances, said to be the first of their kind on the Pacific Coast, played to full houses, and most settlers enjoyed them. A few resented the prelude to the plays: "Modeste is our ship, and modest are we—one word more, and up shall rise the scene; ladies and gentlemen all—God save the Queen."[66]

Ogden also enjoyed the gay atmosphere Fort Vancouver afforded after the arrival of the *Modeste,* but he was still troubled by the question of Cape Disappointment. He was frustrated that he had been swindled by the American Sanler and had been thwarted in the taking of the large Columbian promontory. His attempt to obey Captain Simpson's instructions had caused him to act out of character, and he felt humiliated by the whole affair. So after three months of evaluating the situation, he decided to throw caution to the wind and go back to Cape Disappointment.

On Saint Valentine's Day, 1846, Ogden wrote Warre:

Since our last correspondence having virtually reflected that the principal object of your journey to this country had been frustrated by the prior claim of Wheeler and McDaniell to Cape Disappointment, and our respective instructions, not authorizing us to purchase the Cape, and being fully aware of the importance of securing the Cape for the services of the British Government, I, this day made a purchase of the same for one thousand dollars. Survey was for two hundred dollars forming a total of twelve hundred dollars; and the same had been duly registered in Oregon Register Office in my name and on my own responsibility. May I trust the above information meets with your approbation and that you will on your return to Canada report the same to the Higher Authorities.[67]

On the following day Warre answered Ogden's letter and indicated that he was pleased that Ogden had taken such steps. He then rather gallantly added: "I will not fail to report your proceeding on my return to Canada and I have no doubt from the tenor of Sir G. Simpson's letter to us, he will approve of the measure you have taken for the occupation of the Cape by a British subject, which is evidentally so desirable."[68] Warre was true to his word, but in making his final report, he could not resist suggesting that he and Vavasour had prompted Ogden's actions: "Your Lordship will observe that Mr. Ogden has taken the entire responsibility upon himself, but he was induced to effect this in consequence of the importance we attached to gaining peaceable possession of the Cape. The anticipated arrival of Lieutenant Frémont and the resolutions of the House of Representatives induced us to form this opinion and we trust your Lordship will approve of the expense incurred to gain this object."[69]

Warre and Vavasour were delighted by Ogden's purchase. Now they could go to Cape Disappointment, make their survey, and then, with their mission accomplished, begin thinking about returning to the gay social life of Montreal. Vavasour, the engineer, made an astute analysis of Cape Disappointment and described it graphically for his superiors. He noted that it was "A high, bold headland consisting of two bluffs, having perpendicular scarps toward the sea, connected by a narrow ridge running nearly N. and S., of about 30 feet in width on the top, the face being nearly perpendicular and about 300 feet in height, sloping more gradually to the rear, where it is connected with the mainland by a neck of 30 yards in width."

To fortify the Cape properly, he recommended that the British government lay three batteries of heavy guns on the headland. One battery should consist of four guns and should be laid at the center of the cape; another battery of four guns should be laid on the north bluff. The third battery should consist of two guns and be laid on "the spur running from the north bluff toward the middle sand." To make Cape Disappointment a really strong bastion, he further suggested that a two-story blockhouse overlooking the landing site in Baker's Bay be built close to some running water and that earth be thrown up to form a parapet around it.[70] Vavasour made a drawing of the mouth of the Columbia River, and Warre, who had considerable artistic talent, drew a picture of Cape Disappointment which later appeared in his book published in 1849, *Sketches in North America and the Oregon Territory.*

The two British officers now returned to Fort Vancouver and began their preparations for their journey to Canada. They arranged to make the trip overland with the Express which left for the East every spring. On March 25, 1846, Warre and Vavasour stepped into one of the Company's overlapped boats amid the wild shouts of "good-bye" and "*au revoir*" and the melodious songs of the French Canadian oarsmen. Undoubtedly, Ogden, who always conducted himself in a gentlemanly manner, was on the pier to bid the two British officers farewell, but he must have been delighted to see their boat move up river and out of sight of Fort Vancouver.

On April 3 the Express reached Fort Nez Percés, and Warre and Vavasour decided to visit the Whitman Mission which was a short distance from the Hudson's Bay Company's post. Here they visited with Narcissa Whitman, who was said to have been "a beautiful blonde, of fair form and face and well rounded features" and with her missionary husband.[71] The two officers returned to Fort Nez Percés and pushed eastward with the Express. On May 2 they reached Boat Encampment, where they exchanged their boats for snowshoes and prepared for the trek through the Rockies to Jasper's House, composed of "three miserable log huts,"[72] and then on to forts Assiniboine, Edmonton, and Carlton. On June 7 they finally reached Red River, where they found Governor Simpson waiting for them.

Warre and Vavasour discussed their findings with Simpson, who was thoroughly pleased with Ogden's purchase of Cape Disappointment and the military survey of the headland. Now Simpson was ready to carry the plan one step further. He ordered Fort George on the south side of the mouth of the Columbia removed to the north shore, to Cape Disappointment.[73] Simpson, Warre, Vavasour, and Ogden were satisfied with the results of their mission. Now Great Britain would control Cape Disappointment, which in turn would control the mouth of the Columbia River.

The fate of Oregon, however, was not to be decided by reports, whether favorable or unfavorable. In fact, while Gordon was in the Pacific, while Peel was making the strenuous trip across Mexico, and while Ogden, Warre, and Vavasour were attempting to gain Cape Disappointment, parties in both the United States and Great Britain were moving toward compromise on the "Oregon Question." As early as October 17, 1845, Lord Aberdeen wrote to Peel:

If it should ever be possible to effect a settlement between ourselves upon terms, I think the following might perhaps be accepted; and I should carry the 49th parallel of latitude as the boundary *to the sea* and give to the United

States the line of coast to the south of this degree. This would leave us in possession of the whole of Vancouver's Island, and the northern shore of the entrance into the Straits of John de Fuca [*sic*]. The navigation of the Columbia to its most accessible point, should be common to both parties at all times; and all the ports between the Columbia and the 49th parallel, whether on the mainland, or in the island, should be Free Ports.[74]

By the end of 1845, Peel had come to accept the forty-ninth parallel as the boundary. The only remaining barrier to settlement was the belligerence of President Polk and the unequivocal language he had used when referring to Oregon. Moderates on both sides of the Atlantic realized that an American movement for negotiation could not come from the President because of the position in which he had placed himself. Any compromise would have to be initiated by Congress and the press.

Some uncompromising Democrats wanted territory above the forty-ninth parallel, but most Congressmen by the winter of 1845–46 had come to the conclusion that the United States really did not want or need vast tracts of virgin land, and, therefore, Oregon was only important as a site of Pacific seaports. Because Robert Greenhow's *The History of Oregon and California*, Thomas J. Farnham's *Travels in the Great Western Prairies*, and Charles Wilkes' *Narrative of the United States Exploring Expedition During the Years 1838, 1839, 1840, 1841, and 1842* had all extolled Puget Sound, just south of the forty-ninth parallel, this great inlet was coveted, but no one seemed greatly interested in harbors north of it. Most congressmen believed that Puget Sound and the excellent Mexican harbors of San Francisco and San Diego would be sufficient to develop the American Pacific trade. As Meredith P. Gentry of Tennessee summed it up, "Oregon up to the 49th parallel of latitude, and the province of Upper California, when it can be fairly acquired, is the utmost limit to which this nation ought to go in the acquisition of territory."

By early 1846 the newspapers of the nation were beginning to show the same attitude and were editorializing about California and a negotiation of boundary with Great Britain at the forty-ninth parallel. The *New York Journal of Commerce* was the first to succumb. The *New York Herald* and the *New York Sun* soon followed. Other large metropolitan papers were quick to agree and soon readers in the nation's capital, in St. Louis, and in New Orleans were learning that a peaceful boundary solution with Great Britain at the forty-ninth parallel should be negotiated.[75]

On the other side of the Atlantic, the London *Times* was telling its readers:

We think, then, that every purpose both of honour and interest would be answered if the British Minister, on whom now devolves the duty of making fresh proposals to the Government of the United States, were to renew on his part the offer made to England by Mr. Gallatin in the presidency and under the direction of Mr. Adams. That proposal was to take the 49th degree of north latitude as far as the sea as the boundary line, reserving to Great Britain Vancouver's Island, the harbour of St. Juan de Fuca, and the free navigation of the Columbia. This would be a concession as far as superficial area of ground is concerned. It would leave the United states masters of the greater part of Oregon. But it would secure the principal advantage of the country, the free navigation of the Columbia, to the servants of the Hudson's Bay Company, as well as the harbourage, anchorage, and settlement for English vessels trading with China and our possessions in Australia and New Zealand. It would concede all that the most successful war could acquire—a sovereign but barren domain; but it would secure all the commercial blessing of an honourable compromise and a rational peace.[76]

The Peel government was faced with serious domestic and foreign problems at this time. At home the Corn Law crisis and the great famine in Ireland were creating a realignment of political parties, while the question of the Spanish Marriage was the chief international problem. Early in 1846, consequently, Oregon was not Aberdeen's and Peel's chief concern, and in the face of so many other difficulties, Lord Aberdeen hoped to come to an amiable agreement with the United States. In January, 1846, he instructed Pakenham to offer to arbitrate the "Oregon Question" with the Americans. Pakenham proposed that the boundary settlement should be solved by a mixed commission with a neutral chairman or by a board of distinguished jurists, but Secretary of State Buchanan refused these terms.

On April 26, 1846, while Warre and Vavasour were approaching Boat Encampment on their return to Canada, the United States gave notice to Great Britain that she wished to terminate the treaty of 1827. Although this was not a joyous tiding, it was observed that the phraseology that Polk used in transmitting this notice to Great Britain was courteous and moderate. It was also observed that in the Senate there was a "large majority friendly to a compromise on the basis of the 49th degree,"[77] but English sympathizers in the United States were concerned about how long this "friendly" attitude would last. Robert Dale Owen wrote to Peel:

I feel confident, that, at this moment, and probably for some weeks to come, the government of the United States would accept an offer on the basis of 49°; and that the Senate would ratify such a treaty, by the necessary two-thirds vote, and nothing to spare. But I doubt whether such a treaty can be either signed or ratified, after three months from this date. . . . The warmest friends

of peace, Mr. Calhoun among the number, admit and lament this. Not one, even of them, dare hint at any compromise south of 49°, and the probability is, that nine out of ten legal voters in the United States, would resent the idea, and consign to political death the statesmen who should advocate, or vote for it.[78]

In even more persuasive terms, Richard Crocker wrote Lord Aberdeen:

If you get 49° and the Columbia, you will have done a miracle, but I have no hope of miracles now-a-days, and I shall gladly assent to 49° and half the Straits of Fuca; but for God's sake, end it; for if anything were to happen to Louis Philippe, we should have an American War immediately, and a French one just after, a rebellion in Ireland, real starvation in the manufacturing districts, and a twenty per cent complication in the shape of Income Tax—not pleasant in prospect, and still less so if any portion of the Black Cloud should burst.[79]

These reports probably helped the Cabinet make the decision to try to settle the boundary dispute by negotiation. On May 18, Lord Aberdeen sent Pakenham draft proposals for an Oregon treaty which were in turn submitted by Polk to the United States Senate. The Senate ratified the treaty, and on June 15, 1846, the Oregon Boundary Treaty was signed. The day before, Warre, at Red River, ignorant of the event, was writing his Oregon Report to the colonial secretary.

Shortly after the news of the signing of the treaty reached England, the Peel government fell, primarily because of the furor caused by the repeal of the Corn Laws, and Lord Palmerston returned to the Foreign Office. In America, Warre and Vavasour kept on writing their report, which they thought would determine the final Oregon settlement. In Oregon itself, Ogden, also ignorant of the political developments in Washington and London, was busily directing construction of a warehouse on Cape Disappointment.

South of Ogden, Frémont had crossed the Sierra Nevada Mountains and descended the American River into the Sacramento Valley. After he had been in California for a few weeks, the apprehensive Mexican authorities ordered him to leave their province. Slowly Frémont moved northward into the Klamath Lake region of what is today southern Oregon, which had been first explored by Ogden. Here he was overtaken by Lieutenant Archibald Gillespie of the United States Marine Corps, who had hurried across Mexico to deliver to Frémont various messages as well as letters from his "Manifest Destiny" father-in-law, Senator Benton. The exact contents of the communications that Gillespie delivered to Frémont are not known, but apparently they were encouraging enough to make Frémont believe that he should return to California in order to participate in forthcoming events as circumstances might require. The arrival of Frémont's forces gave heart to the disgruntled American settlers in California. Some of them rose up and declared California the Bear Flag Republic, free and independent of Mexico. The "Bear Flaggers," however, did not have to worry about the question of sovereignty for long. Their "revolution" of June 10, 1846, soon merged into the Mexican War. On July 7, Commodore John D. Sloat and the American Pacific Squadron sailed into Monterey harbor, the Mexican capital of California, and took possession of it without much resistance.

Before Sloat received word that war had broken out between the United States and Mexico on the Texas frontier in May, he was also apprehensive about the "Oregon Question." He dispatched Lieutenant Neil M. Howison in the United States schooner *Shark* to the Columbia. Howison spent April, May, and much of June in the Sandwich Islands while his ship was undergoing repairs, and it was not until July 18 that his twelve-gun schooner entered the Columbia. He made his way up river very carefully and arrived at Fort Vancouver on July 24 in time to see the first horse race on record which was held there, on July 25.

Howison met Ogden and liked him very much. He described him as a "jocose and pleasing companion." During Howison's stay of several months at Fort Vancouver, he and Ogden talked at length about Oregon and about what type of settlement would be worked out between the United States and Great Britain. Neither, of course, realized that over a month before Howison's arrival, the peace treaty setting the boundary had been signed.[80] Before Howison took his departure from Fort Vancouver, however, the news from Washington began filtering to the Columbia in newspapers shipped from the Sandwich Islands. These papers indicated that the United States had given Great Britain notice of the termination of the treaty of 1827; she had done this almost four months before, on April 26, 1846. The newspapers also pointed out that bills were pending in Congress for the establishment of military posts between the Missouri and the Columbia and for the raising of a regiment of mounted riflemen for service along the line of travel to Oregon. Naturally these tidings brought rejoicing in the American camp and depression at Fort Vancouver.

In early September the bark *Toulon* entered the Columbia River carrying packets from the British consul in the Sandwich Islands to Dr. McLoughlin. Among these papers was an extract of a letter from Alexander Forbes, British consul in Tepic, Mexico, to Sir George Seymour, commander of the British Pacific Squadron containing news that the

Hudson's Bay Company steamer, the *Beaver*.

Courtesy Provincial Archives, Victoria, British Columbia

Carving of a beaver reputed to have been made by Indians to serve as the figurehead of the *Beaver*. The figure now stands in Beaver House, London.

Courtesy Hudson's Bay Company

The Dalles, Columbia River. From a drawing by Henry J. Warre,
1845–46.

The Whitman Mission.

Courtesy Oregon Historical Society

Fort Garry. From a drawing by Henry J. Warre, 1845–46.

San Francisco in 1849, two years prior to Peter Skene Ogden's visit to the city.

Courtesy Bancroft Library

Fort Okanagan, an important horse-producing center at the head of navigation on the New Caledonian River.

Sitka, Alaska, headquarters of the Russian American Fur Company. Peter Skene Ogden visited Sitka in 1832 and 1834.

Peter Skene Ogden shortly before his death.

Courtesy Oregon Historical Society

The Ogden family coat of arms.

Oregon boundary had been settled at the forty-ninth parallel. When the Americans heard this news, they fired a salute and raised the American flag, certainly a strange sight to Ogden, Dr. McLoughlin, and the other Company men who had served under the Union Jack for so long.

Ogden was stunned by this news, particularly when he thought back upon his trek across Canada with Warre and Vavasour, about his worry, machinations, and correspondence with Warre regarding possession of Cape Disappointment. All of his efforts during the past year had been for nought, and, as he later wrote to Governor Simpson, "All is ended in giving the Americans all they possibly wished for or required. Far better had they [Peel and Aberdeen] given it at first and then Jonathan would have thanked them for it, on the contrary now they boast and laugh at them. . . . Truly may we say 'put not your trust in Prime Ministers' and thank God Peel is out of power and *long long* may he remain so."[81]

VIII

Ogden the Samaritan

As OGDEN LOOKED AROUND Fort Vancouver in the fall of 1846, he thought about the great changes that he had seen take place on the Columbia in the past twenty-eight years. He recalled that when he had first come to Oregon in 1818 old John Haldane and the North West Company had been a powerful force in the fur trade and he had been an eager young man of twenty-four. Now at fifty-two he was mellower and more disciplined than he had been then, but he was also somewhat cynical and disillusioned after nearly thirty years in the fur trade. So much had happened on the Columbia since he had made that hurried trip from Île à la Crosse. How strange it seemed now that he had been upset in 1821 when he learned that the Hudson's Bay and North West companies had merged and that he had been passed over. After all, both companies had had headquarters in what is now Canada, and the amalgamation had brought relatively few changes. But now the Stars and Stripes instead of the Union Jack waved over the Columbia, and Dr. McLoughlin, whose huge frame and bushy white hair had made a company institution, was no longer at Fort Vancouver.

Ogden recalled that when Warre and Vavasour had been at the Columbia depot, he, Dr. McLoughlin, and James Douglas had received a letter from the Governor and Committee which stated: "We have been informed that the Governor and Council of the Northern Department, in conformity with our opinion that the business of the country, west of the Mountains had become too extensive for individual Superintendance, have placed it under the charge of a Board of Management and have appointed you to constitute that Board for the Current Outfit."[1] Thus the long feud between Governor Simpson and Dr. McLoughlin finally came to an end. The Company treated Dr. McLoughlin well, but the saddened and disgruntled old man left Fort Vancouver in January, 1846, and moved to Oregon City, where he became an American citizen before his death there in 1857.[2] The management of the Hudson's Bay Company affairs in Oregon was now in the hands of Douglas and Ogden.

Virtually all writers and contemporary visitors to the Columbia in the 1840's have indicated that Douglas held a position superior to that of Ogden. This is not true. They were given equal rank by the Governor and Committee. This erroneous opinion developed because the dour Douglas generally stayed at his desk at Fort Vancouver, carrying on much of the Company's correspondence and greeting English and foreign travelers, while Ogden, who hated the confines of an office, was generally in the field handling any problems affecting the Company's interests. The Governor and Committee, however, considered Ogden, the outcast of 1821, a much more valuable employee in Oregon: "The Company have obtained a grant of Vancouver Island from the Crown, and it is considered necessary that in future a member of the Board of Management should be constantly at Fort Vancouver, and Mr. Douglas's services can be better dispensed with at Fort Vancouver than Mr. Ogden's, it is intended that Mr. Douglas should reside at the former place, acting as Governor ad interim under a commission from the Crown."[3] George Roberts, a clerk at the Columbia River depot concurred in this appointment: "James Douglas left Fort Vancouver just in time—he was too unbending and unyielding for the Times."[4]

Now, in 1846, two years before Douglas was to leave for Vancouver Island, his and Ogden's chief problems centered on trying to operate the Company's business in a foreign country. Ironically, even though the United States now owned Oregon, and her nationals—since the large migrations of the past three years—made up the bulk of the Oregon population, the Hudson's Bay Company was still the chief commercial establishment and her officers were greatly respected. With the Mexican War in progress, the United States was slow to provide a government for Oregon. It was not until August 14, 1848, that President Polk signed the bill creating Oregon Territory. Until then, politics in Oregon were in a state of confusion. Prior to the boundary settlement, the main issue in local politics had been the question of the colony's future. One faction had supported immediate intervention by the United States to "protect" the American settlers from the British and the Hudson's Bay Company. Another group had favored the establishment of an independent republic. A third party had advocated co-existence with the Hudson's Bay Company until Congress and the diplomats worked out the Oregon question.

After the boundary settlement, politics degenerated into local antagonisms. Farmers charged both British and American merchants with monopolistic practices. Other groups, similar to temperance movements in the East and in Britain, worried about the regulation of liquor and pressed for prohibition. Still others, particularly newly arrived emigrants, complained that the "Old Timers" manipulated the laws and the lawmakers to protect their own vested interests.[5] Despite the grumbling and political machinations in 1846, the relationship between the provisional government of Oregon and the officers of the Hudson's Bay Company was cordial. The question was how long would this harmony last. Ogden and the Company tried to keep their self-respect and at the same time promote good-will in the difficult transition period.

Their first test came when Lieutenant Neil Howison, the commander of the United States schooner *Shark*, ran his ship aground at the mouth of the Columbia River on September 10, 1846. The vessel was totally wrecked on South Spit, and the officers and men were cast ashore without food or clothing. When Ogden and Douglas received news of this accident two days later, they immediately dispatched a cutter from the *Modeste* with necessary supplies for the poorly sheltered men. They also suggested that Lieutenant Howison apply to Mr. Peers at Fort George "for any articles of food or clothing you may want." The Company was very generous about payment. Generally cash was considered to be worth 12 per cent more than checks, but Howison's requisitions, which were paid for with checks on Baring Brothers bank, were not discounted.

With his new equipment and supplies, Howison tried to make himself and his men comfortable. They erected three houses at Astoria on the south side of the mouth of the Columbia and planted the American flag on its shore. By the end of October, however, Howison felt that his expedition should get underway. He appealed to Ogden and Douglas, and they allowed him to charter the seventy-ton schooner *Cadboro* for £500. Howison thought the price exorbitant, and he would have been even surer about it if he had known that the Company had only paid £800 for the vessel. Undoubtedly the shrewd members of the Board of Management felt that this price was legitimate considering the great risk of crossing the bar at the mouth of the Columbia at this season.[6]

Howison's ill-fated expedition was to be further thwarted. He and his men boarded the *Cadboro* in early November, 1846, but winter storms prevented them from sailing until January 18, 1847. The Hudson's Bay Company's kindness, however, was appreciated by Scottish-born Governor Abernethy of the provisional government of Oregon Territory. He wrote to Ogden: "The timely and needful supply of provisions which were so promptly furnished to the wrecked officers and men of the Lark [Shark], by Captain Baillie of H.B.M.S. 'Modeste' and the Hudson's Bay Company, contributed much to their relief and comfort, and was praiseworthy in the highest degree."[7]

Not everyone felt that the Company was praiseworthy. Soon it was heard that the Hudson's Bay Company was a "large and powerful moneyed institution," and, after all, weren't foreign monopolies against the American way of life? Ogden knew that the peace between the Americans and the Hudson's Bay Company's personnel before the boundary settlement was only temporary, and did not expect it to last: "So far all is apparently tranquil but still we are looked upon with a suspicious eye by one and all."[8]

The Company's men were sure that the first attack upon them would be an attempt to take their land. The Oregon Land Law of 1845 provided that no individual or company could claim more than 640 acres of land. To protect their holdings, the Company invested title to land around Fort Vancouver in nine employees. William Fraser Tolmie, who had been with Ogden during the "Stikine Incident" and who was now at Nisqually, was in a quandary. He did not have enough employees to claim the pasture lands needed for the large Puget's Sound Agricultural Company's herds and flocks. The Governor and Committee, noting that the Foreign Office was not particularly interested in clarifying the Company's treaty position in Oregon, decided that the wisest plan of action was to sell the Hudson's Bay Company property to the United States government. They all knew that the Company's position would deteriorate in the years to come. If £30,000 could be realized from the Puget's Sound Agricultural Company and £70,000 for the Hudson's Bay Company's property and rights south of the forty-ninth parallel, Simpson and the Governor and Committee would be satisfied.[9] The United States, however, was involved in the Mexican War during the late forties, torn by sectional strife during the fifties, and fighting for the survival of the Union in the sixties. American leaders were not interested in negotiating with the Hudson's Bay Company over a problem in remote Oregon.

It was unfortunate for the Hudson's Bay Company not to have been able to sell the Oregon holdings immediately because each year brought greater problems. With the Mexican War raging far to the south and unsettled conditions in California, the emigrant trains which left the Middle West late every spring came in increasing numbers to Oregon. Many Conestoga wagons with their muddy white canopies flapping in the breeze came in 1846, and by 1847 the rate of immigration to Oregon had accelerated greatly. In that year, it has been estimated, between four and five thousand people moved to the Pacific Coast, and very few of them went to California. August was fairly early for immigrants to reach their destination, but on August 23, 1847, the Whitman Mission reported that "probably 80 or 100 wagons have already passed."[10]

As thousands of Americans began to move into Oregon, the Indians became very restive. Prior to 1847, Oregon had had no serious Indian difficulties. The usual problem was the loss of a few cattle or sheep from the Puget's Sound Agricultural Company's holdings,[11] but, on the whole, the officers of the Hudson's Bay Company had great success in dealing with the natives. They were successful because their conception of justice coincided with that of the Indians; an eye for an eye and a tooth for a tooth. Dr. McLoughlin and his subordinates were always careful to punish only the guilty, and whenever possible, they allowed the Indians themselves to determine the guilty party. After long years of experience, the Company men realized that agreements with the Indians had to be made in terms they understood, and, once made, agreements must be adhered to uncompromisingly.

The Americans who came to Oregon were on the whole quite different. They did not have a long tradition of living as a minority thousands of miles from home among large numbers of natives. The Americans felt no need to be considerate about Indian customs. The Indians were their natural enemies. They lurked on the frontiers, impeding the expansion of a growing, aggressive nation. Even the Protestant, American missionaries in Oregon had difficulties. They were often unduly harsh with the Indians when they broke the white man's code, little of which they understood, and when Marcus Whitman was slapped by a native and turned the other cheek, he permitted an indignity that an Indian would never tolerate.

In 1847, with the greatest number of wagons on the trail to date, the emigrants suffered greatly. Water holes were dried up and grass had been depleted by the parties that had arrived earlier. Dysentery and measles began to spread among the emaciated travelers. Many were buried along the trail alongside furniture that had been discarded to lighten the load of suffering oxen. The immigrants, however, believed that all would be well if they could only reach Oregon.

After crossing great stretches of the American West and passing through the lands of hostile Plains Indians, the Oregon-bound immigrants believed that they were out of danger after they left Fort Boise on the Snake River. They had heard stories about the missionaries who worked with the peaceful natives and also that the Indians on the Columbia had been decimated in 1831–32 by malaria, intermittent fever as it was then called. This was true, but the settlers did not take into consideration one tribe, the Cayuses. The Cayuses, who were made up of many small, scattered bands, roamed the country from the foot of the Blue Mountains to a spot approximately twenty-five miles east of Fort Nez Percés. Robert Newell, subagent of Indian affairs for Oregon Territory, described them: "They are unlike any Indians—quite proud and full of themselves—more superstitious than any of their neighbors overbearing and all the surrounding tribes or bands are more or less imposed by them, as they are brave and savage-like disposed. They have never had a good honest feeling towards the Americans."[12] It was among the Cayuses that Marcus and Narcissa Whitman chose to found their mission in 1836.

By the late summer and early autumn of 1847 as wagon after wagon was heading for the Columbia, the Cayuses began attacking unsuspecting travelers. When John Ross and a party of men reached the vicinity of Rock Creek, a branch of John Day River, they saw a startling sight—six women and several children absolutely naked. While their husbands had been away from the wagons searching for strayed cattle, the Indians had struck and stripped every particle of clothing off the bodies of the helpless women and children. Not satisfied with this, the Indians took everything they could carry away. The loss in goods in only one of the wagons was $2,500 according to the owner, Margaret Rodgers. The women had rescued one bolt of muslin, and when John Ross and his companions rode up, the women hastily wrapped strips of this cloth around themselves for clothing. Realizing that muslin would not warm the women, the men made them a bed by building a fire and then pouring mounds of sand over the coals. Soon another wagon train arrived, and the frightened women were given food and clothing. It was a degrading experience, but at least the Rodgers party escaped from Cayuse territory with their lives.

Others were not so fortunate, and in 1847 and 1848 many suffered at the hands of the Cayuses. The emigrants of 1847 brought with them a virulent form of measles and dysentery which spread rapidly throughout Oregon. These epidemics hit the Indians especially hard and made them even more bitter. Actually the situation east of the Cascade Mountains had been growing worse for some time. As early as 1841 several half-bloods began spreading rumors to frighten the Indians. One, Baptiste Dorion, told the Cayuses that "the Americans were coming to make war upon them and take their country." Several Indians informed the missionaries and the Hudson's Bay Company's officers of this rumor and were surprised when their messages were rewarded with gifts. After finding that the game of informing was lucrative, many Indians now passed on irresponsible stories which, of course, grew in the telling. As years passed and more and more American emigrants reached the Columbia, the informers as well as those propagandized began to believe that all the rumors were true.

In 1842 the Cayuses had exhausted the patience of Marcus Whitman, and he made a trip east to plead before the American Board of Commissioners for Foreign Missions which had had misgivings about the site that he had chosen for his missionary work. During his absence, the natives, who greatly resented his growing wheat on "their" land and selling it to the ever increasing number of emigrant trains, burned down his gristmill and frightened Narcissa into taking refuge at The Dalles Methodist mission. Dr. Elijah White, who had been informally appointed Indian subagent for Oregon, tried to handle the situation. He called the Cayuses and Nez Percés together and convinced them to agree to collective tribal responsibility and to manage their young men through the selection of a chief with disciplinary powers. This action seemed wise at the time, but it was only a temporary check on violence, and eventually it weakened the power of the chiefs when they attempted to enforce the code.[13]

Troubles with the Cayuses increased in 1847. The measles epidemic brought in by the emigrants that year took a terrible toll among the Indians, and they became frantic. It is estimated that approximately 197 Cayuses died, and if this figure is correct, almost half of the tribe were killed by the epidemic. As Henry Spalding put it: "It was most distressing to go into a lodge of some 10 fires, and count 20 or 25, some in the midst of measles, others in the last stages of dysentery, in the midst of every kind of filth itself sufficient to cause sickness, with no suitable means to alleviate their inconceivable sufferings, with perhaps one well person to look after the wants of 2 sick ones. Everywhere the sick and dying were pointed to Jesus, and the well were urged to prepare for death."[14]

Dr. Whitman tried to do everything possible both medically and spiritually for the Indians. They could not understand why most white people stricken with the disease recovered and nearly all Indians died. Dr. Whitman tried to explain that, while his medicine would aid the recovery of the Indians, their practice of sitting over the steaming stones in their sweat lodges at the peak of their fever and then plunging into the icy waters of the rivers offset the medical treatment and hastened their deaths.

The Cayuses, who had depended on the ministrations of a medicine man, questioned the power of Dr. Whitman's medicine. Unfortunately for the Whitmans it was a Cayuse custom that relatives kill a medicine man who had treated a patient who died. Archibald McKinlay, Ogden's son-in-law, was fully aware of this custom, for during a period of five years while he was factor at Fort Nez Percés, he saw seven medicine men shot near the fort, and he estimated that "probably over three times that number altogether" were killed.[15] In one of Narcissa's first letters home, she told her family about this practice, not realizing that both she and her husband would be victims of it.

The Cayuses began watching Dr. Whitman even more closely than usual and came to believe that he was using his "evil eye" to harm them. They were completely convinced by what happened to LeGrande, a half-Nez Percé, half-Cayuse, after Dr. Whitman refused to shake hands with him allegedly because LeGrande was a young warrior and Whitman did not believe in fighting. That night while LeGrande was eating a piece of dried buffalo meat, he choked on it and died almost immediately. Many of his friends and members of his family blamed Marcus Whitman for his death.

Much more serious was the superstitious Cayuses' explanation of why more Indians than whites died from the epidemic. Joe Lewis, a half-blood Indian who was employed at the Whitman Mission told a council of Cayuses that one day while he was lying on the settee in Dr. Whitman's room, he had overheard a conversation between Dr. Whitman, Mrs. Whitman, and Henry Spalding. According to Lewis, the Whitmans and Spalding had been writing for two years to their friends in the East to send them poison to kill off the Cayuses and Nez Percés. The first poison to arrive had not been very potent, but better-quality poison had arrived the summer of 1847. In this conversation the mischief-making Indian reported that "the Doctor had said it [was] best to destroy them by degrees, but that Mrs. Whitman said it was best to do it at once, and they would be rid of them, and have all their land and horses as their own." Then Mr. Spalding, he said, asked the doctor why he had not killed the Indians off faster, to which Whitman replied, "Oh, they are dying fast enough; the young ones will die off this winter, and the old ones next spring."[16]

The Indians were greatly aroused by Lewis' story, and for several nights they sat around their council fires and debated what should be done. One contemporary noted that although the Indians were superstitious, they were also fair enough to test the truth of Joe Lewis' story. They asked Dr. Whitman for medicine "for a lad who was then lying sick, and on his fate their decision was to depend. The boy unhappily died."[17] Some of the chiefs still urged caution to the members of the council, but finally a few influential chiefs agreed on a drastic decision—death to the Whitmans.

In late November, 1847, when the Cayuse chiefs were making their decision, Waiilatpu, the Whitmans' mission, was crowded with immigrants who had just come over the Oregon Trail. Every room was filled to capacity. The Saunders family with their five children had two rooms in what was known as Mansion House, and the Nathan Kimballs of Laporte, Indiana, shared a room in the same building with their four children. Also, in the building were the Peter Halls of Illinois, their five children, widow Rebecca Hays of Platte County, Missouri, with her young son, and seven other people, a total of twenty-nine. In the main mission house were twenty-three people, including Dr. and Mrs. Whitman, their children, and school boarders, one of whom was Eliza Spalding and two of whom were the half-blood sons of Chief Factor Donald Manson of the Hudson's Bay Company. Scattered around the cluster of buildings, particularly in the blacksmith shop and sawmill cabin, were twenty-two others.[18] Thus on November 29, 1847, seventy-four people were at Waiilatpu.

Monday, November 29, a cold, dreary morning, began like any other day. Dr. Whitman broiled himself a steak for breakfast and then held the funeral services for three young Indians who had died of measles, one of whom was said to have been the child of Chief Tiloukaikt, who had already lost two other children. Then the doctor made his rounds of the mission and treated his own countrymen who had fallen victim to the epidemic. At noon the midday meal was served. The children then returned to their lessons, and the men went back to work. Dr. Whitman pulled his settee closer to the stove and began to read.

The doctor's reading was soon interrupted. A knock came on the door separating the dining room from the kitchen, and Mrs. Whitman called to her husband that an Indian who wanted some medicine was in the kitchen. When Whitman opened the door, he found Tiloukaikt and Tomahas waiting for him. Apparently while Whitman was talking with Tiloukaikt, Tomahas crept behind him and struck him with his tomahawk. The forty-six-year-old Whitman proved difficult to kill. The Indian struck at him again and again. John Sager saw what was happening and reached for his pistol, but the Indians shot him first. The sound of the gunfire was apparently the signal for the general attack. Indians who had been quietly watching the slaughtering of a steer by the mission men dropped their blankets and revealed guns and tomahawks.

Now all was confusion. Mrs. Whitman tried to drag her semiconscious husband to the settee as the Indians shouted and beat on the doors. Then Narcissa regained her composure and led the thirteen people in the house upstairs hoping to find refuge. But the Indians rushed in, and Chief Tamsucky came up the stairs and appealed to the whites to come down. He told Mrs. Whitman that they were going to set fire to the mission house and that he wanted to save them. Narcissa, full of trust, said "God has raised us up a friend," and led her little band down the stairs.

By this time Mrs. Whitman was so weak that it was decided to carry her down on the settee. As soon as she was outside, the Indians opened fire. One bullet shattered Mrs. Whitman's cheek and another pierced her body. Then her dead body was pushed off the settee and thrown into the mud. As a final act of revenge, Mrs. Whitman's once lovely reddish hair which was always combed back and twisted in a neat knot was yanked back and her upturned face was slapped by a leather quirt. By the end of the massacre, of the seventy-four people who had been at the Whitman Mission, fourteen had been killed, two had died of natural causes, eight including the two half-bloods had escaped, and the Manson and Malin children, who had Hudson's Bay Company parents, had been released. Forty-seven were taken captive.[19]

Fortunately for the captives, Peter Hall, who had been working on the new addition to the mission house, was able to escape during the confusion. He made his way to the river and hid himself in the willows along the banks. When it was dark, he started on foot for Fort Nez Percés and arrived there early the next morning. He told William McBean, the Hudson's Bay Company's factor, what had happened at Waiilatpu and urged him to send out a rescue party. McBean replied that he was under-staffed and his small party of men certainly could not cope with the Cayuses on the rampage. In some accounts, McBean has been severely criticized for his attitude, particularly since he was a Roman Catholic and it was a Protestant mission that had been outraged.

McBean did all that he believed was possible. He wrote immediately to Ogden and Douglas at Fort Vancouver, informed them of the tragedy, and gave instructions to his messenger not to tell anyone along the way about the massacre for fear of arousing the Indians of the lower Columbia. He then sent his interpreter to Waiilatpu to inform Chief Tiloukaikt "that his young men had already gone too far by killing Dr. Whitman, his lady, and the rest," and that he "wanted him to spare the poor women and children."[20]

Ogden and Douglas did not receive news of what had happened at Waiilatpu until December 6, 1847. Undoubtedly they were momentarily in a quandary about what they should do. After all, they were repre-sentatives of a foreign business firm in American territory, and the casualties at the Whitman Mission were American nationals. The Cayuses had released the Manson boys and David Malin out of respect for the Company. Both Ogden and Douglas knew, however, that the Americans could not handle this problem immediately, and time was of the essence in order to save the captives. The United States had not yet formed an Oregon Territorial government although George Abernethy was attempting to bring law and order to the country as head of the provisional governmental organization. It was decided that Ogden should deal with the Indians, but what would happen if he failed? The Hudson's Bay Company and its men were already disliked by many, and if Ogden's entreaties caused the natives to kill their hostages, the Company might be held responsible.

It did not take Douglas and Ogden long to decide that humanity must come first and that they must take the risk. On December 7, 1847, Douglas wrote the Governor:

Having received intelligence last night, by special express, from Walla Walla of the destruction of the missionary settlement at Waiilatpu by the Cayuse Indians of that place, we hasten to communicate the particulars of that dreadful event—one of the most atrocious which darkens the annals of Indian crime . . . Mr. Ogden, with a strong party, will leave this place as soon as possible for Walla Walla, to endeavour to prevent further evil; and we beg to suggest to you the propriety of taking instant measures for the protection of the Rev. Mr. Spalding, who, for the sake of his family, ought to abandon the Clear Water Mission without delay, and retire to a place of safety, as he cannot remain at that isolated station without running imminent risk in the present and irritable state of the Indian population.[21]

Ogden lost no time in trying to rescue the captives. He left Fort Vancouver on December 7, within twenty-four hours of the arrival of the McBean letter. Ogden and sixteen men moved up the Columbia in two boats and reached Walla Walla on December 12.[22] Ogden immediately sent runners to all of the major Indian camps inviting the principal chiefs to a council to discuss the question of the Whitman hostages. He also sent a messenger to Lapwai, the Clear Water Mission, to urge the Spaldings to leave their mission and meet him at Walla Walla, where they would be safe in case the Nez Percés decided to go on the rampage.

When the chiefs were all assembled, Ogden with a serious countenance and deliberate voice, spoke to them in a very straightforward manner:

I regret that all the Chiefs I asked for are not present, two being absent. I expect the words I am about to address you will be reported to them and your young men, on your return to your camps.

We are traders and a different nation from the Americans. But recollect we supply you with ammunition, not to kill the Americans. They are of the same color as ourselves, speak the same language, children of the same God, and humanity makes our hearts bleed when we behold you using them so cruelly. Besides the revolting Butchery, have not the Indians pillaged, ill-treated, and insulted their women when peaceably making their way to the Willamette? As Chiefs, ought you to have connived at such conduct on the part of your young men? You tell me the young men committed these deeds without your knowledge? If you allow them to govern you, you are a set of Hermaphrodites and unworthy of the appelation of men or Chiefs. You young, hot-headed men, I know you pride yourselves upon your bravery and think no one can match you. Do not deceive yourselves. If you get the Americans to commence once, you will repent it, and war will not end until every one of you is cut off the face of the earth. I am aware that a good many of your friends and relatives have died through sickness. The Indians of other places have shared the same fate. It is not Dr. Whitman that has poisoned, but God has commanded that they should die. We are weak mortals and must submit. I trust you avail yourselves of the opportunity by doing so. It may prove advantageous to you, but at the same time remember you alone will be responsible for the consequences. It is merely advice I give you. We have nothing to do with it. I have not come here to make you promises or hold out assistance. We have nothing to do with your quarrels. We remain neutral. On my return, if you wish it, I shall do all I can for you, but I do not promise you to prevent war. If you deliver me up all prisoners I shall pay you for them on being delivered, but let it not be said among you afterwards that I deceived you.

I and Mr. Douglas represent the Company, but I tell you once more we promise you nothing. We sympathize with those poor people and wish to return them to their friends and relatives by paying you for them. My request on behalf of the families concerns you, so decide for yourselves.

With this admonition, Ogden sat down.

The first Indian leader to answer Ogden's speech was Young Chief, and he apparently had been swayed by Ogden's sensible, direct approach:

I arise! to thank you for your words. You white Chiefs command obedience with those that have to do with you. It is not so with us. Our young men are strongheaded and foolish. Formerly we had experienced good Chiefs. These are laid in the dust. The descendants of my father were the only good Chiefs. Though we made war with other tribes yet we always looked, and ever will look, upon the whites as our brothers. Our blood is mixed with yours. My heart bleeds for the death of so many good Chiefs I have known. For the demands made by you, the old Chief Toloquwet is here, speak to him. As regards myself, I am willing to give up the families.

Toloquwet then spoke: "As far as war we have seen little of it. We know the white to be our best friends, who have all along prevented us from killing each other. That is the reason why we avoid getting into war with them, and why we do not wish to be separated from them. Besides the tie of blood, the whites have shown us convincing proof of their attachment to us by burying their dead long side of ours." Then Toloquwet looked at Ogden, the squaw man, with an affection that only long years of acquaintance and understanding could bring and said, "Chief, your words are weighty. Your hairs are gray. We have known you a long time. You have had an unpleasant trip to this place. I cannot therefore keep these families back. I make them over to you, which I would not do to another younger than yourself."[23]

While the messenger from Walla Walla was on his way to inform Ogden and Douglas of the tragedy, the captives were undergoing extreme hardships. To make their punishment even more severe, no one was allowed to gather up the bodies of their dead friends and relatives. In mud and pools of water stained red with blood, the women and children were forced to pass by the mangled bodies of their loved ones.[24] Father Brouillet happened to visit the Whitman Mission on November 31, two days after the murders, and he reported: "I found five or six women and over thirty children in a condition deplorable beyond description. Some had lost their husbands, and the others their fathers, whom they had seen massacred before their eyes, and were expecting every moment to share the same fate. After the first few words that could be exchanged under the circumstances, I enquired after the victims, and was told that they were yet unburied. Joseph Stanfield . . . [who] had been spared by the Indians, was engaged in washing the corpses, but being alone he was unable to bury them. I resolved to go and assist him, so as to render those unfortunate victims the last service in my power to offer them." When the priest saw the Cayuses' victims, he said: "What a sight did I then behold! Ten bodies lying here and there, covered with blood and bearing the marks of the most atrocious cruelty—some pierced with balls, others more or less gashed by the hatchet. Dr. Whitman had received three gashes on the face. Three others had their skulls crushed so that their brains were oozing out."[25]

The Indians found several of the mission women attractive and decided to take them as their wives. Chief Five Crows, who had not taken part in the massacre, did succumb to the beauty of Lorinda Bewley, and eleven days after the Indian attack, he ordered her to be brought to his lodge on the Umatilla River. Hugh Bancroft described her experience: "Having no one to protect her, she was torn from the arms of sympathizing women, placed on a horse, and in the midst of a high fever of both mind and body, was carried through a November snow-storm to the arms of this brawny savage." Five Crows behaved generally in a gentlemanly manner and allowed Miss Bewley to spend part of her time at the home of the Catholic bishop nearby. Soon these virtues gave way to lust, and "nightly she was dragged from Blanchet's presence to the lodge of her lord, the priests powerless to interfere."[26]

While the hostages were experiencing physical indignity and Ogden and his men were pushing up the Columbia on their rescue mission, Governor George Abernethy began to take action. On the afternoon of December 8, after receiving James Douglas' news of the disaster at Waiilatpu, the Governor addressed the legislature. Immediately a resolution was adopted requiring him to raise and equip a company of riflemen, not to exceed fifty men and officers, who were to be dispatched to The Dalles to protect that mission. By noon on December 9 the company was equipped as well as possible from the resources on hand and assembled in front of the City Hotel, where they received a flag from the ladies of Oregon City. The cannon was fired, and the city's inhabitants cheered as the riflemen accompanied by Governor Abernethy and the commissioners, who had been appointed by the legislature to negotiate a loan with the Hudson's Bay Company, moved up the Willamette and headed for Fort Vancouver.

The arrival of the loan commissioners, Jesse Applegate, A. L. Lovejoy, and George L. Curry, put James Douglas in a difficult position. Douglas knew that the Oregon government had no official standing, and he knew, too, that the American settlers with their meager knowledge of native ways were sufficiently well equipped to provoke an Indian war. He and the Hudson's Bay Company had no desire for a war which would ruin the Indian trade and perhaps even cause the destruction of several interior posts. He also believed that a contribution to the American war effort would destroy the mutual understanding that the Company had enjoyed with the natives for so long. Of more immediate importance, the appearance of a well-armed militia in Indian country might jeopardize the success of Ogden's mission. Consequently, Douglas wrote to the commissioners:

With a deep feeling of the importance of the object which has procured me the honor of your present visit, and the necessity of the measures contemplated for the punishment of the Cayuse Indians and for the future protection of the country, I can on the present occasion only repeat the assurance verbally given in our conversation of yesterday, that I have no authority to grant loans or make advances whatsoever on account of the Hudson's Bay Company, my orders on that point being so positive that I cannot deviate from them without assuming a degree of responsibility which no circumstances could justify to my own mind. It is, however, in accordance with the spirit and letter of my instructions from the Hudson's Bay Company, to exert their whole power and influence in maintaining the peace of the country, and in protecting the white population from Indian outrage. The force equipped and despatched, at their sole expense, to Walla Walla, under the command of Mr. Ogden, immediately on receiving the intelligence of the disastrous events at Waiilatpu, is an earnest of our attention to the calls of humanity.[27]

Everyone worried during the latter part of December because little news of Ogden and the Cayuses was forthcoming. At this time, a report began to circulate that the disgruntled Cornelius Gilliam, formerly a captain in the Florida Indian wars and now a colonel-commandant of the Oregon Riflemen, was indignant at the refusal of the Hudson's Bay Company to furnish $100,000 worth of supplies on credit to the Oregon government. Therefore, he was determined to take Fort Vancouver by force and to let his regiment take what they needed from the Company's store. Douglas, hearing this report, placed guns in the bastions and made other preparations for the defense of the great Columbia River depot. Fortunately, through the good offices of Governor Abernethy, Gilliam's bad temper was soothed.

James Douglas, Governor Abernethy, and the captives were not the only ones suffering at this time. Ogden sat apprehensively at Fort Nez Percés. He had held his council with the chiefs on December 24, and although Young Chief and Chief Toloquwet had agreed to release the captives, he had not heard from the other chiefs who must be considered. Each day the tension mounted as the silence continued, and Ogden wrote on December 31, "I have endured many an anxious hour and for the last two nights have not closed my eyes."[28] On that very day, however, the Indians delivered up their sickly and terrified prisoners in exchange for sixty-two three-point blankets, sixty-three cotton shirts, twelve guns, six hundred loads of ammunition, thirty-seven pounds of tobacco, and twelve flints as well as seven oxen and sixteen bags of coarse flour. Ogden considered this to be "a heavy sacrifice in goods, but these are indeed of trifling value compared to the unfortunate beings I have rescued from these murderous wretches, and I feel truly happy."[29]

On the following day, January 1, 1848, the Reverend Spalding, his wife, and other refugees from the Clearwater Mission arrived. Ogden had sent an order to the Nez Percés Indians to deliver them to him at Walla Walla. As a result, the Spaldings, who had not been harmed, moved through the Cayuse country escorted by forty Nez Percés. Upon their arrival, the Spaldings found their "daughter at Fort Walla Walla, with the ransomed captives, too weak to stand, a mere skeleton, and her mind as much impaired as her health." However, "Oh! what a meeting! remnants of large and happy families! But our tears of grief were mingled with those of joy. We had not dared to hope that deliverance would come so soon and complete."[30]

Ogden lost no time in removing the captives and refugees from Walla Walla for fear that the Indians might change their minds. On January 2, the party pushed off in three boats up the Columbia to safety and security. The weather was so good that even with sick passengers aboard, the Ogden party was able to reach Fort Vancouver by January 8.

Douglas was elated, and, as he and Ogden talked, they both thanked God that their calculated risk had been justified. Douglas lost no time in informing Governor Abernethy of Ogden's success: "Mr. Ogden has this moment arrived with three boats from Walla Walla and I rejoice to say he has brought down all the women and children from Waiilatpu, Mr. and Mrs. Spalding and Mr. Stanley [the artist who had been sketching in the interior] ... Mr. Ogden will visit the Falls on Monday and give you every information in his power respecting the Indians in the interior. The Cayuses, Walla Wallas, Nez Percés, and Yakimas are said to have entered into an alliance for mutual defense."[31]

January 8 was a Sunday, and when Douglas' courier arrived in Oregon City, he found the Governor at church. The news, however, was of such great importance to this struggling American colony on the Pacific Coast that the dispatch was immediately delivered to the governor and then read to the entire congregation. On the following day, Ogden delivered the ransomed captives to Governor Abernethy, as James Douglas had promised. When the Ogden party pushed off from Fort Vancouver and down the Columbia into the mouth of the Willamette River, the citizens of Portland cheered and a salute was fired, and even greater rejoicing greeted them as they arrived at Oregon City, the capital of the provisional Oregon Territory.

Ogden was now a regional hero. On January 17, Governor Abernethy wrote to Ogden in an attempt to express the general attitude of the people of Oregon:

I feel it a duty as well as a pleasure to tender you my sincere thanks, and the thanks of this community. . . . From this state I am full satisfied we could not relieve them. A small party of Americans would have been looked upon with contempt; a large party would have been a signal for a general massacre. Your immediate departure from Vancouver on receipt of the intelligence from Waiilatpu enabling you to arrive at Walla Walla before the news of the American party having started from this reached them, together with your influence over the Indians, accomplished the desirable object of relieving the distressed. Your exertions on behalf of the prisoners will no doubt cause a feeling of pleasure to you through life, but this does not relieve them nor us from the obligations we are under to you. You have also laid the American government under obligation to you, for their citizens were the subjects of the massacre.[32]

The Reverend Henry Spalding also praised Ogden and wrote to him annually on the anniversary of the captives' salvation. Spalding believed that Ogden's actions were virtually an Act of God:

I can not but notice the interposing hand of Heaven throughout this great enterprise, without which the strongest earthly man would have been unavailing. We notice it in disposing the ferocious savages to listen to your words and give up the captive women and children, especially the young women the objects of their strongest passions; in disposing the treacherous Nez Percés to allow me to leave their country; in holding back the murderous Cayuse while we were passing through their country, and overcoming the winds and weather so favorably while the boats were passing down the river; and in sparing the lives of all although so many were sick.[33]

Not only Americans applauded Ogden's actions. When Governor Simpson, who usually was grudging in his praise, received the news, he wrote: "The promptitude with which Mr. Chief Factor Ogden went to the assistance of the unfortunate captives is highly commendable and the success that attended his mission reflects much credit to his management. Humanity seemed to dictate that measure: and your determination to maintain a strict neutrality in the subsequent hostile proceedings was highly judicious."[34] An even greater accolade came from the Governor and Committee in London:

We highly approve of the prompt measures which you adopted, and which were so successfully carried into effect by Mr. Ogden, for rescuing the subjects of the United States who had fallen into the hands of the Savages. The cause of humanity required the friendly interposition of the Company in behalf of these unfortunate persons, who, probably could not otherwise have escaped a cruel death, and it had afforded us the sincerest gratification that this interposition proved effectual through the influence possessed over the natives by one of the Company's officers. Such influence is never obtainable without being well deserved, and is therefore highly honourable to Mr. Ogden.[35]

Ogden took all this praise modestly, and, as the Reverend Spalding had predicted, "No earthly treasure or human praise could have any weight in his benevolent mind."[36] He enjoyed a deep inner satisfaction from the rescue, but outwardly he was somewhat embarrassed and deprecatory: "I was the mere acting agent of the Hudson's Bay Company; for without its powerful aid and influence nothing could have been effected, and to them the praise is due."[37] Yet Ogden would have been pleased to know that sixty-nine years after his death, his fearless efforts in 1847 were still remembered. On October 28, 1923, members and friends of the Oregon State Historical Society, the Oregon Pioneer Association, and the Sons and Daughters of Oregon Pioneers gathered at the green and peaceful Mountain View Cemetery in Oregon City to pay homage to Oregon's great benefactor. He would have been even more pleased if he could have seen his granddaughter, Mrs. Thomas Draper, and her husband and his great-grandson, Henry Draper, in the audience. He would also have been delighted to have watched the eighty-six-year-old Gertrude Jane Hall, then Mrs. O. N. Denny, the little ten-year-old girl whom he had rescued from Waiilatpu, unveil the memorial stone which eloquently marked his grave with the simple inscription: "Peter Skene Ogden, 1794–1854. Born at Quebec. Died at Oregon City. Fur trader and explorer in Old Oregon. Arrived Columbia River 1818. Clerk of North West Company. Chief Factor Hudson's Bay Company at Fort Vancouver. Rescued survivors of Whitman Massacre, 1847."[38] What more could a man ask?

The Years of Tension

EVEN THOUGH OGDEN WAS CONSIDERED a hero as a result of his actions following the Whitman Massacre, he found conducting the Company's business in American territory becoming more and more difficult year by year. His popularity of December, 1847, remained in January, 1848, but he still had critics among the Yankee settlers. Now that all the hostages were safe, some people began to question Ogden's motives and methods in securing the release of the captives. W. H. Gray wrote:

> Mr. Ogden, distinctly, and at several times, insisted upon the distinction necessary to be made between the affairs of the Americans and the company, and why? Simply, because the company had determined to suppress and crush the American settlements, if it could be done, by the Indians. They were now in a condition to furnish the Indians directly or clandestinely, through their Jesuit missionaries, all the ammunition required. Hence the liberality of Mr. Ogden, and the care of Mr. Douglas to catch a "rumor" to defend Mr. Ogden's course; to manifest great sympathy for the sufferers, to deceive the settlement in every way possible; and refuse, under the plea of the "stringent rules of the home department," to supply munitions to the provisional troups.[1]

Gray was referring to Ogden's giving ammunition to the Indians at The Dalles who helped him make the portage upstream on his way to Fort Nez Percés, and the guns and six hundred loads of ammunition that he was forced to pay as part of the ransom for the hostages. Too, some settlers were still angry about Douglas' refusal to supply Colonel Gilliam's men with goods from Fort Vancouver. Ogden knew human nature, not only of the red men but of the white men, and he had foreseen widespread repercussions from the Whitman Massacre.

Three days after the news of the atrocities at Waiilatpu had reached the Oregon provisional legislature, a resolution was passed to raise a militia, and by December 14 a peace commission composed of Robert Newell, H. A. G. Lee, and General Joel Palmer had been formed. The peace commission left Champoeg on January 29, 1848, and by February 10 they met Gilliam's forces camped at The Dalles. "On the 11th the field officers and commissioner held a council and agreed on the future plan of carrying on the war,"[2] the so-called Cayuse War. In no Indian war did the white men behave with as much humanity toward the enemy as in the war of the early settlers of Oregon with the Cayuses, mostly on account of the work of the peace commissioners and the growing apathy among the troops. By the summer of 1848 most people were satisfied with having driven many of the Indians into the mountains and having taken possession of Waiilatpu and Wascopam. Skirmishes did continue, however, and it was not until 1850 when the Cayuses surrendered five Indians who were subsequently hanged that the Cayuse War is considered to have ended.[3] Now Indian problems were temporarily solved, and American settlers could return their thoughts to domestic considerations.

The Cayuse War as a military exercise was unimportant, but it seems to have brought the American population in Oregon closer together and developed a greater spirit of nationalism. Antagonism toward the Hudson's Bay Company became greater than it had been in the days before the boundary settlement. The old economic and political antagonisms were now joined by an even stronger force—religion. Ogden and many of his fellow officers were Anglicans, but most of the Hudson's Bay Company's employees with their French Canadian background were Roman Catholics. When Dr. McLoughlin converted to Catholicism, many of his fellow citizens of Oregon City who were Protestants became convinced that he and the Company were their religious enemies. It was easy for many of the evangelical Americans to combine ancient animosities into a charge that the Hudson's Bay Company had conspired with Roman Catholic priests to massacre the Protestant Whitmans.

Fortunately for the Company, men of the stature of Ogden and Douglas were on the Board of Management. They could not prevent the growth of American hostility, but they certainly retarded it. In a region where they represented a "foreign monopoly" and were a minority,[4] their personalities and conduct commanded the respect of the more responsible Americans. Such comments as that by the prominent Jesse Applegate, "I hope to visit the white settlements in the course of the summer and the greatest pleasure of the visit I expect to derive from paying my respects to you,"[5] were not uncommon. Also, because of their co-operation with the American military forces in Oregon, the company leaders gained the support of the army. The commanding general, Persifer Smith, had nothing but praise for Ogden and the Hudson's Bay Company: "We and our fellow citizens who have proceeded us have experienced so much and such immeasurable kindness from the officers of your company, and yourself in particular, that we must always rejoice when an opportunity occurs of recording our acknowledgements."[6]

Again fortunately for the Hudson's Bay Company, a continuing population increase in Oregon that would have made the Company's position even more difficult was checked by an event which took place at Captain John Sutter's sawmill at Coloma, California, on January 24, 1848—the discovery of gold.

News of the discovery of gold in California was slow to reach the eastern United States, and attention was not focused on it until Lieutenant Lucien Losser arrived in Washington, D.C., with Governor Mason's official report and a tea caddy containing $3,000 worth of gold. Then on December 5, 1848, President Polk officially notified Congress of the discovery, and the rush was on. The Oregonians learned of the discovery much earlier when Captain Newell in the little schooner *Honolulu* arrived on the Columbia on July 31, 1848. His report was corroborated on August 9 when the brig *Henry* arrived from San Francisco. When he reached Fort Vancouver aboard the Company's brig *Mary Dare*, James Douglas was skeptical about the gold discoveries, but gold madness had already seized Oregon's citizens. On August 24, the *Oregon Spectator* reported: "Quite a number of our fellow-citizens are leaving and preparing to leave for the gold mines of the Sacramento."[7] Certainly many more people were ready to leave for the mines than had volunteered to fight the Cayuses.

The first persons to leave Oregon for California used pack trains, but in September a wagon company was organized. Fifty ox-drawn wagons were loaded with provisions and mining equipment, and Peter H. Burnett, who was later California's first governor, was elected captain. The party followed the Old South Road through the Umpqua and Rogue River valleys, then went southward to Klamath Lake. From here they moved southward and were soon following Peter Lassen's new Lassen Cutoff.[8] On October 1, 1848, after watching the hysteria sweeping the Northwest, Ogden estimated that two thousand people had already left Oregon for the Sacramento area.[9]

By the spring of 1849 the gold fever had reached the East, and men were throwing up their jobs and rushing westward, either overland or by the various water routes. Almost 40,000 forty-niners came to California in that year. Ogden, at Fort Vancouver, was pleased that the discovery of gold had changed the direction of immigration from Oregon to California. He calculated that only 200 Americans had come to Oregon that year, whereas 20,000 immigrants had passed Fort Hall on the way to California.[10]

The Company also suffered from the California gold rush. Prices of much needed equipment and food stuffs rose steeply, and people clamored to buy regardless of cost. The price of lumber rose from $16 to $65 per thousand feet, and wages skyrocketed. Unskilled laborers received from $5 to $10 per day. Sailors demanded and received $150 a month. Still there was a shortage of labor. Many Company servants deserted, and Indians were employed in their place.

On the plus side, California gold flowed into Fort Vancouver, creating a very favorable balance of trade. On the whole, 1849 was a good year for Ogden and the Hudson's Bay Company. They faced the usual difficulties of a corporation in a foreign land, but the first territorial governor, Joseph Lane, who arrived in March, 1849, was personally friendly to the Company. Governor Lane had 161 regular troops at his disposal. He meant to keep law and order, and he intended to see that the Company's rights under the Oregon treaty were respected. Thus, in 1849, Ogden and Douglas, the latter of whom had since departed for his new post on Vancouver Island, had a feeling of well-being.

Although the Governor remained friendly toward the Company, during his long political career, Oregon settlers and certain other officials harassed Ogden and the Company. As early as 1847, William Fraser Tolmie at Fort Nisqually complained that "one Smith" (Lyon A. Smith) had squatted on land owned by the Puget's Sound Agricultural Company. By 1851 there were twenty-eight alleged trespassers, and by 1853 the number had increased to fifty. In 1851 the Company's land around Fort Vancouver had virtually all been taken over by squatters. More would have been taken sooner if Colonel W. W. Loring, commander of the troops and a friend of Ogden's and the Hudson's Bay Company had not designated Fort Vancouver and the land immediately around it as a military reservation.

Even more vexing than squatters were tax collectors. In the spring of 1849, John Adair arrived at Astoria to serve as the first American collector of customs. The zealous Adair decided in April, when the Hudson's Bay Company's bark *Columbia* entered the river after which she was named, to levy duties not only on the goods destined for Fort Vancouver, but also on those destined for New Caledonia in Company territory. Ogden, Simpson, and the Governor and Committee were outraged. In February, 1850, Simpson placed the problem before William M. Meredith, the American secretary of the treasury, who agreed to let goods in bond destined for delivery north of the forty-ninth parallel pass duty free.

Ogden's problems were by no means settled. He had to reckon with the machinations in Washington of Samuel R. Thurston, the first Oregon delegate to Congress. Thurston was said to have "introduced into Oregon the vituperative and invective style of debate, and mingled with it a species of coarse blackguardism such as no Kentucky ox driver or Missouri flatboatman might hope to excell." Too, "he was a man of such impulsive, harsh traits, that he would often carry college feuds to extremities."[11] Thurston hated the Hudson's Bay Company, and he now began to put pressure on Secretary Meredith. As a result, in May, 1850, the Treasury Department prohibited any trade between Fort Victoria on the English Vancouver Island and Fort Nisqually on the American Puget Sound. This order hurt the Company considerably. It forced all Company vessels to visit Astoria first for custom inspection. This took them 350 miles off course, subjected them to crossing the hazardous Columbia sandbar twice, and made them pay heavy piloting fees at the custom's port.

The Company had also another enemy, Simpson P. Moses, the first customs collector at Olympia in what is now the state of Washington.[12] Moses was unscrupulous, and he wanted to be popular with the extreme "patriots" in the Puget Sound area. His first opportunity came when the Company's ships *Beaver* and *Mary Dare* arrived at Fort Nisqually on November 27, 1851. Chief Factor John Work and his family as well as Rose Birnie, sister of James Birnie, who had recently arrived from England, disembarked at the Puget Sound post. The next day Work went back on board, and the two ships set out for Olympia for customs inspection. Several days later when William Fraser Tolmie, who was in charge of the Company's business in this area, visited Moses, he was shocked to learn that Moses had confiscated the *Mary Dare* because she had a package of refined sugar on board weighing less than six hundred pounds. According to Moses, this was a violation of an act of Congress, passed in 1799, which provided for the forfeiture of the vessel in such a case.

Tolmie was even more shocked when he learned that the Company's steamer *Beaver* had been confiscated on the pretext of having entered Olympia with ballast when in fact she had no ballast aboard. To make his case stronger, Moses later added that he had seized the *Beaver* because Miss Birnie and the Work family had disembarked at Nisqually without having first been cleared at the port of entry. Tolmie quickly appealed to the courts for a hearing, but Moses released the *Beaver* before a hearing could take place. Eventually the Company received $1,000 as compensation for its losses connected with the seizure of the *Beaver*. While Tolmie's attorney, Samuel B. Marye of Olympia, was preparing an appeal to the American secretary of the treasury, Moses released the *Mary Dare* under a $13,000 bond. By this time William Meredith had been succeeded by Thomas Corwin as secretary of the treasury. Corwin ordered that the bond and the over two hundred pounds of sugar that had been seized be returned to the Company if the Company would pay the legal fees involved.[13]

Ogden and Simpson undoubtedly realized that such difficulties might arise after the boundary settlement, but even though navigation on the Columbia remained open to the nationals of both countries, they had not anticipated the difficulties in supplying the interior posts that arose after the Whitman massacre and during the Cayuse War. Consequently attention again turned to the Fraser River as a supply point for New Caledonia. Governor Simpson had envisioned this in 1828, but the terrain that he had explored had proved too difficult to be negotiated by brigades carrying supplies. In May, 1846, Alexander Caulfield Anderson also tried to find an easy route from Thompson River to Fort Langley near the mouth of the Fraser. He, too, found the journey to be very arduous, but in early 1848 he received word from Fort Vancouver "that we must break our way through to Langley, whither the supplies for the several Districts would be forwarded to meet us." The brigades of New Caledonia, Thompson River, and Colvile, with four hundred horses, many of them unbroken, and fifty men under Donald Manson made their way to Langley. In the following year a small post was built at Hope, and a rough trail was cut across the mountains.[14] Thus some strain was taken off the coastal trade, for this route was used until 1860, when it was greatly improved by the building of a government road.

Ogden found 1850 and 1851 to be distressing years. In addition to operational and international problems, he had been having continual labor difficulties since the beginning of the California gold rush. In May, 1850, he wrote that the *Mary Dare* had arrived and had begun unloading, but that four of the crewmen had already deserted and that the rest would probably go within the next few days, leaving him without any prospects of hiring new hands. His taut nerves and frustration began to show in some of his correspondence. Governor Simpson was shocked when Ogden criticized him in a letter, something that no one had ever had the temerity to do, and in reply Simpson wrote: "You are the first person, I believe with whom I have had business relations, who has complained of a want of punctuality on my part in correspondence, and I think you will find you have, in your own impatience, taxed me unjustly with neglecting to advise you on matters of importance."[15]

Ogden's troubles increased in 1851. Twenty years after the first epidemic, virulent malaria again struck the Columbia. In 1831, Ogden had just returned from the Snake country, and in his run-down condition, easily contracted the disease. Now, in 1851, at the age of sixty-one, he was in a weakened condition from overwork and tension, the reward of a position of responsibility, and in late summer once more he came down with malaria. With better treatment and medical facilities than during the previous epidemics, Ogden was sick for only two months.

When Ogden recovered from his illness, he found the situation brighter in that the Hudson's Bay Company's claim for compensation for their posts and rights south of the forty-ninth parallel might finally be settled by negotiation. Since July, 1850, when Daniel Webster had become the American secretary of state, the British prospects had looked more promising. In the fall of 1851, Justin Butterfield, the federal land commissioner, suggested that Congress take action for the "prompt, summary and final adjustment" of the Company's claims, and Anson Dart, the superintendent of Indian affairs, concurred.[16] Ogden was pleased that he might be going on Company business and perhaps play a role in selling the Company's "possessory rights" in a region that he had worked so long to develop.

In December, Ogden left Fort Vancouver in charge of John Ballenden and prepared to go East. He decided that a ship's voyage would be less arduous than an overland trip. Shipping traffic between San Francisco and New York City had developed greatly during the past few years. In 1848 mail contracts had been awarded to the United States Steamship Company for the New York to Chagres route and to the Pacific Mail Steamship Company for the Panama to San Francisco route. Better means of transportation had been developed, and traffic had greatly increased during the gold rush. Ogden sailed down the West Coast and arrived in San Francisco, about which he had often heard but had never really visited. San Francisco Bay had a very different appearance than when he had first seen it in 1831, twenty years earlier. San Francisco was now a thriving metropolis with hundreds of ships moored in her bay. And when he went to the Pacific Mail docks at First and Brannan streets, many hacks and drays were lined up, waiting for customers.[17]

Ogden's journey was not as pleasant as he had hoped. The ship was crowded, and the weather on the Pacific Coast was not particularly good. In fact, he wondered, like so many mariners before and since, why the Pacific was so named; he found it anything but pacific. As the ship proceeded southward and came adjacent to Costa Rica, the weather became much warmer and more humid, something Ogden had never experienced before. He had thought that eastern Oregon, Utah, and Nevada could be hot, but the heat in these southern waters was quite different; the high humidity made sweat cling to the skin and produced a sense of lethargy. When the ship arrived at Panama City even though Ogden was uncomfortably warm, he was intrigued by this sixteenth-century port as he looked at it through a maze of clotheslines.

From Panama City the travelers took mules over the trail that had been well worn by the forty-niners, an ancient footpath with many dangerous descents. When they finally reached Cruces in the Isthmian area, the mules were exchanged for "bongos," dugout canoes between fifteen and twenty-five feet long, dug out from a single mahogany log. Ogden was surprised that these boats were "operated" by Negroes who wore little clothing; sometimes the captain wore only a straw hat. How different they were from his own *voyageurs*, who donned their most elegant and colorful clothing before arriving at a Company post. As the bongos were poled down the Chagres, Ogden was amazed that the jungle on either side of the river was virtually impenetrable with its heavy vine covering which came down to the water's edge. Here and there he could see what were pointed out to him as banana trees with their yellow fruit pointing upward. The silence of the rain forest was interrupted by an occasional parrot call or the scrambling of monkeys, who peered curiously out from their leafy hiding places. This river was different from the mighty St. Lawrence or the Columbia, which were arteries for their given regions. The Chagres was more like the river that Ogden had discovered, the Humboldt—it was a small stream that led overland travelers across difficult country.

The trip in the bongo to Aspinwall at the mouth of the Chagres was hot and steamy, and Ogden was relieved when he finally reached his point of embarkation on the Caribbean and prepared to board a Pacific Mail Steamship Company's vessel to carry him on the next leg of his journey. Once out to sea, the weather became cooler, but not enough to suit Ogden: "I suffered from the heat. All I ever experienced before was a trifle compared with it. I now know what heat is—a hot burning sun accompanied us to within three days' sail of New York."

When Ogden reached New York City on January 20, 1852, the weather was a great contrast to that of Panama. He was greeted by freezing temperatures characteristic of the East Coast in winter. Thoughts of the weather of any kind left him when he saw his brother Henry standing on the pier. Henry, who was eight years older than he, had been born in New York City after the Ogden family had fled from their New Jersey home during the Revolutionary War. He had later returned to his birthplace, where he was the collector of customs for many years. Henry handled governmental funds efficiently, but he had trouble taking care of his own. On April 17, 1845, when Ogden was returning from England with his niece, he had loaned Henry money,[18] and he probably loaned him more now. He was fond of his older brother, and when he made out his will, he instructed his executors not to take any action to recover for his estate the money that Henry owed him; Henry was to consider the cancellation of the debts "as a Legacy."[19]

Ogden did not spend much time in New York City. He was eager to reach Canada and to visit the rest of his family, whom he had not seen for almost seven years. He set out posthaste and arrived at Lachine about January 27 or 28. There he had pleasant and informative visits with Sir George and Lady Simpson and with Edward Hopkins, Simpson's capable secretary. Ogden always thought of Edward not merely as part of the Company, but as the husband of his favorite niece, Annie. During the course of these conversations they all, especially Ogden, reminisced about the pleasant times that they had had in London together in 1845, and Lady Simpson reported: "When I told him [Ogden] this morning that I was writing home, he begged me to remember him most kindly there."[20]

Much had happened since those pleasant, yet apprehensive days in 1845. Then Ogden and Simpson had been enthusiastic about the prospect of taking possession of Cape Disappointment and had planned Warre and Vavsour's journey across the plains. In spite of all their efforts, Oregon had been lost to the United States, and the Company now was trying to hold on to its land and trade south of the forty-ninth parallel long enough to be able to sell out at a reasonable price, a time-consuming and frustrating task.

The life of his dearest relative had also greatly changed. Annie Ogden, at the time of her trip to the British Isles with her uncle Peter, had been only twenty-one years old. Now, seven years later, she was the wife of Edward Hopkins and lived comfortably at Lachine. Her health was not good, but she worked ardently to improve it after a miscarriage in 1848 which had been "quite a disappointment to them both, but especially to Edward." Her health did improve, and she gave birth to three sons, Edward Gouverneur, Peter Ogden, and Manley, the last named after Edward's well-known brother, the poet Gerard Manley Hopkins. Annie was a good wife and helped her husband greatly, and Edward's employer, Sir George, was "very fond of Annie, and admires her housekeeping talents so much that he consults her upon all points."[21]

When Ogden arrived at Lachine, however, Annie was not there. She had gone to Three Rivers to visit her parents during the last days of her pregnancy. Her father, Isaac, an old and respected inhabitant of this St. Lawrence town, had been born in New York City in 1783, but had preferred Canada to America. He was commissioned in the 56th Regiment of Foot and gained the rank of captain before he resigned his commission and became sheriff of Three Rivers.[22]

Annie's last days of confinement were ones of great sadness. About the middle of January, 1852, her mother, Elizabeth Walker Ogden, died suddenly after an illness of only twenty-four hours. When Ogden reached Three Rivers, even though Annie had just given birth to another son a few days before,[23] he found such sorrow in the family that he left immediately: "It was all gloom and did not suit me."[24] Ogden decided that since he could not enjoy a peaceful visit with his family at Three Rivers, he might as well go back to work. At Lachine, Ogden and Simpson had discussed seriously the question of a negotiated sale of the Company's possessory rights south of the forty-ninth parallel to the United States. Simpson told him that in January when he was planning to make a trip up the Ottawa River to the Fort Coulonge District, he had received word from London to visit Washington, D.C. While Ogden was at Lachine, Simpson began preparing for his February 2 departure.[25] It seems quite clear that during their conversations Simpson asked Ogden to accompany him to the United States capital.

The question of the sale of the Hudson's Bay Company's lands and rights had been brought up immediately after the boundary settlement, but discussion was postponed by the Mexican War. In 1850, when Daniel Webster became secretary of state, Ogden and higher Company officials had hoped for settlement, but for almost two years Webster's attention was engaged by other problems. Finally in the spring of 1852 conditions for a settlement seemed propitious, and Simpson was ordered to Washington with Ogden soon to follow him.

Webster's new interest in the Hudson's Bay Company sale was undoubtedly the result of the efforts of Robert J. Walker, the former zealous secretary of the treasury in the Polk cabinet. In March, 1852, the Company made an agreement with Walker to attempt to sell the Company's possessory rights to the United States government for the sum of one million dollars. If he was successful, he would receive a commission of 10 per cent. Walker worked hard, and soon Webster agreed. He insisted, however, that the settlement must be set forth in a convention specifying the relinquishment of British rights of navigation on the Columbia River. In England the Derby ministry had taken office in February, 1852, at the time that Simpson and Ogden were departing for Washington. It was a weak government destined to remain in power for less than a year. The ministers did not want to risk criticism for recalcitrance, especially at a time when Anglo-American relations were strained over the question of American fishing rights off the coast of British North America.[26]

Simpson traveled directly to Washington, but Ogden first visited New York City to conduct some Company business there. Simpson had asked him to purchase a cargo of stores to send out to the Columbia to John Ballenden, who was taking Ogden's place at Fort Vancouver during his absence. Ogden was amazed at the high prices of goods in the booming Atlantic port, but in his usual shrewd way, he took "great pains to select the best articles." One of his purchases was an extremely large cook stove for Fort Vancouver; Ogden thought it would be more economical to operate because it would use less wood than several smaller ones. He did not forget members of his family while conducting Company business. He took time off to buy clothes for his wife and two daughters, Sarah and Euretta. His effort illustrates a different side of Ogden's personality. The strong, self-willed Ogden was considerate and sentimental about his women folk: "I have selected the very best articles and hope they will give satisfaction." And like so many men through the ages, he added: "I had no time to get the dresses made nor could I with certainty give the proper sizes so they must excuse me." Then Ogden chartered the four-hundred-ton *Robert Benton* to carry the goods to the Columbia, and the ship started loading on May 29, 1852.

Ogden left for Washington to join Governor Simpson on that same day. He hoped not only to be able to aid in the sale of the Hudson's Bay and Puget's Sound Agricultural companies' claims, but to gain satisfaction and remuneration for the Company's losses from the Whitman Massacre and the Cayuse War. His discussions with the Secretary of the Treasury and with the Superintendent of Indian Affairs on the subject were unrewarding. Also, because of failure to agree on the question of the British relinquishment of navigational rights on the Columbia, Simpson and Ogden were unable to secure a settlement for the sale of the Company's possessory rights. Even though they failed, both Simpson and Ogden worked faithfully, and Ogden even visited the White House in an effort to influence Millard Fillmore, who had become President of the United States upon the death of Zachary Taylor in 1850. Ogden did not realize that six years later Fillmore would marry a distant relative of his, Carolyn Carmichael. Carolyn was the daughter of Lieutenant Alexander Carmichael and Mary Ogden, who like Ogden was descended from the eighteenth-century David Ogden of Morristown, New Jersey.[27] Fillmore was unsympathetic, and the question of the Hudson's Bay Company sale dragged on, through the Civil War and Reconstruction. Simpson and Ogden did all they could to bring about a settlement in 1852, but Ogden had been in his grave for almost seventeen years and Simpson in his for eleven, before a solution was finally reached.[28]

In Washington, Ogden met many people, one of whom was Elwood Evans, who later wrote a history of Oregon and Washington. The nation's capital was still a relatively small city in 1852, and most of the politicians, military officers, and members of the elite frequented the same restaurants. One evening Ogden was delighted to see in a hotel dining room Mr. Drayton, who had been a close companion of his when the Wilkes Expedition was on the Columbia in 1841. He was further pleased that "Old Drayton . . . at first sight recognized me." He also met again many of the army officers with whom he had become acquainted when they were stationed at Fort Vancouver. With the renewal of these old associations his stay in Washington was made somewhat more pleasant. Ogden, however, was eager to leave the American capital, and, as he made his preparations to depart, he said, "trust I bid adieu to Washington forever."[29]

On June 6, 1852, Ogden left Washington and began his return trip to Lachine. He looked forward to visiting with his friends and relatives in Canada, but he was becoming impatient to return to his own family on the Columbia. He wrote to London asking permission to go back to the Pacific Coast, but word was slow in coming because of the death of John Pelly, governor of the Hudson's Bay Company and director of the Bank of England, on August 13.[30] One month after Pelly's death, on September 13, 1852, Ogden wrote his son-in-law Archibald McKinlay: "I can therefore at present say nothing decisive, in what capacity or when it will be in my power to return *back*. I shall therefore not disappoint you by stating any particular date. I wish to have all finally settled before." Then in typical Ogden fashion, he added: "Remember me kindly to all; to Allan Campbell Holbrook—tell the latter to have some good Brandy ready for me when I arrive—I intend to take him by surprise."[31]

It was some time before Ogden could again enjoy Holbrook's brandy. It was not until February 5, 1853, that Ogden was again in New York City and ready to board the *Georgia* for his trip home. He undoubtedly dreaded the thought of the long voyage—2,500 miles to the uninspiring little port of Aspinwall (named for William H. Aspinwall who pioneered Isthmian transportation), then 60 miles across Panama, and 3,500 miles from Panama City to San Francisco before he could begin the last leg of his journey to the Columbia. Too, conditions were crowded. Thousands of people in the East were still intrigued by the thought of California gold, and it is estimated that over seventeen thousand people made the same trip that Ogden took in 1853.[32]

The *Georgia* sailed from New York City on February 7 and arrived at Aspinwall in good time, on the morning of February 16. Then Ogden

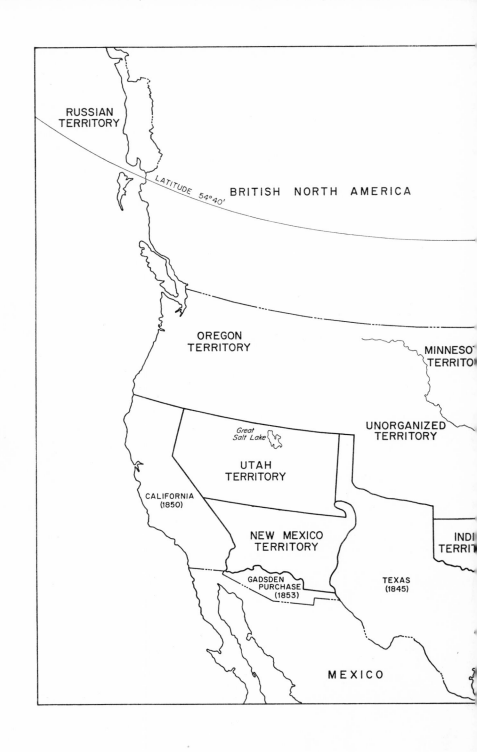

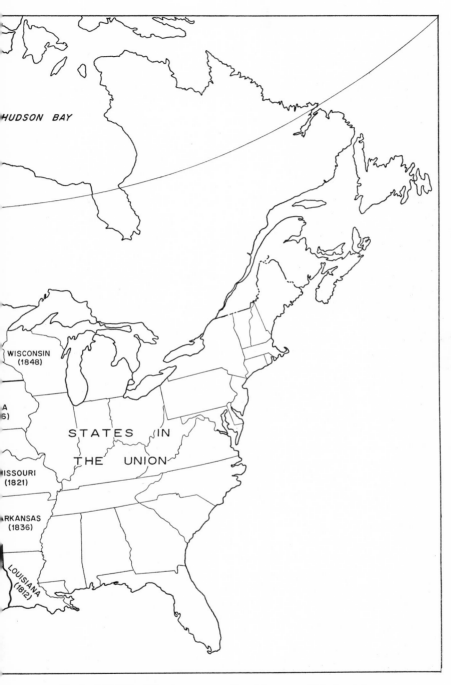

HUDSON BAY

WISCONSIN
(1848)

A
6)

STATES IN

THE UNION

MISSOURI
(1821)

ARKANSAS
(1836)

LOUISIANA
(1812)

Ogden's Political Environment, 1854 (the year of his death)

and his fellow passengers began the arduous boat and mule trek across the Isthmus to Panama City. By the afternoon of February 19, he, along with six hundred other travelers, were jamming the deck of the *Tennessee* as she pushed out into the Pacific and headed north. On February 26 the *Tennessee* entered the beautiful, natural harbor of Acapulco and made her way between the shoals bathed in sea spray and the spectacular rocky cliffs that have attracted modern-day tourists. Ogden saw the sun-drenched, white beaches stretching for miles and the little fort perched on top of the hill that once protected the Manila galleons as they came and went from the New Spanish coast with their exotic cargoes.

After rapidly recoaling, the *Tennessee* was again on her way, and by the early hours of Sunday morning, March 6, she was groping her way through a shroud of fog which hid the entrance to San Francisco Bay. Shortly after nine o'clock as Ogden was sitting down to his breakfast, he heard a great crash and felt the little steamer shudder as she was halted abruptly. Then pandemonium broke out. Officers shouted orders. The paddlewheels were thrown into reverse, and people and dishes in the saloon were thrown about while bells clanged the alarm. The *Tennessee* had gone aground on the rocky California coast just four and one-half miles north of the Golden Gate.

A camp was made on shore and passengers were told that they could either stay there to wait for transportation or walk over the steep hills to San Francisco Bay to a boat for San Francisco. Ogden, now sixty-three years old, elected to push on, although most of the passengers, approximately five hundred in number, remained behind. He was, however, in a dilemma. He had several thousand dollars in gold coins in a locked valise. It was too heavy for him to carry to San Francisco Bay. Finally he unlocked his suitcase, put soiled clothing on top of the coins, and let a pair of old, half-worn shoes hang out in plain sight, hoping that anyone with thieving tendencies would believe that an unlocked case contained nothing of value. Ogden was right. When he returned to the camp, he found that the trunks had all been opened and rifled, "but the thieves had not touched his satchel, which lay on the ground just as he had left it." Ogden took a particular delight in outsmarting the thieves and loved to tell the story. When he repeated this incident to General James C. Strong, he chuckled and twisted his lips as he always did when he was pleased.[33]

On March 13, Ogden headed for home. He boarded the steamer *Columbia*, and on the evening of March 16 he arrived at Astoria at the mouth of his beloved Columbia River, after an absence of fourteen months. He was delighted to be home again with his wife, Julia, and to see his favorite daughter, Sarah Julia McKinlay, and to welcome into the family her fifth child, a daughter, Sarah Ellen, who had been born during his absence.

Taking over the Company's business once more was not quite so pleasant. The stillness of the forest was now broken almost constantly by the resounding blows of axes, and the blue sky was overcast by the billowy smoke clouds which rose from the fires the farmers set to tree stumps and underbrush in order to clear the land for cultivation. Oregon City was becoming a "metropolis" with three hotels, and Portland, across the river from Fort Vancouver, was a beehive of construction activity. Also, while Ogden had been away, gold had been discovered in the Rogue and Umpqua valleys, and miners from California, who had been displaced by the shift from placer to quartz mining in that region moved in. The Indians were dislocated, and the result was the short but bloody Rogue River War.

Political developments were keeping pace with settlement and population expansion. While Ogden was sailing up the Pacific Coast in the ill-fated *Tennessee,* President Fillmore signed the bill creating Washington Territory. This did not have any great immediate effect upon Ogden and the Company. Soon, however, Governor Isaac I. Stevens, a West Point graduate who had been in the Corps of Topographical Engineers, began making treaties with the Indians, and in 1854 he warned Ogden to wind up Company affairs in his territory. At the same time the Bureau of Indian Affairs pointed out to Ogden and the Company that the right to trade with Indians was not a corollary of the right to possess trading posts. In the face of all of this opposition, Ogden kept on trying to distribute goods to the inland posts as far away as Fort Hall near present-day Pocatello, Idaho.

After the strenuous trip home in the early months of 1853, the shipwreck off San Francisco, and the many political and economic difficulties in Oregon and Washington territories, Ogden's health began to deteriorate. In mid-July, 1854, he began to complain of feeling ill. One month later he felt no better, and on the advice of medical friends, particularly Dr. Barclay, he left Fort Vancouver on August 18,[34] never again to see the post that he had for so long called home. He moved to Oregon City to stay with his daughter and son-in-law, Sarah and Archibald McKinlay. McKinlay had become a member of the firm of Allan, McKinlay and Company and lived comfortably in a home, "The Cliffs," which overlooked the cascading falls of the Willamette.

Dr. McLoughlin, long a citizen of Oregon City, came to visit Ogden's bedside often, and all his friends hoped that the respite from Company worries and the change of scenery would help his health, but "in this hope they have been disappointed as he gradually became weaker." By September, Ogden was noticeably worse, and Governor Simpson wrote: "By last advices he was in a very reduced state and his friends very anxious respecting him—Dugald McTavish speaks despondingly reflecting the prospects of his ultimate recovery."[35] Dugald MacTavish was correct. As the days of September wore on, Peter Skene Ogden "at length sunk under his complaint, which was evidently disease of the brain,"[36] and on September 27, 1854, the man who had done so much to develop the North American West departed from it.

The Indelible Mark

As the funeral cortege bearing Peter Skene Ogden's body passed to the lovely Mountain View Cemetery in Oregon City, a large group of mourners, each with a deep sense of grief in his heart, followed the coffin. Julia, Ogden's widow, who was to outlive him by thirty-two years, moved with stoical face but remembered a thoughtful and loving husband. The young Peter, who had patterned himself so much after his father and was now an integral part of the Hudson's Bay Company, felt the loss greatly. The McKinlays who had been so very close to Ogden were also there. The other children, Charles, Cecilia, Michael, David, Euretta, and Isaac all felt the void in a different way.

Survivors from the Whitman Massacre whom Ogden had rescued were at the graveside to pay their last respects. Citizens of Oregon City turned out to give tribute to a man who, though stern, had been honest, trustworthy, and generous. The Company's servants, many of whom had been Ogden's intimate friends for years, watched the coffin lowered into the ground, and, although death was a common sight to them, they could scarcely believe that Peter Skene Ogden was gone.

The Argyllshire Scot, Dugald MacTavish, who had succeeded Ogden at Fort Vancouver, said: "It is quite unnecessary for me to point out, the very severe loss the business has sustained—by the death of Mr. Ogden— their Honors being fully aware—of the able and distinguished services he has rendered to the Fur Trade, during his long connection with it. I may however state that it will be impossible to replace him here, as there is no man in the Service, with whom I am acquainted—possessed of the same qualifications as Mr. Ogden for the charge of this Department."[1]

Six weeks after Ogden's death, Governor Simpson wrote one of his rare sentimental letters to Ogden's brother, Henry:

As your son William will have already communicated to you the fatal termination of your worthy brother Peter's illness on the 27th September last, I am spared the painful task of being the first to break the sad intelligence to you and your family. His loss will be felt by a very large circle of friends and acquaintances not only in the Service of which for so many years he had been a distinguished member, but in the Territory of Oregon where his urbanity and personal influence in a conspicuous position had gained him the good will of the whole population. Out of his own family, few persons I believe knew him so well or esteemed his friendship more highly than myself—our regard for each other had been the growth of years, on my side increasing as I became more and more intimately acquainted with his character and worth; his loss to me is greater than I am able to express more particularly as I had been looking forward to his early return from Oregon in the hope that for years to come we might enjoy much of each other's Society.[2]

Thus, in his sixty-fifth year, Peter Skene Ogden passed from the North American scene leaving an indelible mark upon his family, business associates, and all who knew him.

Ogden's final sickness and death had come quickly, but he had been prepared. After the murder of Sam Black in 1841 and the subsequent dispute between his widow and his Scottish relatives over the disposition of Black's estate, Ogden had made careful preparations for his own death and provisions for his family. In June, 1851, he had drawn upon his own legal experience to make a will as thoughtful and meticulous as an inventory of supplies for a Snake Country Expedition. He had had this document witnessed by his fellow Hudson's Bay Company officers, Joseph Hardisty, James Birnie, and George T. Allen.

In his will Ogden tried to foresee every eventuality. Although he considered Julia his lawful wife and his children legitimate, a Christian marriage ceremony had never been performed. As old age set in, he apparently became more conscious of his early religious training, and in his will he spoke of his children as "adopted." To his "adopted sons Peter, Charles and Michael Ogden," he bequeathed "each and several the sum of two hundred pounds Stg. . . . to be paid them at the rate of fifty pounds Stg. per annum until the whole be paid." He had favorite grandchildren, and so to his "Grandson Peter Ogden, son of my adopted son Peter Ogden, and to my Granddaughter Janette McKinlay daughter of Archibald and Sarah Julia McKinlay each and severally one hundred pounds Stg."

In his will Ogden also showed his great fondness for Annie Ogden Hopkins. To her he bequeathed "the dividends or interest accruing from one thousand pounds Halifax Currency . . . invested in Bank Stock or other investment in my name by Thomas B. Anderson, Esqr. Annie, however, did not have an opportunity to enjoy her uncle's bequest. When Ogden was lying on his deathbed at "The Cliffs" in Oregon City, Annie was dying at Lachine. An error in the Ogden family history indicates that she lived until 1867,[3] but Annie, who was never robust, died of cholera in late July, 1854.[4] Four years later Edward Hopkins married the artistic Frances Anne Beechey,[5] the daughter of an admiral in the Royal Navy.[6]

Ogden's land, some 5,320 acres, was designated "to be sold or disposed of" and the proceeds divided into equal portions among his children, Sarah Julia, Peter, and Isaac, and his "wardrobe, horses, cattle, and house or houses, furniture, landed property appertaining to me at my death in the Columbia and in the County of Champoeg now I believe called Marion County in Oregon Territory be made over and given to the Mother, commonly called Julia."

His daughter Euretta received stock in the Puget's Sound Agricultural Company, while the grandchildren who were minors received "money sufficient for their comfort without extravagance." Almost no one was forgotten. Ogden's half-sister, Mary Browne Ogden, who was also his godmother, received dividends from Bank of Montreal stock which Charles Richard had bought for Ogden. Continuing his meticulous provisions, Ogden specified that upon Mary's death these fifty shares were to be divided, forty going to Sarah Julia McKinlay and ten to Henry Ogden's youngest daughter. Elizabeth Anderson, daughter of his friend and business aid in Montreal, Thomas B. Anderson, was also remembered. The orphaned Fabian Rivet, grandson of François Rivet who had accompanied Ogden on his Snake Country Expeditions, was bequeathed one hundred pounds, to be paid twenty pounds per annum "as a mark of my regard for him." Finally, his oldest son, Peter, was to receive his watch and seals. With Sam Black's example before him and perhaps fearful of his greedy brother, Charles Richard, who has become the attorney general of the Isle of Man and the district registrar at Liverpool, Ogden added, "Now I have to request should any relation of mine or any other individual attempt to dispute this my Last Will and Testament I declare that with the exception of the legacies already fully stated and mentioned I do hereby declare that I disinherit them as fully as the law authorises me and should there appear an ambiguity or misapprehension as to my real meaning or intention I desire the same may be cleared up by the decision of my said Executors."[7] The executors were Governor Simpson, Archibald McKinlay, Thomas B. Anderson, and Dugald MacTavish.[8]

Ogden's evaluation of human nature was accurate. Soon after his death his brother, Charles Richard, and his sister made their move. Charles Richard was a pious man, a pillar in the Church of England. The sister is remembered by a tablet in St. James Church at Three Rivers which is inscribed: "Sacred to the memory of Harriet Lawrence Ogden, beloved wife of General Thomas Evans, C.B., who departed this life on the 27th November, 1858 in the 71st year of her age to the great grief of her sorrowing husband and bereaved children and truly regretted by her many relatives and friends."[9] All their piety and goodness, however, did not prevent their writing Governor Simpson and demanding that Ogden's "wife" and bastards be cut off with nothing. They pointed out that under English law, the common-law child had no rights. After years of litigation, a compromise was worked out, but Julia and the children received only part of what Ogden had so carefully provided for them. Many of the other provisions, however, did stand up. Marguerite Fraser (Mrs. Pierre Ladouceur) successfully claimed her mother's legacy from the Ogden estate,[10] and the will of Governor Simpson, one of Ogden's executors, left fourteen shares of Bank of Montreal stock in trust for Euretta Ogden and two shares for her mother, Julia. Other accounts in Simpson's name showed that he held trust shares in the Commercial Bank and the Bank of Toronto for Isaac, Peter, Euretta, and Julia.[11]

After Ogden's death his family dispersed. Archibald and Sarah Julia McKinlay gave up the mercantile trade and turned to wheat farming, but the disastrous floods of 1860, 1861, and 1862 ruined them financially, and they moved to Lac la Hache in what is now British Columbia, taking Julia with them. Their last days were spent with their daughter Sarah Ellen. Sarah Ellen had married A. B. Ferguson, owner of the Lakeview Hotel at Savona's Ferry at the southern end of Lake Kamloops, and here, in the little cemetery overlooking Thompson River, Archibald and Sarah Julia McKinlay were buried,[12] in 1891 and 1892 respectively.[13] Celia Ogden Fraser lived for a time at Red River. Euretta and Isaac lived at Champoeg and were the only ones to remain near to their father's home.

Ogden's oldest son, Peter, spent his entire career with the Company. He became Chief Trader in the Hudson's Bay Company in 1854, and his son Peter Skene, who was ten years old at the time of his grandfather's death, followed in the footsteps of the two preceding generations. Peter relived the days of his father and his own childhood when he directed Company affairs from Stuart's Lake. Happily for Peter, his son, Peter Skene, was relatively close by, the clerk in charge of Hudson's Bay Company's establishment at Fraser Lake.[14]

Peter Skene Ogden bequeathed more than money and stock to his son and grandson. They both inherited his warmth, sense of humor, and ability. His namesake grandson "was very popular with all who knew him. He possessed great strength, and was fond of athletic sports." He loved to hunt, and in the fall of 1870, with a group of Indian companions, he followed his dogs in pursuit of a bear. He became so engrossed in the chase that he soon outdistanced his companions, but he became overheated and when his fellow hunters overtook him, "they found Peter and the lolling dogs lying on the ground beside the dead bear."[15] Influenza was sweeping the New Caledonia District at this time, and thus Peter Skene, suffering from overexertion quickly contracted it and died on October 3, 1870. Six days later Peter Ogden was dead from the same virus. Roderick Finlayson reported: "Influenza is mentioned as the complaint which caused the death of both father and son at different Stations within so short a time of each other." Continuing, Finlayson wrote about Peter as he would have about the elder Peter Skene: "The sad death of such an old and efficient officer as Mr. Ogden and the want of his intimate knowledge of the language, trade and of the hunters of New Caledonia will, I fear, prove a serious injury to the trade of that valuable district, as it is difficult to replace him."[16]

Although sons, daughters, grandchildren, and Ogden descendants to the present day have made important contributions, it was Peter Skene Ogden who would not be deterred from adventure by a well-born family and who felt that his destiny lay in Canada and not on the United States frontier. It was Peter Skene Ogden who as a Nor'wester fought the Hudson's Bay Company, then as a "Gentleman Adventurer" fought the Americans and the Russians with every available resource. It was Peter Skene Ogden who faced hostile Indians from southeastern Alaska to the Mojave Desert and who virtually singlehandedly rescued the survivors of the Whitman Massacre. "The humourous, honest, eccentric, law-defying Peter Ogden, the terror of Indians, and the delight of all gay fellows"[17] was a little known but an important contributor to the exploration and development of the continent of North America.

OGDEN FAMILY TREE
Elizabeth Town, New Jersey, Branch

First generation:
John Ogden (1609–82) m. Jane Bond
Second generation:
David Ogden (1639–92) m. Elizabeth (Swaine) Ward
Third generation:
Colonel Josiah Ogden (1679–92) m. Catharine Hardenbroeck
Fourth generation:
Judge David Ogden (1707–98) m. Gertrude Gouverneur
Fifth generation:
Judge Isaac Ogden (1740–1824) marries twice:

Mary Browne (1st)   Sarah Hanson (2nd)

Sixth generation:

children: children:
David   Catharine
Harriet   Charles
Henry   Isaac
                                Mary
                                Sarah
                                *Peter Skene Ogden

PETER SKENE OGDEN (descendants)

Cree woman (1st)   Julia Rivet (2nd)

Seventh generation:
child: *children:*
Peter (1817–70) m.   Charles (1819–80)
    Phrisine Brabbant   Cecelia (b. 1822) m. Hugh Fraser
                                Michael (b. 1824)
                                Sarah Julia (1826–92) m. Archibald
                                    McKinlay
                                David (b. 1828)
                                Euretta (1836–61)
                                Isaac (1839–69) m. Anne Manson

Eighth generation:
Peter Skene Ogden II
    (1844–70)

Bibliography

ABBREVIATIONS

B.L.: The Bancroft Library, Berkeley, California
H.B.C.A.: The Hudson's Bay Company Archives, London
Lilly Lib.: Lilly Library, Bloomington, Indiana
N.L.: Newberry Library, Chicago, Illinois

MANUSCRIPTS AND MAPS

Abernethy, George. MSS, primarily uncatalogued. Oregon Historical Society, Portland, Oregon.
Allan, Alexander. "Cariboo and the Mines of British Columbia," Victoria, 1878. MS P–C 1. B.L.
Anderson, William Caulfield. "History of the Northwest Coast," Victoria 1878. MS P–C 2. B.L.
Applegate, Jesse. "Applegate's Views of History." MS. B.L.
———. "Views of Oregon History." MS. B.L.
Archives of the Puget's Sound Agricultural Company (microfilm–5 reels), Film Z-G5. B.L.
Arrowsmith, Aaron. "A Map exhibiting all the new discoveries in the interior parts of North America." London, 1795. Lilly Lib.
———. "A New Map of Mexico and Adjacent Provinces." London, 1810. Lilly Lib.
———. "Map of North America." London, 1822. Lilly Lib.
Arrowsmith, John. "British North America." London, 1834. Lilly Lib.
———. "British North America." London, 1837. Lilly Lib.
Barrington, Daines. "Miscellaneous." MS 125,B2,1781, Ayer Collection, N.L.
Bayley, C. A. "Early Life on Vancouver Island." MS P–C3. B.L.
Bidwell, John. "California in 1841–8." MS. B.L.
Biggar, H. P., ed. *A Collection of Documents Relating to Jacques Cartier and Sieur de Roberval*. Ottawa, Public Archives of Canada, 1931.
Bird, James. Edmonton District Journal, 1814–1815. MS B.60/a/13. H.B.C.A.
Birnie, Robert. "Personal Adventures of Robert Birnie." MS C–E 65:33. B.L.
Brightly, C. "North America from the Best Authorities" (Suffolk, 1806). Lilly Lib.

Brown, Charles. "Statement of Recollection of Early Events in California." MS. B.L.

Campbell, Robert. "Journal, 1808–1851." MS P–C 209. B.L.

Compton, Pyms Nevins. "Forts and Fort Life in New Caledonia under Hudson's Bay Company regime," Victoria, 1878. MS P–C 5. B.L.

Cooper, James. "Maritime Matters on the Northwest Coast and Other Affairs of the Hudson's Bay Company in Early Times," Victoria, 1878. MS P–C 6. B.L.

Cridge, E. "Characteristics of James Douglas." MS. B.L.

Cruden, Davina Ruth. "Early Fur Trade in California." Unpublished M.A. thesis, University of California, 1922.

Cumberland House Journal. MS B.49/a/38. H.B.C.A.

Davis, William Heath. "Glimpse of the Past in California." MS. B.L.

———. Heath Papers. The Henry E. Huntington Library, San Marino, California.

Deans, James. "Settlement of Vancouver Island," Victoria, 1878. MS P–C 9. B.L.

De Cosmos, Amor. "The Governments of Vancouver Island and British Columbia," Victoria, 1878. MS. B.L.

Douglas, Sir James. "Extracts and paraphrase of transcribed journals in Alaska Miscellany, 1840." MS P–K 28:2. B.L.

———. "Fort Vancouver and the Northwest Coast." MS. B.L.

———. "Journal, 1840–41." MS. Archives of British Columbia, Victoria. An imperfect copy is in B.L.

———. "Journals, 1840–1843." MS P–C 11. B.L.

———. "Private Papers, 1827–1861." MS P–C 12–13. B.L.

Edmonton Accounts, 1823–24. MS B.60/d/15. H.B.C.A.

Engelson, Lester Gordon. "Interests and Activities of the Hudson's Bay Company in California, 1820–1846." Unpublished M.A. thesis, University of California, 1939.

Evans, Ellwood. "History of Oregon." MS. B.L.

"Extract from memorial from J. Berens, Gov. H.B.C. to Lord Bathurst" in Selkirk Papers, No. 158(a), included in a series of H.B.C. Photostats and copies. H.B.C.A.

Fidler, Peter. The Île-à-la-Crosse Journal. MS B.89/a/12. H.B.C.A.

Finlayson, Roderick. "History of Vancouver Island and the Northwest Coast," Victoria, 1878. B.L.

Flathead Post Journal. MS B.69/a/1. H.B.C.A.

Foreign Office Papers. MS 5/457. Public Record Office, London.

Fort Colvile Journal. MS B.45/a/1. H.B.C.A.

Fort Edmonton Journal of Occurrences. MS B.60/a/22. H.B.C.A.

Fort Nisqually, Washington, Journal of Occurrences, May 30, 1833–59. MS. Lilly Lib.

Fort Simpson Post Journal. MS B.201/a/3. H.B.C.A.

Harvey, Eloisa McLoughlin Rae. "Life of John McLoughlin, Governor of the Hudson's Bay Company's Possessions on the Pacific Slope at Fort Vancouver." MS P–B 12. B.L.

Hudson's Company Deed Poll, 1834. MS P–C 42. B.L.

Jackson, David E. Letter dated Dec. 24, 1831, in Vallejo Documents, Vol. XXX, Doc. 280. B.L.

Johnson, Alexander Smith. "Correspondence and papers." MS P–B 208. 2 vols. B.L.

Journal . . . kept at Fort Langley during the years 1827–30. MS P–C 22. B.L.

Journal at Fort Simpson, 1834–37. MS P–C 23. B.L.

"Journals of the Travels of Jonathan Carver in the Years 1766 and 1767." MSS 142 & 143, Ayer Collection. N.L.

Lac La Pluie Journal, 1822–23. MS B.105/2/8. H.B.C.A.

"Larkin Account with Hudson's Bay Company, (1842–44)." MS C–5, 105:65, Larkin Collection of Accounts, Box 11. B.L.

Leader, Herman Alexander. "The Hudson's Bay Company in California." Unpublished Ph.D. dissertation, University of California, 1927.

Log of the *Dryad*. MS C.1/281. H.B.C.A.

Logan, Île-à-la-Crosse Journal. MS B.89/a/3. H.B.C.A.

McKay, Joseph William. "Recollections of a Chief Trader in the Hudson's Company," Fort Simpson, 1878. MS P–C 24. B.L.

McKinlay, Archibald. "Narrative of a Chief Factor of the Hudson's Bay Company." MS P–C 25. B.L.

McLoughlin, John. "An Account of his relations with Americans, 1825–1845." MS P–A 155:2. B.L.

———. "An Account of his Services in Oregon." MS P–A.155:5. B.L.

———. "Interview with Bancroft—June 15, 1878." MS P–A 70. B.L.

———. "Memorial to the Congress of the United States." MS. B.L.

———. "Notes and Copies of correspondence concerning property at the Falls of the Willamette and controversies with American settlers," March 1, 1844. MS P–A 155:1. B.L.

———. Private Papers—1825–1856. MS P–A 155. B.L.

———. "Remarks on Messrs. Warre's and Vavasour's Report," submitted to the Hudson's Bay Company, March 16, 1847. MS P–A 155:3. B.L.

Melish, John. "Map of the United States with the contiguous British and Spanish possessions (engraved by J. Vallance and H. S. Tanner)." Philadelphia, 1818. Ayer Collection. N.L.

Minutes of the Council of the Northern Department. MS B.229/k/3. H.B.C.A.

Moss, Sydney W. "Pictures of Pioneer Times." MS P–A 52. B.L.

Norway House Journal. MS B.154/a/43. H.B.C.A.

"Notes and Extracts from Journal of the Hudson's Bay Company at Fort Simpson, 1834–37." MS P–C 23. B.L.

O'Fallon, Benjamin. "Documents relating to the fur trade from records of the Adjutant General's Office and Office of the Sec. of War in the National Archives" (1818–32). Film P–W 16. B.L.

———. "Items relating to the fur trade from Secretary of War and Adjutant General's Office, 1823–1830." Film P–W 5. B.L.

Ogden, Peter Skene. "Snake Country Journals, 1828–29." MS B.202/a/8. H.B.C.A.

Papers relating to the Red River Settlement, 1815–1819. Printed by order of the House of Commons, July 12, 1819. H.B.C.A.

Ritz, Phillip. "Settlement of the Great Northern Interior," San Francisco, 1878. MS. B.L.

Roberts, George B. "Recollections of George B. Roberts." MS P–A 83. B.L.

Robinson, W. "The British Possessions in North America from the Latest Authorities." 1814. Lilly Lib.

Ross, Alexander. "Snake Country Journal, 1824." MS B.202/a/1. H.B.C.A.

———. "The Fur Hunters of the Far West," (ca.1850). MS for the printer for the book published in 1855 with deletions and corrections. Film P–W 3:1. B.L.

"Russian America: Collections of Translations." MS P–K 1:7. B.L.

Simpson, Sir George. "Character Book." MS A.34/2. H.B.C.A.

Strong, William. "History of Oregon," Portland, 1878. MS P–A 68. B.L.

Sutter, John. "Personal Reminiscences of General J. A. Sutter." MS. B.L.

Thornton, Jesse Quinn. "Oregon History," Salem, 1878. MS. B.L.

Tolmie, William Fraser. "History of Puget Sound and the North West Coast." MS P–B 25, microfilm. B.L.

Treasury Papers. MS 480. Public Record Office, London.

Work, John. "Journal—1824–1834." MS P–C 30, microfilm. B.L.

York Factory Journal. MS B.239/a/131. H.B.C.A.

ARTICLES, GOVERNMENT DOCUMENTS, NEWSPAPERS, AND PERIODICALS

Abel-Henderson, Annie. "[Letters of] General B.L.E. Bonneville," *Washington Historical Quarterly*, Vol. XVIII (July, 1927), 208–30.

Adams, Ephraim D. "English Interests in the Annexation of California," *American Historical Review*, Vol. XIV (July, 1909), 744–63.

Alexander, W. D. "The Steamer 'Beaver,'" *Fourth Annual Report of the Hawaiian Historical Society* (1896), 9–10.

American Monthly Magazine, Vol. XXXIII (Jan., 1906).

Andrews, Clarence L. "Russian Plans for American Dominion," *Washington Historical Quarterly,* Vol. XVIII (April, 1927), 83–92.

[Anon.]. "Northern Coast of America," *The Times* (London), November 2, 1835.

Atkin, W. T. "Snake River Fur Trade, 1816–24," *Oregon Historical Quarterly*, Vol. XXXV (Dec., 1934), 295–312.

Bagley, Clarence B., ed. "Letter by Daniel N. Lownsdale to Samuel R. Thurston, First Territorial Delegate from Oregon to Congress," *Oregon Historical Quarterly*, Vol. XIV (Sept., 1913), 213–49.

Barker, Burt Brown. *The Dr. John McLoughlin House, a National Historic Site*. Published by the McLoughlin Memorial Association, Oregon City, 1949.

Bates, Henry L. "The Occasion of the Unveiling of the Memorial Stone on the Grave of Peter Skene Ogden," *Oregon Historical Quarterly* Vol. XXIV (Dec., 1923), 361–63.

Beaver, Herbert. "Experience of a Chaplain at Fort Vancouver, 1836–1838," ed. by R. C. Clark, *Oregon Historical Quarterly*, Vol. XXXIX (March, 1938), 22–38.

Blossom, Robert H. "First Things Pertaining to Presbyterianism on the Pacific Coast," *Oregon Historical Quarterly*, Vol. XV (June, 1914), 81–103.

Blue, George Verne, ed. "A Hudson's Bay Company Contract for Hawaiian Labor," *Oregon Historical Quarterly*, Vol. XXV (March, 1924), 72–75.

———. "The Oregon Question, 1818–1828," *Oregon Historical Quarterly*, Vol. XXIII (Sept., 1922), 193–219.

Bradley, Marie Merriman. "Political Beginnings in Oregon," *Oregon Historical Quarterly*, Vol. IX (March, 1908), 42–72.

Brown, Judge William C. "Old Fort Okanagan Trail," *Oregon Historical Quarterly*, Vol. XV (March, 1914), 1–38.

Burns, Thomas P. "The History of a Montgomery Street Lot in Yerba Buena from November 4, 1837, to June 14, 1850," *California Historical Quarterly*, Vol. XI (March, 1932), 69–72.

Chapin, Jane Levins, ed. "Letters of John McLoughlin, 1805–49," *Oregon Historical Quarterly*, Vol. XXXVII (March & Dec., 1936), 45–75, 293–300.

Clark, General William. "1830 Report on the Fur Trade," *Oregon Historical Quarterly*, Vol. XLVIII (March, 1947), 25–33.

Clark, R. C. "How British and American Subjects Unite in a Common Government for Oregon Territory in 1844," *Oregon Historical Quarterly*, Vol. XIII (June, 1912), 140–59.

Cline, Gloria Griffen. "Jedediah Smith: Leading Contender in the Anglo-American Fur Rivalry," *The Pacific Historian*, Vol. V (Aug., 1961), 95–103.

———. "Peter Skene Ogden," *Nevada Highways Centennial Issue* (1964), 18–20.

———. "Peter Skene Ogden's Nevada Explorations," *Nevada Historical Quarterly*, Vol. III (July–Sept., 1960), 3–11.

Commager, Henry S. "England and the Oregon Treaty of 1846," *Oregon Historical Quarterly*, Vol. XXVIII (March, 1927), 18–38.

Cowan, Ian McTaggart. "The Fur Trade and the Fur Cycle: 1825–1857," *British Columbia Historical Quarterly*, Vol. II (Jan., 1938), 19–30.

Crampton, C. Gregory. "The Discovery of the Green River," *Utah Historical Quarterly*, Vol. XX (Oct., 1952), 299–312.

———. "Humboldt's Utah, 1811," *Utah Historical Quarterly*, Vol. XXVI (July, 1958), 268–81.

———, and Gloria Griffen [Cline]. "The San Buenaventura, Mythical River of the West," *Pacific Historical Review*, Vol. XXV (May, 1956), 163–71.

Cree, Muriel R., ed. "Three Simpson Letters: 1815–1820," *British Columbia Historical Quarterly*, Vol. I (April, 1937), 115–21.

Current, Richard N. "Webster's Propaganda and the Ashburton Treaty," *Mississippi Valley Historical Review*, Vol. XXXIV (Sept., 1947), 187–200.

Dale, Harrison Clifford. "A Fragmentary Journal of William L. Sublette," *Mississippi Valley Historical Review*, Vol. VI (June, 1919), 99–110.

Davidson, Donald C. "Relations of the Hudson's Bay Company with the Russian American Company on the Northwest Coast, 1829–1867," *British Columbia Historical Review*, Vol. V (Jan., 1941), 37–46.

Davis, William L. "Pierre Jean DeSmet: The Journey of 1840," *Pacific Northwest Quarterly*, Vol. XXXV (Jan., 1944), 29–43; Vol. XXXV (April, 1944), 121–42.

———. "Pierre Jean DeSmet: The Years of Preparation, 1801–1837," *Pacific Northwest Quarterly*, Vol. XXXII (April, 1941), 167–96.

Dee, Henry Drummond. "An Irishman in the Fur Trade: The Life and Journals of John Work," *British Columbia Historical Review*, Vol. VII (Oct., 1943), 229–68.

Douglas, David. "Second Journey to the Northwest Parts of the Continent of North America During the Years 1829, '30, '31, '32, '33," *Oregon Historical Quarterly*, Vol. VI (Sept., 1905), 288–309.

———. "Sketch of a Journey to the Northwestern Parts of the Continent of North America During the Years 1824, '25, '26, '27," *Oregon Historical Quarterly*, Vol. VI (June, 1905), 206–27.

DuFour, Clarence John. "The Russian Withdrawal from California," *California Historical Quarterly*, Vol. XII (Sept., 1933), 240–76.

Elliott, T. C., ed. "The Coming of the White Women, 1836," *Oregon Historical Quarterly*, Vol. XXXVII (Sept., 1936), 250–63.

———. "Corrections," *Oregon Historical Quarterly*, Vol. XI (Dec., 1910), 415.

———. "Dedicatory Address by T. C. Elliott," *Oregon Historical Quarterly*, Vol. XXIV (Dec., 1923), 379–82.

———, ed. "Facsimile of a Marriage Certificate," *Oregon Historical Quarterly*, Vol. X (Dec., 1909), 325–28.

———. "The Fur Trade in the Columbia River Basin Prior to 1811," *Oregon Historical Quarterly*, Vol. XV (Dec., 1914), 241–51.

————. "Indian Expeditions," *Oregon Historical Quarterly*, Vol. XLIII, (September, 1942), 294.

————. "Peter Skene Ogden, Fur Trader," *Oregon Historical Quarterly*, Vol. XI (Sept., 1910), 229–78.

————. "The Surrender at Astoria in 1818," *Oregon Historical Quarterly*, Vol. XIX (Dec., 1918), 271–82.

————. "Wilson Price Hunt, 1783–1842," *Oregon Historical Quarterly*, Vol. XXXII (June, 1931), 130–34.

Ermatinger, C. O. "A Tragedy on the Stikine in '42," *Oregon Historical Quarterly*, Vol. XV (June, 1914), 126–32.

————. "The Columbia River under Hudson's Bay Company Rule," *Washington Historical Quarterly*, Vol. V (July, 1914), 192–206.

Farquhar, Francis P. "Exploration of the Sierra Nevada," *California Historical Quarterly*, Vol. IV (March, 1925), 3–58.

————. "Jedediah Smith and the First Crossing of the Sierra Nevada," *Sierra Club Bulletin*, Vol. XXVIII (June, 1943), 36–53.

"Fort Langley Correspondence," *British Columbia Historical Quarterly*, Vol. I (July, 1937), 187–94.

Fort Ross State Historical Monument. Published under the direction of Division of Beaches and Parks, State of California (Dec., 1955).

Fort Vancouver National Monument. Washington, National Park Service, U.S. Department of the Interior, 1957.

Fullerton, John. "My Days Aboard the 'Beaver,'" *British Columbia Historical Quarterly*, Vol. II (July, 1938), 185–88.

Galbraith, John S. "British-American Competition in the Border Fur Trade of the 1820's," *Minnesota History*, Vol. XXXVI (Sept., 1959), 241–49.

————. "France as a Factor in the Oregon Negotiations," *Pacific Northwest Quarterly*, Vol. XLIV (April, 1953), 69–73.

————. "George N. Sanders, 'Influence Man' for the Hudson's Bay Company," *Oregon Historical Quarterly*, Vol. LIII (Sept., 1952), 159–76.

————. "The Little Emperor," *The Beaver*, Outfit 291 (Winter, 1960), 22–28.

Gallatin, Albert. "A Synopsis of the Indian Tribes within the United States East of the Rocky Mountains, and in the British and Russian Possessions in North America," *Transactions and Collections of the American Antiquarian Society*, Vol. II. Worcester, Mass., 1836.

Garry, Nicholas. "Diary of Nicholas Garry," *Proceedings and Transactions of the Royal Society of Canada,* Ser. II, Vol. II, sec. II (1900), 3–204.

Gill, John. "Superstitions and Ceremonies of Indians of Old Oregon," *Oregon Historical Quarterly*, Vol. XXIX (Dec., 1928), 311–22.

Goodfellow, J. C. "Furs and Gold in Similkameen," *British Columbia Historical Quarterly*, Vol. II (April, 1938), 67–88.

Goodwin, Victor O., and John A. Hussey. "A History of the Sawtooth

Range" (History Substudy Report), prepared jointly by the U.S. Forest Services and the National Park Services (Oct., 1964), 1–56.

Gough, Barry M. "H.M.S. 'America' on the North Pacific Coast," *Oregon Historical Quarterly*, Vol. LXX (Dec., 1969), 293–311.

Graebner, Norman A. "Maritime Factors in the Oregon Compromise," *Pacific Historical Review*, Vol. XX (Nov., 1951), 331–45.

——. "Politics and the Oregon Compromise," *Pacific Northwest Quarterly*, Vol. LII (Jan., 1961), 7–14.

——. "Polls, Politics, and Oregon," *East Tennessee Historical Society's Publications*, No. 24 (1952).

Grant, Louis S. "Fort Hall under the Hudson's Bay Company, 1837–1856," *Oregon Historical Quarterly*, Vol. XLI (March, 1940), 34–39.

Hafen, LeRoy R. "Mountain Men before the Mormons," *Utah Historical Quarterly*, Vol. XXVI (Oct., 1958), 307–26.

Haines, Francis D., Jr. "The Relations of the Hudson's Bay Company with the American Fur Trade in the Pacific Northwest," *Pacific Northwest Quarterly*, Vol. XXXX (Oct., 1949), 273–94.

Harvey, A. G. "David Douglas in British Columbia," *British Columbia Historical Quarterly*, Vol. IV (Oct., 1940), 221–43.

——. "Meredith Gardner: Doctor of Medicine," *British Columbia Historical Review*, Vol. IX (April, 1945), 89–111.

Hill, Joseph J. "Ewing Young in the Fur Trade of the Far Southwest, 1822–1834," *Oregon Historical Quarterly*, Vol. XXIV (March, 1923), 1–35.

Himes, George H., ed. "Letter by Burn Osborn, Survivor of the Howison Expedition to Oregon, 1846," *Oregon Historical Quarterly*, Vol. XIV (Dec., 1913), 355–65.

Holman, Frederick V. "A Brief History of the Oregon Provisional Government and What Caused Its Formation," *Oregon Historical Quarterly*, Vol. XIII (June, 1912), 89–139.

——. "Address," *Oregon Historical Quarterly*, Vol. XXIV (Dec., 1923), 363–79.

——. "Life and Services of Peter Skene Ogden," *Oregon Historical Quarterly*, Vol. XXIV (Dec., 1923), 363–79.

Howay, F. W. "Authorship of Traits of Indian Life," *Oregon Historical Quarterly*, Vol. XXXV (March, 1934), 42–49.

——. "Brig Owyhee in the Columbia, 1829–30," *Oregon Historical Quarterly*, Vol. XXXV (March, 1934), 10–21.

——. "Early Settlement on Burrard Inlet," *British Columbia Historical Quarterly*, Vol. I (April, 1937), 101–14.

Howison, Neil M. "Report of Lieutenant Neil M. Howison on Oregon, 1846," *Oregon Historical Quarterly*, Vol. XIV (March, 1913), 1–60.

Ireland, Willard E., ed. "James Douglas and the Russian American Company, 1840," *British Columbia Historical Quarterly*, Vol. V (Jan., 1941), 53–66.

Jackson, Ian. "The Stikine Territory Trade and its Relevance to the Alaska Purchase," *Pacific Historical Review*, Vol. XXXVI (Aug., 1967), 289–306.

Johnson, Alice M. "Simpson in Russia," *The Beaver* (Autumn, 1960), 4–12, 58.

Johnson, F. Henry. "Fur Trading Days at Kamloops," *British Columbia Historical Quarterly*, Vol. I (July, 1937), 171–85.

Kemble, John Haskell. "Coal from the Northwest Coast, 1848–1850," *British Columbia Historical Quarterly*, Vol. II (April, 1938), 123–30.

Kelly, Charles. "Jedediah Smith on the Salt Desert Trail," *Utah Historical Quarterly*, Vol. III (Jan., 1930), 23–27, 35–52.

Koch, Elers. "Lewis and Clark Route Retraced across the Bitterroots," *Oregon Historical Quarterly*, Vol. XLI (June, 1940), 160–74.

Lamb, W. Kaye. "Early Lumbering on Vancouver Island, Part 1:1844–1855," *British Columbia Historical Quarterly*, Vol. II (Jan., 1938), 31–53.

———. "Early Lumbering on Vancouver Island, Part 11:1855–1866," *British Columbia Historical Quarterly*, Vol. II (April, 1938), 95–121.

———. "The Advent of the 'Beaver,' " *British Columbia Historical Quarterly*, Vol. II (July, 1938), 163–84.

———. "The Governorship of Richard Blanshard," *British Columbia Historical Quarterly*, Vol. XIV (Jan.–April, 1950), 1–40.

———, ed. "The James Douglas Report on the 'Beaver Affair,' " *Oregon Historical Quarterly*, Vol. XLVII (March, 1946), 16–28.

Longstaff, F. V., and W. Kaye Lamb. "The Royal Navy on the Northwest Coast, 1813–1850," *British Columbia Historical Review*, Vol. IX (Jan., 1945), 1–24, and (April, 1945), 113–28.

MacLaurin, D. L. "Education before the Gold Rush," *British Columbia Historical Quarterly*, Vol. II (Oct., 1938), 247–63.

McGregor, D. A. "Old Whitehead, Peter Skene Ogden," *British Columbia Historical Review*, Vol. XVII (July–Oct., 1953), 161–95.

McKelvie, B. A. "Sir James Douglas: A New Portrait," *British Columbia Historical Review*, Vol. VII (April, 1943), 93–101.

McLoughlin House, National Historic Site. Published by the National Park Service in co-operation with the McLoughlin Memorial Association and the Municipality of Oregon City, 1957.

McLoughlin, John. "Copy of a Document found among the Private Papers of the late Dr. John McLoughlin," *Transactions of the Oregon Pioneer Association*, 1880, 46–55.

———. "Dr. McLoughlin's Last Letter," ed. by Katherine B. Judson, *American Historical Review*, Vol. XXI (Oct., 1915), 104–35.

———. "Letter of Dr. John McLoughlin to Sir George Simpson, March 20, 1844," ed. by Katherine B. Judson, *Oregon Historical Quarterly*, Vol. XVIII (Oct., 1916), 215–39.

———. "Letters of Dr. John McLoughlin, 1835–37, to Edward Ermatinger," ed. by T. C. Elliott, *Oregon Historical Quarterly*, Vol. XXIII (Dec., 1922), 365–71.

Maloney, Alice B. "The Hudson's Bay Company in California," *Oregon Historical Quarterly*, Vol. XXXVII (March, 1936), 9–23.

———. "Peter Skene Ogden's Trapping Expedition to the Gulf of California, 1829–30," *California Historical Quarterly*, Vol. XIX (Dec., 1940), 308–16.

Martig, Ralph Richard. "Hudson's Bay Company Claims, 1846–69," *Oregon Historical Quarterly*, Vol. XXXVI (March, 1935), 60–70.

Mazour, Anatole. "Doctor Yegor Scheffer: Dreamer of a Russian Empire in the Pacific," *Pacific Historical Review*, Vol. VI (March, 1937), 15–20.

———. "The Russian-American and Anglo-Russian Conventions of 1824–25: An Interpretation," *Pacific Historical Review*, Vol. XIV (Sept., 1945), 303–10.

Meinig, Donald W. "Wheat Sacks Out to Sea," *Pacific Northwest Quarterly*, Vol. VL (Jan., 1954), 13–18.

Merk, Frederick. "British Party Politics and the Oregon Treaty," *American Historical Review*, Vol. XXXVII (July, 1932), 653–77.

———. "Presidential Fevers," *Mississippi Valley Historical Review*, Vol. XVII (June, 1960), 3–33.

———. "Snake Country Expedition, 1824–25: An Episode of Fur Trade and Empire," *Mississippi Valley Historical Review*, Vol. XXI (June, 1934).

———. "The British Corn Crisis of 1845–46 and the Oregon Treaty," *Agricultural History*, Vol. VIII (July, 1934), 95–123.

———. "The Genesis of the Oregon Question," *Mississippi Valley Historical Review*, Vol. XXXVI (March, 1950), 583–612.

———. "The Ghost River Caledonia in the Oregon Negotiations of 1818," *American Historical Review*, Vol. LV (April, 1950), 530–51.

———. "The Oregon Pioneers and the Boundary," *American Historical Review*, Vol. XXIX (July, 1932), 681–99.

Miller, David E. "Peter Skene Ogden's Explorations in the Great Salt Lake Region; A Restudy Based on Newly Published Journals," *The Western Humanities Review*, Vol. VIII (Spring, 1954), 139–50.

———. "Peter Skene Ogden's Journal of His Expedition to Utah, 1825," *Utah Historical Quarterly*, Vol. XX (April, 1952), 159–86.

———. "William Kittson's Journal Covering Peter Skene Ogden's 1824–25 Snake Country Expedition," *Utah Historical Quarterly*, Vol. XXII (April, 1954), 125–42.

Minto, John. "Dr. McLoughlin, What I Know Of, and How I Know It," *Oregon Historical Quarterly*, Vol. XI (June, 1910), 177–200.

———. "The Influence of Canadian French on the Earliest Development of Oregon," *Oregon Historical Quarterly*, Vol. XV (Dec., 1914), 277–82.

Morison, Samuel E. "New England and the Opening of the Columbia River Salmon Trade, 1830," *Oregon Historical Quarterly*, Vol. XXVIII (June, 1927), 111–32.

Ogden, Peter Skene. ". . . Journals," ed. by T. C. Elliott, *Oregon Historical*

Quarterly, Vol. X (Dec., 1909), 331–65; Vol. XI (June, 1910), 201–22; Vol. XI (Dec., 1910), 355–96.

———. "Letter to Reverend Elkanah Walker," *Oregon Historical Quarterly*, Vol. XI (Dec., 1910), 398–99.

———. "Ogden's Report of His 1828–30 Expedition," ed. by John Scaglione, *California Historical Quarterly*, Vol. XXVIII (June, 1949), 117–24.

———. "Peter Skene Ogden's Notes on Western Caledonia," ed. by W. N. Sage, *British Columbia Historical Review*, Vol. I (Jan., 1937), 45–56.

———. "The Snake Country Expedition, 1824–25," ed. by Frederick Merk, *Oregon Historical Quarterly*, Vol. XXXV (June, 1934), 93–122.

Oregon Spectator, August 24, 1848; February 6, 1849.

Pipes, Nellie B. "Indian Conditions in 1836–1838," *Oregon Historical Quarterly*, Vol. XXXII (Dec., 1931), 333–42.

Pratt, Julius W. "James K. Polk and John Bull," *Canadian Historical Review*, Vol. XXIV (Dec., 1943), 341–49.

Reid, Robie L. "Early Days at Old Fort Langley," *British Columbia Historical Review*, Vol. I (April, 1937), 71–85.

Rolle, Andrew F., ed. "Jedediah Strong Smith: New Documentation," *Mississippi Valley Historical Review*, Vol. XXXX (Sept., 1953), 305–308.

Ross, Alexander. "Journal of the Snake Country Expedition of 1824," ed. by T. C. Elliott, *Oregon Historical Quarterly*, Vol. XIV (Dec., 1913), 366–88.

Ross, Frank E., ed. "Sir George Simpson at the Department of State," *British Columbia Historical Review*, Vol. II (April, 1938), 131–35.

Russell, Carl P. "Trapper Trails to the Sisk-Kee-Dee," *Chicago Westerners Brand Book for 1944* (1946), 57–79.

Sage, W. N. "A Note on the Change in Title of Fort St. James," *British Columbia Historical Review*, Vol. II (Jan., 1938), 55–56.

Schafer, Joseph. "Documents Relative to Warre and Vavasour's Military Reconnaisance in Oregon, 1845–46," *Oregon Historical Quarterly*, Vol. X (March, 1909), 1–99.

Scott, Leslie M. "Indian Diseases as Aids to Pacific Northwest Settlement," *Oregon Historical Quarterly*, Vol. XXIX (June, 1928), 144–61.

———. "Influence of American Settlement upon the Oregon Boundary Treaty of 1846," *Oregon Historical Quarterly*, Vol. XXIX (March, 1928), 1–19.

———. "Report of Lieutenant Peel on Oregon in 1845–46," *Oregon Historical Quarterly*, Vol. XXIX (March, 1928), 51–76.

Simpson, Sir George. "Letters of Sir George Simpson, 1841–1843," ed. by Joseph Schafer, *American Historical Review*, Vol. XIV (Oct., 1908), 70–94.

———. "Simpson to Tolmie, January 28, 1856," *British Columbia Historical Review*, Vol. I (Oct., 1937), 241–42.

Slater, G. Hollis. "New Light on Herbert Beaver," *British Columbia Historical Review*, Vol. VI (Jan., 1942), 13–29.

Spry, Irene M. "Routes through the Rockies," *The Beaver* (Autumn, 1963), 26–39.

Stacey, C. P. "The Hudson's Bay Company and Anglo-American Rivalries during the Oregon Dispute," *Canadian Historical Review*, Vol. XVIII (Sept., 1937), 281–306.

Stewart, Edgar I. "Peter Skene Ogden in Montana, 1825," *Montana Magazine of History* (Autumn, 1953), 32–45.

Strong, William. "Knickerbocker Views of the Oregon Country: Judge William Strong's Narrative," *Oregon Historical Quarterly*, Vol. LXII (March, 1961), 57–87.

Sutter, John A. "Letter to Don Juan Alvarado, Governor of California, November, 1841," *San Francisco Examiner*, March 22, 1925.

Tolmie, S. F. "My Father, William Fraser Tolmie," *British Columbia Historical Review*, Vol. I (Oct., 1937), 227–40.

Tyler, S. Lyman. "The Myth of the Lake of Copala and Land of Teguaya," *Utah Historical Quarterly*, Vol. XX (October, 1952), 313–29.

———. "The Spaniard and the Ute," *Utah Historical Quarterly*, Vol. XXII (October, 1954), 343–61.

United States Senate. *Executive Documents*, 20 Cong., 2 sess., Vol. I, No. 67.

Van Alstyne, Richard W. "International Rivalries in the Pacific Northwest," *Oregon Historical Quarterly*, Vol. XLVI (September, 1945), 185–218.

Warner, Colonel J. J. "Reminiscences of Early California from 1831–1846," *Annual Publications of the Historical Society of Southern California, 1907–1908*, Vol. VII, pp. 176–93.

Warre, Henry, M. Vavasour, *et al.* "Secret Mission of Warre and Vavasour," *Washington Historical Quarterly*, Vol. III (April, 1912), 131–53.

Warren, Governor K. "Bonneville's Expedition to the Rocky Mountains, 1832, '33, '34, '35, '36," *Annals of Wyoming*, Vols. XV–XVI (1943–44), 220–28.

Work, John. "Journal of John Work . . . Covering the Snake Country Expedition of 1830–31," ed. by T. C. Elliott, *Oregon Historical Quarterly*, Vol. XIII (Sept., 1912), 280–314.

———. "Journal of John Work . . . April 30 to May 31, 1830," ed. by T. C. Elliott, *Oregon Historical Quarterly*, Vol. X (Sept., 1909), 296–313.

Yarmolinsky, Abraham. "A Rambling Note on the 'Russian Columbus,' Nikolai Petrovich Rezanov," *Bulletin of the New York Public Library*, Vol. XXXI (Sept., 1927), 707–13.

BOOKS

Adam, G. Mercer. *The Canadian North-West*. Toronto, Rose Publishing Co., 1885.

Adams, Randolph G. *A History of the Foreign Policy of the United States.* New York, Macmillan, 1924.

Alaska Boundary Tribunal Atlas Accompanying the Case of the United States before the Tribunal Convened at London. Washington, D.C., Government Printing Office, 1903.

Alden, John R. *Rise of the American Republic.* New York, Harper & Row, 1963.

Alter, J. Cecil. *James Bridger, Trapper, Frontiersman, Scout, and Guide: A Historical Narrative.* Salt Lake City, Shepard Book Co., 1925; Norman, University of Oklahoma Press, 1962.

Atherton, William Henry. *Montreal under British Rule.* Montreal, Vancouver, Chicago, S. J. Clarke Publishing Co., 1914.

Atwood, Wallace W. *The Physiographic Provinces of North America.* Boston, Ginn & Co., 1940.

Bailey, Thomas A. *America Faces Russia: Russian American Relations from Early Times to Our Day.* Ithaca, Cornell University Press, 1950.

Baillie-Grohman, W. A. *Fifteen Years' Sport and Life in the Hunting Grounds of Western America and British Columbia.* London, Horace Cox, 1900.

Bancroft, Hubert Howe. *The Works of Hubert Howe Bancroft.* 39 vols. San Francisco, The History Company, 1886–91.

Barck, Oscar Theodore, Jr., and Hugh Talmage Lefler. *Colonial America.* New York, Macmillan, 1958.

Barker, Burt Brown. *The McLoughlin Empire and Its Rulers.* Glendale, Arthur H. Clark, 1959.

Barnes, Major R. Money. *A History of Regiments and Uniforms of the British Army.* London, Seeley Service, 1954. 3d ed.

Barrow, John. *A Chronological History of Voyages into the Arctic Regions: undertaken chiefly for the purpose of discovering a Northeast, Northwest, or Polar Passage between the Atlantic and Pacific.* London, J. Murray, 1818.

Beaver, Herbert. *Reports and Letters of Herbert Beaver, 1836–38.* Thomas E. Jessett, ed. Portland, Oregon, Champoeg Press, 1958.

Beckwourth, James G. *The Life and Adventures of James P. Beckwourth.* New York, Harper & Bros., 1856.

Benton, Thomas Hart. *Thirty Years' View.* 2 vols. New York, D. Appleton & Co., 1854–56.

Billington, Ray Allen. *Westward Expansion: A History of the American Frontier.* New York, Macmillan, 1960. 2d ed.

Binns, Archie. *Peter Skene Ogden, Fur Trader.* Portland, Oregon, Binfords & Mort, 1967.

Black, Samuel. *A Journal of a Voyage from the Rocky Mountain Portage in Peace River to the Sources of Finlays Branch and Northwestward in Summer, 1824.* E. E. Rich, ed. Introduction by R. M. Patterson. Vol. XVIII. London, Hudson's Bay Record Society, 1955.

Blanchet, Francis Norbert. *Historical Sketches of the Catholic Church in Oregon*. Portland, Oregon, 1878.

Boorstin, Daniel J. *An American Primer*. 2 vols. Chicago, University of Chicago Press, 1966.

———. *The Americans: The Colonial Experience*. New York, Random House, 1958.

Boswell, James. *Boswell's London Journal, 1762–1763*. New Haven, Yale University Press, 1950.

Brewster, William. *The Pennsylvania and New York Frontier*. New York, Theo. Gaus, 1954.

British and American Joint Commission for the final settlement of the claims of the Hudson's Bay Company and Puget's Sound Agricultural Company. Washington, D.C., Government Printing Office, 1867.

Bryce, George. *Remarkable History of the Hudson's Bay Company, including that of the French Traders of N. W. Canada and of the N. W., X. Y., and Astor Fur Companies*. London, S. Low, Marston & Co., 1910.

Burnett, Peter H. *An Old California Pioneer*. Oakland, California, Biobooks, 1946.

Burpee, Lawrence J. *An Historical Atlas of Canada*. Toronto and New York, Thomas Nelson & Sons, 1927.

———, ed. *Journal de Larocque de la rivière Assiniboine jusqu'à la rivière "Aux Roches Jaunes."* Ottawa, Public Archives, 1911.

Buss, Claude E. *Asia in the Modern World*. New York, Macmillan, 1964.

Camp, Charles L., ed. *James Clyman, American Frontiersman, 1792–1881*. San Francisco, California Historical Society, 1928.

Caughey, John Walton. *California*. New York, Prentice-Hall, 1940.

———. *History of the Pacific Coast of North America*. New York, Privately published, 1933.

Chapman, Charles Edward, ed. *Expedition on the Sacramento and San Joaquin Rivers in 1817: Diary of Fray Narciso Durán*. Berkeley, University of California Press, 1911.

Chevigny, Hector. *Russian America, the Great Alaskan Venture, 1741–1867*. New York, Viking Press, 1965.

Chittenden, Hiram Martin. *The American Fur Trade of the Far West*. 3 vols. New York, Francis P. Harper, 1902.

———, and Alfred Talbot Richardson. *Life, Letters, and Travels of Father Pierre-Jean DeSmet, S.J., 1801–1873*. 4 vols. New York, Francis P. Harper, 1905.

Chitwood, Oliver Perry. *A History of Colonial America*. New York, Harper & Bros., 1961. Revised ed.

Christie, Robert. *History of the Late Province of Lower Canada*. 6 vols. Quebec & Montreal, 1848–56.

Clark, Robert C. *History of the Willamette Valley, Oregon*. 2 vols. Chicago, S. J. Clarke, 1927.

Cline, Gloria Griffen. *Exploring the Great Basin.* Norman, University of Oklahoma Press, 1963.

Colocoressess, Lieut. George M. *Four Years in the Government Exploring Expedition Commanded by Captain Charles Wilkes.* New York, J. M. Fairchild, 1855.

Cook, James. *A Voyage to the Pacific Ocean undertaken by the Command of His Majesty for Making Discoveries in the Northern Hemisphere . . . Performed under the Direction of Captain Cook, Clarke, and Gore, in His Majesty's Ships, the Resolution and Discovery in the Years 1776, 1777, 1778, 1779 and 1780.* 3 vols. London, W. & A. Strahan for G. Nicol & T. Cadell, 1784.

Coues, Elliott, ed. *Forty Years a Fur Trapper on the Upper Missouri.* 2 vols., New York, Francis P. Harper, 1898.

————, ed. *The Journals of Lewis and Clark.* 4 vols. New York, Francis P. Harper, 1893.

Cox, Ross. *Adventures on the Columbia River.* 2 vols. London, H. Colburn & R. Bentley, 1831. New edition, University of Oklahoma Press, Norman, 1957. (Introduction by Edgar I. Stewart and Jane R. Stewart.)

Crouse, Nellie M. *In Quest of the Western Ocean.* New York, William Morrow & Co., 1928.

————. *La Verendrye, Fur Trader and Explorer.* Ithaca, Cornell University Press, 1956.

————. *The Search for the Northwest Passage.* New York, Columbia University Press, 1934.

Currie, A. W. *Economic Geography of Canada.* Toronto, Macmillan of Canada, 1945.

Dale, Harrison Clifford. *The Ashley-Smith Explorations and the Discovery of a Central Route to the Pacific, 1822–1829.* Cleveland, Arthur H. Clark, 1918.

Davidson, Donald Curtis. *Relations of the Hudson's Bay Company with the Russian American Company on the Northwest Coast, 1829–1867.* Victoria, B. C., the author, 1941.

Davidson, Gordon Charles. *The North West Company.* Berkeley, University of California Press, 1918.

Dellenbaugh, Frederick S. *Frémont and '49.* New York, G. P. Putnam & Sons, 1914.

Denison, Merrill. *Canada's First Bank.* Toronto and Montreal, McClelland and Stewart, 1966.

Dennett, Tyler. *Americans in Eastern Asia.* New York, Barnes & Noble, 1941.

Dent, John Charles. *The Last Forty Years: Canada Since the Union of 1841.* 2 vols. Toronto, George Virtue, 1881.

DeSmet, Pierre Jean. *Letters and Sketches, with a Narrative of a Year's*

Residence among the Indian Tribes of the Rocky Mountains. Philadelphia, M. Fithian, 1843.

Dobbs, Arthur. *An Account of the Countries Adjoining the Hudson's Bay.* London, printed for J. Robinson, 1744.

Douglas, David. *Journal Kept by David Douglas During His Travels in North America, 1823–1827.* London, published under the direction of the Royal Horticultural Society, 1914.

Drury, Clifford M. *First White Women over the Rockies.* 3 vols. Glendale, Arthur H. Clark, 1963–65.

———. *Henry Harmon Spalding: Pioneer of Old Oregon.* Caldwell, Idaho, Caxton Printers, 1936.

———. *Marcus Whitman, M.D., Pioneer, and Martyr.* Caldwell, Idaho, Caxton Printers, 1937.

Duchaussois, Fr. P. *Mid Snow and Ice: The Apostles of the North-West.* Dublin, Lourdes Messenger Office Irish Lourdes, 1937.

Dunn, John. *History of the Oregon Territory and British North American Fur Trade.* London, Edwards & Hughes, 1844.

———. *The Oregon Territory and the British North American Fur Trade.* Philadelphia, G. B. Zieber & Co., 1845.

Edwards, Major T. J. *Military Customs.* Revised by Arthur L. Kipling. Aldershot, England, Gale & Polden, 1961.

———. *Regimental Badges.* Revised by Arthur L. Kipling. Aldershot, England, Gale & Polden, 1963.

Ermatinger, Edward. *Edward Ermatinger's York Express Journal.* Introduction and Notes by Judge C. O. Ermatinger. *Transactions of the Royal Society of Canada,* Vol. VI. Ottawa, 1912.

Farnham, Thomas J. *Travels in the Great Western Prairies, the Anahuac, and Rocky Mountains.* Poughkeepsie, N.Y. 1841.

Fleming, Harvey, ed. *Minutes of Council Northern Department of Rupert Land, 1821–31.* Hudson's Bay Record Society, Vol. III. London, 1940.

Frémont, John Charles. *Memoirs of My Life.* New York, Clark & Co., 1887.

———. *Report of the Exploring Expedition to the Rocky Mountains in the Years 1842, and to Oregon and North California in the Years, 1843–44.* Washington, Government Printing Office, 1845.

"Fur Trader." *Traits of American Indian Life and Character.* London, Smith & Elder, 1853.

Galbraith, John S. *The Hudson's Bay Company as an Imperial Factor, 1821–1869.* Berkeley, University of California Press, 1957.

Gates, Charles M., ed. *Five Fur Traders of the Northwest.* Minneapolis, University of Minnesota Press for the Society of the Colonial Dames of America, 1933.

———, ed. *Messages of the Governors of the Territory of Washington to the Legislative Assembly, 1854–1889.* University of Washington *Publica-*

tions in the Social Sciences. Seattle, University of Washington Press, 1940.

Ghent, W. J. *The Road to Oregon.* London & New York, Longmans, Green & Co., 1929.

Glazebrook, G. P., ed. *The Hargrave Correspondence, 1821–1843.* Toronto, Champlain Society, 1938.

Glover, Richard, ed. *David Thompson's Narrative, 1784–1812.* Toronto, Champlain Society, 1962.

Graebner, Norman A. *Empire on the Pacific: A Study in American Continental Expansion.* New York, Ronald Press, 1955.

Gray, William H. *A History of Oregon, 1792–1849, Drawn from Personal Observation and Authentic Information.* Portland, Oregon, Harris & Holman, 1870.

Greenhow, Robert. *Geography of Oregon and California and the Other Territories on the North-West Coast of North America.* New York, M. H. Newman, 1845.

――――. *History of Oregon and California.* London, John Murray, 1844.

――――. *The History of Oregon and California and the Other Territories on the Northwest Coast of North America.* Philadelphia, D. Appleton, 1845.

――――. *Memoir, Historical and Political, on the Northwest Coast of North America and the Adjacent Territories.* New York & London, Wiley & Putnam, 1840.

Hafen, LeRoy R., ed. *The Mountain Men and the Fur Trade of the Far West.* 8 vols. Glendale, Arthur H. Clark, 1965–70.

――――, and W. J. Ghent. *The Life Story of Thomas Fitzpatrick, Broken Hand.* Denver, Old West Publishing Co., 1931.

――――, and Ann W. Hafen, eds. *To the Rockies and Oregon, 1839–1842.* Glendale, Arthur H. Clark, 1955.

Hastings, Lansford. *Emigrant's Guide to Oregon and California.* Cincinnati, G. Conclin, 1845.

Heizer, Robert F. *Aboriginal California and Great Basin Cartography, University of California Archaeological Survey Report, No. 41.* Berkeley, 1958.

Henry, Alexander. *New Light on the Early History of the Great Northwest.* Elliott Coues, ed. 2 vols. New York, F. P. Harper, 1897.

Hill, Joseph J. *Ewing Young in the Fur Trade of the Far Southwest, 1822–1834.* Eugene, Oregon, Koke-Tiffany Co., 1923.

Hines, Rev. Gustavus. *Oregon and its History, Condition and Prospects containing a Description of the Geography, Climate and Productions with Personal Adventures among the Indians.* New York & Auburn, Miller, Orton and Mulligan, 1857.

Hines, Rev. H. K. *An Illustrated History of the State of Oregon.* Chicago, Lewis Publishing Co., 1883.

Hodge, Frederick Webb. *Handbook of American Indians North of Mexico.* 2 vols. Washington, D.C., Bureau of American Ethnology, 1907–10.

Hofstadter, Richard, William Miller, and Daniel Aaron. *The United States: The History of a Republic*. Englewood Cliffs, New Jersey, Prentice-Hall, 1957.

Holmes, Kenneth L. *Ewing Young, Master Trapper*. Portland, Oregon, Binfords and Mort for the Peter Binford Foundation, 1967.

Huish, Robert, ed. *A Narrative of the Voyages and Travels of Captain Beechey . . . to the Pacific and Behring's Straits*. London, W. Wright, 1836.

Hussey, John A. *The History of Fort Vancouver and Its Physical Structure*. Portland, Oregon, Abbott, Kerns & Bell Co. for the National Park Service and Washington State Historical Society, 1957.

Innis, Harold A. *Essays in Canadian Economic History*. Mary Q. Innis, ed. Toronto, University of Toronto Press, 1956.

————. *The Fur Trade in Canada*. New Haven, Yale University Press, 1930.

Irving, Washington. *Astoria*. New York, G. P. Putnam, 1849.

————. *The Adventures of Captain Bonneville, U.S.A. in the Rocky Mountains and the Far West*. New York, G. P. Putnam, 1868.

Johansen, Dorothy O., ed. *Robert Newell's Memoranda: Travels in the Territory of Missouri: Travels to the Kayuse War, Together with a Report on the Indians South of the Columbia River*. Portland, Oregon, Champoeg Press, 1959.

————, and Charles Gates. *Empire of the Columbia*. New York, Harper & Bros., 1957.

Kane, Paul. *Wanderings of an Artist among the Indians of North America*. London, Longman, Brown, Green, & Roberts, 1859.

Kemble, John Haskell. *San Francisco Bay: A Pictorial Maritime History*. New York, Cornell Maritime Press, 1957.

Lillywhite, Bryant. *London Coffee House: A Reference Book of Coffee Houses of the Seventeenth, Eighteenth, and Nineteenth Centuries*. London, George Allen & Unwin Ltd., 1963.

McCain, Charles W. *History of the S.S. 'Beaver.'* Vancouver, Evans & Hastings, Printers, 1894.

MacDonald, Ronald. *Ronald MacDonald*. Ed. & annotated by William S. Lewis and Naojiro Murakami. Spokane, Eastern Washington State Historical Society, 1923.

McGillivray, Simon. *A Narrative of Occurrences in the Indian Countries of North America*. London, B. McMillan, 1817.

MacKay, Douglas. *The Honourable Company*. London, Cassell, 1937.

Mackenzie, Alexander. *Voyages from Montreal on the River St. Lawrence, through the Continent of North America, to the Frozen and Pacific Oceans in the Years 1789 and 1793*. 2 vols. Philadelphia, John Morgan & R. Carr, 1802.

Mackenzie, Cecil W. *Donald Mackenzie, King of the Northwest*. Los Angeles, I. Black, Jr., 1937.

McInnis, Edgar. *Canada: A Political and Social History.* New York, Holt, Rinehart & Winston, 1961.

McLeod, Malcolm. *Oregon Indemnity: Claim of Chief Factors and Chief Traders of the Hudson's Bay Company,* Ottawa, 1892.

McLoughlin, John. *Letters of Dr. John McLoughlin.* Burt Brown Barker, ed. Portland, Oregon, Binfords & Mort for the Oregon Historical Society, 1948.

———. *The Letters of John McLoughlin, from Fort Vancouver to the Governor and Committee, First Series, 1825–38.* E. E. Rich, ed. London, Hudson's Bay Record Society, Vol. IV, 1941.

———. *The Letters of John McLoughlin from Fort Vancouver to the Governor and Committee, Second Series, 1839–44.* E. E. Rich, ed. London, Hudson's Bay Record Society, Vol. VII, 1943.

———. *The Letters of Dr. McLoughlin from Fort Vancouver to the Governor and Committee, Third Series, 1844–46.* E. E. Rich, ed. London, Hudson's Bay Record Society, Vol. VI, 1944.

Madsen, Brigham. *The Bannock of Idaho.* Caldwell, Idaho, Caxton Printers, 1958.

Malloy, W. M., C. F. Redmond, and E. J. Treworth, eds. *Treaties, Conventions, International Acts, Protocols, and Agreements between the United States and Other Powers, 1776–1937.* 4 vols., Washington, Government Printing Office, 1910–38.

Maloney, Alice Bay, ed. *Fur Brigade to the Bonaventura.* San Francisco, California Historical Society, 1945.

Manning, Clarence A. *Russian Influence on Early America.* New York, Library Publishers, 1953.

Martin, R. M. *The Hudson's Bay Territories and Vancouver's Island.* London, T. & W. Boone, 1849.

Melish, John. *The Traveller's Directory through the United States.* Philadelphia, the author, 1815.

———. *The Traveller's Manual: and Description of the United States . . . .* New York, A. T. Goodrich, 1831.

Merk, Frederick. *Albert Gallatin and the Oregon Problem.* Cambridge, Harvard University Press, 1950.

Michael, Franz H., and George E. Taylor. *The Far East in the Modern World.* New York, Henry Holt & Co., 1956.

Miller, David Hunter, ed. *Treaties and Other International Acts of the United States.* 8 vols. Washington, Government Printing Office, 1931–48.

Morgan, Dale L. *The Great Salt Lake.* Indianapolis & New York, Bobbs-Merrill Co., 1947.

———. *Jedediah Smith and the Opening of the West.* Indianapolis, Bobbs-Merrill Co., 1953.

———. *The West of William H. Ashley.* Denver, Old West Publishing Co., 1964.

————, and Carl I. Wheat. *Jedediah Smith and His Maps of the American West*. San Francisco, California Historical Society, 1954.

Morice, Rev. Adrien Gabriel. *The History of the Northern Interior of British Columbia, Formerly New Caledonia*. Toronto, W. Briggs, 1904.

Morton, Arthur S. *A History of the Canadian West to 1870–71*. London, Nelson & Co., 1939.

Morton, W. L. *The Kingdom of Canada*. Toronto, McClelland & Stewart, 1963.

Mowry, William A. *Marcus Whitman and the Early Days of Oregon*. New York, Boston, & Chicago, Silver Burdett & Co., 1901.

Nunis, Doyce B., Jr., ed. *The California Diary of Faxon Dean Atherton, 1836–1839*. San Francisco & Los Angeles, California Historical Society, 1964.

Ogden, Adele. *The California Sea Otter Trade, 1784–1848*. Berkeley, University of California Press, 1941.

Ogden, Peter Skene. *Ogden's Snake Country Journals, 1824–26*. E. E. Rich, ed. Introd. by Burt Brown Barker. London, Hudson's Bay Record Society, Vol. XIII, 1950.

————. *Peter Skene Ogden's Snake Country Journal, 1826–27*. Frederick Merk, ed. London, Hudson's Bay Record Society, Vol. XXIII, 1961.

————. *Peter Skene Ogden's Snake Country Journals, 1827–28 and 1828–29*. Glyndwr Williams, ed. Introduction and notes by David E. Miller and David L. Miller, London, Hudson's Bay Record Society, Vol. XXVIII, 1971.

Okun, S. B. *The Russian-American Company*. Trans. by Carl Ginsburg. Cambridge, Harvard University Press, 1951.

Ormsby, Margaret A. *British Columbia: A History*. Vancouver, Evergreen Press, 1958.

Parker, Reverend Samuel. *Journal of an Exploring Tour beyond the Rocky Mountains . . . 1835, '36, and '37*. Boston, Crocker & Brewster, 1842.

Perkins, Bradford. *Castlereagh and Adams: England and the United States, 1812–1823*. Berkeley, University of California Press, 1964.

Phillips, Paul Chrisler, and J. W. Smurr. *The Fur Trade*. 2 vols. Norman, University of Oklahoma Press, 1961.

Rich, E. E., ed. *Colin Robertson's Correspondence Book, September 1817 to September 1822*. London, Hudson's Bay Record Society, Vol. II, 1939.

————, ed. *The History of the Hudson's Bay Company, 1670–1870*. 2 vols. London, Hudson's Bay Record Society, Vols. XXI–XXII, 1958, 1959.

Richman, Irving B. *California under Spain and Mexico, 1535–1847*. Boston, Houghton Mifflin, 1911.

Rolle, Andrew F. *California: A History*. New York, Thomas Y. Crowell Co., 1963.

Ross, Alexander. *The Fur Hunters of the Far West: A Narrative of Adventures in Oregon and the Rocky Mountains*. 2 vols. London, Smith,

Elder & Co., 1855. New edition, Kenneth A. Spaulding, ed. Norman, University of Oklahoma Press, 1956.

Rossiter, Clinton. *The First American Revolution.* New York, Harcourt Brace & World, Inc., 1956.

Russell, Carl P. *Firearms, Traps, and Tools of the Mountain Men.* New York, Alfred A. Knopf, 1967.

Sabine, Lorenzo. *Loyalists of the American Revolution.* 2 vols. Boston, Little Brown, 1947.

Savage, James, ed. *A Genealogical Dictionary of First Settlers of New England, Showing Three Generations of Those Who Came before May, 1692, on the Basis of Farmer's Register.* 4 vols. Baltimore, Genealogical Publishing Co., 1965.

Simpson, George. *Simpson's 1828 Journey to the Columbia.* E. E. Rich, ed. Intro. by W. W. Stewart Wallace. London, Hudson's Bay Record Society, Vol. X, 1947.

————. *Fur Trade and Empire: The Journal of Sir George Simpson.* Frederick Merk, ed. Cambridge, Harvard University Press, 1931.

Scidmore, Eliza Ruhamah. *Alaska, Its Southern Coast and the Sitkan Archipelago.* Boston, D. Lothrop and Co., 1885.

Stewart, Omer Call. *Northern Paiute Bands. University of California Publications in Anthropological Records,* Berkeley, University of California Press, 1939.

Sullivan, Maurice S. *The Travels of Jedediah Smith.* Santa Anna, Calif., Fine Arts Printing Co., 1934.

Tolmie, William Fraser. *The Journals of William Fraser Tolmie, Physician and Fur Trader.* Vancouver, Mitchell Press, 1963.

Townsend, John K. *Narrative of a Journey across the Rocky Mountains to the Columbia River and a Visit to the Sandwich Islands, Chile, etc.* Reuben Gold Thwaites, ed. Philadelphia, Henry Perkins, 1839.

Van Alstyne, Lawrence. *The Ogden Family History, Elizabethtown Branch: Charts.* New Haven, Tuttle, Morehouse and Taylor Press, 1907.

Wallace, William Stewart, ed. *The Macmillan Dictionary of Canadian Biography.* 3rd edition. London & Toronto, Macmillan, 1963.

Warre, Henry J. *Sketches in North America and the Oregon Territory.* London, Dickinson and Co., 1849.

Wheeler, William Ogden. *The Ogden Family in America, Elizabethtown Branch, and their English Ancestry.* Philadelphia, printed for private circulation by J. B. Lippincott, 1907.

Wilkes, Charles. *Narrative of the United States Exploring Expedition During the Years 1838, 1839, 1840, 1841, 1842.* 5 vols. Philadelphia, C. Shuman, 1844.

Winther, O. O. *The Old Oregon Country. University of Indiana Publications in Social Science, No. 7.* Bloomington, 1950.

Notes

PROLOGUE

1. William Ogden Wheeler, *The Ogden Family in America, Elizabethtown Branch, and Their English Ancestry*, 25.

2. *Ibid.*, 68.

3. Clinton Rossiter, *The First American Revolution*, 238–39.

4. Judge David Ogden was married to Gertrude Gouverneur, and their son, Samuel, married Euphemia Morris in 1754. Wheeler, *Ogden Family*, 67, 104.

5. *Ibid.*, 69.

6. Lorenzo Sabine, *Loyalists of the American Revolution*, II, 124.

7. Samuel Ogden sold some of his land to Judge William Cooper, who was the father of James Fenimore Cooper, author of *Leatherstocking Tales*. Wheeler, *Ogden Family*, 105.

8. Daniel J. Boorstin, *The Americans: The National Experience*, 207.

9. Wheeler, *Ogden Family*, 103–105.

Chapter I

THE CALL OF THE BEAVER

1. Wheeler, *Ogden Family*, 102–103.

2. Letter from A. E. Williams, vestry clerk, Cathedral of the Holy Trinity, Quebec, to the author, October 7, 1970.

3. Wheeler, *Ogden Family*, 180.

4. *Peter Skene Ogden's Snake Country Journals, 1824–25 and 1825–26* (ed. by E. E. Rich), xv.

5. The canoe and much of the baggage were cached in the upper reaches of the Fraser River to make traveling to the Pacific easier. See Alexander Mackenzie, *Voyages from Montreal . . . in the Years 1789 and 1793*.

6. See H. P. Biggar, *The Voyages of Jacques Cartier*.

7. Paul Chrisler Phillips and J. W. Smurr, *The Fur Trade*, I, 15.

8. Carl P. Russell, *Firearms, Traps, and Tools of the Mountain Men*, 5–6.

9. See E. E. Rich, *The History of the Hudson's Bay Company, 1670–1870*, I, 52–60; John S. Galbraith, *The Hudson's Bay Company as an Imperial Factor, 1821–1869*, 4.

10. For the best discussion, see Gordon Charles Davidson, *The Northwest Company*.

11. The area between the Ohio and Mississippi rivers and south of the relatively undefined Canadian boundary.

12. Phillips and Smurr, *The Fur Trade*, I, 157–66.

13. Nicholas Hoffman died in 1800, but respect for him and his family remained. Wheeler, *Ogden Family*, 103.

14. William Caulfield Anderson, "History of the Northwest Coast," MS, Bancroft Library; T. C. Elliott, "Peter Skene Ogden, Fur Trader," *Oregon Historical Quarterly*, Vol. XI (Sept., 1910), 235.

15. Peter Fidler, Île à la Crosse Journal, September 21, 1810, mentions that Ogden is to winter at the North West Company's post there. B.89/a/12, fo. 11, Hudson's Bay Company Archives (hereafter cited as H.B.C.A.).

16. The Saskatchewan District stretched from at least Cumberland House on Cumberland Lake between the drainage of the Churchill and Saskatchewan rivers to the Rocky Mountains.

17. For the most authoritative description of Fidler, see J. G. MacGregor, *Peter Fidler: Canada's Forgotten Surveyor, 1769–1822*.

18. Fidler's Île à la Crosse Journal, entries for October 12 and 25, 1810, fos. 13, 13d, 14.

19. *Ibid.*, entry for March 27, 1811, fo. 26d.

20. *Ibid.*, entries for June 4 and 10, 1811, fos. 36–37.

21. Edmonton District Journal, 1814–15, entry for February 1, 1815, B.60/a/13, fos. 14d–15d, H.B.C.A.

22. *Ibid.*

23. Ogden is undoubtedly referring to his encounter with Hudson's Bay Company men on Paint River in December, 1814.

24. Edmonton House District Journal, 1814–15, entry for April 1, 1815, B.60/a/13, H.B.C.A.

25. Logan, Île à la Crosse Journal, entry for September 13, 1815, B.89/a/3, fo. 2, H.B.C.A.

26. *Ibid.*, entry for March 20, 1816, fo. 16.

27. The Hudson's Bay Company often used the term *house* instead of *post* or *fort* for its establishments. In this case, the writing was done by a Hudson's Bay Company employee and refers to both companies' posts.

28. James Bird, Edmonton House Journal, entry for May 16, 1816, B.60/a/15, fos. 37–38, H.B.C.A.

29. "Extract from memorial from J. Berens, Gov. H. B. C., to Lord Bathurst," February 4, 1818, Letters from Red River Settlement, Vol. V, Selkirk Papers, No. 158(a), in series of Hudson's Bay Company photostats and copies, H.B.C.A. (hereafter referred to as Selkirk Papers).

30. "Inclosure in Sir J. C. Sherbrooke's of 20th July, 1818; viz. Mr. Coltman's Report, etc.," *Papers Relating to the Red River Settlement, 1815–1819*, printed by orders of the House of Commons, July 12, 1819, 242–44, H.B.C.A.

31. *Ibid.*

32. Ross Cox, *Adventures on the Columbia River*, II, 24–44.

33. Mr. Gale to Lady Selkirk, Bas de la Rivière, August 8, 1817, Vol. IV, Selkirk Papers, No. 157(b).

Chapter II

ACROSS THE GREAT DIVIDE

1. Lawrence J. Burpee (ed.), *Journal de Larocque de la rivière Assiniboine jusqu'à la rivière "Aux Roche Jaunes,"* 16–42.

2. Davidson, *The Northwest Company*; *David Thompson's Narrative, 1784–1812* (ed. by Richard Glover).

3. Early in its history the North West Company employed Iroquois Indians from the St. Lawrence region and sent many of them west. Although good trappers, they were unruly and difficult to manage, so their introduction into the western fur trade was not generally considered a successful experiment.

4. Hubert Howe Bancroft, *History of the Northwest Coast, 1800–1846,* II, 287–89.

5. Ogden's movements at this time are rather difficult to follow, but J. F. La Rocque, writing to J. G. McTavish from Thompson River on March 22, 1819 (F.3/2, fo. 190, H.B.C.A.), mentions "Mr. Ogden who had charge of Spokan last Fall."

6. Alexander Ross, *The Fur Hunters of the Far West,* I, 138–39.

7. T. C. Elliott, in "Peter Skene Ogden, Fur Trader," *loc. cit.,* 245, suggests that Ogden took a wife "from the Spokane tribe of Indians (if family tradition is correct)"; and Archie Binns, in *Peter Skene Ogden, Fur Trader,* 93, is adamant that she was a "full blooded Flathead." Dale Morgan, in *Jedediah Smith and the Opening of the West,* 135, substantiates this writer's theory that Julia Rivet was a Nez Percé.

8. Roderick McKenzie, Jr., June 26, 1819, B.105/a/7, fo. 14, H.B.C.A.

9. Colin Robertson to William Williams, Fort Cumberland, August 26, 1819, in *Colin Robertson's Correspondence Book* (ed. by E. E. Rich), 257.

10. Colin Robertson to William Williams, Île à la Crosse, September 6, 1819, *ibid.,* 258–59.

11. Colin Robertson's journal, entry for May 24, 1820, as quoted in Samuel Black, *A Journal of a Voyage from the Rocky Mountain Portage in Peace River to the Sources of Finlays Branch and Northwestward in the Summer of 1824* (ed. by E. E. Rich), xxxvi.

12. Wheeler, *Ogden Family,* 183.

13. John Dugald Cameron to the Governor and Council of the Northern Department, April 3, 1822, D.4/116, fos. 49–50, H.B.C.A.; see also *Ogden's Journals, 1824–26* (Rich), xx–xxi.

14. J. L. Lewes to Governor Simpson, letter begun at Fort George on April 2, 1822, and completed at Fort Nez Percés on April 22, D.4/116, fo. 57, H.B.C.A.

15. Peter Skene Ogden to Finan McDonald, May 3, 1822, B.208/a/1, H.B.C.A.

16. Cumberland House Journal, entries for June 15 and 16, 1822, B.49/a/38, H.B.C.A.

17. George Simpson to Andrew Colvile, York Factory, August 16, 1822; see Black's *Journal*, xlvi.

18. John Dugald Cameron to the Governor and Council of the Northern Department, April 3, 1822, D.4/116, fos. 49d–50, H.B.C.A.

19. The Governor and Committee to Governor Simpson, March 8, 1822, A.6/20, fo. 36, H.B.C.A.

20. George Simpson to John Dugald Cameron, York Factory, July 18, 1822; see *Minutes of Council Northern Department of Rupert Land, 1821–31* (ed. by Harvey Fleming), 412–13 (hereafter cited as Fleming, *Minutes of Council*).

21. John Halkett was a member of the London Committee of the Hudson's Bay Company.

22. Selkirk Papers, fo. 637, No. 112. See *Ogden's Journals, 1824–26* (Rich), xxii–xxiii.

23. Nicholas Garry, in *Diaries of Edward Ermatinger and Nicholas Garry, Transactions of the Royal Society of Canada*, Vol. VI, Section 11, p. 93, bound copy in H.B.C.A.

24. The North West Company ledger indicates that Ogden's credit in 1821 was almost two thousand North West livres, F.4/32, fo. 763, H.B.C.A. Thirteen and one-third North West livres were equal to one pound sterling. See *Ogden's Journals, 1824–26* (Rich), xvi, n.1.

25. William Younger's pub, Ye Olde London, was located on the site at the time of this writing.

26. Description given in *Roach's London Pocket Pilot, 1793*, as quoted in Bryant Lillywhite, *London Coffee Houses*, 339.

27. *Ibid.*, 339–44.

28. J. D. Cameron to Governor Simpson, April 13, 1822; see Black's *Journal*, xiv.

29. Meeting of the Board for Consulting and Advising on the Management of the Trade, February 27, 1823, A.3/1, fo. 20d, H.B.C.A.

30. At the beginning of the nineteenth century, excavations on and around the site of the London Coffee House revealed many Roman ruins.

31. A pharmacy stood on the site at the time of this writing.

32. T. C. Elliott, "Peter Skene Ogden, Fur Trader," *loc. cit.*, 243; Binns, *Peter Skene Ogden*, 73–74.

33. William Smith, Secretary, to P. S. Ogden, Care of Wm. McGillivray, Hudson's Bay House, London, March 6, 1823, A.6/20, H.B.C.A.

34. A. Colvile to George Simpson (?), letter headed "(Copy to George Simpson)," dated London, March 10, 1823, Selkirk Papers, No. 112.

35. Governor Simpson to Andrew Colvile, September 8, 1823. See *Fur Trade and Empire: The Journal of Sir George Simpson* (ed. by Frederick Merk), 203 (hereafter referred to as Merk, *Fur Trade and Empire*); *Ogden's Journals, 1824–26* (Rich), xxiv.

36. Bird was also on Company business and was carrying a box.

37. See A.6/20, fos. 154–68, H.B.C.A.

38. "Diary of Nicholas Garry," in *Diaries of Edward Ermatinger and Nicholas Garry*, Section 11, 83–88.

39. Lac la Pluie Journal, 1822–23, B.105/2/8, fo. 15d, H.B.C.A.

40. Since only chief factors, of whom James Bird was one, were allowed to attend council meetings, Ogden was not included.

41. Fleming, *Minutes of Council*, 39.

42. York Factory Journal, B.239/a/131, H.B.C.A. See Black's *Journal*, xlvi–xlvii.

43. Fleming, *Minutes of Council*, 52–54.

44. York Factory Journal, entry for July 18, 1823, B.39/a/131, H.B.C.A.

45. Arthur S. Morton, *A History of the Canadian West to 1870–71*, 712.

46. Governor Simpson to Andrew Colvile, York Factory, September 8, 1823, Selkirk Papers, No. 112.

47. Morton, *History of the Canadian West*, 711–12; John Work, "Journal —1823–1827," MS, Provincial Archives of British Columbia. There are also some imperfect copies in the Bancroft Library at Berkeley, California.

48. John Rowand's Journal of Occurrences, Edmonton District, 1823–24, B.60/a/22, H.B.C.A.

49. *Ibid.*, entries for November 4–6, 1823, fos. 8d–20d. It is known that Mrs. Ogden was still at Edmonton House on October 28, for on that day she bought goods amounting to £ 4.19.8d., which included a 2½-point blanket, colored thread, blue beads, and Indian awls and knives. Edmonton Accounts, 1823–24, MS, B.60/d/15, H.B.C.A.

50. At this time it was known as Jasper's House, but it was later called Jasper House.

Chapter III

JOHN BULL MEETS UNCLE SAM

1. *The Fur Hunters of the Far West*, I, 184.

2. T. C. Elliott Collection, Oregon Historical Society, Portland.

3. Finan McDonald to J. G. McTavish, April 4, 1824, B.239/c/1, H.B.C.A., as quoted in Galbraith, *Hudson's Bay Company*, 84.

4. Alexander Ross, Snake Country Journal, 1824, B.202/a/1, H.B.C.A.

5. The Governor and Committee to John Haldane and John D. Cameron, September 4, 1822, in Merk, *Fur Trade and Empire*, 187–88.

6. Entry in Simpson's diary for October 28, 1824, *ibid.*, 44–47.

7. *Ibid.*, Appendix A, 198.

8. Ross, Snake Country Journal, entry for October 12, 1824, B.202/a/1, H.B.C.A.

9. 20 Cong., 2 sess., *Sen. Exec. Doc. 67.*

10. Alexander Ross, Flathead Post Journal, entry for November 26, 1824, B.69/a/1, H.B.C.A.

11. *Ibid.*, entry for November 27.

12. Governor and Committee to the Chief Factors in charge of the Columbia Department, July 27, 1825, A.6/21/fo. 56, H.B.C.A.

13. Simpson's entry for October 28, 1824, Merk, *Fur Trade and Empire,* 44–47.

14. Ross, Flathead Post Journal, B.69/a/1, H.B.C.A.

15. *Ibid.*

16. *Ogden's Journals, 1824–26* (Rich), 2–3. There is a discrepancy regarding the size of the party, for the Flathead Journal, B.69/a/1, H.B.C.A., as summarized by T. C. Elliott in "Journal of Alexander Ross—Snake Country Expedition, 1824," *Oregon Historical Quarterly,* Vol. XIV (Dec., 1913), 386–88, gives the figures as "25 lodges, 2 gentlemen, 2 interpreters, 71 men and lads, 80 guns, 364 beaver traps and 372 horses."

17. Carl P. Russell, *Firearms, Traps, and Tools of the Mountain Men,* 151.

18. *Ogden's Journals, 1824–26* (Rich), 7, entry for December 24, 1824.

19. *Ibid.*, entry for January 1, 1825.

20. *Ibid.*, entry for February 1, 1825.

21. *Ibid.*, entry for February 2, 1825.

22. *Ibid.*, 23, entry for February 17, 1825; William Kittson's Journal, entries for February 17 and 27 included in *ibid.*, 218–19.

23. *Ibid.*, 24, entry for February 22, 1825.

24. *Ibid.*, 24–26, entries for February 23 and 28, 1825.

25. *Ibid.*, 37, entry for April 17; David E. Miller, "Peter Skene Ogden's Explorations in the Great Salt Lake Region: A Restudy Based on Newly Published Journals," *The Western Humanities Review,* Vol. VIII (Spring, 1954), 141.

26. *Ibid.*, 146; *Ogden's Journals, 1824–26* (Rich), 43–44, entries for May 4 and 5, 1825.

27. S. Lyman Tyler, "The Myth of the Lake of Copala and Land of Teguayo," *Utah Historical Quarterly,* Vol. XX (Oct., 1952), 343–61.

28. Morgan, *Jedediah Smith,* 142–43, and Miller, "Ogden's Explorations in the Great Salt Lake Region," *loc. cit.,* 141.

29. Ogden says "early in the day" while Kittson says "in the afternoon." See *Ogden's Journals, 1824–26* (Rich), entry for May 23, 1825, and Kittson's journal, *ibid.,* 233.

30. If this were the case, Provost deserves the honor of discovering the Great Salt Lake; Bridger did not see it until early in 1825.

31. *Ogden's Journals, 1824–26* (Rich), 51; Kittson's journal, *ibid.,* 233–34; Gloria Griffen Cline, *Exploring the Great Basin,* 141–42.

32. *Ogden's Journals, 1824–26* (Rich), 51, entry for May 24, 1825.

33. Ross, "Journal of the Snake Country Expedition, 1824," *loc. cit.*, 375.

34. Ogden says that he now has only twenty trappers, *Ogden's Journals, 1824–26* (Rich), 54, entry for May 25, while Kittson states, "Our party is now reduced to the number of 22 Freemen, 11 Engages and 6 Boys besides Mr. Ogden and I" (*ibid.*, 235).

35. Dale L. Morgan, *The West of William H. Ashley*, 286, states that 700 furs were taken. However, McLoughlin in a letter written to the Governor and Committee, October 6, 1825, places the number between 2,000 and 3,000. See *The Letters of John McLoughlin from Fort Vancouver, First Series*, 9.

36. Letter, Dr. McLoughlin to the Governor, Chief Factors, and Chief Traders, Fort Vancouver, August 10, 1825, B.223/b/1, H.B.C.A.

37. Dr. McLoughlin to Peter Skene Ogden, Fort Vancouver, November 3, 1826, B.223/b/2, H.B.C.A.

38. Harrison Clifford Dale, *The Ashley-Smith Explorations and the Discovery of a Central Route to the Pacific, 1822–29*, 152–53.

39. McLoughlin to the Governor and Committee, October 6, 1825, *The Letters of John McLoughlin from Fort Vancouver, First Series*, 9. See also C. Gregory Crampton and Gloria Griffen [Cline], "The San Buenaventura, Mythical River of the West," *Pacific Historical Review*, Vol. XXV (May, 1956), and Cline, *Exploring the Great Basin*.

40. Peter Skene Ogden, "The Snake Country Expedition, 1824–25," (ed. by Frederick Merk), *Oregon Historical Quarterly*, Vol. XXXV (June, 1934), 99.

41. Kittson Map, B.202/a/3b, H.B.C.A., which has been reprinted in *Ogden's Journals, 1824–26* (Rich).

42. Smith drew this map, which has since been lost, for Dr. McLoughlin in August, 1828, when he had taken refuge at Fort Vancouver following the Umpqua Massacre. See Morgan, *Jedediah Smith and the Opening of the West*, and Morgan and Carl I. Wheat, *Jedediah Smith and His Maps of the American West*.

43. *Ogden's Journals, 1824–26* (Rich), 56, entry for May 29, 1825.

44. *Ibid.*, 59–60, entry for June 12, 1825.

45. Entry for October 19, 1825, Edmonton House Journal, B.60/a/23, H.B.C.A.

46. This letter, dated June 27, 1824 (1825), has been reprinted by the Hudson's Bay Record Society in *The Letters of John McLoughlin from Fort Vancouver, First Series*, 296–97, and in "*The Snake Country Expedition, 1824–25*" (Merk), *loc. cit.*, 115–16.

47. *Ogden's Journals, 1824–26* (Rich), 70, entry for July 30, 1825.

48. *Fur Trade and Empire* (Merk), 54–57, entry for November 2, 1824.

49. Governor and Committee to Simpson, March 12, 1827, A.6/21, fo. 117d, H.B.C.A.

Chapter IV

OUR MAN IN THE SNAKE COUNTRY

1. It is impossible to trace the numbers and identities of the men who accompanied Ogden on this second Snake expedition, but undoubtedly the number was fairly small, for Simpson in his 1826 report to the Governor and Committee indicated that the combined strength of Ogden's and McDonald's parties consisted of "about 50 gentlemen and servants." D.4/89, fos. 2d–3, H.B.C.A., and *Ogden's Journals, 1824–26* (Rich), 95.

2. Russell, *Firearms*, 97–113, 147–50.

3. *Ogden's Journals, 1824–26* (Rich), 128, entry for February 16, 1826.

4. When the name of the Sandwich Islands was changed to Hawaii, the name of the river also changed, but the new name was a corrupted form of "Hawaii."

5. Hawaiians took part in the western fur trade. Their first contact with the trade came as a result of the extensive shipping traffic between Oahu and the posts at the mouth of the Columbia.

6. *Ogden's Journals, 1824–26* (Rich), 143–44, entry for March 20, 1826.

7. Dale, *The Ashley-Smith Explorations*, 165–66.

8. 1/2 denotes a baby or very small beaver.

9. *Ogden's Journals, 1824–26* (Rich), 154, entry for April 10, 1826.

10. Morgan, *Jedediah Smith*, 170.

11. *Ogden's Journals, 1824–26* (Rich), 155, entry for April 11, 1826.

12. *Ibid.*, 166, entry for May 15, 1826.

13. *Ibid.*, 169, entry for May 23, 1826.

14. *Ibid.*, 194–95, entry for July 27, 1826.

15. The McDonald party made good time. They separated from Ogden on June 29, stopped at Fort Nez Percés, and were met by Hudson's Bay Company men at The Dalles on July 10. See letter, William Connolly to the Governor, Chief Factors, and Chief Traders, July 18, 1826, D.4/120, fo. 9d, *ibid.*, 195.

16. The date of Gervaise's arrival at Fort Vancouver is unknown, but he did arrive in time to accompany Ogden on his third expedition. *Ibid.*, 204, entry for July 16, 1826.

17. John A. Hussey, *The History of Fort Vancouver and Its Physical Structure.*

18. David Douglas, *Journal Kept by David Douglas During His Travels in North America, 1823–1827*, 106–107, 152.

19. William Smith, Secretary of the Committee, to the Chief Factors of the Columbia Department, November 14, 1823, A.6/20, 236–37, H.B.C.A., in which he lists the recent library material that he was sending out to the Columbia.

20. *Ogden's Journals, 1824–26* (Douglas), 205.

21. Rich, in *Hudson's Bay Company*, II, 592, states that Ogden brought out 3,800 beaver and otter.

22. McLoughlin to the Governor, Chief Factors, and Chief Traders, August 8, 1826, B.223/b/1, and McLoughlin to John Dease, August 8, 1826, B.223/b/2, H.B.C.A.

23. "Ogden's Snake Country Report 1825–26," written at Fort Vancouver, August 20, 1826, in *Ogden's Journals, 1824–26* (Rich), 264.

24. McLoughlin to the Governor, Chief Factors, and Chief Traders, Northern Factory, July 4, 1826, D.4/120, fo. 7, H.B.C.A.

25. "Snake Country Report, 1826," Fort Vancouver, August 10, 1826, in *Ogden's Journals, 1824–26* (Rich), 263–64.

26. *Ibid.*, 263.

27. McLoughlin to the Governor and Committee, September 1, 1826, in *The Letters of John McLoughlin from Fort Vancouver, First Series*, 33.

28. Jedediah Smith to the United States Plenipotentiary at Mexico (City), December 16, 1826, in Andrew F. Rolle (ed.), "Jedediah Strong Smith: New Documentation," *Mississippi Valley Historical Review*, Vol. XXXX (Sept., 1953), 308.

29. *American Monthly Magazine*, Vol. XXXIII (Jan., 1906), 329. Undoubtedly Smith was confused about the latitude of San Francisco Bay; 43 degrees north latitude lies in southern Oregon.

30. For more detailed information about the Smith route, see Morgan, *Jedediah Smith*; Dale, *The Ashley-Smith Explorations*; Maurice Sullivan, *The Travels of Jedediah Smith*; and Irving Richman, *California under Spain and Mexico, 1535–1847*.

31. In 1830, McLoughlin described Ogden's return trip from the Gulf of California: Ogden "ascended the North Branch of the Buenaventura till he came to the head of it, where he hunted winter 1826 and 7." McLoughlin to the Governor and Committee, October 11, 1830, in *The Letters of John McLoughlin from Fort Vancouver, First Series*, 85–86.

32. Peter Skene Ogden, "Journals of the Snake Country Expedition, 1826–27," (ed. by T. C. Elliott), *Oregon Historical Quarterly*, Vol. XI (June, 1910), 201, entry for July 18, 1827, 134. See also McLoughlin to Simpson, March 20, 1828, D.4/121, fo. 35, in *The Letters of John McLoughlin from Fort Vancouver, First Series*, 49–51.

33. *Peter Skene Ogden's Snake Country Journals, 1827–28 and 1828–29* (ed. by Glyndwr Williams).

34. Ogden's "Snake Country Journal, 1828–29," B.202/a/8, H.B.C.A., entries for October 28 and November 1, 1828.

35. *Ibid.*, entry for December 10, 1828.

36. *Ibid.*, entry for March 30, 1829.

37. Dr. McLoughlin to the Governor and Committee, Fort Vancouver, August 5, 1829, B.223/b/5, H.B.C.A.

38. Peter Skene Ogden to the Governor, Chief Factors, and Chief Traders,

March 21, 1831, in "Ogden's Report of His 1829–30 Expedition" (ed. by John Scaglione), *California Historical Quarterly*, Vol. XXVIII (June, 1949), 121–22.

39. "Fur Trader," *Traits of Indian Character*, 3.

40. *Ibid.*, 4–10.

41. Mexico had declared her independence from Spain in 1821, and California was now a Mexican province.

42. Letter, Dr. McLoughlin to the Governor and Committee, July 23, 1830, as quoted in *The Letters of Dr. John McLoughlin* (ed. by Burt Brown Barker), 119–20; see also "Warner's Reminiscences," MS, Bancroft Library; Bancroft, *History of California, 1825–40*, 174; Kenneth L. Holmes, *Ewing Young, Master Trapper*.

43. McLoughlin to the Governor and Committee, July 23, 1830, *McLoughlin Letters* (Barker), 119–20.

44. Letter, Peter Skene Ogden to John McLeod, March 10, 1831, T. C. Elliott Collection, Oregon Historical Society.

Chapter V

THE THREAT OF THE NORTH

1. Rich, *Hudson's Bay Company*, II, 612–13. Also Robie L. Reid, "Early Days at Old Fort Langley," paper read before the Royal Society of Canada and reprinted in the *British Columbia Historical Quarterly*, Vol. I (April, 1937), 70–85.

2. B.239/c/1, H.B.C.A.; *Simpson's 1828 Journey*, 248.

3. Governor and Committee to Dr. McLoughlin, October 28, 1829, A.6/22, H.B.C.A.

4. There has always been a question about what really happened. Were all of the men drowned or were they murdered by the Clatsop Indians? See *Simpson's 1828 Journey*, 622–23. See also McLoughlin to the Governor and Committee, *The Letters of John McLoughlin from Fort Vancouver, First Series*, 71–74.

5. Brigs owned by Josiah Marshall and Dixey Wildes of Boston.

6. McLoughlin to the Governor and Committee, July 23, 1830, in *McLoughlin Letters* (Barker), 117–19.

7. McLoughlin to Æmilius Simpson, July 7, 1830. *Ibid.*, 109–10.

8. *Simpson's 1828 Journey*, 626–27, and McLoughlin to Francis Heron, October 14, 1830, in *McLoughlin Letters* (Barker), 149.

9. James Douglas Journal, 1840–41, MS in the Archives of British Columbia, Victoria, British Columbia. There is an imperfect copy in the Bancroft Library, Berkeley, California. See also H. H. Bancroft, *History of the Northwest Coast, 1800–1846*, 502–504.

10. McLoughlin to the Governor and Committee, October 11, 1830, in *McLoughlin Letters* (Barker), 140.

11. A. G. Harvey, "Meredith Gardner: Doctor of Medicine," *British Columbia Historical Quarterly*, Vol. IX (April, 1945), 98.

12. *Simpson's 1828 Journey*, 250–52.

13. *McLoughlin Letters* (Barker), 316–17.

14. McLoughlin to the Governor and Committee, October 11, 1830, in *The Letters of John McLoughlin from Fort Vancouver, First Series*, 88.

15. The child, Ogden's favorite daughter, was born January 1, 1836, and was named Sarah in honor of Ogden's mother and Julia after her own mother.

16. McLoughlin to Captain Simpson, April 11, 1831, B.223/b/7, H.B.C.A.

17. Entry in the Fort Colvile Journal for January 5, 1831, B.45/a/1, H.B.C.A.

18. On May 29, 1831, according to one source, Ogden's newly born son, Peter, was baptized by the Reverend D. T. Jones, E.4/a/1, fo. 82, H.B.C.A. There is a discrepancy here. The Peter Ogden who became so well known in the fur trade was born on January 18, 1817. Too, according to Wheeler, *Ogden Family*, 183, no child was born to the Ogdens in 1831.

19. Entry in the William Fraser Tolmie Journal for June 15, 1834. The original journals are in the Provincial Archives of British Columbia, Victoria, but they have been published under the title *The Journals of William Fraser Tolmie, Physician and Fur Trader*. See also William Caulfield Anderson, "History of the Northwest Coast," MS, Bancroft Library.

20. Vassili Berg, "Historical Review of the Russian American Company from 1799 to 1863, compiled by the Department of Imperial Archives," MS, P–K, Bancroft Library.

21. Galbraith, *Hudson's Bay Company*, 120–34.

22. Eliza R. Scidmore, *Alaska, Its Southern Coast and the Sitkan Archipelago*, 157; Hector Chevigny, *Russian America, the Great Alaskan Venture, 1741–1867*; and Rich, *Hudson's Bay Company*, II, 625.

23. *Journals of W. F. Tolmie*, 283.

24. Ogden informed Dr. McLoughlin of Æmilius Simpson's death and of what had happened at Fort Simpson on both September 2 and 7. This is known from references in McLoughlin's reply to Ogden's letters, McLoughlin to Ogden, October 16, 1831, B.223/b/7, H.B.C.A.

25. Simpson was buried "on shore there," but when the fort was moved to a more pleasant site on Dundas Island, Simpson's casket was exhumed and "re-interred at the present Fort Simpson." Anderson, "History of the Northwest Coast," MS, Bancroft Library.

26. McLoughlin to Ogden, October 16, 1831, B.223/b/7, H.B.C.A.

27. Governor and Committee to George Simpson, June 8, 1832, A.6/22, fo. 130d, H.B.C.A.

28. McLoughlin indicates that he sent the remainder of Ogden's supplies in the *Cadboro* in August, 1831; McLoughlin to Ogden, August 14, 1831, B.223/b/7, fo. 5, H.B.C.A. He ordered Ogden to send the *Dryad* to Fort

Vancouver to pick up a "supply as will enable you to devote the whole of your attention to the Coasting Trade." McLoughlin to Ogden, October 16, 1831, B.223/b/7, H.B.C.A.

29. McLoughlin to Ogden, December 15, 1831, B.223/b/7, fo. 10d, H.B.C.A.

30. McLoughlin to Ogden, December 15, 1831, B.223/b/7, fo. 10d, H.B.C.A.

31. Simpson's Report, D.4/99, fo. 15, H.B.C.A.; see W. Kaye Lamb's introduction to *The Letters of John McLoughlin from Fort Vancouver, First Series*, lxxxvii–viii.

32. McLoughlin to James Birnie, January 10, 1832, B.223/b/7, fo. 11, H.B.C.A.

33. McLoughlin to Ogden, December 15, 1831, B.223/b/7, fo. 10d, H.B.C.A.

34. McLoughlin to Duncan Finlayson, July 17, 1832, B.223/b/8, and Governor and Committee to Simpson, March 1, 1833, A.6/23, fo. 9, in which the Governor and Committee mention receiving a letter from Ogden dated "Sitka, 8th May."

35. Log of the *Dryad*, C.1/281, entries for September 27 and 28, 1834.

36. Hector Chevigny, *Russian America*, 127 and 189; Lamb's introduction to *The Letters of John McLoughlin from Fort Vancouver, First Series*, lxxxvii–viii; *Alaska Boundary Tribunal*, Appendix to the Counter Case of the United States, 1–2.

37. Chevigny, *Russian America*, 131.

38. McLoughlin to Governor Simpson, September 12, 1832, B.223/b/8, H.B.C.A.

39. Governor and Committee to Dr. McLoughlin, May 1, 1833, A.6/22, fo. 23, H.B.C.A.

40. Dr. McLoughlin to Duncan Finlayson, July 17, 1832, B.223/b/8, H.B.C.A.

41. Dr. McLoughlin to Governor Simpson, September 12, 1832, B.223/b/8, H.B.C.A.

42. Donald Manson's Journal, B.201/a/2, fos. 5, 7d, and 8, H.B.C.A.

43. *Ibid.*

44. The *Lama* had been bought by Duncan Finlayson in the Hawaiian Islands. She was a bargain, for Finlayson paid only £750 for her, of which £250 was paid by the Company with timber and salmon.

45. McLoughlin to Ogden, December 8, 1832, B.223/b/8, H.B.C.A.

46. The baby Charles, son of "Peter Ogden and a native woman," was baptized by the Reverend D. T. Jones, the same minister who was supposed to have baptized young Peter in May, 1831, E.4/19, H.B.C.A.

47. McLoughlin to Simpson, March 20, 1833, D.4/42, H.B.C.A.

48. McLoughlin to Ogden, March 4, 1833, B.223/b/8, H.B.C.A.

49. Duncan Finlayson to William Smith, Secretary, January 11, 1834, B.223/b/7, H.B.C.A.

50. McLoughlin to Francis Heron, November 20, 1833, B.223/b/9, H.B.C.A.

51. Governor and Committee to McLoughlin, December 4, 1833, A.6/33, fo. 50–50d, H.B.C.A.

52. Log of the *Dryad*, C.1/281, fo. 185, H.B.C.A.

53. *Journals of W. F. Tolmie*, 281, entry for June 4, 1824.

54. Log of the *Dryad*, C.1/281, fo. 186, H.B.C.A.

55. *Ibid.*, fo. 187, H.B.C.A.; *Journals of W. F. Tolmie*, 283.

56. Wrangel's statement, May 15/27, 1834, B.223/c/1, No. 1, H.B.C.A.

57. Ogden to the "Superintendent of the Russian Establishment," June 18, 1834, B.223/c/1, No. 2, H.B.C.A.

58. *Journals of W. F. Tolmie*, 283.

59. Ogden to Wrangel, June 20, 1834, B.223/c/1, No. 3, H.B.C.A.

60. Log of the *Dryad*, June 19, 1834, fo. 187d, H.B.C.A.; *Journals of W. F. Tolmie*, 284–85.

61. "Notes and extracts from Journal of the Hudson's Bay Company at Fort Simpson, 1834–37," entry for July 30, 1834, MS, P–C, Bancroft Library.

62. Log of the *Dryad*, entries for August 21–29, fos. 12–13, H.B.C.A.

63. *Ibid.*, entries for September 2–16, fos. 13–14d; P. N. Compton, "Forts and Fort Life in New Caledonia under the Hudson's Bay Company," MS, Bancroft Library.

64. Some authorities say September 8, 1834. See Galbraith, *Hudson's Bay Company*, 147. The dates presented here are based on the Log of the *Dryad*, fo. 20, and the Fort Simpson Post Journal, B.201/a/3, fo. 7d, H.B.C.A.

65. Donald C. Davidson, "Relations of the Hudson's Bay Company with the Russian American Company on the Northwest Coast, 1829–1867," *British Columbia Historical Quarterly*, Vol. V (January, 1941), 37–46.

66. John K. Townsend, *Narrative of a Journey Across the Rocky Mountains to the Columbia River and a Visit to the Sandwich Islands, Chile, etc.*, 185.

67. Log of the *Dryad*, entries for October 2–December 11, fos. 20d–48d; Fort Simpson Post Journal, entries for October 14–22, fos. 9–9d, H.B.C.A.

68. McLoughlin to Peter Warren Dease, January 18, 1835, B.223/b/10, H.B.C.A.

69. McLoughlin to Dease, December 13, 1834, B.223/b/10, H.B.C.A.

70. Ogden to McLoughlin, December 20, 1834, B.223/c/1, H.B.C.A.

71. A.11/69, fos. 7–10d, H.B.C.A.; also McLoughlin to Simpson, March 14, 1835 in *The Letters of John McLoughlin from Fort Vancouver, First Series*, 134–36.

72. Simpson to Ogden, July 3, 1834, D.4/20, fos. 10d–11, H.B.C.A.

Chapter VI

NEW CALEDONIA, 1835–1844

1. Ogden remained at Fort Vancouver until at least the latter part of June, 1835, for he delivered to Dr. McLoughlin at the Columbia River Depot a letter written by Pierre Pambrun, June 15, 1835, B.223/b/1, H.B.C.A.

2. Townsend, *Narrative*, 98.

3. With the exception of the Kelley-Young party—Governor Figueroa of California had warned McLoughlin against them.

4. McLoughlin to Samuel Black, June 16, 1835, B.223/b/11, H.B.C.A.

5. Eloisa McLoughlin Rae Harvey, "Life of John McLoughlin, Governor of the Hudson's Bay Company's Possessions on the Pacific Slope at Fort Vancouver," MS, Bancroft Library. William Heath Davis Papers, Henry E. Huntington Library; "Personal Reminiscences of Gen. J. A. Sutter," MS, Bancroft Library.

6. McLoughlin to Samuel Black, June 16, 1835, B.22/b/11, H.B.C.A.

7. Governor Simpson's "Character Book," A.34/2, fos. 12–13d, H.B.C.A.; also see R. M. Patterson's introduction to Black's *Journal*.

8. See Ross, *The Fur Hunters of the Far West*, I, 61; typewritten copy of the "Journals and Correspondence of John McLeod Senior . . . from 1812–44" in the Archives of British Columbia, 8–9, and F. Henry Johnson, "Fur Trading Days at Kamloops," *British Columbia Historical Quarterly*, Vol. I (July, 1937), 171–85.

9. Margaret A. Ormsby, *British Columbia: A History*, 72–73; H. H. Bancroft, *The History of British Columbia*, 59.

10. Judge William C. Brown, "Old Fort Okanagan Trail," *Oregon Historical Quarterly*, Vol. XV (March, 1914), 24, 33, 35. Much of the old Okanagan Trail could be seen as late as the latter part of the nineteenth century, but most of it was washed away by the floods of 1894.

11. See *Simpson's 1828 Journey*, 25; "Peter Skene Ogden's Notes on Western Caledonia" (ed. by W. N. Sage), *British Columbia Historical Quarterly*, Vol. I (January, 1937), 51.

12. *Simpson's 1828 Journey*, 19.

13. See *Simpson's 1828 Journey*, 19; "Ogden's Notes on Western Caledonia," *loc. cit.*, 52; Rev. A. G. Morice, *History of the Northern Interior of British Columbia, Formerly New Caledonia*, 174; Thomas Dears to Edward Ermatinger, March 5, 1831 in Ermatinger Papers, 288, Public Archives of Canada, Ottawa.

14. "Ogden's Notes on Western Caledonia," *loc. cit.*, 52.

15. "Fur Trader," *Traits of American Indian Life*, 35.

16. Paul Kane, *Wanderings of an Artist among the Indians of North America*, 243–44; see also Morton, *History of the Canadian West*, 361–62; "Ogden's Notes on Western Caledonia," *loc. cit.*, 48.

17. "Ogden's Notes on Western Caledonia," *loc. cit.*, 49–50.

18. Harold A. Innis, *The Fur Trade of Canada*, 303; Rich, *Hudson's Bay Company*, II, 367–68; "Ogden's Notes on Western Caledonia," *loc. cit.*, 51.

19. *Ibid.*, 53.

20. *Ibid.*, 52–53.

21. Johnson, "Fur Trading Days at Kamloops," *loc. cit.*, 181–82.

22. Anderson, "History of the Northwest Coast," 29–30.

23. Those who were attached to the brigade always received more liberal allowances than those who remained "inland."

24. "Ogden's Notes on Western Caledonia," *loc. cit.*, 50, 54.

25. *John McLean's Notes of Twenty-Five Years in the Hudson's Bay Territory* (ed. by W. Stewart Wallace), 147–48; Ormsby, *British Columbia*, 72; "Ogden's Notes on Western Caledonia," *loc. cit.*, 49.

26. Ogden mentions that "I generally take my departure from this place the 22nd April." "Ogden's Notes on Western Caledonia," *loc. cit.*, 55.

27. *Ibid.*

28. Simpson to the Governor and Committee, August 10, 1832, D.4/99, fos. 16d–17d, H.B.C.A.; McLoughlin to the Governor and Committee, April 9, 1836, in *The Letters of John McLoughlin from Fort Vancouver, First Series*, 144; McLoughlin to the Governor and Committee, June 17, 1836, *ibid.*, 150; W. Kaye Lamb, "The Advent of the *Beaver*," *British Columbia Historical Quarterly*, Vol. II (July, 1938), 165–71.

29. Archibald McDonald in a letter to Edward Ermatinger, January 25, 1837, MS, Archives of British Columbia, states that the date was June 11, 1836; Samuel Parker, *Journal of an Exploring Tour beyond the Rocky Mountains . . . 1835, '36, and '37*, 314, states that it was January 14. See Lamb, "Advent of the *Beaver*," *loc. cit.*, 172–73.

30. "Extract of a correspondence from Lord Palmerston, Secretary of State of Foreign Affairs to John Henry Pelly, Esq.," dated Foreign Office, January 28, 1836, included in the Governor and Committee to McLoughlin, February 10, 1836, A.6/24, fos. 13d–14d.

31. McLoughlin to Simpson, August 29, 1837, D.5/4, fo. 322 d, H.B.C.A.

32. Ray Allen Billington, *Westward Expansion: A History of the American Frontier*, 521–22; Oscar O. Winther, *The Old Oregon Country*, 97–98; Dorothy O. Johansen and Charles Gates, *Empire of the Columbia*; T. C. Elliott (ed.), "The Coming of the White Women, 1836," *Oregon Historical Quarterly*, Vol. XXXVII (September, 1936), 250–63; Clifford M. Drury, *Marcus Whitman*; Drury, *Henry Harmon Spalding*; Drury, *First White Women over the Rockies*.

33. William H. Gray, *The History of Oregon, 1792–1849*, 162.

34. *Reports and Letters of Herbert Beaver, 1836–1838* (ed. by Thomas E. Jessett).

35. *Journals of W. F. Tolmie*, 260, entry for January 2, 1834.

36. Beaver to the Governor and Committee, October 10, 1837, *Reports and Letters of Beaver*, 49.

37. Beaver to Ogden, Fort Vancouver, June 17, 1837, *ibid.*, 49.

38. Johansen and Gates, *Empire of the Columbia*, 176–77.

39. Winther, *The Old Oregon Country*, 90, and Washington Irving, *The Adventures of Captain Bonneville, U.S.A. in the Rocky Mountains and the Far West.*

40. Rich, *Hudson's Bay Company*, II, 684.

41. Bancroft, *History of Oregon, 1834–1848*, 99–103.

42. Elliott, "Peter Skene Ogden, Fur Trader," *loc. cit.*, 253–54.

43. James Douglas to the Governor and Committee, October 18, 1838, *The Letters of John McLoughlin from Fort Vancouver, First Series*, 257.

44. Governor and Committee to McLoughlin or officer in charge of Fort Vancouver, January 25, 1837, A.6/24, fo. 68; Governor and Committee to Simpson, February 15, 1837, D.5/4, fo. 239d, H.B.C.A.

45. Simpson's private diary of this journey in H.B.C.A., quoted in Alice M. Johnson, "Simpson in Russia," *The Beaver* (Autumn, 1960), 4–12, 58; Chevigny, *Russian America*, 160; Rich, *Hudson's Bay Company*, II, 642–51.

46. Rich, *Hudson's Bay Company*, II, 651–55.

47. James Douglas to the Governor and Committee, October 14, 1839, A.11/69, fo. 83, H.B.C.A.

48. T. C. Elliott (ed.), "Facsimile of the Marriage Certificate," *Oregon Historical Quarterly*, Vol. X (December, 1909), 325–28; Archibald McKinlay, "Narrative of a Chief Factor of the Hudson's Bay Company," MS, Bancroft Library.

49. Black's *Journal*, xcii–vii; McLoughlin to Simpson, March 20, 1841, in *The Letters of John McLoughlin from Fort Vancouver, Second Series*, 247–49; Bancroft, *History of the Northwest Coast*, 511–13; Johnson, "Fur Trading Days at Kamloops," *loc. cit.*, 179.

50. "Fur Trader," *Traits of American Indian Life*, chap. XII. There has always been a great deal of discussion about the true identity of the author of this book. It is quite possible that the anonymous fur trader was Peter Skene Ogden. See pp. 91–92.

51. In 1842 the body was exhumed and was to be reinterred at Fort Vancouver, but when the party was crossing Monte Creek, either a pack horse or Indians carrying Black's coffin slipped, and all went into the water. Because the body was completely soaked, it was impossible to carry it on to Fort Vancouver. Thus Sam Black was finally buried under a big ponderosa pine on land that was later part of the ranch of Senator Bostock. Black's *Journal*, xciv–v.

52. "Fur Trader," *Traits of American Indian Life.*

53. See A.10/13, fos. 446–47, H.B.C.A.; R. G. MacBeth, "A British Columbia Study," *The Beaver* (May, 1922), 2; Black's *Journal*, xcii–ix.

54. Ogden's will is housed in "Wills and Admins, 1855," D.L.C. 415, No. 78, Record Room, County Hall, London, England.

55. Charles Wilkes, *Narrative of the United States Exploring Expedition, During the Years 1838, 1839, 1840, 1841, 1842,* IV, 389, 395–98, 419–20.

56. P. Fraser to McGillivray (?), New Caledonia, January 20, 1842, McGillivray Papers, IV, Ottawa, Public Archives of Canada, and No. 112 in series of photostats and copies, fo. 728, H.B.C.A.

57. Hiram Martin Chittenden and Alfred Talbot Richardson, *Life, Letters, and Travels of Father Pierre-Jean DeSmet,* 384; see also Father William L. Davis, "Pierre Jean DeSmet: The Years of Preparation, 1801–1837," *Pacific Northwest Quarterly,* Vol. XXXII (April, 1941), 167–96; "Pierre Jean DeSmet: The Journey of 1840," *Pacific Northwest Quarterly,* Vol. XXXV (January, 1944), 29–43; *ibid.* (April, 1944), 121–42; *DeSmet's Oregon Missions,* 38; Bancroft, *History of Oregon, 1834–1848,* 323–26.

58. McLoughlin to the Governor and Committee, June 24, 1842, *McLoughlin's Fort Vancouver Letters, Second Series,* 57.

59. Simpson to McLoughlin, June 21, 1843, B.223/c/1, H.B.C.A.

60. McLoughlin to the Governor and Committee, November 15, 1843, as quoted in *The Letters of John McLoughlin from Fort Vancouver, Second Series,* 128.

61. *Ibid.,* 128; McLoughlin to the Governor and Committee, August 2, 1843, *ibid.,* 108.

62. The Brigade arrived at Fort Vancouver on June 4, 1844. McLoughlin to the Governor and Committee, July 4, 1844, *ibid.,* 199.

63. Alexander Caulfield Anderson to Peter Skene Ogden, Fort Alexandria, April 26, 1844, in Elliott, "Peter Skene Ogden, Fur Trader," *loc. cit.,* 260.

Chapter VII

DISAPPOINTMENT AT THE CAPE

1. Minutes of the Council of the Northern Department, June, 1844, B.239/k/3, 315, H.B.C.A.

2. *Ibid.,* 334.

3. Norway House Journal, entry for June 25, 1844, B.154/a/43, H.B.C.A.

4. "Fur Trader," *Traits of American Indian Life,* 61.

5. Wheeler, *Ogden Family,* 177–80; John Charles Dent, *The Last Forty Years; Canada Since the Union of 1841,* I, 80–88, 246.

6. John McKenzie to Archibald Barclay, Liverpool, September 28, 1844, A.10/18, fo. 659, H.B.C.A.

7. Ogden to Simpson, Hudson's Bay House, London, dated Edinburgh, November 7, 1844, D.5/12, H.B.C.A.

8. *Ibid.,* November 11, 1844.

9. *Ibid.,* November 7, 1844.

10. "Simpson's Character Book, 1832," A.34/2, fos. 13d–14, H.B.C.A.

11. Simpson to Henry Ogden, New York, dated Lachine, D.4/83, pp. 219–20, H.B.C.A.

12. Simpson to Ogden, August 30, 1850, private correspondence, D.4/71, p. 377, H.B.C.A.

13. Letter written by Archibald Barclay in the name of the Governor and Committee to McLoughlin, November 30, 1844, B.223/c/1, H.B.C.A.

14. Archibald McDonald to Edward Ermatinger, Colvile, March 15, 1843, in C. O. Ermatinger, "A Tragedy on the Stikine in 1842," *Oregon Historical Quarterly*, Vol. XV (June, 1914), 132.

15. Galbraith, *Hudson's Bay Company*, 220.

16. Bancroft, *History of Oregon*, 292.

17. The livestock of the Oregon settlers were harassed by wolves. Meetings were held to decide what action should be taken against these animals. The large groups assembled at these meetings soon turned to discussing political topics also.

18. Simpson to Aberdeen, March 29, 1845, D.4/66, H.B.C.A.; see also Galbraith, *Hudson's Bay Company*, 233–37.

19. Henry U. Addington, Foreign Office, to Simpson, April 1, 1845, D.5/13, H.B.C.A.

20. Simpson to Pelly, April 4, 1845, confidential, D.4/66; Simpson to Pelly, May 4, 1845, D.4/67, H.B.C.A.

21. In Boston on April 17, 1845, Ogden drew a bill of exchange on the Hudson's Bay Company in favor of his brother Henry Ogden, who lived in New York City. Ogden to Archibald Barclay, Boston, April 17, 1845, A.10/10, fo. 190, H.B.C.A.

22. Simpson to Pelly, confidential, May 4, 1845, A.12/2, fos. 514–15, H.B.C.A.

23. *Ibid*.

24. Stewart Wallace, ed., *The Macmillan Dictionary of Canadian Biography* (3d ed.), 343, 729–30.

25. Dent, *The Last Forty Years*, I, 263–77; *Dictionary of National Biography*.

26. *Harte's Army List*, 1864.

27. Colonel H. Vavasour, Mervin's father, was stationed in Ireland in 1847 and wrote to the Treasury in an attempt to collect the allowance granted to his son for "Services in Oregon." Col. H. Vavasour, Dublin, March 10, 1847, Treasury Papers, 480, Public Record Office, London.

28. Lt. Col. F. T. Stear, head librarian, Royal Engineer Corps Library, Chatham, to Brigadier Michael Crosthwait, May 20, 1970; Brigadier Michael Crosthwait to the author, May 22, 1970.

29. Simpson to the Governor and Committee, Lachine, May 4, 1845, A.12/2, fo. 516, H.B.C.A.

30. Governor Simpson to H. J. Warre and M. Vavasour, Encampment Lac la Pluie, confidential, May 30, 1845, D.4/65, 60, H.B.C.A.

31. Joseph Schafer, "Documents Relative to Warre and Vavasour's Mili-

tary Reconnaissance in Oregon, 1845–46," *Oregon Historical Quarterly*, Vol. X (March, 1909), 22–24.

32. "Confidential Instructions for Lieut. Vavasour Royal Eng.," fo. 4/457, Public Record Office. Simpson to Pelly, "confidential," May 4, 1845, D.4/67, fo. 14–15, H.B.C.A.

33. Colonel Halloway to Lt. Vavasour, Montreal, May 3, 1845, in Schafer, "Documents," *loc. cit.*

34. Governor Simpson, "To the Gentleman conducting the H.B. Co.'s affairs at all their Settlements and posts situated between Red River Colony and the Pacific Ocean," Encampment, Lac la Pluie, May 30, 1845, D.4/67, fo. 64–65, H.B.C.A.

35. Henry J. Warre, *Sketches in North America and the Oregon Territory*, 1.

36. Simpson to Ogden, Encampment Lac la Pluie, May 30, 1845, confidential, D.4/67, fo. 66–68, H.B.C.A.

37. Warre, *Sketches in North America*, 1.

38. *Ibid.*, 2.

39. Simpson to Pelly, July 8, 1845, D.4/67, fo. 192, H.B.C.A.

40. Simpson to Ogden, Encampment Lac la Pluie, confidential, May 30, 1845, D.4/67, fo. 69, H.B.C.A.

41. Father DeSmet to Bishop Hughes, Station of the Assumption, Flatbow country, August 17, 1845, in Chittenden and Richardson, *Life, Letters, and Travels of DeSmet*, II, 485.

42. McLoughlin to the Governor and Committee, Fort Vancouver, September 1, 1845, B.134/c/60, fo. 241, H.B.C.A.

43. Simpson to H. J. Warre and M. Vavasour, Esqrs., Encampment Lac la Pluie, confidential, May 30, 1845, D.4/67, fo. 60.

44. Ogden to Simpson, Fort Vancouver, March 20, 1846, private and confidential, D.5/16, H.B.C.A.; see *The Letters of John McLoughlin from Fort Vancouver, Third Series*, 146–47.

45. Report to "The Right Hon. the Secretary of State for the Colonies," Fort Vancouver, October 26, 1845, in Schafer, "Documents," *loc. cit.*, 58.

46. *Ibid.*, 10.

47. "Fur Trader," *Traits of American Indian Life*, 3.

48. Ogden had arrived at Fort Vancouver on August 26, and before September 1 he had already departed "to take possession of Cape Disappointment." McLoughlin to the Governor and Committee, September 1, 1845, B.134/c/60, fo. 241, H.B.C.A.

49. Warre and Vavasour's Report, June 15, 1846, to the "Right Honble. the Secretary of State for the Colonies," in Schafer, "Documents," *loc. cit.*, 72.

50. Captain Gordon to Chief Factor McLoughlin, H.M. Ship *America*, Port Discovery, 2nd September, 1845, in Leslie M. Scott, "Report of Lieuten-

ant Peel on Oregon in 1845–46," *Oregon Historical Quarterly*, Vol. XXIX (March, 1928), 51–71.

51. "The Recollections of George B. Roberts," MS P–A 83, 6, Bancroft Library; for an excellent detailed discussion of this expedition, see Barry M. Gough, "H.M.S. *America* on the North Pacific Coast," *Oregon Historical Quarterly*, Vol. LXX (Dec., 1969), 293–311.

52. Roberts' "Recollections," 6.

53. Jesse Applegate, "Views of Oregon History," MS, 15, Bancroft Library.

54. Lt. Peel to Minister Pakenham, The Steamship *Trent*, January 2, 1846, between Vera Cruz and Havana in Scott, "Report of Lt. Peel," *loc. cit.*, 65; McLoughlin to the Governor and Committee, Fort Vancouver, November 20, 1845, *The Letters of John McLoughlin from Fort Vancouver, Third Series*, 146–47.

55. Captain Gordon to the Admiralty H.M. Ship *America* at sea, October 19, 1845, in Scott, "Report of Lieut. Peel," *loc. cit.*, 70.

56. Ogden to H. J. Warre, Esq., Fort Vancouver, October 2, 1845, private, F.O.5/457, 137, Public Record Office, London (hereafter cited as P.R.O.).

57. Ogden to Warre, Fort Vancouver, November 17, 1845, private, P.R.O., *loc. cit.*, 137d.

58. Warre and Vavasour to Lord Metcalfe, Fort Vancouver, November 2, 1845, P.R.O., *loc. cit.*, 63–64.

59. Warre to Ogden, Fort Vancouver, November 17, 1845, confidential, P.R.O., *loc. cit.*, 138–138d.

60. Ogden to Warre, Fort Vancouver, November 18, 1845, confidential, P.R.O., *loc. cit.*, 138d–139.

61. Warre to Ogden, Fort Vancouver, November 19, 1845, confidential, P.R.O., *loc. cit.*, 139d.

62. Ogden to Warre, Fort Vancouver, November 19, 1845, confidential, P.R.O., *loc. cit.*, 140–140d.

63. Warre to Ogden, Fort Vancouver, November 19, 1845, confidential, P.R.O., *loc. cit.*, 140d.

64. McLoughlin to the Governor and Committee, Fort Vancouver, November 20, 1845, *The Letters of John McLoughlin from Fort Vancouver, Third Series*, 147; McLoughlin to the Governor and Committee, December 12, 1845, *ibid.*, 152.

65. Ogden to Simpson, April 4, 1846, private, D.5/17, fos. 72d–73, H.B.C.A.

66. Bancroft, *History of Oregon, 1834–1848*, 573–77; Roberts MS, 38.

67. Ogden to Warre, Fort Vancouver, February 14, 1846, private and confidential, P.R.O., *loc. cit.*, 141.

68. Warre to Ogden, Fort Vancouver, February 15, 1846, private, P.R.O., *loc. cit.*, 141d.

69. Warre and Vavasour Report, June 16, 1846, to "The Right Honble. The Secretary of State for the Colonies," P.R.O. *loc. cit.*, 73.

70. Lieut. Vavasour's (engineering) report, Fort Vancouver on the Columbia River, Oregon Territory, March 1, 1846, P.R.O., *loc. cit.*, 89.

71. Drury, *Marcus Whitman*, 127.

72. Paul Kane, *Wanderings of an Artist*, 153.

73. Warre to Ogden, Red River, June 16, 1846, P.R.O., *loc. cit.*, 141d–42.

74. Aberdeen to Peel, October 17, 1845, Peel papers, in Frederick Merk, "The Oregon Pioneers and the Boundary," *American Historical Review*, Vol. XXIX (July, 1932), 698–99.

75. See Norman A. Graebner's excellent article, "Maritime Factors in the Oregon Compromise," *Pacific Historical Review*, Vol. XX (November, 1951), 331–45.

76. *The Times* [of London], January 3, 1846, in Galbraith, *Hudson's Bay Company*, 244.

77. Edward Everett to Peel, April 28, 1846, *ibid.*, 245. See Rich, *Hudson's Bay Company*, II, 728–29.

78. Robert Dale Owen to Peel, March 23, 1846, in Galbraith, *Hudson's Bay Company*, 246.

79. Richard Crocker to Aberdeen, May 13, 1846, *ibid.*, 246; see also Robert C. Clark, *History of the Willamette Valley, Oregon*, I, 859.

80. Neil M. Howison, "Report of Neil M. Howison on Oregon, 1846," *Oregon Historical Quarterly*, Vol. XIV (March, 1913), 1–60.

81. Ogden to Simpson, March 15, 1847, D.5/19, H.B.C.A.; in Galbraith, *Hudson's Bay Company*, 250.

Chapter VIII

OGDEN THE SAMARITAN

1. The Governor and Committee to McLoughlin, Ogden, and James Douglas, October 8, 1845, B.223/c/1, H.B.C.A.

2. H. H. Berens to Simpson, London, October 1, 1845, D.5/15, fo. 251, H.B.C.A.; see also Rich, *Hudson's Bay Company*, II, 710–11.

3. Archibald Barclay, Secretary, to Ogden, September 30, 1848, and "Extracts from Dispatch of the Governor and Committee of the Hon. Hudson's Bay Company to the Board of Management," Fort Vancouver, London, September 8, 1846, B.223/c/1, fo. 325, H.B.C.A.

4. Roberts' "Recollections," 7.

5. *Robert Newell's Memoranda: Travels in the Territory of Missourie: Travels to the Kayuse War, together with a Report on the Indians South of the Columbia River* (ed. by Dorothy O. Johansen), 86.

6. Howison, "Report on Oregon" *loc. cit.*, 67; Bancroft, *History of Oregon, 1834–1848*, 587–88.

7. Abernethy to Ogden, Oregon City, August 7, 1847, B.223/c/1, H.B.C.A.

8. Ogden to Simpson, March 20, 1846, private and confidential, D.5/16, H.B.C.A.; in Galbraith, *Hudson's Bay Company*, 252.

9. For an excellent discussion, see *ibid.*, 254–82, and Galbraith, "George N. Sanders, 'Influence Man,' for the Hudson's Bay Company," *Oregon Historical Quarterly*, Vol. LIII (September, 1952), 159–76.

10. Drury, *Marcus Whitman*, 380.

11. Simpson to Ogden, June 19, 1845, Red River, D.4/67, fo. 127–28, H.B.C.A.

12. *Robert Newell's Memoranda*, 150.

13. *Ibid.*, 92–94.

14. H. H. Spalding, writing in the *Oregon American*, July 19, 1848, in Bancroft, *History of Oregon, 1834–1848*, 653.

15. Drury, *Marcus Whitman*, 395.

16. There are many versions to the Joe Lewis story. See Drury, *Marcus Whitman*, 393–94, and Bancroft, *History of Oregon, 1834–1848*, 652–53.

17. Anderson, "History of the Northwest Coast," 266. Catholic and Protestant rivalry also figured in the causes of the Whitman Massacre.

18. Drury, *Marcus Whitman*, 385–89.

19. *Ibid.*, 400–11; William A. Mowry, *Marcus Whitman and the Early Days of Oregon*, 302.

20. Drury, *Marcus Whitman*, 407.

21. Douglas to Abernethy, Vancouver, December 7, 1847, in Mowry, *Marcus Whitman*, 321–22.

22. Some historians have contended that Ogden reached Walla Walla on December 19, 1847; see Ogden to E. Walker, Walla Walla, December 31, 1847, in Mowry, *Marcus Whitman*, 316–17.

23. The record of these speeches is found in a letter written to Rev. David Greene, Secretary, American Board of Commissioners for Foreign Missions, from Rev. Cushing Ells, Tshimshain near Fort Colvile, Oregon Mission, January 29, 1848, in the Congregational House, Boston, in Mowry, *Marcus Whitman*, 312–15.

24. Rev. H. H. Spalding to Rev. David Greene, Fort Vancouver, January 8, 1848, *ibid.*, 301–302.

25. Bagley, *Early Catholic Missions in Old Oregon*, 192, in Drury, *Marcus Whitman*, 410.

26. Bancroft, *History of Oregon, 1834–1848*, 662–63.

27. Douglas to Applegate, A. L. Lovejoy, and George L. Curry, Fort Vancouver, December 11, 1847, *ibid.*, 673.

28. Ogden to Rev. E. Walker, Walla Walla, December 31, 1847, in Mowry, *Marcus Whitman*, 316–17.

29. *Ibid.*, 317; Spalding to Rev. David Greene, *ibid.*, 310; Bancroft, *History of Oregon, 1834–1848*, 687.

30. Spalding to Mr. and Mrs. Stephen Prentiss (Narcissa Whitman's

mother and father), Oregon City, April 6, 1848, in Mowry, *Marcus Whitman*, 326–27.

31. Douglas to Abernethy, Fort Vancouver, January 8, 1848, in Bancroft, *History of Oregon, 1834–1848*, 686.

32. *Oregon Spectator*, January 30, 1848, *ibid.*, 687–88.

33. Spalding to Ogden, Tualatin Plains, January 12, 1849, B.223/c/1, fos. 339–40. There is a disagreement about the date of arrival at Oregon City, whether it was January 9 or 12, 1848.

34. Simpson to Ogden, Work, and Douglas, Norway House, June 24, 1848, B.223/c/1, H.B.C.A.

35. Governor and Committee to Ogden, Work, and Douglas, September 8, 1848, B.223/c/1, H.B.C.A.

36. Spalding to Rev. Greene, Oregon City, January 24, 1848, in Mowry, *Marcus Whitman*, 311.

37. Ogden to Abernethy, Fort Vancouver, January 26, 1848, in the *Oregon Spectator*, February 16, 1848.

38. Henry L. Bates, "The Occasion of the Unveiling of the Memorial Stone on the Grave of Peter Skene Ogden," *Oregon Historical Quarterly*, Vol. XXIV (December, 1923), 361–63; Frederick V. Holman, "Address," *ibid.*, 363–79; T. C. Elliott, "Dedicatory Address," *ibid.*, 379–82.

Chapter IX

THE YEARS OF TENSION

1. Gray, *History of Oregon*, 558–59.

2. *Robert Newell's Memoranda*, 105–106.

3. Governor Abernethy's statements, *Oregon Spectator*, February 6, 1849; *Robert Newell's Memoranda*, 81–139; Bancroft, *History of Oregon, 1834–1848*, 700–54.

4. The census of 1849 revealed that the population of Oregon was 9,083; 8,785 inhabitants were Americans, and 298 were foreigners. Winther, *The Old Oregon Country*, 100.

5. Applegate to Ogden, Yoncalla, Umpqua, February 19, 1850, B.223/c/1, H.B.C.A.

6. Gen. Smith to Ogden, October 6, 1849, B.223/c/1, H.B.C.A.

7. *Oregon Spectator*, August 24, 1848.

8. Winther, *The Old Oregon Country*, 120–21; Bancroft, *History of Oregon, 1848–1888*, 42–45; John Walton Caughey, *California*, 285–92; Peter H. Burnett, *An Old California Pioneer*.

9. Ogden to the Governor and Committee, October 1, 1848, B.223/b/38, H.B.C.A., in Galbraith, *Hudson's Bay Company*, 462.

10. Ogden to Simpson, September 15, 1849, private, D.5/26, H.B.C.A.; Caughey, *California*, 295.

11. Bancroft, *History of Oregon, 1848–1888*, 115.

12. Roberts said of him that he "took almost every British ship that came. His conduct was beneath the government, and was probably from beneath, also." Roberts' "Recollections," 16.

13. Galbraith, *Hudson's Bay Company*, 265–67; Rich, *Hudson's Bay Company*, II, 742; Bancroft, *Oregon, 1848–1888*, 104–108.

14. Anderson, "History of the Northwest Coast," 110–98.

15. Simpson to Ogden, Lachine, August 30, 1850, private, D.4/17, H.B.C.A.

16. Galbraith, *Hudson's Bay Company*, 269.

17. See John Haskell Kemble, *San Francisco Bay: A Pictorial Maritime History*.

18. Ogden to Barclay, Boston, April 17, 1845, A.10/19, fo. 190, H.B.C.A.

19. "Wills and Admins, 1855," D.L.C. 415, No. 78, Record Room, County Hall, London.

20. Lady Simpson to William Scott Simpson (her brother), Lachine, January 30, 1852, D.6/1, H.B.C.A.

21. Lady Simpson to Louisa Barkley Simpson, Lachine, September 15, 1849, D.6/1, H.B.C.A.

22. Major R. Money Barnes, *A History of Regiments and Uniforms of the British Army*, 322; Wheeler, *Ogden Family*, 176–77.

23. Lady Simpson to William Scott Simpson, Lachine, January 30, 1852, D.6/1, H.B.C.A.

24. An Ogden letter, dated Montreal, January, 1852, as quoted in Binns, *Peter Skene Ogden*, 343–44.

25. Lady Simpson to William Scott Simpson, Lachine, January 30, 1852, D.6/1, H.B.C.A.

26. For an excellent discussion, see Galbraith, *Hudson's Bay Company*, 269–71.

27. Wheeler, *Ogden Family*, 73, 111, 216.

28. President Grant signed the settlement bill in February, 1871, which paid $650,000 to the Hudson's Bay and Puget's Sound Agricultural companies for the final extinguishment of their possessory claims south of the forty-ninth parallel.

29. Elliott, "Peter Skene Ogden, Fur Trader," *loc. cit.*, 270, and Ogden to A. McKinlay, Washington, June 2, 1852, in Binns, *Peter Skene Ogden*, 346–48.

30. Galbraith, *Hudson's Bay Company*, 15–16.

31. Ogden to A. McKinlay, Lachine, September 13, 1852, in Binns, *Peter Skene Ogden*, 348–50.

32. Andrew F. Rolle, *California*, 212–13.

33. General Strong noted how Ogden twisted his lips when he recalled this story, Elliott, "Peter Skene Ogden, Fur Trader," *loc. cit.*, 271–72.

34. Dugald MacTavish to Barclay, dated Vancouver, Washington Terri-

tory, October 4, 1854, F. G. Box 701—Ft. Van. Correspondence—B.K. 1853/57, H.B.C.A.

35. Governor Simpson to F. Jos. Hargrave, Lachine, October 18, 1854, Simpson Correspondence, D.N. 521 (March–October, 1854), 200, H.B.C.A.

36. MacTavish to Barclay, October 4, 1854, F. G. Box 701—Ft. Van. Correspondence—B.K. 1853/57, H.B.C.A.

Chapter X

THE INDELIBLE MARK

1. MacTavish to Barclay, October 4, 1854, F. G. Box 701—Ft. Van. Correspondence—B.K. 1853/57, H.B.C.A.

2. Simpson to Henry Ogden, N.Y., Lachine, November 14, 1854, D.4/83, 219–20, H.B.C.A.

3. Wheeler, *Ogden Family*, 291.

4. Simpson to Barclay, Lachine, July 31, 1854, A.12/7, H.B.C.A.

5. Frances Anne painted, and several of her pictures now hang in Beaver House, until 1970 the Hudson's Bay Company's headquarters, in London.

6. Duncan Finlayson wrote to the editor of the *Montreal Herald*, September 18, 1858, asking him to announce this marriage of August 31, 1858, B.134/b/15, fo. 250b, H.B.C.A.

7. "Wills and Admins, 1855," D.L.C. 415, No. 78, Record Room, County Hall, London.

8. Wills, entry for October 24, 1854, A.44/3, p. 96, and A.44/4, p. 38, H.B.C.A.

9. Wheeler, *Ogden Family*, 177.

10. Statement by Marguerite Fraser of "Lac la Hache, Ruperts Land," indicating that she had received from Edward Hopkins all of the money that she was due from her grandfather's estate. See A.36/11, fo. 72 (watermark, 1859), H.B.C.A.

11. Governor Simpson's will.

12. Elliott, "Peter Skene Ogden, Fur Trader," *loc. cit.*, 277–78; Elliott (ed.), "Facsimile of Marriage Certificate," *loc. cit.*, 325–28.

13. Wheeler, *Ogden Family*, 295.

14. For details of Peter Ogden, Jr.'s activities, see Minutes of the Council, Northern Department, B.239/k/3 (1851–1870), 46, 59, 71, 97, 98, 110, 119, 120, 139, 140, 159, 161, 179, 180, 199, 200, 218, 219, 239, 241, 261, 262, 283, 285, 305, 307, H.B.C.A.

15. Wheeler, *Ogden Family*, 294.

16. Roderick Finlayson to W. G. Smith, October, 1870, B.226/b/43, fo. 59a, H.B.C.A.

17. Cox, *Adventures on the Columbia River*, II, 243.

Index